AN·ET·HIB·REX·FIDEI·

Reverendissimo in Christo Patri
D.no GILBERTO SHELDON Archiep.
Cantuariensi totius Angliæ Primati
& Metrop. &c. Theatri hujus Funda
tori Munificentissimo
D.D.C.Q. Dav: Loggan.

THE
ILLUSTRATED HISTORY
OF
OXFORD UNIVERSITY

THE
ILLUSTRATED
HISTORY OF
OXFORD
UNIVERSITY

Edited by
JOHN PREST

Oxford   New York
OXFORD UNIVERSITY PRESS
1993

Oxford University Press, Walton Street, Oxford ox2 6dp

Oxford New York Toronto
Delhi Bombay Calcutta Madras Karachi
Kuala Lumpur Singapore Hong Kong Tokyo
Nairobi Dar es Salaam Cape Town
Melbourne Auckland Madrid
and associated companies in
Berlin Ibadan

Oxford is a trade mark of Oxford University Press

Published in the United States by
Oxford University Press Inc., New York

British Library Cataloguing in Publication Data
Data available

Library of Congress Cataloging in Publication Data
The Illustrated history of Oxford University / edited by John Prest.
p. cm.
Includes bibliographical references.
1. University of Oxford—History. 2. University of Oxford—
History—Pictorial works. I. Prest, John M.
LF510.I45 1993
378.425'7—dc20
92–35199
CIP
ISBN 0–19–820158–3

Datacapture to Alliance Typesetters, Pondicherry
Typeset by Oxuniprint, Oxford
Printed in Great Britain
on acid-free paper by
Butler & Tanner Ltd,
Frome, Somerset

Front endpaper: The Sheldonian Theatre from *Oxonia Illustrata* (1675), by David Loggan (Bodleian Library, Oxford, Arch Antiq, A II 13). *Back endpaper*: The Bodleian Library, Arts End, engraved by J. Le Keux for *Memorials of Oxford* (1873), by James Ingram (Bodleian Library, Oxford, GA Oxon 4° 795)

Editor's Foreword

THE University has been successively a part of the Western Christian Church, an Anglican university, and a (more or less) non-denominational one, and its history can be divided into three periods.

The first began in the twelfth century, when scholars took up residence in the town and began to teach there. Their arrival led to bitter struggles with the citizens. Every time there was a new outbreak of violence involving town and gown, the University, as it was soon called, appealed to the king for protection. The town was humbled and required to supply the University with everything it needed, from bread and beer to service, at prices the Masters and the poor students could afford. The University had come to stay. The resident Masters of Arts, who were all in holy orders, turned houses into halls where groups of students could lodge together. Monasteries set up hostels for members of their own orders, and the friars arrived. Oxford became a very clerical place, whose studies revolved round the exposition of sound religion, as defined by the Roman Catholic Church, and the refutation of heresy.

The second period dates from the Reformation. The monasteries and friaries disappeared. Queen Elizabeth consolidated her position as head of the Church of England, and the University, with some misgivings, identified itself with the new regime. The halls vanished, and the more spacious endowed colleges became the norm. In the seventeenth century the University itself began to resemble a federation of colleges. Oxford became a fashionable place for the children of the aristocracy and gentry to complete their education. In 1642, when the Civil War broke out, the Court moved to Oxford, and Charles I made his headquarters there. In 1681 Charles II summoned Parliament to meet at Oxford. It was for the last time. In the eighteenth century the University contracted in numbers. Undergraduate life became expensive and the dons grew indolent. Sir Hans Sloane left his collection, which forms the basis of the British Museum, not to Oxford, but to London—the greatest rebuff Oxford has ever suffered. Among the professions, the study of law and of medicine became concentrated in London, where there were more briefs and higher fees. Oxford remained training the clergy.

The third period starts in the early nineteenth century, when a new university was, at last, founded in London, and many of the formal links between the English State and the Anglican Church were broken (in 1828–9). Oxford had either to reform itself or be remodelled from outside. In 1850 Lord John Russell's Government appointed the first

Royal Commission of Inquiry into the University. The Commission's report was published in 1852, and two years later Parliament opened the way for religious dissenters to matriculate and to obtain Bachelor's degrees. In 1871 college fellowships, too, were freed from religious tests. The sons of the middle classes began to crowd in through the gates. In 1878 the gender barrier was broken and the first women students were matriculated.

The second and third Royal Commissions appointed in 1871 and 1919 wanted to see the government of the University released from the stranglehold of the colleges. By the time Sir Charles Mallet published his history of the University in 1924–7, University faculties had assumed responsibility for the organization of syllabuses, and the Science departments were striving to achieve a status comparable with that accorded to them in other countries. Oxford was recovering the ground lost in the eighteenth and early nineteenth centuries, and that process may now be said to have been completed.

This new history is organized thematically. The contributors were asked to consider what Oxford has given to the world, and each of the chapters can be read separately. But the sequence of the chapters is significant. The book has a rolling centre of gravity, and it is intended to be read as a whole.

Oxford is (with Cambridge) the leading example of a university town, as opposed to a town with a university (Chapter 1). It has furnished Church and State with trained minds, and it has played an important role in creating a homogeneous governing élite. Oxford has united Oxford men—at the expense, sometimes, of dividing the nation (Chapter 2). An unbroken existence has allowed the University and colleges to create, over the centuries, the greatest feast of architecture of different styles north of the Alps. The buildings of Oxford are the most impressive of all the records of its past. They are both Gothic and Classical. They reflect the religious aspirations and the aristocratic pretensions of previous generations, the simple life of the medieval scholar and the attempt to create a new Athens and a new Rome (Chapter 3). Generation after generation has dreamt, read, talked, and revelled beneath the spires and the towers, and glimpses of the romance of Oxford will be found among the illustrations.

The University began as a religious institution, and everything from Logic and Mathematics to Natural History was studied within a framework established by the Fathers of the Church (Chapter 4). From concern with a Christocentric universe, the primacy was slowly transferred to the study of the ancient classics, where it remained (if we are to judge by the records of candidates admitted to the civil service) until the beginning of the twentieth century (Chapter 5). From the Classics it has been passing, in the Arts, to the modern studies, Law, Modern History, English, Modern Languages, Philosophy, Politics, and Economics (Chapter 6).

The bridge between the Arts and the Sciences is provided by the University collections, the libraries and museums. In addition to the books, sculptures, and paintings which are the staple of so much academic study in the Arts, the collections contain the anthropological remains, which are used by both Arts and Sciences, and the anatomical, astronomical, botanical, geological, and meteorological holdings which lie at the heart of the natural sciences (Chapter 7).

Among the life sciences many practitioners were able to work happily within the traditional Oxford ethos (Chapter 8). The physical scientists, on the other hand, found that the prejudices of their colleagues in the Arts were the greatest of all the obstacles they had to overcome. In order to win themselves a place in the sun, they had to represent themselves as 'pure' scientists. Then, in their turn, they became infected with the early twentieth-century snobbery of Oxford, and set their faces against the applied sciences. To their shame Professors of Physics and Chemistry fought a rearguard action against the introduction of Engineering, Metallurgy, and Management (Chapter 9). Fortunately, throughout the twentieth century Oxford has never fallen more than one step behind the times. First the Arts were persuaded to make room for the pure sciences, and then the pure sciences were won round and prevailed upon to acknowledge the intellectual qualities of the applied sciences.

A university must be judged by its studies, and successive chapters show that Oxford has always thought of itself as a teaching university with a responsibility to instruct its undergraduates in accepted doctrines rather than speculative opinions. In the Middle Ages teaching was focused upon the oral disputation proceeding according to formal rules. Since the Reformation tuition has been based upon printed texts, the Bible, the Prayer Book, and the Greek and Latin classics (and in the middle of the nineteenth century Cardinal Newman still thought that a university ought not to concern itself with anything else). The consequence was that modern studies, if they were to make any headway at all, had to present themselves in the same format as the instruction already being given. For Modern History this meant learning Stubbs's *Charters* by heart, for English it necessitated mastering Anglo-Saxon. This was never as suffocating as it sounds, for originality could still flourish within the decentralized system of college teaching. And in one important respect, at least, the policy has paid off. The concentration upon texts has enabled the University Press to build its reputation on the publication of standard editions. Oxford has not, since the departure of the Stuarts, had any pretensions to becoming the capital of the nation, but it has become the home of major projects (some of which did not originate in Oxford) like the *New English Dictionary* and the *Dictionary of National Biography*. The University rules the printed page, and the rights and wrongs of the English language, such as they be, are laid down in Oxford.

Many generations of college fellows acknowledged no duty to carry out original enquiries. German universities preserved, and American universities established, a different tradition, in which research was given a high priority. When Oxford began to change its ways, this was largely the work of the Natural Scientists. The most significant event in the history of the University during the twentieth century was Professor Perkin's insistence that every undergraduate reading Chemistry should have to complete an additional year's research before being allowed to qualify for a degree. Rhodes

Scholars, too, contributed something to the change. The scholarships may have been founded, within the Oxford teaching tradition, to promote the formation of a global governing class of healthy, moral generalists. But Rhodes Scholars were recruited from a world in which the value of higher degrees was taken for granted. Their demands helped to convince the University that to every undergraduate School there should be added a School of Graduate Studies, and that graduate colleges should find a place alongside undergraduate ones (Chapter 10). Now, towards the end of the twentieth century, the most important question we have to ask about a university is 'What has it added to the sum of human knowledge?' This is the point to which, more than any other, we have addressed ourselves in this book.

J. P.

ACKNOWLEDGEMENTS

The Editor has relied upon E. H. Cordeaux and D. H. Merry's bibliographies of printed works relating to the University of Oxford and the City of Oxford, and the knowledge of the staff of the Local History Section in the Central Library in Westgate. He also wishes to thank Tony Simcock, of the Museum of the History of Science, who provided guidance, correction, and confirmation, Susan Le Roux, the illustrations editor, who sensed the authors' inexperience and added gradually and tactfully to the illustrations suggested to her, John Waś, who patiently and skilfully brought the copy to a state of consistency and made it fit for the printer, and Vivien McKay who prepared the maps. Without them there would have been no book.

Contents

List of Colour Plates

Note to the Reader

THE GLOSSARY There are many terms used in everyday speech in Oxford which may not be familiar outside the University. These are explained in the Glossary towards the back of the book, pp. 384–8.

PARENTHETICAL DATES All the chapters except two cover many centuries, and throughout the text parenthetical dates are inserted after names—'Walter de Merton (d. 1277)', 'Archbishop Laud (1573–1645)', 'Edward Heath (b. 1916)'. Dates are not given after the names of royalty and a few other exceptionally famous persons, nor in the small number of cases where the authors have been unable to find any. The dates are inserted upon the first occasion a name is mentioned in each chapter, and are not repeated within the chapter. Parenthetical dates are not used in the captions, where they would be too obtrusive, but the dates of persons named in captions can be found in the index.

Maps

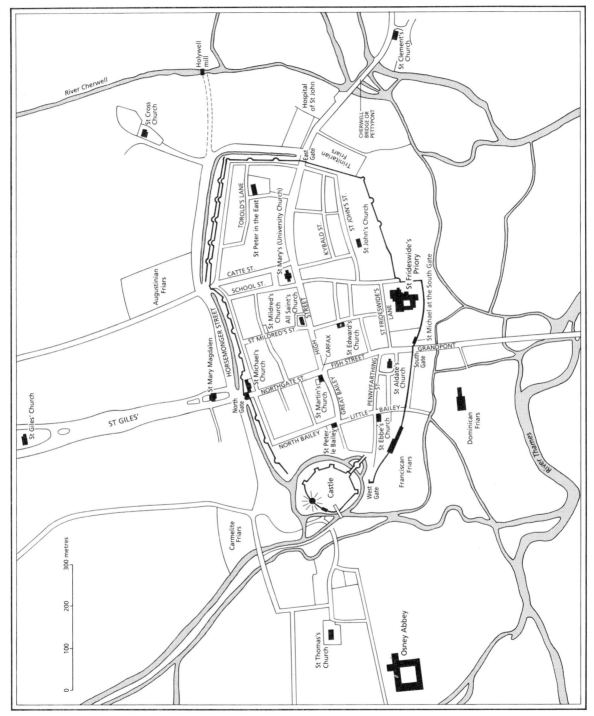

River Cherwell

Holywell mill

St Cross Church

St Clement's Church

Hospital of St John

CHERWELL BRIDGE OR PETTYPONT

East Gate

Trinitarian Friars

TOROLD'S LANE

St Peter in the East

ST JOHN'S ST.

St Mary's (University Church)

KYBALD ST.

St John's Church

CATTE ST.

SCHOOL ST.

Augustinian Friars

St Frideswide's Priory

St Mildred's Church

All Saint's Church

ST FRIDESWIDE'S LANE

St Michael at the South Gate

St Mary Magdalen

St Michael's Church

St Mildred's St.

STREET

St Edward's Church

HIGH

CARFAX

HORSEMONGER STREET

St Giles' Church

FISH STREET

PENNYFARTHING ST.

Grandpont

GRANDPONT

ST GILES'

North Gate

NORTHGATE ST.

St Martin's Church

GREAT BAILEY

South Gate

St Aldate's Church

LITTLE BAILEY

St Peter le Bailey

NORTH BAILEY

St Ebbe's Church

Dominican Friars

Castle

West Gate

Franciscan Friars

River Thames

Carmelite Friars

St Thomas's Church

Osney Abbey

300 metres

200

100

0

OXFORD c.1250

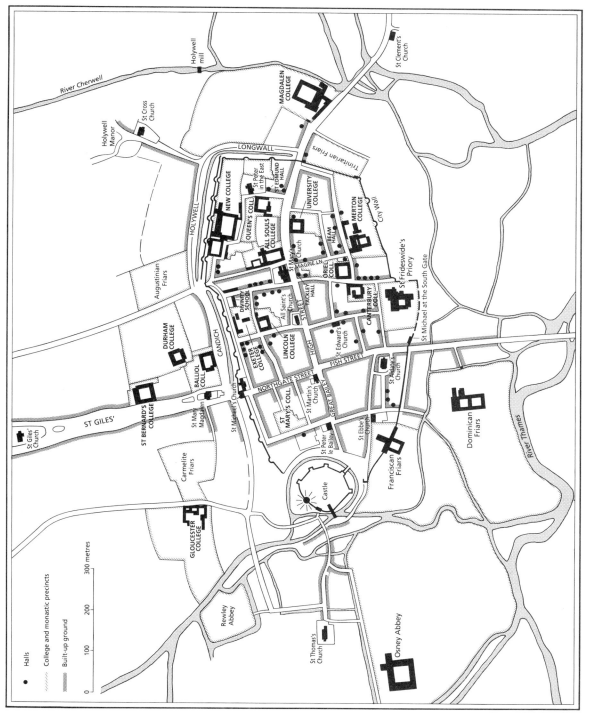

Halls
•
College and monastic precincts
Built-up ground

0   100   200   300 metres

St Giles'
Church

ST GILES'

Carmelite
Friars

ST BERNARD'S
COLLEGE

St Mary
Magdalen

DURHAM
COLLEGE

BALLIOL
COLL.

CANDICH

St Michael's Church

ST
MARY'S COLL.

St Martin's
Church

GREAT BAILEY

St Peter
le Bailey

Rewley
Abbey

GLOUCESTER
COLLEGE

Castle

Franciscan
Friars

St Ebbe's
Church

Osney Abbey

St Thomas's
Church

River Thames

Dominican
Friars

St Aldate's Church

NORTHGATE STREET

EXETER
COLLEGE

LINCOLN
COLLEGE

HIGH

DIVINITY
SCHOOL

All Saint's
Church

St Mary's
Church

Augustinian
Friars

HOLYWELL

NEW COLLEGE

St Peter
in the East

ST EDMUND
HALL

QUEEN'S COLL.

ALL SOULS
COLLEGE

UNIVERSITY
COLLEGE

MERTON
COLLEGE

City Wall

MAGPIE LN
PACKLEY
HALL

ORIEL
COLL.

BEAM
HALL

FISH STREET

CANTERBURY
COLL.

St Edward's
Church

St Frideswide's
Priory

St Michael at the South Gate

River Cherwell

Holywell
mill

Holywell
Manor

St Cross
Church

LONGWALL

Trinitarian Friars

MAGDALEN
COLLEGE

St Clement's
Church

OXFORD IN 1500

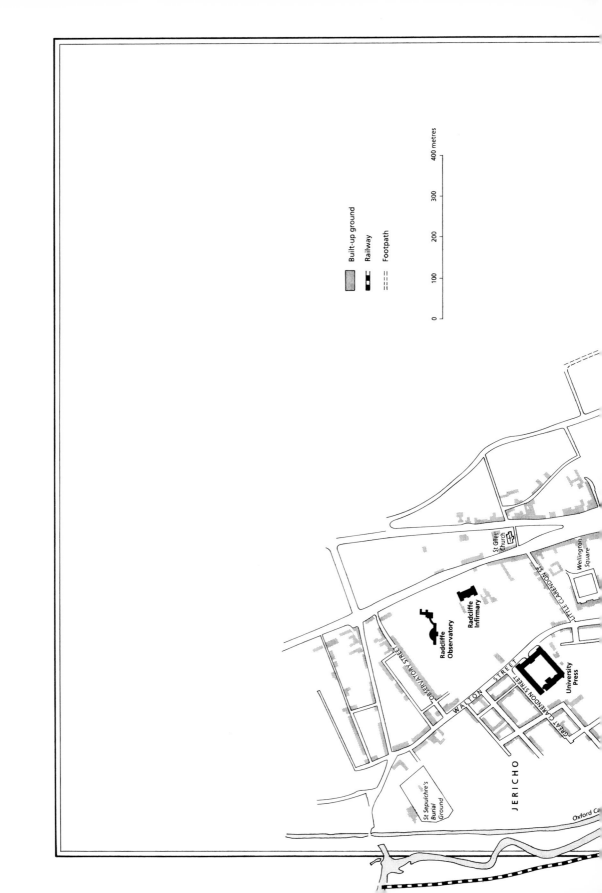

Built-up ground

Railway

Footpath

0   100   200   300   400 metres

St Giles's
Church

Radcliffe
Observatory

Radcliffe
Infirmary

Wellington
Square

OBSERVATORY STREET

GREAT CLARENDON STREET

LITTLE CLARENDON ST

University
Press

WALTON STREET

JERICHO

St Sepulchre's
Burial Ground

Oxford Ca

OXFORD IN 1850

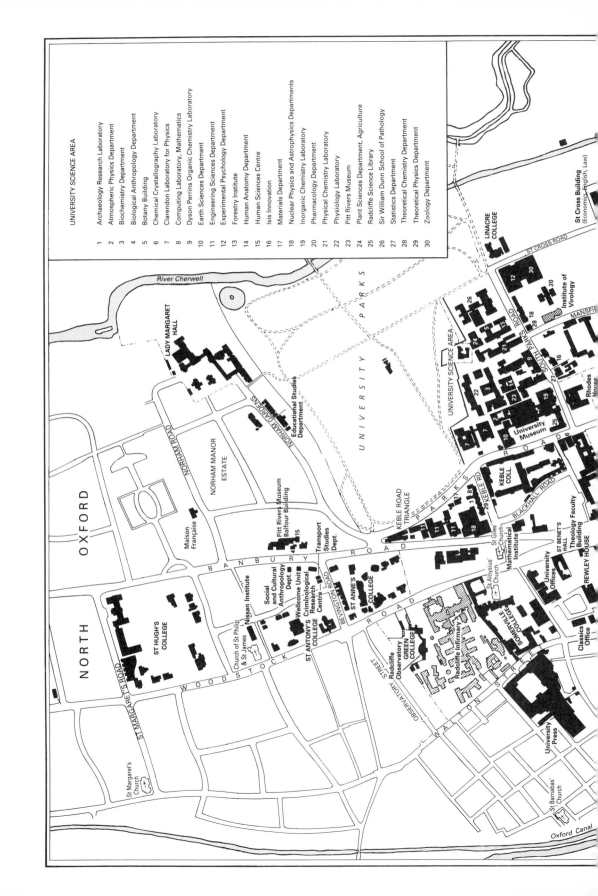

UNIVERSITY SCIENCE AREA

1 Archaeology Research Laboratory
2 Atmospheric Physics Department
3 Biochemistry Department
4 Biological Anthropology Department
5 Botany Building
6 Chemical Crystallography Laboratory
7 Clarendon Laboratory for Physics
8 Computing Laboratory, Mathematics
9 Dyson Perrins Organic Chemistry Laboratory
10 Earth Sciences Department
11 Engineering Sciences Department
12 Experimental Psychology Department
13 Forestry Institute
14 Human Anatomy Department
15 Human Sciences Centre
16 Isis Innovation
17 Materials Department
18 Nuclear Physics and Astrophysics Departments
19 Inorganic Chemistry Laboratory
20 Pharmacology Department
21 Physical Chemistry Laboratory
22 Physiology Laboratory
23 Pitt Rivers Museum
24 Plant Sciences Department, Agriculture
25 Radcliffe Science Library
26 Sir William Dunn School of Pathology
27 Statistics Department
28 Theoretical Chemistry Department
29 Theoretical Physics Department
30 Zoology Department

OXFORD IN 1990

ST CATHERINE'S COLLEGE

St Cross Church

Florey Building (Queen's Coll.)

GREYFRIARS

MAGDALEN BRIDGE

River Cherwell

ST HILDA'S COLLEGE

River Cherwell

MAGDALEN COLLEGE

LONGWALL STREET

Dept. of Fine Art

School of Geography

City wall

NEW COLLEGE

ST EDMUND HALL

HOLYWELL STREET

MANCHESTER COLLEGE

...AD

HERTFORD COLL.

QUEEN'S COLL.

ALL SOULS COLL.

Examination Schools

Faculty of Modern History Building (b)

HIGH STREET

UNIVERSITY COLLEGE

MERTON COLLEGE

CORPUS CHRISTI COLLEGE

...COLL.

CHRIST

CHURCH

MEADOW

CATTE STREET

St Mary's Church

New Bodleian

Museum of the History of Science

BRASENOSE COLL.

ORIEL COLL.

TRINITY COLLEGE

BROAD ST.

EXETER COLL.

LINCOLN COLL.

Town Hall

Music Faculty Building

FOLLY BRIDGE

TURL STREET

BALLIOL COLL.

St Michael's Church

JESUS COLL.

CHRIST CHURCH

ST ALDATES

Blackfriars

GILES'

St Mary Magdalen

GEORGE ST.

CORNMARKET STREET

CARFAX

St Aldate's Church

PEMBROKE COLL.

SPEEDWELL STREET

River Thames

Oriental Institute (a)

Ashmolean Museum

Archaeological Institute (a)

BEAUMONT STREET

Social Studies Faculty Building (c)

Oxford Union

NEW INN HALL ST.

QUEEN STREET

St Ebbe's Church

Westgate Centre

CAMPION HALL

RUSKIN COLLEGE

ST PETER'S COLLEGE

NEW ROAD

CASTLE STREET

Thames

WORCESTER COLLEGE

NUFFIELD COLLEGE

Castle Mound

PARK END ST.

St Thomas's Church

Railway Station

University building

Institution associated with the University

Railway

Footpath

a   Formerly Barnett House

b   Formerly Indian Institute

c   Formerly City of Oxford High School for Boys

0   100   200   300 metres

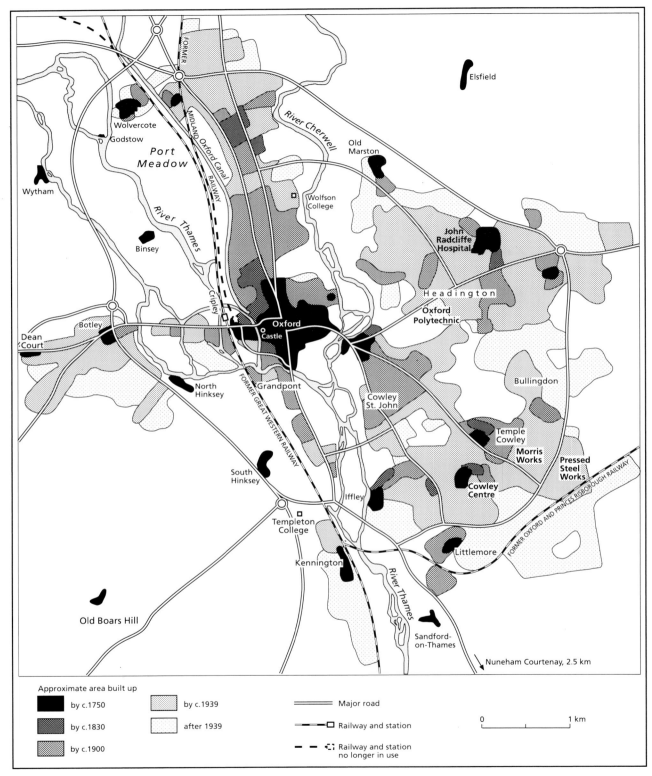

GROWTH OF THE URBAN AREA

Map labels:

Elsfield

Wolvercote
Godstow

Port Meadow

Wytham

Binsey

River Cherwell

Old Marston

Wolfson College

John Radcliffe Hospital

River Thames

MIDLAND OXFORD CANAL RAILWAY

FORMER

Osney

H e a d i n g t o n

Oxford Polytechnic

Dean Court

Botley

Oxford Castle

North Hinksey

Grandpont

Bullingdon

FORMER GREAT WESTERN RAILWAY

Cowley St. John

Temple Cowley

Morris Works

Pressed Steel Works

South Hinksey

Cowley Centre

FORMER OXFORD AND PRINCES RISBOROUGH RAILWAY

Iffley

Templeton College

Littlemore

Kennington

River Thames

Old Boars Hill

Sandford-on-Thames

Nuneham Courtenay, 2.5 km

Legend:

Approximate area built up

by c.1750
by c.1830
by c.1900
by c.1939
after 1939

Major road

Railway and station

Railway and station no longer in use

0   1 km

THE
ILLUSTRATED
HISTORY OF
OXFORD
UNIVERSITY

I

City and University

JOHN PREST

OXFORD is a county town and a borough. It grew up at the southern tip of a promontory lying between the River Thames and the River Cherwell, at a place where it was easy for men to drive cattle through the water. It was, and to this day still is, almost encircled by meadows which are liable to flood. Archaeological excavation suggests that continuous settlement began in the eighth century, and the first written reference occurs early in the tenth, when the Saxons erected a fortified *burg* with earthen ramparts. From Carfax one can see how the streets were (by English standards) laid out according to a remarkably rectilinear pattern. By 1066 there were more than a thousand houses, and Oxford was the sixth largest town in the kingdom after London, York, Norwich, Lincoln, and Winchester. In 1071 the western approaches to the town were

ST FRIDESWIDE fled to Oxford to avoid marriage to a bad King Algar. She established a nunnery, died *c*.735, and became the patron saint of city and University. Her foundation was suppressed by Wolsey in 1525, but this thirteenth-century representation has survived in the chapter house of the Cathedral.

WILLIAM DE BRAILES, who worked in Catte Street 1230–60, was one of the many scribes and illuminators attracted to Oxford. A scene from the life of St Catherine (*above*), who converted the philosophers sent to reason with her in her prison cell, was tortured on the wheel, and became the patron saint of learning, shows her body being buried by angels on Mount Sinai.

OXFORD was an important centre for the manufacture of stained glass. A late-thirteenth-century window (*left*) in St Michael at the Northgate shows St Edmund of Abingdon, who taught the new logic where St Edmund's Hall now stands and later became Archbishop of Canterbury.

changed by the construction of the Norman castle, and the Domesday Book of 1086 recorded 583 houses as having been laid 'waste'. Whatever this term meant, the town appears to have recovered rapidly. In the twelfth century there was a cloth industry, and the first charter, of *c*.1155, gave the members of the 'guild merchant' the privilege of moving their goods and offering them for sale free of tolls and customs throughout England and Normandy. This was the heyday of the 'busy, prosperous borough'. The Saxon defences were replaced by stone walls, and the freemen elected their own mayor, bailiffs, and aldermen. The historian J. R. Green (1837–83) was not far out when he wrote that Oxford 'had already seen five centuries of borough life before the first student appeared within its streets'.

Osney Abbey, founded in 1129, may have provided a focal point for learning, but nobody knows how the University began. Scholars were footloose, and in the twelfth century the University just grew, as first one teacher and then another settled in the town. Lectures are mentioned for the first time in 1116–20. Seventy years later, in 1187, when Gerald of Wales (1146?–1223) spent three days in Oxford reading his *Topographia*

Hibernica to the doctors, he recorded the existence of several different faculties. By this time the University was on its way to becoming a *studium generale*, whose members were attracted to Oxford from all over the country. By the beginning of the thirteenth century the University was acquiring a coherent structure. It was an ecclesiastical organization, and its prime function was to train an educated clergy. The students, who were clerks in minor orders, were required to place themselves under 'Regents', who met regularly in a body known later, and to this day, as Congregation. Senior members of the University, both Regents and non-Regents, gathered together in another assembly subsequently called Convocation. The whole was placed under a resident Chancellor elected by the Masters (the change to a non-resident Chancellor and a resident Vice-Chancellor took place in the fifteenth century), and the University became a corporation, so that there were then two rival bodies, civic and academic, in the same town.

Even at the best of times students disturbed the peace. We may doubt whether, as the *Oxford Protestant Magazine* expressed it in 1847, 'under the opposing banners of the Realists and Nominalists' the clerks decided 'by issue of bloody conflicts the speculative question, whether universals . . . have a real essence, and exist independent of particulars'. But it was soon recognized within the University that the students had formed

FISTS WERE THE LANGUAGE OF TOWN AND GOWN. In this illustration from C. E. Bradley's *College Life* (1850) the undergraduates appear to be getting the better of the skirmish. But some contests between town and gown were fought out over many hours, and in 1867 the Grenadier Guards were called from Windsor to put a stop to a town-and-gown brawl.

THE TOWN WAS PUNISHED for the St Scholastica's Day riots in 1355, and the University gained control over the assizes of bread and ale. By the time this photograph was taken in 1909 the assize was tolerated rather than resented, and the Clerks of the Market were more concerned with weights and measures than with price-fixing.

themselves into 'nations' of Northerners and Southerners (the dividing-line was the River Nene). The Welsh and Irish went in with the Southerners, whose ranks they strengthened when it came to battles between North and South. When not engaged in fighting each other, students complained about the local bread and ale and the cost of lodgings. The citizens began to regret having offered hospitality to the University, and for a century and a half they fought back. Between 1209, when a student killed his mistress and the townspeople seized some of his companions and hanged them, and St Scholastica's Day (10 February) 1355, when a dispute in the Swindlestock Tavern at Carfax sparked off a riot in which sixty-three members of the University died, the townsmen reacted to their situation like a native people resisting the encroachments of an imperial power. As Hastings Rashdall (1858–1924), the historian of European universities, once said of the High Street in Oxford, there are historic battlefields on which less blood has been spilt.

The townsmen were gradually overborne by superior power. At a very early stage in the conflict the members of the University invoked the authority of the Church and secured an interdict against the town. In the thirteenth century they vindicated their claim to clerical immunity, which meant that a clerk who fell into the hands of the city authorities would have to be delivered up to the University for trial. Every year after 1248 the mayor and bailiffs were obliged to swear an oath, upon taking office, to observe the privileges of the University; and every year after 1355 the mayor, bailiffs, and sixty burgesses were required to proceed, upon the anniversary of the riots, to the University Church, where they were to say a mass for the souls of the sixty-three slaughtered scholars, bow to the Chancellor, and lay one penny each upon the altar.

While other towns were advancing towards civic independence, Oxford was moving in the other direction. Every show of resistance upon the town's part ended with the

PARTS OF GLOUCESTER COLLEGE, which was established for the benefit of the Benedictine monks of the southern province, are preserved in Worcester College. Each of these fifteenth-century houses was kept for use by the scholars of a particular monastery: Hyde, Pershore, Tewkesbury, Winchcomb, and Worcester.

THESE HOUSES IN HOLYWELL (*left*) are among the small number of old town houses which survive after the expansion of the colleges. On the opposite side of the street others like them were demolished to make way for the looming mass of New College's Scott building of 1872.

THE FRIARS WERE PIONEERS IN LEARNING. The illustration (*right*) comes from a fifteenth-century manuscript of *Piers Plowman*, and the author, William Langland, was no friend of theirs. But many of the most famous Oxford-trained scholars of the thirteenth and fourteenth centuries, including Roger Bacon, Duns Scotus, and William of Ockham, were friars.

University acquiring new privileges. By the middle of the fourteenth century the University had, through the favour of successive kings, achieved uneasy dominion over the town. To the disadvantage of the citizens, it had won control of the market, of the licensing of alehouses, and of the various assizes for regulating the prices of provisions and for checking weights and measures. The Chancellor possessed the power to 'dis-common' tradesmen with whom the University fell into disagreement (that is, to prohibit members of the University from trading with them), and thereby to deprive them of their livelihood. The University circumvented the clause in the town's charter which restricted trade to persons born and apprenticed in Oxford, brought in favoured clients of its own, and declared them to be privileged persons. Finally, the University was given exclusive power to police the town at night. The students, all of whom were male and

THE ENDOWED COLLEGE
lived off its estates, and as
recently as 1945, when this
photograph (*left*) was taken,
every scholar in his room was
supported by eleven agricul-
turalists labouring in the fields,
like these tenants of St John's
College on the estate nearby at
Long Wittenham.

EVERY YEAR, AFTER THEY
HAD PAID THEIR RENTS, the
tenants were treated to a dinner
in the college like this one
(*below*), of about 1900 (when
they were served venison from
the park?), in the hall of
Magdalen College.

living away from home, had to be saved from the perils of experimental sex. An evening curfew was imposed upon the inhabitants, and any woman who ventured out on to the streets was liable to be arrested and detained as a prostitute. While the town authorities were forbidden to enter University property, the University Proctors, in pursuit of a suspect, could force their way into any house they chose.

In the fourteenth century, following the Black Death, English towns contracted, and the population of Oxford fell below the level recorded in the eleventh century. Property became derelict, and this in turn prepared the way for the development of a collegiate structure which was ultimately to distinguish Oxford (and Cambridge) from all other European universities, and to determine the future of the city. When the first scholars arrived in the twelfth century, some of them lived in lodgings, like Chaucer's clerk of Oxenford, while others gathered together with their teachers in what became known as halls of residence. Monastic orders set up houses for their own members, and the friars followed. A hall was not unlike other property. It could be sold, and with the passage of the generations it would probably change hands and might be converted to another use. Even when there were hundreds of halls, as there were before the end of the fourteenth century, it was still not inconceivable that University teaching might one day, like any other trade, decline or migrate. Before that could happen, however, everything was changed by the introduction of the endowed college. In the twelfth and thirteenth centuries there were endowed colleges in France and Italy, but they were to vanish while a majority of those in England survived and grew. Oxford colleges have not, upon the whole, expanded quickly, but then they have been able to afford to wait. Seen from the point of view of the town, the colleges appear like cancers, slowly eating away century after century at the homely timber frames and studded partitions of Oxford's indigenous architecture, and substituting obtrusive purpose-built student palaces in their stead. There are dozens of places in the city where a guide can say 'Houses stood here and were pulled down to make way for a college': none where he can point to the remains of a college whose lands were returned to town use. (The sites of colleges which did fail, Durham, Canterbury, Gloucester, St Bernard's, and St Mary's Colleges, have been absorbed into colleges which still exist.)

The colleges changed the University from a society of scholars with no fixed address to a permanent, and ultimately overwhelming, physical presence. The earliest colleges—University College, Balliol, and Merton, dating from the thirteenth century—were chiefly founded to house what we would now call graduates, reading for higher degrees, and Merton was the first to erect staircase accommodation, a chapel, and a dining-hall around a quadrangle, in the manner that is now held throughout the world to be characteristic of Oxford. In the fourteenth century three more colleges—Exeter, Oriel, and Queen's—were endowed before William of Wykeham (1324–1404) began, in 1369, to take advantage of the collapse of house prices in Oxford to buy up a site for a 'New' college, which did indeed set new standards of opulence which were to become the norm, and therefore condition the accessibility of higher education in England.

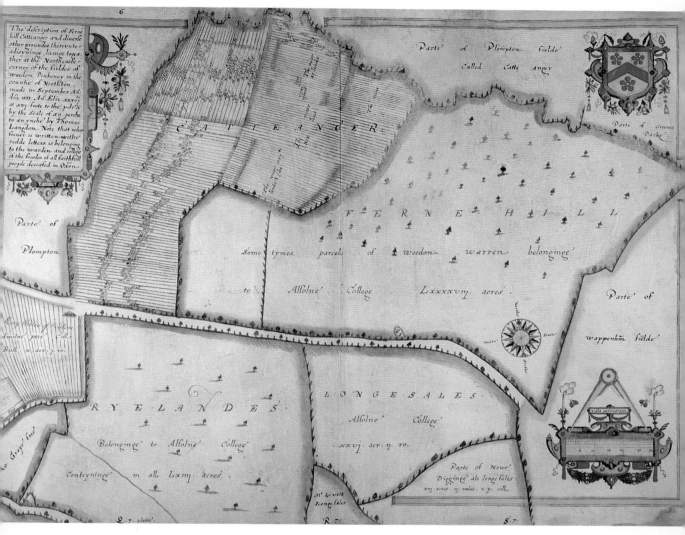

A THOROUGH SURVEY made it easier for an endowed college to manage a distant estate. This map of the lands belonging to All Souls College at Weedon in Northamptonshire was commissioned by the Warden, Robert Hovenden, and made by Thomas Langdon in 1594.

VIEW OF OXFORD from South Park: rising above the houses in St Clements, the legendary spires are framed between Magdalen tower on the left and Hawksmoor's towers at All Souls on the right.

In the fifteenth century the number of students fell, and in the sixteenth the halls began to decline as residence in an endowed college became common among undergraduates as well as graduates. For century after century existing colleges enlarged their premises and additional colleges were founded: Lincoln, All Souls, and Magdalen in the fifteenth century, Brasenose, Corpus Christi, Christ Church, Trinity, St John's, and Jesus in the sixteenth, Wadham and Pembroke in the seventeenth, Worcester and Hertford, which had to struggle for existence, in the eighteenth (to these should be added St Edmund Hall, which survived without an endowment from the thirteenth century). As the colleges expanded, they took up more and more of the eastern two-thirds of the town, on one side of the line running from north to south and joining St Giles' to St Aldate's. Business property became concentrated on the other side, in the western third, between Cornmarket and the Castle, while the borough and county offices and, last of all, the inhabitants fitted in wherever they could.

It is not easy to estimate just how humiliating the town's position remained between the middle of the fourteenth and the middle of the eighteenth century. Apologists for the University argue that its powers were exercised only occasionally. That may be true, but the townsmen never ceased wishing to be rid of them, and there were occasions, in the sixteenth and seventeenth centuries, when it appeared that their prayers might be granted. In the 1530s there was a chance that Henry VIII might follow up the destruction of the monasteries by dissolving the colleges, many of which had links with monastic foundations. Upon reflection, the King decided that he valued Oxford as a nursery of statesmen, and informed the town that he judged 'no money better bestowed than that which is given to our Universities, for by their maintenance our Realm shall be well governed when we are dead and rotten'. The original endowment for Cardinal College had come from the lands of St Frideswide's, a house of secular canons, which was dissolved by Wolsey (1475?–1530) in 1525. In 1546 the college emerged with a share in the spoil of Osney Abbey as the new joint foundation of Christ Church and the Cathedral of Oxford, thus adding diocesan politics to Oxford's already complicated affairs. Then, at the beginning of Elizabeth's reign, it became illegal to say mass in England, and the town thankfully assumed that the St Scholastica's Day ceremony would be allowed to

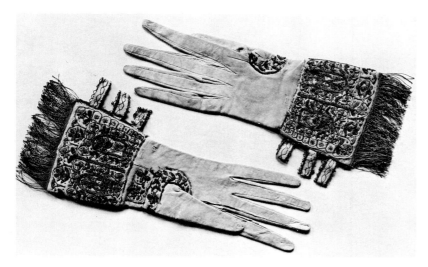

QUEEN ELIZABETH VISITED OXFORD IN 1566, and was presented by the Vice-Chancellor with six pairs of gloves (this pair in the Ashmolean Museum is believed to be one of them). Gloves made in Oxford and Woodstock were renowned for their pliability and high-quality decoration. The Vice-Chancellor still presents white gloves to the Crown Court judges when they come to Oxford.

The Cheife places in the Citie obserued *by seuerall letters*

A S Giles
B S Iohns Colledg
C Trinitie Colledg
D Balliol Colledg
E Magdalen Colled
F S Michaell
G Iesus Coll
H Exeter Colledg
I Vniuersitie scho
K Lyncolne Colle
L All Hallowes
M S Martins
N Corne Markett
O S Peters in Baile

P The Castle
Q S Thomas
R S Ebbes
S S Aldates
T Christ Church Coll
V Christ Church
W Corpus Chr. Col
X Merton Coll
Y S Maries
Z All Soules Coll
1 Vniuersitie Col
2 Brasenose Col
3 Oriall Col
4 Eastgate

THE ROYALIST FORTIFICATIONS around Oxford were formidable. Readers who find it difficult to reconcile this plan (*above*), drawn in 1645, with the city they know should hold the picture up to a mirror—not an early attempt at military disinformation, just a printer's error.

UPON THE OUTBREAK OF WAR the Royal Mint moved to Oxford. In January 1642 (the date is Old Style and would now be rendered 1643) the King asked the colleges to surrender their plate. Loyal Oriel agreed (*right*), but St John's, thinking to save its treasures, offered £800 instead. The King accepted the money and took their plate as well.

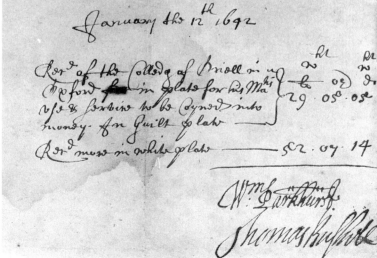

lapse. But the University substituted a sermon for the mass and, with the power of the Tudor State behind it, compelled the town to resume its annual penance.

The University survived into the new era of the Anglican Establishment, and in 1604 it was invited to elect its own Members to serve in the House of Commons. It still remained primarily a nursery of clergymen, but the student body included an increasing proportion of the sons of the secular aristocracy and gentry, with long purses and expensive lifestyles. New statutes were adopted by the University at the prompting of Archbishop Laud (1573–1645) in 1636. In the town these were resented as an 'Ocean or Great Sea of Privilege'. Within the University, where the colleges had already taken over most of the teaching, the innovation lay in the setting up of a Hebdomadal Board, composed of Heads of Houses (i.e. colleges), who chose the Vice-Chancellor and became the ruling cabinet of the University. In this way the University became a loose federation of colleges, the complexity of whose operation has baffled enquiry ever since. For the next three hundred years the colleges were to be more important than the University, and the townspeople, understandably, began to use the expression 'the colleges' when they wished to refer to the University.

When the Civil War broke out, town and gown took opposite sides: Oxford became the headquarters of the King's army, the colleges were turned into barracks for the Cavaliers, and the townspeople, who sympathized with Parliament, were disarmed. Following the execution of the King in 1649, the town authorities hoped to be relieved from their 'most intollerable sufferings and oppressions'. Once again they were to be disappointed. Parliament turned the royalist Heads out of the colleges, and having changed the personnel, omitted to do anything about the privileges. A generation later the town led the way in resisting the illegal exercise of James II's prerogative. But it could scarcely expect William III to take its side in any struggle against the University, and the only possible ally, the county of Oxfordshire, had seldom made common cause with the borough. Now, the sympathies of the landed gentry of the shire lay with the University, and nothing could be changed.

Oxford was not a town with a university, as it might have been in Italy, France, or Germany, but a university town. In the eighteenth century the lowly status of the town authorities led to a loss of civic morale. The annual elections of the mayor and other officers degenerated into a ritual of beer and bribes, in which only 'the most indigent, illiterate and worthless inhabitants' cared to participate, and the town fell into debt. The corporation started selling off some of its house properties (in Kybald Street, for example). Then in 1768 it sold the Parliamentary representation of the borough, with its two seats, to the fourth Earl of Abingdon (1740–99) and the fourth Duke of Marlborough (1739–1817) for £5,670 (the earl retained control of his seat till 1796, the duke till 1812).

Happily, at this point an alternative model began to take shape, and the University and town agreed to come together in new bodies. The feeling that England's oldest university required a more appropriate urban setting led, in 1771, to the creation of a new

IN 1687 THE TOWN WAS MORE READY EVEN THAN THE UNIVERSITY to resist James II's illegal attempts to remodel corporate bodies. This propaganda painting by Egbert von Heemskerk the younger shows the King's messenger delivering an instruction to the mayor. In the foreground James's nominee for the position of alderman, abused by the spectators, mops his brow.

board of Commissioners, to amend 'certain of the Mile-Ways leading to Oxford', to repair Magdalen Bridge, to make 'commodious Roads from the said Bridge, through the University and City', and to make provision for cleansing and lighting the streets. The Commissioners, whose names were placed in order of social and academic rank, were drawn from both town and University. A majority came from the latter, but one of the first acts of this new body was to erect a new (now the covered) market in 1774, and to set up a joint market committee upon which the University and town were represented equally. The novel experience of working together initiated a process of change in the relations between town and gown, and in 1825 the University ceased to require the town to give penance on St Scholastica's Day.

That is not to say that everything ran smoothly thereafter—far from it. Under the Commissioners' Act the town was required to pay three-fifths of the improvement rates and the University two-fifths. There was no equality in that, and in the nineteenth century there was a series of disputes about rates. The colleges did not pay poor-rates. The University argued that 'it had no poor, and that it made no poor'. The townsmen pointed to the presence of large numbers of prostitutes who resorted to the workhouse when they were to be confined, and dumped their illegitimate children upon the parishes for support. Who used these women, if not the members of the University? And yet overseers who tried to levy poor-rates from the colleges were threatened, so it was alleged, with discommoning.

In 1843 a fresh attempt was made to compel Exeter College, which was unpopular with local tradesmen because it provided supplies to undergraduates from its own store, to pay poor-rates. The college's defence, which was that it had once been in the parish of St Mildred, that St Mildred's Church had been demolished to make way for Lincoln College, and that it was now therefore extra-parochial, succeeded. Worse still, the University's riposte to this initiative was to secure an Act of Parliament, of 1848,

THE TAUNTON FAMILY came from Cornwall. William Taunton was Clerk of the Peace for Oxfordshire and Town Clerk of Oxford, and was knighted in 1814 when the allied sovereigns came to Oxford. He dwelt in St Aldate's, and married the daughter of the sub-Treasurer of Christ Church. Three sons matriculated at the University.

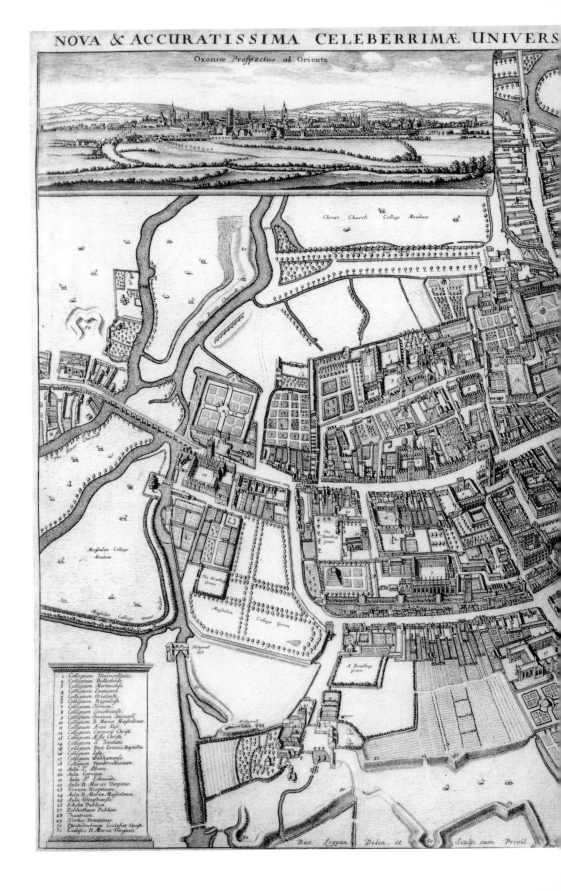

Oxoniæ *Prospectus ab Oriente*

Christ Church College Meadow

Magdalen College
Meadow

Magdalen College Water

Magdalen College Grove

The Bowling
Green

The Bowling
Green

A Bowling
Green

Holywell
Hill

Holywell

1 Collegium Universitatis.
2 Collegium Balliolense.
3 Collegium Mertonense.
4 Collegium Exoniense.
5 Collegium Orientale.
6 Collegium Reginense.
7 Collegium Novum.
8 Collegium Lincolniense.
9 Collegium Omnium Animarū.
10 Collegium B. Mariæ Magdalenæ.
11 Collegium Ænei Nasi.
12 Collegium Corporis Christi.
13 Collegium Ædis Christi.
14 Collegium S. Trinitatis.
15 Collegium Divi Ioannis Baptistæ.
16 Collegium Iesu.
17 Collegium Wadhamense.
18 Collegium Pembrochianum.
19 Aula S. Albani.
20 Aula Cervina.
21 Aula S. Edmundi.
22 Aula B. Mariæ Virginis.
23 Novum Hospitium.
24 Aula B. Mariæ Magdalenæ.
25 Aula Glocestrensis.
26 Schola Publicæ.
27 Bibliotheca Publica.
28 Theatrum.
29 Hortus Botanicus.
30 Parochæcium Ecclesia Christi.
31 Ecclesia B. Mariæ Virginis.

Dav. Loggan Delin. et Sculp. cum Privil.

Reverendissimo in Christo
Patri, natalium splendore, vir
tutum meritis, literarum Scien
tia, Sacris demum infulis consum̄a
tissimè Illustri, D.no HENRICO COMPTON
Episcopo Oxoniensi; sedis suæ (quæ
tanto Præsule quasi novo fastigio
aucta altius assurgit) Ichnogra
phiam hanc in obsequij debitissi
mi tesseram. D.D.C.Q.
Dav. Loggan.

The Black Fryers

Castle

Broken Hayes

Beaumont

Gloucester green

1	University College.	27	The Publick Library.
2	Balioll College.	28	The Theater.
3	Merton College.	29	The Phisick Garden.
4	Exeter College.	30	Christ Church Almshous.
5	Oriell College.	31	St Maries Church.
6	Queens College.	32	Carfax.
7	New College.	33	Allhallowes.
8	Lincoln College.	34	St Aldats.
9	Allsoules College.	35	St Ebbs.
10	Magdalen College.	36	St Peters in the Bayly.
11	Brazen-nose College.	37	St Michaels.
12	Corpus Christi College.	38	St Magdalen.
13	Christ Church College.	39	St Peters in the East.
14	Trinity College.	40	St Clements.
15	St Johns College.	41	Hollywell.
16	Iesus College.	42	St Giles.
17	Wadham College.	43	St Thomas.
18	Pembrock College.	44	The Town Hall.
19	Alban Hall.	45	Bocardo and North gate.
20	Hart Hall.	46	The East gate.
21	Edmond Hall.	47	Frier Bacons Study.
22	St Mary Hall.	48	Paradise garden.
23	New Inn.	49	The Gray Friers.
24	Magdalen Hall.	50	The Ruins of the
25	Glocester Hall.		Forresication.
26	The Publick Schools.		

DAVID LOGGAN was appointed engraver to the University in 1669. The pages of his *Oxonia Illustrata* were cross-referenced to the *Historia et Antiquitates Universitatis Oxoniensis* compiled by the antiquarian Anthony Wood, and for many years the University used to present copies of the two works to its distinguished visitors.

reducing its contribution to the improvement rates from two-fifths to one-third. The University's case was that the proportions had become 'inequitable', because the population of the town had grown from 12,279 in 1801 to nearly 30,000 while that of the University had not increased at all. There had been a thousand undergraduates in 1800, and in the mid-century there was still the same number.

The argument served its turn, but it was one which the University might have done better not to have employed. Townsmen were dependent upon the University for their livelihoods. If the University remained stationary while the town grew, how were the townspeople to exist? For the first time since disputes between town and gown began the town's complaint found a response in high places. The population of England doubled between 1801 and 1851, and Parliament too thought that the University ought to be expanding and putting its endowments to better use. In the changed atmosphere created by the appointment of the first Royal Commission of Inquiry into the University in 1850 and the termination of the restriction upon matriculation and entry to Anglicans in 1854, the colleges (except Christ Church, which did not surrender extra-parochial status until 1875) were at last shamed into agreeing, in 1854, to pay poor-rates. The University then sought to be allowed to appoint half the members of the new Board of Guardians. But Parliament stepped in, took the University at its own valuation of 1848, and imposed a formula according to which the University contributed a third of the poor-rates and received a third of the representation, the other two-thirds being divided equally between the town council and the parishes. Under the watchful eyes of the nation, the colleges were being taught how to behave towards the town, and in 1859 the University agreed to an Act releasing the mayor and other officers of the city from the oath, imposed in 1248, requiring them to observe its privileges.

The Board of Guardians worked well, and the sides gained confidence in each other. The Mileways Commissioners too were infected with the new spirit, and in 1864 they resolved by a majority of 60 to 9 to adopt the Local Government Act of 1858. In this way they terminated their own existence, and voluntarily exchanged an organization upon which the University had enjoyed a majority for a new Local Board of Health, upon which the University, the town council, and the parishes were, once again, to be equally represented. As the *Chronicle* said, 'city and university have, for once, been found in perfect accord . . . the preponderating influence of the University . . . is totally destroyed, while on the other hand the representation assigned to it is that to which it is justly and fairly entitled'. The new body, which would enjoy enormously increased powers of borrowing, would be able to cope with the public-health problems of the growing town and construct the much-needed sewer outfall at Sandford. Once again the University was required to pay a third of the rates.

The establishment of the Local Board of Health was followed in 1868 by that of a single joint police force, which replaced both the town constables, who had looked after the streets by day, and the uniformed, professional night police, recruited and paid by the University, who had had sole jurisdiction from 9 p.m. to 4 a.m. Upon this occasion

Watch & Ward in the Semi-detached House – Oxford.

Explan. The University long ago wrested from the City the prerogative of keeping the Police under their direction and — on their pay. The prerogative became an incumbrance. Now the University is trying to shift the burden on to the shoulders of the City.

PROXIMUS SUM EGOMET MIHI

Two Neighbours 'Fast Asleep' Watch! Always out — Never at home to Party.

What's the odds so long as you're happy?

TO HUGO'S WATER PIPE

PARTY WALL

'SITY FORCE

TRUNCHEON

MR TOWN

S CAVE CANEM

Eligible Sites in the Banbury & Wood[...] Roads To be Let

On Esthetic Building & Ornamental Dog Kennel

TAXES
On Dogs
— Hair Powder
— Liveries
— Crests
— Vanity

Mr Gown. There now — you may call him yours, dear Mr Town.
Mr Town. No, dear Mr Gown — I couldn't think of it. Call him yours as heretofore. And (Aside) Pay the tax.

VICE-CHANCELLOR AND MAYOR dispute the shares of town and gown (the 'semi-detached house' of the title) in the costs of the new joint police force which began patrolling on 1 January 1869. There were thirty-five men commanded by a superintendent and two inspectors recruited from the Metropolitan Police. Whenever the officers expected trouble reinforcements were brought in from London.

it was the University which made the running, and its one-third share of the cost of the new police represented a substantial saving upon the sole costs of its own night force. The new arrangements did not, however, mean that everything changed at once. The vast majority of undergraduates were minors. If gilded and powerful parents were to continue to entrust their sons to the University, the latter, for its part, had to be able to reassure them that offences committed by their offspring would be trivialized as high spirits. After the riots of 2 May 1883 (following the visit of the Prince of Wales), 'A number of University men were taken to the [police] Station, and were afterwards handed over to the Proctors to be dealt with by them, whilst the citizens who were arrested will have to answer for their conduct before the City Magistrates.'

AFTER THE PRINCE OF WALES had opened the new Town Hall in 1897 the undergraduates went on the rampage. F. E. Smith, who was a young fellow of Merton College, was charged with disorderly conduct and with assaulting two (Metropolitan) policemen. He cross-summonsed PC Bird, the charges were dismissed, and Smith later became Lord Chancellor. The drawing is by A. N. Prentice.

There were still going to be grievances against the University lasting well into the twentieth century. In the meantime, the joint police force was followed, in 1870, by the establishment of a School Board, where, yet again, the University secured a third of the representation and paid a third of the rates. In 1874 the philosopher T. H. Green (1836–82) became a member of the Board. Two years later he was elected by the North ward to a seat on the town council. Green's temperance politics probably deepened the divide in city politics between the Liberals and Nonconformists on one side and the Conservative brewers, the Halls and the Morrells, on the other. But Green felt ashamed that Oxford, with a university in its midst, lacked a place of education for the people. He threw himself into a 'project for a Grammar School', where a number of free places would be reserved for poor scholars from the elementary schools—thus opening up a route along which the sons of ordinary Oxford citizens could reach the University. His initiative led to the foundation of the City of Oxford High School for Boys, which opened in 1881. When Green died, prematurely, in 1882, 'the Mayor and Corporation, wearing their official robes . . . walked in procession from the Council Chamber to Balliol College' and thence, in pouring rain, with 2,000 other people, to the burial in St Sepulchre's. 'A more impressive sight has never perhaps been witnessed in Oxford than at the funeral of Professor Green.'

Green 'was the first University teacher to break through the tradition which separated the official life of Oxford City from the official life of Oxford University'. With him was buried the worst of the centuries-old antagonism of town and gown. In the years following his death University and town co-operated to place all the powers and responsibilities of the various joint bodies which had grown up in the course of the nineteenth century (with the exception of the Poor Law Guardians, who continued in existence until 1929) in the hands of a new town council with the status of a county borough. The town was divided into four wards, and the University was formed into an additional ward of its own, so that it elected a fifth of the councillors. The regime began with a competition for the design of a new town hall, won by Henry T. Hare (1861–1921). When the building was opened in 1897, Alderman Robert Buckell (1841–1925) became the first citizen to receive an honorary degree of the University. In 1913 a University councillor was elected mayor for the first time.

The period in the middle of the nineteenth century, when the relationship between town and gown was being redefined, was also the great age of the public meeting. For the first time the authentic voices of the ordinary people of Oxford can be heard in the local newspapers, whose reports convey the clarity with which the inhabitants understood their position. The citizens of Oxford knew that they were in thrall to a finishing-

The D·I·A
Cautionary Guide to
~ OXFORD ~
With an introduction by
Clough Williams-Ellis, F.R.I.B.A.

THE TWO OXFORDS—A contrast by composite photographs

PRICE SIXPENCE

Published by the Design and Industries Association and sold by Sidgwick & Jackson, 44 Museum St., London, W.C.1

CLOUGH WILLIAMS-ELLIS drew attention to the continuing existence of two Oxfords and to the ugliness and degradation by which the University and the colleges were surrounded. He is more often remembered today for the planning and building of Portmeirion in North Wales.

school for the sons of the privileged élite, and compared themselves to the inhabitants of Windsor, where everything was subordinated to the castle. Tradesmen with seats upon the town council pointed out, rhetorically, that many of the colleges had been founded by people of their own kind. 'It was an Alderman and Merchant Tailor of London who established St. John's.' Now, 'The Colleges occupied the best and most advantageous sites throughout the city.' One alderman invited his audience to consider how every improvement to the University involved damage to the town, and another lamented that this was an irreversible process. By the middle of the century the University and colleges held 77 of the 150 acres in the city centre. The consequence was that the mass of the townsmen had been forced to take refuge either in the 'stived up alleys' behind the High Street or among the unhealthy suburbs in the 'low-lying situations' under the Castle.

Middle-class sentimentalists pictured Oxford as a casket of architectural jewels in mellowed stone rising out of the unspoilt countryside, and it is true that, looked at from Boars Hill or Elsfield, it appeared as though one could pass 'straight from the woods and meadows into the heart of the University'. But the reality was that between the two lay the 'base and brickish skirt' deplored by Gerard Manley Hopkins (1844–89), where the inhabitants knew as much about deprivation and fever as any in England. Oxford was a place of sharp contrasts. In the centre of the city, as Mr Faulkner said in 1848, 'the

BUYING GOODS ON CREDIT was a temptation to undergraduates. The nightmare shown in *College Life* (1850) was not so much the fear of accumulated interest, for few shopkeepers (except of course the moneylenders) would have stayed in business had they asked for that, but the prospective showdown with one's father.

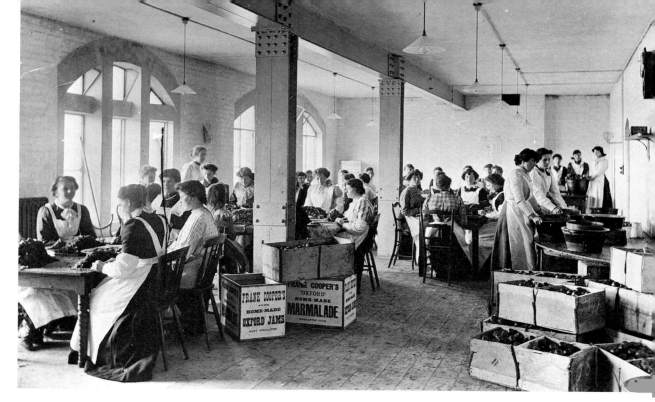

THE CUTTING-ROOM at Cooper's marmalade factory in Victoria Buildings opposite the Midland Railway station offered much-needed employment and companionship for women.

bells were going ting-tang, ting-tang everlastingly'. But where, he asked, was 'the justice and mercy?' The two Universities were called the two eyes of England: he 'could not say whether they had a squint or not', but certainly 'they all looked one way'. The University 'had learned the 11th commandment "to get all they can and keep all they can"'. Mr Faulkner was supported by Mr Dobney, who alleged that imbalance was marked even among the works carried out by the Mileways Commissioners. 'In the vicinity of the colleges there was plenty of light, while in St. Ebbe's and other places there was just light enough to make darkness visible. The same might be said also as to cleansing and paving in those places; it amounted to just nothing; but when they came to those parts of the city near the university, there was broad pavement and plenty of light.' The city was stirring. It was beginning to show 'a spirit of independence, somewhat foreign to that which had been exhibited in Oxford for many generations', and in 1852 one of the many hundreds of townspeople who voted in favour of the adoption of the Public Libraries Act said that what was wanted was 'A Public Library . . . Not the one at Blenheim, not the Radcliffe, not the Bodleian . . . but one in which everyone may stand, and . . . exclaim, it is mine!'

It was a great gain to the town when its local government was transformed in the middle of the nineteenth century. But there was still something missing, which was variety of employment, regular work, and decent wages. There were two kinds of citizen who had been able to accommodate themselves to conditions in a university town, the tradesmen and the college servants. The tradesmen were not always loved even by those they served. In 1847 a University magazine condemned the succession of persons presenting themselves with offers of service to varsity freshers. First, 'a pale-faced, low-voiced tailor, who combined in a marvellous degree the qualities of servility and audacity, displayed his patterns of the newest and most fashionable things . . .': fifth, another offered 'Sherry, Sir, bright as a sunbeam . . . and our Port, Sir! I assure you such as even the Portuguese themselves don't know the taste of.' A few years later the Royal Commission of 1850 criticized the tradesmen who enmeshed gullible students in credit (the only aspect of town-and-gown relations which it explored). But there was another side to the story. There were many undergraduates in Oxford 'to whom the expenditure of three, four, or five hundred pounds, more or less, in a term' was of no consequence. Competition for their custom was keen, and Oxford may not have been a town in which all tailors and all grocers and all wine merchants and silversmiths made fortunes. But it

A PORTER ejects a student who is not a member of the college with the words 'Non intrabis hic' ('You shall not enter here')—from a revised version of the New College statutes of about 1400, making changes required by William of Wykeham himself. The scene puts one in mind of representations of the angels banishing Adam and Eve from the Garden of Eden.

JOHN BOSSOM was porter at Brasenose, the college described in *The Adventures of Mr. Verdant Green* (1853–7), when this photograph was taken on 14 April 1860. The fictitious image conveyed in the book was not an easy one for either University or college to lose.

IN REGENCY ENGLAND dining could be a boisterous affair, and Robert Cruikshank's drawing of 1824 leaves no doubt that undergraduate parties where bumper succeeded bumper called for great tact on the part of the servants.

was one in which some tradesmen did exceptionally well. The names of Grimbley and Hughes were, and that of Basil Blackwell (1889–1984) is, legendary. Many of the connections, once formed, lasted for life, and it was not unknown for a former member of the University, in the course of fifty years, to order two hundred pairs of shoes from a cobbler who had fashioned him an individual last while he was an undergraduate. The name 'Oxford' upon a label became a recommendation, and Cooper's Oxford marmalade, for example, which was offered for sale in 1874, was soon being shipped to every corner of the British Empire. Successful tradesmen bought large houses on Headington hill and in North Oxford, found their way on to the town council, and, as we have seen, gradually reached a *modus vivendi* with the University.

The college servants identified totally with the young men they looked after. They welcomed them when they arrived: 'Hidges, looking kindly on an old master's son, "hoped his father was well", remarking, "you're very much like him, Sir".' The college scout 'softened that sense of embarrassment, discomfort, and isolation' which oppressed the freshmen who had left home for the first time. Servants loved to enthuse about their charges, knowing full well that 'Parliaments shall be as clay in their hands'

SHELDONIAN THEATRE.

Enormous attraction for the coming Commemoration.

THE SHAM LIBERAL UNVEILED!

THIS NEW SENSATION PIECE

Will open with a Scene of

CRIPLEY MEADOW AND PORT MEADOW

The Spires of OXFORD in the Distance.

First Act.

G. W. R. ENGINEERS

APPEAR SURVEYING.

Enter GOLDWIN SMITH on Horseback, singing "Yankee Doodle."

His sudden Dismay and Collapse on seeing a "BRITISH ARTIZAN" so near Oxford.

Second Act.

Scene changes to a House near the Parks,

The PROFESSOR in SERIOUS AGITATION discovers that he never was a LIBERAL,

Seizes Paper, and writes to the "Daily News" his Recantation.

Before the Curtain drops, the Memorialists, led by TOMMY SHORT, will sing in Dutch Concert

"ODI PROFANUM VULGUS ET ARCEO,"

Those who have forgotten their Latin will sing Professor CONINGTON's Translation

"I HATE THE SMELL OF FUSTIAN, I DO, I DO."

To the Air "I wish I was with Nancy."

Third Act.

GOLDWIN SMITH in the last stage of Exhaustion, trying in vain to get sensible men to sign his Memorial.

INTERLUDE BY THE CORPS DE BALLET—

First Danseuse - THE PRESIDENT OF TRINITY.

Ably seconded by PROFESSOR WALL, F. of Corpus, and Dr. FISHER, &c., &c.

Fourth Act.

Storm, Sham Thunder, and Sheet Lightning !

Under the able management of "THE TIMES."

The Scene for this Act, Painted by GOLDWIN SMITH, represents

"THE BRITISH ARTISAN DRUNK & DISORDERLY"

The UNIVERSITY & PUBLIC BUILDINGS **IN RUINS.**

Fifth Act.

Enter the FAIRY QUEEN

COMMON SENSE !

BETWEEN THE VICE-CHANCELLOR AND MAYOR,

With a large attendance of Members of the University, and Citizens of Oxford, escorting the

CHAIRMAN OF THE GREAT WESTERN RAILWAY ON AN ENGINE !

With Banners and Figures Emblematical of

PROGRESS, PROSPERITY, SOBRIETY, INTEGRITY, FREE TRADE AND FRIENDSHIP

TO THE ARTIZANS AND ALL MANKIND !

Last Scene.

GENERAL JOY!

In the midst of which, PROFESSOR SMITH leaves Oxford in a

DISSOLVING VIEW !

And Oxford appears with

NEW & HANDSOME ARCHITECTURAL BUILDINGS

THE UNIVERSITY EXTENDED!

THERE'S MORE A'COMING.

GOLDWIN SMITH was Regius Professor of Modern History. Not long after he had lost his character by opposing the proposed carriage works he resigned his chair and went to Cornell University. He found anti-British feeling running high in the United States (it was the time of the *Alabama* dispute), and three years later he migrated to Toronto.

and that 'the broad lands of England shall be theirs'. Service in college enjoyed a high status because, unlike household service, it was a predominantly male occupation, and the college servant did not live in, but returned every evening to his own home. The wages were modest, and in the eighteenth and nineteenth centuries servants were generally laid off in the vacations. But the perks were good, and in the second half of the nineteenth century many college servants owned their own homes in Jericho or beside the Cowley Road. Recruitment was by personal recommendation. Fathers secured positions for their sons, and dynasties of college servants were not unknown.

Tradesmen and college servants apart, the prospects for employment were grim, and there was 'a background of low wages to the labour of the place'. Even among the building trades, where the demand for stonemasons was high, 'trade-union rates of pay are low, and labourers' wages . . . are quite inadequate to support a large family . . . unless the wife or children earn money'. Wives and children heeded the message. The place was full of needlewomen, laundrywomen, and chars. Young girls became domestic servants, and the more fortunate ones found situations in the moneyed middle-class suburbs rising upon the St John's College estates in North Oxford. Throughout the nineteenth century domestic service was the largest single occupational category at 27 per cent, twice the national average. For boys Oxford offered 'abundant blind-alley occupations', running errands and attending to the college grounds. Most remarkable of all was the case of the University Press. Printing was one trade which the University had attracted to the town. The Press was founded in 1585, and between 1826 and 1830 it moved from the Clarendon Building in Broad Street to a new factory, complete with steam engines, chimney, and smoke, in Jericho. A suburb grew up around it. Many of the employees were highly skilled and earned good wages, but scores, hundreds even, were mere boys. No Factory Act applied to printing, and the works was conducted, as the Revd R. Greswell (1800–81) informed Convocation in 1865, 'as no Manchester man-ufactory was allowed to be'. The children were hired at the age of ten, 'were worked 12 hours a day', and were paid five shillings—some alleged two shillings and sixpence—a week. 'Nothing was done towards educating them', and to avoid paying them adult wages 'they were turned adrift at 16'.

The townspeople wished to increase their chances of employment, and in the middle of the nineteenth century two opportunities appeared for them to do this. The first involved the railway. Town and gown alike had welcomed the opening of the canal to Banbury in 1778, and to Coventry in 1790, and the prospect of cheap coals. In 1837–40, however, the projected railway from London to Bristol caught both sides in two minds. Tradesmen feared that members of the University would go to London to make their purchases; the University was alarmed lest undergraduates find their way to the capital to take their pleasures. The uncertainty did the town harm: instead of coming direct to Oxford, the railway swung west at Didcot, and Oxford was relegated to a branch line, opened in 1844 as far as Grand Pont. The Midland Railway arrived from Bletchley in 1851, and the following year the Great Western opened a station on the present site, and began to extend its line towards Worcester.

In 1865 the Great Western resolved to move its carriage works away from Padding-ton. Oxford Council, acting in a way that would have reflected credit upon a twentieth-century development corporation, found a site in Cripley, ascertained that St John's College would sell land for housing, fought off rival bids from Reading, Didcot, Abing-don, and Banbury, and appeared to have clinched the deal. The townspeople knew that tradesmen and mechanics 'did better in large towns than in small ones', and looked for-ward to 'these carriage builders' requiring 'a vast number of apprentices'. But that was what the members of the University feared, and the Regius Professor of Modern History, Goldwin Smith (1823–1910), raised an opposition. In vain did Mr Neate (1806–79), one of the Members for the borough, warn that if the town 'lost the boon through the interference of the University', it 'would rankle' for years to come. Convocation sent a delegation to wait upon the directors of the GWR. Throughout the summer the directors held faithfully to their compact with the town. They were vilified in *The Times*, and *Punch* lampooned them for aiming to take the University's pride down a peg, 'those what you call Dons—those aughty scholars . . . The time as come for a hend of logic and Greek and Latin . . . Cost what it may, we'll set up our factory at Hoxford . . . It's a question of Railways against Colleges. This sort of thing is going to squash that sort of thing'. The sarcasms of the respectable press proved too much for Richard Potter (1826–92), the chairman of the GWR, who resigned. He was succeeded by Daniel Gooch (1816–89), who had always advocated relocating the works at Swindon, and lost little time in abandoning the Oxford project.

OPPONENTS OF THE PROPOSED CARRIAGE WORKS pointed out that the Thames overflowed its banks almost every year, and that the factory and the artisans, represented here in Sydney Hall's cartoon by *faber* (a smith), might be flooded.

THE FOURTH BATTALION of the Oxfordshire Light Infantry on parade in Broad Street in 1875. The most famous engagement in the whole history of the regiment was the seizure from the air of the Benouville (now Pegasus) and Ranville bridges over the River Orne in the early hours of 6 June 1944 as the invasion of Normandy began.

The second occasion on which the town enjoyed a prospect of obtaining alternative employment came eight years later, when the Army was being reorganized and the War Office required a site for a new depot somewhere in Oxfordshire or Buckinghamshire. Edward Cardwell (1813–86), the Secretary of State for War, who was a Member of Parliament for the town, selected Oxford 'because it had a larger population among which enlistments for the army could be made than any other town which could be selected'. Twenty-four professors and eighty-nine tutors petitioned against 'the too probable collision between academic and military discipline'. Cardwell stood firm, and Pembroke College agreed to sell land at Bullingdon. The contractors were already on site when there was a change of Government and Gathorne Gathorne-Hardy (1814–1906), one of the two Members for the University, succeeded Cardwell. Hopes and fears ran high that he would cancel the project, and in a maiden speech Lord Randolph Churchill (1849–95), the Member for Woodstock, raised the spectre of

Working-men of Oxford,

If you like this sort of thing vote for Mr HALL, who voted for it July 18.1879, in the House of Commons.

If you do not, then vote for Sir WILLIAM HARCOURT, who voted against it on the same day.

Oxford's becoming another Aldershot. The proposal to attach regiments to counties had turned into a battle between the local MPs, and Churchill was answered by A. W. Hall (1838–1919), the brewer (Member for Oxford), who pointed out that cancellation would 'undo the good relations established on the Board of Guardians and the Local Board'. Gathorne-Hardy was caught, the project went ahead, and Cowley barracks became the base for the 43rd and 52nd Foot Regiments of the Oxfordshire and Buckinghamshire Light Infantry. But the number of recruits stationed there remained small, and the town's hopes of securing increased employment were once again dashed.

In the second half of the nineteenth century numbers in the University doubled. Existing colleges were enlarged, one new college, Keble, was founded in 1868, Hertford was refounded by Act of Parliament in 1874, and a decree was passed allowing non-collegiate students to live in lodgings. Four halls, which later became colleges, were founded for women—Lady Margaret Hall (1878), Somerville (1879), St Hugh's (1886), and St Hilda's (1893)—together with a Society of (women) Home Students, which ultimately, in 1942, became St Anne's. These again were followed, in a development reminiscent of the thirteenth century, by a new wave of private religious halls, three Nonconformist—Mansfield (Congregationalist, 1886), Manchester (Unitarian, 1889), and Regent's Park (Baptist, 1927)—and three Roman Catholic—Campion Hall (1896), St Benet's (1897), and Greyfriars (1910).

In the meantime the town grew even faster. North Oxford continued its measured, zoned, and genteel expansion under the controlling hand of St John's College, and became a residential resort both for dons, who were now allowed to marry and retain their fellowships, and for retired civil servants and Indian Government officials. In South-East Oxford, where the politically motivated Freehold Land and Building Societies operated, the Liberals erected many of the houses in Alma Place and Temple Street, upon either side of the Cowley Road, and the Conservatives those at the corner

EARLY IN SEPTEMBER ST GILES' FAIR offers the town a chance to enjoy itself during the University long vacation. In 1830 soldiers in charge of forty-four prisoners from Otmoor rashly attempted to conduct them through the crowd to Oxford Castle. The convoy was attacked and the prisoners released. This photograph was taken in 1905.

OXFORD'S OLDEST STREET: St Aldate's runs from Thames to town. The top end was once the site of the fish market. These shops and houses at the lower end, photographed in 1904, were demolished to make way for Christ Church Memorial Gardens, St Catherine's Society (now the Music Faculty), and the police station.

of Iffley Road and Magdalen Road. To the south and west of the town the old Great Western station in Grand Pont was redeveloped, and Christ Church put up a block of model dwellings in St Thomas's. In 1879 the suburbs were being extended 'in every direction'. The University, which had formed 10 per cent of the total population of 12,279 in 1801, accounted for only 7 ½ per cent of the 49,336 inhabitants in 1901. Oxford remained a distributive rather than productive town, and in 1907 the *Victoria County History* said that 'the county is prevented, as if by fate, from ever attaining to the position of a great industrial or commercial centre'. In that year William Richard Morris (1877–1963) was thirty years old. He had already progressed from bicycle repairs in the back yard of his father's house in Cowley St John to the sale of bicycles at 48 High Street, and was now manufacturing motor bicycles at 100 Longwall. In 1909–10 he began servicing motor cars and opened the Morris Garage. In 1912 he made his first car, and in 1914 visited the Ford plant in Detroit.

Morris knew that there was a shortage of skills in Oxford, and when the Great War ended in 1918 he restarted production by purchasing fully manufactured parts from outside suppliers (mainly in Coventry and Birmingham) and employing local labour to assemble them in Temple Cowley. In the autumn of 1920 the motor industry went into a recession, and unsold cars were piling up in the yard. In 1921 Morris slashed his prices. In 1922 he sold 6,956 cars, in 1923 20,048, in 1924 32,918, and in 1925, when he took 41 per cent of the United Kingdom market, 55,582. In the early 1930s Morris was badly caught between replacement demand (from those who had cars already and wanted more powerful ones) and expansion demand (from first-time buyers looking for small cars). But his market share stabilized at about 30 per cent. The moving production line was introduced in 1933–4. In 1939 he made his millionth car; his two millionth came off the line in 1951.

In 1912 Violet Butler (1884–1982), who was an economics tutor at St Anne's, had drawn attention to the existence in Oxford of a pool 'of unskilled men with no training'. The 1938 *Survey* referred instead to the disappearance of the unskilled worker, and his replacement by the semi-skilled one. Work at Cowley was repetitive and interrupted by seasonal stand-offs, but Morris paid good wages. A man on the line could earn up to 120*s*. in a busy week, and over the year averaged 70*s*.–80*s*. This put him almost on a par with a skilled printer, and well above a college servant. Women, who were employed mainly in small pressing, upholstery, and trimming, were paid 45*s*. a week—more than they could earn in domestic service. There were, as Morris expressed it, 'no marble halls at Cowley', but within a few years there were instead full-time medical officers, free treatment, and holidays with pay. These, as the *Survey* said, were very unusual features 'in industrial welfare in this country'. Morris had liberated a whole social group, comprising a third of the population, for whom it was a new experience to be able to buy their own and their children's clothes first hand. For them 'a new class of shop, fixed-price stores and ready-made tailors' made its appearance in Oxford.

University men themselves loved the Morris Oxford with the city arms on its bonnet. Others perceived it as 'a Ford with a University education'. In the course of a few years the motor industry absorbed Oxford's surplus labour and drew men from the surrounding villages. In the 1920s Oxford grew faster than any other town in Great Britain except Watford and Bournemouth, and in 1929 the city boundaries were extended. There was no repetition of the events of 1865. Everything happened so quickly that in 1925 the University 'did not make any representations to the inquiry which zoned the Cowley area for industrial development'. The following year the Pressed Steel Company came to Oxford to make car bodies, and Morris's and Pressed Steel spilled out over the fields and reached the railway line between Oxford and Princes Risborough.

The first sign of a backlash appeared in 1927, with the setting up of the Oxford Preservation Trust, which bought South Park and other parcels of land to save them

WILLIAM RICHARD MORRIS (*above*) with the Laurels Cycling Club on its annual boating party in 1900. Sadly, the motor magnate was never to look so relaxed again, and late in life he passed a joyless semi-retirement at Nuffield Court along the road to Henley.

THE MORRIS GARAGES were a retail outlet for cars made at Cowley (*right*). But in 1924 they began to manufacture two-seater sports cars on their own account and market them under the slogan 'Safety Fast'. Five years later the MG works was moved to Abingdon, and in the 1950s 91,547 out of the 101,081 MGAs produced were exported.

from the builders. But the Trust was not powerful enough to stem the growth, and even after the city engineer, whose roads and sewers had become overloaded, began to argue in favour of balanced development, the motor industry continued to expand. In the 1930s Morris and Pressed Steel together employed 10,000 people (29.4 per cent of the workforce registered under the National Insurance Acts), and Oxford stood out as a boom town in a country suffering from a depression. A new population, which was 'unfamiliar with the life and traditions of a university town', was attracted from places further afield, and in the six years after 1931 there was a further net immigration of 21,800 people. By 1939 Oxford had nearly 100,000 inhabitants. Morris has often been blamed for destroying the beautiful university city, and turning it into a place indistinguishable from Neasden or Tooting Bec. But, as John Betjeman (1906–84) said, 'the genius of William Morris . . . could hardly have been expected to extend to town-planning'. It was not his fault that the 6,000 houses built by private developers and the 3,000 built by the city council between 1919 and 1939 (even the exceptionally high-quality council houses in Morrell Avenue) appeared to sensitive eyes like a 'tawdry, empty suburbia'. If anyone is to be blamed for the erosion of the countryside round Oxford between the wars, it is the individual colleges which sold land without caring what happened to it afterwards, when, as Betjeman said, you would have thought that, with all their learning, 'they could have planned an industrial town . . . which would have been worthy of the University City beside it'.

Morris himself became Lord Nuffield in 1938. Throughout his life he took the view that 'You can only wear one suit at a time. You can only eat one meal at a time', and that the best thing you could do with money was to give it away. 'Rich men', he said, 'don't give nearly enough money away.' Nuffield himself gave away well over £36 million, a large part of it to what by this time was often called the Oxford region. There is nothing about the distribution of his bounty to suggest that he was indifferent either to the appearance of Oxford or to the fortunes of the University. One of his early gifts, made in 1926, helped to save the Chair of Spanish Studies, and another much larger one, in 1939, provided the department of physical chemistry with a new building. Upon other occasions he seems to have sought to assist both University and town simultaneously. Noting the contrast between the two Oxfords which lay on either side of the line between St Giles' and St Aldate's, he resolved to improve the appearance of the western third of the old town. To this end he championed the forlorn and beleaguered colleges on the wrong side of the line, gave money to Pembroke, St Peter's (founded in 1928), and Worcester Colleges, and became an honorary fellow of all of them (and of no other college on the more favoured side). When he wanted to perpetuate his name, he chose to site his own college in the derelict canal basin, lying on the site of the castle bailey between Worcester College and St Peter's.

Nuffield's greatest gift to Oxford served to bring the University and town closer together. He always said that he would have liked to have been a surgeon, and in 1936 he was asked whether he would help to establish a postgraduate medical school. His comment when he heard how much money would be required—£1,250,000—was to say 'they have opened their mouths widely this time'. But his considered response was remarkable. First he presented himself to the University as the autocrat of the motor works, and insisted that, in addition to Chairs in Medicine, Surgery, and Obstetrics, there should be a Chair in Anaesthetics, which was not at that time considered an academic subject, and that he himself should make the first appointment. (This was despite the opposition of Sir Hugh Cairns, 1896–1952, the Regius Professor of Medicine. Morris was right and Cairns was wrong.) Then, having shown who was boss, he attended the meeting of Convocation at which his gift was to be formally accepted, and dramatically increased it to £2 million. Having raised University medicine to the front rank, he then funded first-class hospitals for his Nuffield Professors to work in. In this way the citizens gained some of the best medical facilities in the country, as the Nuffield Orthopaedic Centre testifies to this day.

During the Second World War the idea took hold that the motor industry could somehow be halted at the point it had reached, and the beauties of Oxford saved by the designation of a green belt lying at a distance of between four and twelve miles from the city centre. Further development could then be diverted to Swindon or South Wales while Oxford addressed itself to the problems which the first half of the twentieth century had brought, and in particular to the traffic in the city centre. Two ways of ridding the High Street of vehicles attracted attention. The first was to turn Oxford into a 'twin city', by building a new shopping centre at Cowley. The second, devised by Thomas Sharp (1901–78), was a plan, published in 1948, to drive a relief road across 'the dank, inaccessible acres' of Christ Church meadow. The controversies surrounding the proposed meadow road lasted for fifteen years. While the city council and the Ministry of Town and Country Planning gradually became more and more committed to the scheme, the University split. Colleges fronting the High voted in favour. But those facing the meadow resisted the proposal and, when they were outvoted in Congregation, spoke foolishly of their intention to exploit their personal friendships with ministers of the Crown to have the scheme thrown out by the Cabinet. The University had shown itself unable to make up its mind, and willing to frustrate others who had found that they could, after equal deliberation, make up theirs. City planning had been paralysed, and the opprobrium lasted long after the plan for a meadow road was abandoned in the mid-1960s and a new shopping centre grew up in Westgate. The result was that in 1974, when local government was reorganized, Parliament extinguished the University's right to separate representation on the city council. After six hundred years senior members of the University had at last become ordinary citizens, no more and no less.

The change has not been regretted in the University, where students attending courses in the Department of External Studies at Rewley House and members of the

OXFORD TRAFFIC: in the 1930s vibration caused by road traffic was held to damage college buildings. In the 1950s, when this photograph of the High Street was taken from Carfax Tower, the issue became that of congestion. Following the disappearance of the domestic coal fire traffic is now perceived as the main source of air pollution.

common rooms of the new graduate colleges, St Antony's College and Wolfson, St Cross, Linacre, Green, and Templeton, care little about ancient quarrels. Undergraduates too now fit much more easily into the town than they used to. For sixty years after the First World War educational privilege retreated in the face of egalitarian values. This began with the institution of State scholarships by H. A. L. Fisher (1865–1940), later Warden of New College, in 1920, and proceeded, slowly between the wars but with gathering momentum after 1945, as undergraduate numbers were expanded from 2,000 to 10,000. Non-collegiate students disappeared when the State accepted the responsibility for meeting Oxford college fees; the non-collegiates' society, St Catherine's, was converted into a college and relocated, with 400 residential places, in 1956. Most of the remainder of the expansion has been taken up by existing colleges erecting new buildings and substituting the bedsitting room for the separate study and bedroom. This in turn has helped to render students less lordly. The losers were the old generation of tradesmen and college servants, many of whom did not understand and were not understood by the new type of student. But the gains have, in the long run, become apparent even in the town. The majority of the post-1945 generation bought

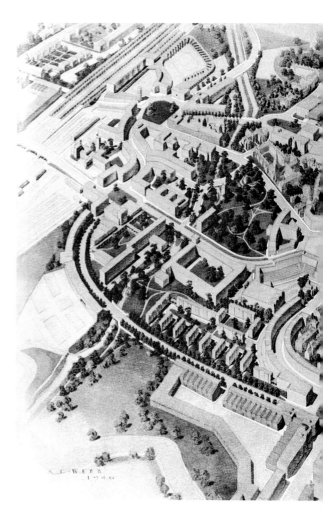

THOMAS SHARP'S PROPOSED MEADOW ROAD, or Merton Mall, of 1948 would have made it possible for the City Council to close the High Street to traffic. But had this relief road been built it would have been found to lie too close to the centre of the city.

everything from clothes to gramophone records in the same shops as the Cowley workers. They were happy to see the separate representation of the University in Parliament disappear in 1950 and, when the University attempted to open a register of recent graduates who would be entitled to vote if the seat were restored, they replied almost to a man and woman that they did not think it right that it should be. There were few young bloods to be found after the 1950s, seeking to go out and do battle with the town on Guy Fawkes night, and the deplorable tradition of town-and-gown brawls appears to have been broken in the early 1960s (though individual students are still from time to time attacked in the streets). When a period of student protest began in the late 1960s, the rebels ceased to wish to be protected by the University Proctors, and preferred to take their chance with the police and the magistrates' courts like anyone else.

Turning for the last time to the economy of the town, we may note that Morris had built his business up by keeping control in his own hands and reinvesting the profits. But tax law nudged him towards a public flotation and the dissipation of profits by way of dividends, and between 1936 and 1950 nothing was reinvested. When the easy conditions of the period after 1945 vanished, the merger with Austin, which led to the

formation of the British Motor Corporation in 1952, compounded the problems rather than solved them. It is difficult to know where to lay the responsibility for this state of affairs. Some blame the restrictionist policies of the city planning authorities for destroying the incentive to expand, while others say it lies with Lord Nuffield himself for indulging in philanthropy. A third school of economists point a finger at the University, which refused to allow Nuffield College to become a college of technical engineering as its founder wished, and turned it instead into a graduate college for the social sciences, or 'a bloody Kremlin' as the donor once called it. A fourth interpretation lays the blame on the bad labour relations which, in the 1950s, began to spread from Pressed Steel—where American bosses encountered a trade-union culture brought to Oxford from South Wales—into the Morris works, which between the wars had been a nest of hard-working, grateful countrymen. At all events the Oxford factories began to fall behind the competition. However many times the business was reorganized in the late 1960s and early 1970s, the slide continued. By the time the State was ready to provide the massive investment that was needed, in the late 1970s, the motor industry in Oxford was in irreversible decline.

When one asks whether the disappearance of volume car production will mean that Oxford returns to the unhappy state of affairs which existed before the 1920s, then the answer is that this is unlikely. Part of the explanation lies in the creation of the National Health Service, and the construction of the John Radcliffe Hospital in Headington, which turned the Regional Health Authority into the largest employer in the area. Another part is to be found in the development of University science. In the early twentieth century the natural sciences were still a poor relation to the arts. But the Great War effected a change, and in 1919 central Government decided to set up a University Grants Committee and to support the universities, especially the natural sciences, upon which the safety of the State was, in the century of total war, going to depend. The University Science Area has expanded ever since, all along South Parks Road and into the Keble Road triangle. A new generation of 'high-tech' businesses, like Oxford Instruments, is springing up in and around Oxford, within easy reach of the science departments and the John Radcliffe Hospital, and the University has set up a company, Isis Innovation, to exploit discoveries made in its laboratories. Large-scale manufacturing may be a thing of the past, but smaller-scale enterprises are appearing to take its place. And the most important reason why they are doing so lies in the growth of the Polytechnic. In 1954–6 the city's existing training schools in Art, Commerce, and Technology were amalgamated to form a new College of Technology on the present site in Gipsy Lane, Headington. The opening ceremony was performed by Lord Nuffield, and in 1970 the college was awarded polytechnic status. It has since become, in all but name, the city's own university, with over 4,000 full-time and many more part-time students. Thanks to the two universities, the city's workforce, which in the 1920s and 1930s made the transition from unskilled to semi-skilled, is as well placed as any in England to enter the twenty-first century fully trained and skilled.

2

The University and the Nation

VIVIAN GREEN

FOR centuries Oxford and Cambridge were England's only two universities. As the cathedral and monastic schools, old-fashioned in their outlook and curriculum, declined, so Oxford was well placed to become a principal centre for advanced education. This was more especially so as it was receptive to the intellectual changes arising from new interpretations of the system of Christian philosophy known as scholasticism, upon which all higher education was then based, which had been fostered by the

THE UNIVERSITY SEAL, which replaced an earlier seal of about 1220, dates from the late thirteenth century. It is made of gilt bronze, and shows the Chancellor in academic dress with three scholars on either side of him and six below. The cast which is shown here is in the Ashmolean Museum.

MERTON COLLEGE. A sculpture of the fifteenth century above the front entrance to Merton College. It depicts the Agnus Dei (Lamb of God) on the left, and the kneeling founder, Walter de Merton, Bishop of Rochester, and St John Baptist, to whom the college was dedicated, on the right. The Book of Seven Seals is in the foreground.

revived study of the works of the Greek philosopher Aristotle in thirteenth-century Europe. Within decades of their foundation, obscure as this undoubtedly was, the universities were providing Church and State with the professional pastors and administrators whom both required for their efficient operation.

With the support of Church and Crown, Oxford was soon to acquire an identity as a national institution, enjoying a prestige comparable to that of Paris, the leading European university. As a society of clerks, most of whom were to be ordained if they were not already priests, the University was protected by the Church against secular interference and jurisdiction. But it was soon to outgrow its role as an ecclesiastical seminary or school in the diocese of Lincoln, becoming a genuine *studium generale* and an autonomous corporation of graduates who had taken the degree of Master of Arts, with its own complex administrative structure which in its bare outlines still exists today. Simultaneously the University gradually shed the oversight of the Bishop of Lincoln, its independence from his jurisdiction finally confirmed in 1370. In the early fifteenth century the Masters had to defend the University against an attempt by Thomas Arundel (1353–1414), Archbishop of Canterbury, to interfere in University affairs by making a metropolitical visitation, inquiring into the University's conduct—something which he believed he had a right to do as Archbishop of Canterbury but which the Masters resented as a threat to their cherished privileges; at long last Oxford's independence from all external ecclesiastical jurisdiction was confirmed by papal bull in 1489.

ROBERT DUDLEY, EARL OF LEICESTER, a portrait, 1587, attributed to William Seager. Favourite of Queen Elizabeth I, and Chancellor of Oxford University from 1564 to 1585, Leicester was the first Chancellor to use English in writing to the University.

pis hic BACVLVS Patrii moderaminis ARCTOS
Hoc vno ingratos quod beet ipse miser.

F R A

T R E S

Qui gloriatur: in domino glorietur. Non enim qui seipsum comendat, ille probatus est: sed quem D E V S commendat. Vtinam sustineretis modicum quid insipientie mee: sed et supportate me. Emulor enim vos D E I emulatione. Despondi eñ vos vni viro virginem castam exhibere C H R I S T O.

In die sancti Cuthberti epi et conf. Lect' libri sapie.. Eccia. xliii.

A D V I T O R

D O M I N V S M I H I

The Crown too afforded Oxford its protection, confirming and extending its privileges, and supporting it in any conflict with its detractors, more especially the townspeople. So favoured, it was soon to attract significant benefactions, most notably from bishops holding high offices in the State. Walter de Merton (d. 1277), Bishop of Rochester, twice Chancellor, founded Merton College in 1264; Walter de Stapledon (1261–1326), Bishop of Exeter, Treasurer to Edward II, Exeter College in 1314; William of Wykeham (1324–1404), Bishop of Winchester, Chancellor of Edward III, New College in 1379; Richard Fleming (d. 1431), Bishop of Lincoln, Lincoln College in 1427; Henry Chichele (1362?–1443), Archbishop of Canterbury, All Souls College in 1438; and William Waynflete (1395?–1486), Bishop of Winchester, Henry VI's Chancellor, founded Magdalen College in 1458. In setting up colleges the episcopal founders were concerned above all to train the future clergy for service in Church and State (Bishop Fleming designed that Lincoln should train clergy to refute the Lollard heretics), and to ensure that masses should be said for their souls and the souls of other benefactors by the fellows. Although the University, unlike the colleges, had as yet negligible endowments, cosseted by the good and great in Church and State, it was soon to acquire a national, even an international, reputation as a home of scholastic learning, among its scholars men of such distinction as Robert Grossetesste (1175–1253), one of Oxford's first Chancellors and Bishop of Lincoln, the logicians Duns Scotus (1265?–1308) and William of Ockham (1300?–49?), Thomas Bradwardine (1290?–1349), Archbishop of Canterbury and theologian, known as the 'doctor profundus', and the religious reformer and Lollard leader John Wyclif (1329?–84).

As a consequence of its growing reputation, it was soon attracting scholars from all parts of England, and even from further afield—Scotland, Wales, Ireland, and the Continent; by the late Middle Ages Scotland had its own universities, which catered for the majority of its students, though after the eighteenth century an increasing number of Scots came south. The very diversity of the intake shows how wide was the catchment area from which Oxford was drawing its students. Most colleges had regional connections which were long to persist: such as Exeter, with the west country, and Queen's, with the north country. Once their studies were complete, the young graduates, some of whom stayed on in Oxford as teaching masters, were to be widely distributed throughout the country, exercising an integral influence at every stage of professional life in Church and State.

Since the great majority of the students were destined for the priesthood, Oxford men were to provide an increasing number of parish priests and a fair segment of the episcopate. Through the establishment of monastic halls at Oxford, the University's influence percolated into the monasteries and friaries. Between 1200 and 1500, 2,104 out of 4,614 scholars had taken a degree in the Faculty of Theology, an essential

THOMAS WOLSEY commissioned an epistolary, 1528, as a gift to his new foundation of Cardinal College. This page depicts St Frideswide, the patron saint of Oxford, with the city itself in the background. The artist was probably a member of the Herenbouts family.

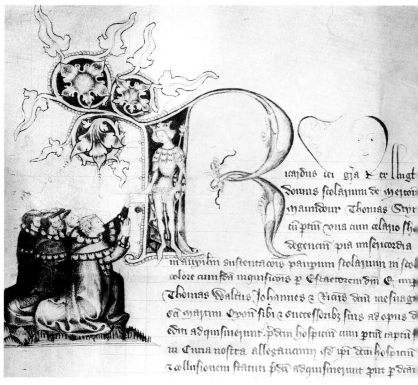

NEW COLLEGE. A misericord in the chapel (*above*) shows the founder of New College, William of Wykeham, welcoming scholars to Oxford; they apparently emerge as dignitaries of the Church.

A ROYAL CHARTER (*right*). The fellows of Merton College kneel before Richard II to receive a charter confirming a grant of land in Oxford, dated 1380. The grant of a royal charter was an essential ingredient in the foundation of a college. The University owed much to firm support from the Crown, as, for instance, in the struggle between the students and the townspeople in the reign of Edward III.

qualification for senior ecclesiastical preferment. When in the fifteenth century legal studies became a bonus for such high preferment, there was an increasing shift in that direction. This suggests that even in the late Middle Ages Oxford's studies were adapted to what might be construed to be the national needs. Not only were there more episcopal founders of colleges at Oxford than there were at Cambridge, but between 1216 and 1500 the episcopal bench was dominated by Oxford-trained men, some 57 per cent by comparison with 10 per cent from Cambridge. Even in the fifteenth century, when the number of Cambridge-trained bishops increased, Cambridge supplied only sixteen bishops to Oxford's thirty-one.

A similar situation prevailed in other high ecclesiastical appointments. In the fourteenth and fifteenth centuries no fewer than 58 per cent of cathedral deans came from Oxford, in comparison with 10 per cent from Cambridge. Since a large proportion of the Crown's ministers and civil servants were drawn from the higher ranks of the clergy, Oxford's influence extended to the most influential echelons of the nation. The advantages of an Oxford training, spiritually and intellectually, were so appreciated by servants of the Crown who had not themselves been at the University that, like William of Wykeham, founder of New College, some were ready to found and endow colleges.

THE FOUNDATION OF NEW COLLEGE. This portrays William of Wykeham, Bishop of Winchester, and luminaries associated with the college. On Wykeham's right Henry Chichele, Archbishop of Canterbury, and Thomas Beckington, Bishop of Bath and Wells; on his left Thomas Cranley, Archbishop of Dublin, and William Waynflete, Bishop of Winchester. Below, distinguished fellows and benefactors of the college.

The social spread of these early Oxford graduates seems to have been as wide as their geographical distribution. While some colleges were founded more especially with the object of providing for 'poor scholars', the majority of the students, who lived in halls run by Masters rather than the colleges, seem to have been men of intermediate social status, the sons of lesser gentry and landowners, merchants, officials. In the fourteenth and fifteenth centuries there was, however, a slow trickle of men of aristocratic lineage: Henry Beaufort (d. 1447), the second illegitimate son of John of Gaunt, who studied at Queen's, Oxford, as well as Peterhouse, Cambridge. Robert (later Lord) Hungerford (1409–59) and John Tiptoft (1427?–70), later Earl of Worcester and a patron of early humanists, had been at University College. The founder of Magdalen, Bishop Waynflete, doubtless influenced by Wykeham's example at New College, made provision in the college statutes for twenty places for the sons of nobles and gentlemen who would pay fees for their residence and teaching.

In the sixteenth century there was a shift in the University's relationship with the nation. In the Middle Ages the Crown had acted as a patron of the University but had exercised only a loose control. It was mainly concerned to support the University's privileged position, for the University served what Crown and Church construed to be the interests of the nation. Before the fifteenth century had ended, the Crown was acquiring an instrument of indirect control through a change which was occurring in the character of the University's chancellorship. Hitherto the Chancellor, who, in spite of opposition from the Bishop of Lincoln, was elected by the Regent Masters, had usually

A UNIVERSITY CHEST. Made *c.*1412, burgled and damaged in 1544, restored 1546, the chest housed University records and moneys. It was called the chest of five keys because it required the keys in the possession of the Chancellor, the two Proctors, and two annually elected heads of colleges to open it.

been a scholar residing in the University. In future, however, he was to be a non-resident, at first a great dignitary in the Church but after the mid-sixteenth century more often a royal servant, such as the Earl of Leicester (1532?–88), who, under Elizabeth I, interfered constantly in college elections and University affairs to further the interests of the Crown, acting through the Vice-Chancellor, whom he nominated as his deputy. Though the chancellorship continued to be an elective office, it came to be closely associated with the Government and on occasion an appointment might be made in response to a mandate from the Crown. The Chancellor did not necessarily subordinate the University's well-being to the policy of the Government: in William Laud (1573–1645), for instance, Archbishop of Canterbury, Chancellor from 1630 to 1641, Oxford had a very devoted and loyal servant. Moreover, that the Chancellor was likely to have patronage and preferment at his disposal could be advantageous to Oxford's loyal dons. None the less, the fact that the office of Chancellor was invariably held by a great churchman or nobleman underlined the extent to which Oxford had become aligned to the established order in Church and State.

The onset of the Reformation had provided an opportunity for further strengthening the Crown's control. The Reformation fomented an ideological debate which could eventually be resolved only by the intervention of the Crown, for the Crown could not step aside and leave its critics in the University free to propagate theological doctrines, whether conservative or radical, of which it disapproved. While Oxford did not lack Protestant propagandists—the pamphleteer and translator of the Bible William Tyndale (d. 1536) is probably the best known—it was Cambridge which gave Protestantism the more sympathetic hearing. Oxford's inclinations were conservative; if its dons approved the suppression of Lutheran preachers and literature, they deplored also the ending of the study of canon law, the dissolution of the religious houses, the declining hold of scholastic philosophy, and the liturgical changes. But the Tudor Governments, more especially after Elizabeth I became Queen, exerted a slow but steady pressure to ensure that the University toed the line they wanted.

This was not only achieved by disciplining Nonconformists but also by setting up an outside commission for the visitation of the University. The first such commission was issued by Thomas Cromwell (1485?–1540) in 1535. A further commission under Edward VI had wide powers to change statutes and syllabuses and to reform University and college finances. The visitors provided new statutes, eliminated the surviving symbols of Romanism, and encouraged Protestantism; an Italian Protestant Peter Martyr (1500–62) was appointed to the Chair of Divinity in 1548. But Oxford opinion remained confused and bewildered, so that many dons greeted the return to the old religion under Mary, by whose visitors the Edwardian statutes were declared null and void.

The accession of Elizabeth restored an equilibrium, for a further commission, acting for the most part with discretion and moderation, rooted out the supposedly unorthodox and disloyal and established the University on a firm Protestant footing. The ousting of Roman influence was slow but ultimately thorough. Catholic supporters were

CHRIST CHURCH HALL. Built by Cardinal Wolsey, it was completed in 1529. The Cardinal was commemorated by most of the 600 or more coats of arms and badges in the fine hammerbeam roof. It is the largest hall in Oxford, and is reproduced here from a coloured engraving in Ackermann's *History of the University of Oxford* (1814).

weeded out; some fled abroad and a few, such as Edmund Campion (1540–81), paid the ultimate penalty for their faith. Mandates from the Chancellor, sometimes stoutly resisted by fellows who cherished an independence seemingly guaranteed by college statutes, were dispatched, nominating the heads and fellows of colleges whom the Government could trust for their obedience and religious conformity. The University was hitched to the new order in Church and State.

Although the growth of a more extreme Protestant or Puritan faction, small if loquacious, located in the surviving academic halls rather than in the colleges, remained a tantalizing challenge to the established order, the Crown as well as the governing classes recognized the essential services which the University provided in training clergy and administrators. The Crown continued to act as the University's patron. Henry VIII founded the most prestigious college in Oxford, Christ Church, on the basis of Cardinal Wolsey's (1475?–1530) quondam foundation, Cardinal College (see above, p. 9), and set up Regius Professorships in Divinity, Greek, Hebrew, and Medicine. Queen Mary proved to be the University's most princely benefactor to date by appropriating to it the livings of South Petherwyn in Cornwall, of Syston in Leicestershire, and of Hulme Cultram in Cumberland; though it was under the aegis of her Government that two bishops, Latimer (1485?–1555) and Ridley (1500?–55), and Archbishop Cranmer (1489–1556) were burnt at the stake in Broad Street outside Balliol in 1555/6. Her sister Elizabeth I made two ceremonial visits, in 1566 and 1592, apparently much gratified by protracted sycophantic orations and some tedious drama, and was acclaimed as the founder of Jesus College—a trifle dishonestly, since the real founder was a Welshman, Dr Hugh Price (1495?–1574). James I, an amateur scholar himself, much relished his visit to Oxford, declaring after he had visited the handsome new library set up by Sir Thomas Bodley (1545–1613) that if he were not a king he would be an Oxford scholar; and his son Henry, Prince of Wales, actually matriculated at Magdalen in 1605. To a greater extent than ever before the sons of the gentry and rich merchants (as well as a new class, the children of the married clergy) were drawn to the University. Between 1575 and 1639 sons of the gentry made up roughly 50 per cent of the University

THREE UNIVERSITY STAVES, with wooden cores covered in silver, were purchased for Queen Elizabeth's visit to Oxford in 1566. They were carried by the beadles of the three faculties, Arts and Medicine, Civil Law, and Theology, as emblems of their authority. This is the head of the Theology stave.

ARCHBISHOP LAUD, by Anthony Van Dyck. William Laud became President of St John's College in 1621, Chancellor of the University in 1629, and Archbishop of Canterbury in 1633. He built the Canterbury Quad in St John's at his own expense, and then spent as much again in entertaining Charles I and Henrietta Maria when they came to open it. He was executed in 1645 and his remains were reinterred in St John's in 1663.

entry, some 41 per cent were of plebeian birth, and 9 per cent were sons of the clergy. In the eyes of Church and State Oxford had certainly attained respectability.

Oxford men were to be increasingly to the fore in the nation's life as the sixteenth century wore on. In 1563 only eighteen Members of Parliament as against forty-nine from Cambridge were Oxford-educated. By 1584 Oxford supplied eighty-three to Cambridge's sixty-two. In 1604 the Universities of Oxford and Cambridge became themselves entitled each to elect Members of Parliament, a right which they enjoyed until the Parliament of 1945–50. The University saw such representation as a means of defending its own interests, which might be 'pretermitted to its own hindrance', to 'serve', as Glanville (1586–1661) put it, 'for those students, who though useful members of the community, were neither concerned in the landed or trading interest; and to protect in the Legislature the Rights of the Republic of Letters'.

High preferment was once more coming Oxford's way. The primacy of Canterbury, which had not been held by an Oxford graduate since Warham's death in 1532—apart from the short-lived archiepiscopate of Reginald Pole (1500–58)—was bestowed in 1611 on George Abbot (1562–1633), a former Master of University College. Abbot was succeeded by William Laud, a former President of St John's, one of the most active and philanthropic of the University's Chancellors.

Other equally important changes in the relationship of University and nation had been taking place. At the beginning of the sixteenth century the student community had been mainly housed in small halls under the supervision of Masters. By the end of the century most of the halls had disappeared, and all junior members were required to live in colleges, hitherto largely reserved for young graduates. Magdalen College had been the first to open its doors specifically to undergraduates. Religious, economic, and political factors brought about the dissolution of most of the halls, for they lacked the endowments which enabled the colleges to survive a period of economic stress. Moreover, the Government, suspicious of unsupervised groups of young men, capable of forming a seed-bed for religious and political subversion, made membership of a recognized society—a college—a necessary condition for membership of the University. In 1565 matriculation became the essential preliminary to entry to the University; and after 1581 an oath to accept the Thirty-nine Articles of the Church of England, drawn up in 1571, had to be taken on admission (if of the age of sixteen or over) and before the taking of a degree.

A society trimmed of irregularity, if never to the extent of stifling completely its independence of judgement, and bound to the support of the established order, had great attraction for the Elizabethan and Jacobean governing class, eager for the higher education of its sons. While the academic fodder remained traditional in character, still focused on logic and Aristotelian learning, it had been modified by the insertion of Protestant, more particularly Calvinistic, theology; and it was possible to engage in a wide series of extra-curricular activities, ranging from science and mathematics to music and dancing. The young undergraduate no longer lived in lodgings or in a hall but in college, his life supervised even down to the payment of his bills, and disciplined by a tutor—a paternalistic formula but not necessarily lacking intellectual rigour.

There can be little doubt that in the late sixteenth and early seventeenth centuries the social range of the University was widened as noblemen and gentry, together with the emergent mercantile classes, sent their sons to Oxford in greater numbers than before; but not to the exclusion of the children of poorer people, for whom in several colleges, through a system of quaintly termed scholarships—battlerships, sizarships, and servitorships, by which in return for some menial duties the holders paid lower fees—special financial provision was made. The first three decades of the seventeenth century saw an astonishing increase in the population, popularity, and prosperity of the University, with colleges rebuilding and extending their accommodation.

The great majority of Oxford's graduates were still, as for centuries to come, to seek a career in the ministry of the Church of England, and many enjoyed high preferment. Of William Laud's successors as Archbishop, Juxon (1582–1663) had been President of St John's, Gilbert Sheldon (1598–1677), who built the Sheldonian Theatre at his own expense, had been Warden of All Souls, and John Potter (1674?–1747) was a fellow of Lincoln and Regius Professor of Divinity. But the clerical complexion of Oxford's graduates was more diluted than it had been in the past by men who won distinction in the secular professions, some as Members of Parliament, others as lawyers or even doctors—such as John Radcliffe (1650–1714), who had a great reputation as a physician in the late seventeenth century and proved to be one of the University's most notable benefactors.

The outbreak of the Civil War and the subsequent Government of the Commonwealth acted as a hiatus. While the townsmen adhered for the most part to Parliament, the influence exerted by the University's Chancellor, Archbishop Laud, his allies, and

A CHARLES I CROWN PIECE OF 1643–4. In all 2,000 lbs. in gold and silver given by the colleges was melted down and made into the new coinage needed during the Civil War. Charles holds a sword and an olive-branch, and a view of Oxford can be seen in the background.

the natural social conservatism of the University ensured its loyalty to the Crown; Charles I had been entertained with prodigal splendour by Laud after the completion of the Canterbury Quad at St John's College in 1636. When, therefore, Charles made Oxford the royalist headquarters in 1642, it was a step supported by the colleges and the majority of their fellows, though it would be incorrect to suppose that Oxford graduates were uniformly loyal; Puritan and Parliamentary policies had some support, for instance, in the surviving halls as well as among some non-resident graduates. Some 280 of the 552 Members of the Long Parliament had been to either Oxford or Cambridge. The colleges were perhaps a trifle reluctant to melt down their silver for the royal coffers, but they emptied their rooms of students to house the King and Queen, their Court, advisers, and cavaliers. Christ Church became the King's headquarters, Merton the Queen's. The University tried to keep up an appearance of normality, but there were far fewer young men to pursue their studies, and the quads and fields echoed to the drilling of soldiers. As the royal cause began to fail, and the University's Chancellor suffered execution, so increasingly dons must have become apprehensive as to the University's future. College bursars began to gather provisions to withstand a possible siege by the Parliamentary army. Perhaps fortunately, Charles realized that his situation was becoming desperate and so retreated, leaving the colleges to pick up the pieces and the unpaid bills which the cavaliers left behind. It was fortunate for Oxford that Fairfax held his hand and did not bombard the city with his artillery.

But Oxford's apprehensions were in some sense justified. It had identified itself with what was momentarily a failing cause, the Church of England as well as the Crown; and in the next fourteen years it had to pay a forfeit for its loyalty. Its royalist heads and fellows were for the most part displaced; the only head to keep his position through this turbulent time was Paul Hood (1586?–1668), the Rector of Lincoln, who by a masterful policy of sitting on the fence managed more or less to satisfy both parties and emerged as the first Vice-Chancellor after the restoration of Charles II. Parliament replaced the heads and fellows with nominees of its own, whom the colleges were forced willy-nilly to elect. The Puritan form of worship was imposed on college chapels, and a Puritan discipline tried to ensure that the students did not indulge in unbecoming conduct, directions doubtless in the long run no more strictly heeded than the paternalistic legislation of Laud.

But if some of Parliament's supporters were sufficiently critical of Oxford to wish it brought low—William Dell (d. 1664), for instance, once Laud's secretary and later the Puritan Master of Gonville and Caius College, Cambridge, arguing that university education should be placed within the reach of the inhabitants of the larger towns, was strongly condemnatory of Oxford's élitism and argued for the establishment of other universities, one of which, at Durham, had a brief shadowy existence—Oxford was too strongly entrenched and too serviceable to the Government to be dissolved. Pruned and reformed, it would remain a centre of higher education. Its representative in Parliament, the humane scholar John Selden (1584–1654), was its effective defender

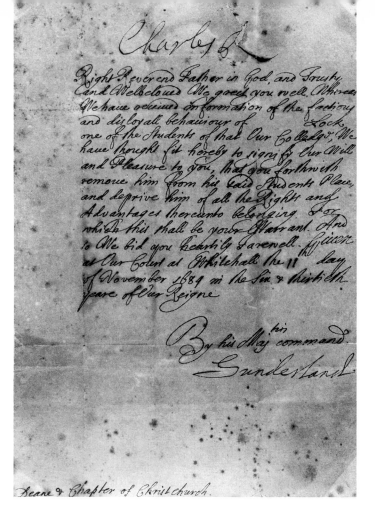

EXPULSION OF JOHN LOCKE.
Locke was appointed Censor of
Moral Philosophy at Christ Church
in 1663. His patron, the politician
Lord Shaftesbury, was suspected of
disaffection, and the royal mandate
seen here ordered the Dean and
Chapter to remove Locke's name
from the Students of Christ Church.
This was promptly done,
15 November 1684.

In 1650 Oliver Cromwell himself became the University's Chancellor. The Vice-Chancellor John Owen (1616–83), Dean of Christ Church, who shocked the conservatives by his secular mode of dress, was much in Cromwell's confidence.

With a zest for survival which has brought the University through many crises, Oxford showed signs of a renaissance of learning even before the Restoration, its resurgence in this respect signified by the meetings of a group of men who formed the nucleus of the future Royal Society: Cromwell's brother-in-law John Wilkins (1614–72), Warden of Wadham (and later Master of Trinity, Cambridge), who in 1638 had published a book with a prescient title *The Discovery of a World in the Moon*, Christopher Wren (1632–1723) of Wadham, Nathaniel Crewe (1633–1721) of Lincoln, and John Wallis (1616–1703), a Cambridge man who had been appointed Savilian Professor of Geometry in 1649.

The restoration of Charles II meant a virtual elimination of the new order, at least as far as the personnel of the colleges were concerned, and a return of the heads and fellows who had been expelled by the Parliamentarians a decade earlier. The garrulous if learned antiquary and historian Anthony Wood (1632–95) saw in Restoration Oxford an expression of a decline in morals and manners characteristic of the royal Court itself, yet in other respects the University prospered as a centre for learning and advanced study. Its colleges were full. The formidable Dean of Christ Church, John Fell (1625–86), developed the University printing-press. Thomas Marshall (1621–85), the erudite Rector of Lincoln, with other scholars promoted the study of language, including Old English. Wren, who was Savilian Professor of Astronomy from 1661 to 1673, was to enrich Oxford (and Cambridge) with some of its finest buildings. Yet the late seventeenth century saw signs of contraction, and with it some decline in the University's centrality in the nation and even a threat of parochialism. The partial disintegration of Anglicanism with, as its corollary, a rise in dissent—Congregationalists, Presbyterians, Roman Catholics, Baptists, and Quakers—meant that those who could not accept the Thirty-nine Articles would henceforth be excluded from membership of the University.

The University's loyalty to the Crown could hardly be doubted. It readily piled subversive works containing 'damnable doctrines destructive to the sacred persons of princes', such as *Leviathan* by Thomas Hobbes (1588–1679), on to a bonfire in the Bodleian quadrangle, to the hurrahs of the bystanders, dons and students. James Parkinson (1653–1722), a fellow of Lincoln, who had described the ministers of the Crown as 'fooles' and 'dunces', was deprived of his fellowship for his seditious republican principles: 'H'ant the king bum-fodder enough?', he commented when the question of sending a loyal address was raised. At the request of the Government the Dean of Christ Church erased the name of the philosopher John Locke (1632–1704) from the college books for his 'whiggisme'. It was to Oxford as a centre of loyalty that Charles II summoned Parliament in 1681. In 1683 the University reaffirmed its belief in the divine right of monarchy and passive obedience to any ruler. The University also helped in the suppression of Monmouth's rebellion against James II, Magdalen, like other colleges, raising troops to put it down.

The close alliance between Oxford and the Crown, which had made the University after the Commonwealth a pillar of the political and social order in Church and State, was to be challenged by James II's ill-conceived use of his prerogative powers, more especially to suspend statutes and to dispense individuals from their statutory obligations. The King believed that if the universities could be brought under Roman Catholic control what he held to be the Anglican heresy could be counteracted. To bring this about he sought to nominate to headships and fellowships by using his dispensing power and by appointing special commissioners in the name of supposed religious toleration.

James II's attempt to impose Roman Catholic sympathizers and Roman Catholics on Magdalen College (see below, p. 140) became a national *cause célèbre*, encapsulating all the issues which ultimately brought about his downfall. The fellows of Magdalen defied the king. 'We have', as Dr Hough (1651–1743), whom they had elected as President, told William Penn (1644–1718), 'our Statutes and Oaths to justify us; but setting this aside, we have a Religion to defend, and I suppose you yourself would think us knaves if we should tamely give it up. The Papists have already Christ Church and University College; the present struggle is for Magdalen and they threaten that in a short time they will have the rest.'

Although the defence of the Church of England was of the essence of the conflict, even more fundamental was the belief of the King's critics that James II, by using the royal mandate to nominate to headships and fellowships and by expelling Protestant fellows, was not merely contravening the statutes of the college (as he may have believed, following earlier royal precedents, he was entitled to do, and which the fellows by oath were bound to uphold) but was seeking to impose an arbitrary system of government which threatened the liberties as well as the property of his subjects. When James came down to Oxford to confront the fellows of Magdalen, he angrily told

JAMES II AND MAGDALEN COLLEGE. The college buttery-book records how, in his attempt to Catholicize Oxford, James deprived the fellows of Magdalen and replaced them by pro-Catholic ones. Then, in a vain attempt to propitiate his critics, he changed tack and ordered the college's Visitor to 'settle the College legally and statutably'. Crosses were placed against the names of the Catholic fellows, and the former fellows' names reinscribed.

them, 'you have been a stubborn, turbulent College . . . You have affronted me. Is this your Church of England loyalty? . . . Go back and shew yourselves good members of the Church of England . . . Get you gone . . . Know that I am your King. Go and admit the Bp. of Oxford [as President] or else you must expect to feel the heavy hand of an angry king.' Even if James had been within his rights in respect of the letter of the law, he was acting in violation of its spirit and intent. If the King could override existing law, as represented by the college statutes, then all offices in Church and State and all rights of property were in peril.

But the King's power was fast crumbling, and in an attempt to save the situation he ordered the restoration of the expelled President and fellows. In lighting their bonfires and ringing their bells, the fellows of Magdalen, as of other colleges, were not merely extolling their cherished if somewhat dented autonomy but also celebrating their defence of the constitutional liberties of the nation itself.

In a sense what followed was something of an anti-climax. Some at least of the more precisian among the dons refused the oath to William III and Mary, and joined the ranks of the Nonjurors. The 'Toryism' of the University became more pronounced, and the death of Queen Anne and the succession of the Elector of Hanover, George I, in religion a Lutheran, portended ill for Oxford. For half a century Oxford was to be out of favour with the established order. In 1715 the University's Chancellor, the Duke of Ormonde (1665–1745), a committed Jacobite, fled abroad, but the dons elected in his stead his brother the Earl of Arran (1671–1758), who secured 140 votes to the 3 of the Whig candidate, the Earl of Pembroke (1656–1733). Arran remained in office until he died, in his eighty-eighth year. While he had no influence at Court, at least no Whig head of a college was called to serve as Vice-Chancellor in his forty-four years of office. The Whig Government suspected Oxford of aiding and abetting the Jacobite pretender:

> King George, observing with judicious eyes
> The state of both his universities,
> To Oxford sent a troop of horse; and why
> That learned body wanted loyalty.
> To Cambridge books he sent, as well discerning,
> How much that loyal body wanted learning.

It tried to infiltrate Whig sympathizers into colleges, and managed to win three bastions, Christ Church, Merton, and Wadham. It instituted in 1724 a Professor of Modern History, who was also to nominate lecturers to give instruction in modern languages, in the hope—hapless as it turned out—of strengthening the links between Government service and the University.

The University became the target of astringent critics, such as Nicholas Amhurst (1697–1742), who in his periodical pamphlet *Terrae Filius* attacked the University not only as a nest of political subversion but as corrupt, indolent, and ineffectual. At one stage the Whig Government seriously considered a bill to restrict its freedom. This could not happen without repercussions on its admissions and on the nature of the influence it exerted in national life. Tory dons could no longer look as they had in the past for high preferment in the Church, which was now reserved for Whig sympathizers. There was a striking drop in the number of admissions to the University, which most affected the classes at the top and bottom levels of the social scale—noblemen and gentlemen-commoners on the one hand, who in return for higher fees enjoyed greater amenities, poor scholars and servitors on the other. In the first case the fall may have represented a lack of confidence felt by the governing class in the political integrity of the University, which seemed tainted with questionable Toryism if not treasonable Jacobitism. It had become less fashionable, less able to dispense the social graces which could be better acquired by a grand tour on the Continent. The fall in the number of poor scholars reflected different social features, among them some decline in the grammar schools and the rising costs of a university education. Even for graduates, in an age of growing pluralism it could prove difficult to get a benefice in the Church without an influential patron, unless the poor boy became a fellow of a college and so eligible for a college living.

After the accession of George III Oxford's relations with the Government improved. When Arran died in 1758 the ministry had tried to secure the election of a Whig Chancellor but failed until, on the death of Lord Lichfield (b. 1718) in 1772, the University chose the King's chief minister, Lord North (1732–92), an appointment which George III approved of, calling it 'a compliment to me'.

In spite of what was admittedly a low period in Oxford's history, it is wrong to overstress the decline. Eighteenth-century Oxford educated the founders of Methodism John Wesley (1703–91) and Charles Wesley (1707–88), William Blackstone (1723–80), the greatest legal luminary of his age, and the writer Samuel Johnson (1709–84), though Johnson had to leave before completing his course through lack of funds. Of a sample 590 Members of Parliament between 1715 and 1754, 176 were Oxford men as against 70 from Cambridge, fairly evenly divided between Government supporters and their opponents; of another sample 660 Members between 1754 and 1770, 157 were Oxford-educated, 123 from Cambridge. In addition to Lord North, such notable politicians as Carteret (1690–1763), Henry Pelham (1695?–1754), William Pitt the Elder (1708–78), Shelburne (1737–1805), and Charles James Fox (1749–1806) had been at Oxford. Of 158 bishops in the eighteenth century in the province of Canterbury, 85 were Oxford graduates (compared with 67 from Cambridge), and in the province of York 14 out of 22 bishops were Oxford men. If the University was in some decline, the decline was relative to its nature. When a motion was introduced in the House of Commons to abolish or modify the compulsory subscription to the Thirty-nine Articles, it was defeated. Oxford still had powerful friends at Court and in Parliament.

But the University's reconciliation with the Crown, and the faltering steps that it was taking in the direction of reform, could not still the rising tide of criticism in some quarters of the nation. Oxford graduates like Jeremy Bentham (1748–1832) and Adam Smith

THE VICTORY OF TORYISM. The symbolic figures in the Oxford Almanack for 1712 represent the Tory and High Church Party triumphing over Toleration and the Whigs. The building in the background resembles New College. The helmeted figure has her hand on a shield bearing the University arms, and her foot and shield on a monster.

UNIVERSITY ENCAENIA, the name given to the vestigial part of the longer ceremonial known as the Act, the festivities at the end of the academic year when honorary degrees are conferred, as upon this occasion in 1761. Presided over by the Chancellor, it takes place in the Sheldonian Theatre.

JEREMY BENTHAM, who had matriculated at The Queen's College in 1760 at the age of twelve, was in later life a prominent critic of Oxford: 'mendacity and insincerity, in these I found the effects—the only sure effects of an English University education.'

(1723–90) were severely critical of its deficiencies. There was a growing chorus of complaint about the inadequacy of the tuition, the indolence and drunkenness of its dons, and its narrow attachment to the Church of England. The historian Edward Gibbon (1737–94) painted a sombre and somewhat unjust portrait of his time as a gentleman-commoner of Magdalen. In the last sermon which he preached before the University (in 1744) John Wesley denounced dons and students alike as indolent and irreligious. The sniping became more intensive as the eighteenth century drew to its close.

'You cannot', growled Lord Hugh Cecil (1869–1956), a later Member of Parliament for the University, 'reform a university any more than you can reform a cheese.' Yet a slow move in this direction had already started before the end of the century. Three colleges—Christ Church, Balliol, and Oriel—had already taken themselves in hand and were providing better tuition. Under a series of able Deans, culminating in the princely Cyril Jackson (1746–1819), Christ Church had once again taken the lead as the most prestigious college with a reputation for effective tutors and genuine scholarship; among its alumni were the eminent statesmen Canning (1770–1827), Peel (1788–1850), and Gladstone (1809–98). Peel and Gladstone were in fact graduates of a new vintage, for they had actually taken an examination and been awarded first-class honours instead of performing the nominal oral exercises which for the most part led to a degree in eighteenth-century Oxford. For the Hebdomadal Board, Oxford's governing body, had in 1801 introduced a new statute providing for an honours examination, partly, it would seem, to stem the growing criticism of the University and partly because the experience of the French Revolution had seemed to demonstrate that ignorance and indolence could foster subversion and irreligion. The new examination system was the start of a steady but at first very slow advance towards the making of the modern University.

In the nineteenth century British society was changing rapidly, and though the professional classes which formed the main recruiting-ground for undergraduates long remained a dominant influence in a society that was still at its top aristocratic in composition, mercantile and industrial interests were increasingly to the fore. The Church of England, with which the University was identified, was itself fragmented by sectional interests and had its monopoly challenged by dissenters, Roman Catholics, and agnostics. The foundation of London University, freed from doctrinal attachments, showed the way the wind was blowing.

OXFORD DEBAUCHERY. In the eighteenth century the senior members of the University were much criticized, not always justly, for their sloth and drunkenness, conveyed by William Hogarth in his depiction of a scene from the play *The Humours of Oxford*, written by a Whig clergyman, James Miller, in 1730.

A FRENCH CARTOON of the visit of the allied sovereigns to Oxford on 15 June 1814 to receive honorary degrees and to dine in the Radcliffe Camera. From left to right, the Duchess of Oldenburg (the Tsar's sister), the Tsar, the Prince Regent, the King of Prussia, and Marshal Blücher. Russians, Prussians, and English (in the foreground) are hideous, and two handsome Frenchmen stand with their backs to the proceedings.

Changes were taking place at Oxford in the first three or four decades of the nineteenth century: better tuition, the opening of fellowships, as at Oriel, to free competition, more emphasis on research, and a somewhat token attention to science; but to critics outside the University these changes seemed cosmetic rather than radical. In general Oxford remained fundamentally Protestant and Tory, its life ordered by the Laudian statutes of 1636, its colleges governed by statutes dating from their foundation and looking backward to past traditions rather than forward to future needs. The University had been intensely critical of the movement for Roman Catholic emancipation. Sir Robert Peel had been elected the University's Member of Parliament in preference to Canning because he was thought to be the safer man. 'We are all, Sir, greatly indebted to you', the vicar of Bengeworth wrote, 'for that weight of arguments by which when the House of Commons was in a state of portentous equipoise, you inclined it on behalf of the "Protestant Ascendancy".' But eleven years later Peel had 'ratted', and the dons rejected his candidature and elected the genial Sir Robert Inglis

(1786–1855) as the champion of the concept that 'the constitution of England ought to be preserved fundamentally and exclusively Protestant'.

The dons watched the passing of the Reform Bill of 1832 with apprehension; one of its most unpopular opponents in Parliament, Sir Charles Wetherell (1770–1846), was the son of a former Master of University College. Young William Gladstone spoke at the newly formed debating society, the Oxford Union, against the bill. In the years that followed the University sent petitions against the profanation of the Lord's Day, against the Irish Church Bill of 1833, and against the coming of the Great Western Railway to Oxford. It was appropriate that a High Tory, the Duke of Wellington (1769–1852), should have been elected the University's Chancellor. The Irish Church Bill had given John Keble (1792–1866) the occasion to preach an Assize Sermon (a sermon preached before the visiting Judge of Assize) in St Mary's Church which initiated the Tractarian or Oxford Movement, a clerical revival which scarcely assisted the cause of University reform; basically it was a backward-looking movement, and though it later contrived to inject some warmth into the liturgy and teaching of the Established Church, at the time it so immersed Oxford in religious controversy that attention was diverted from the task of reform.

Criticism of the University outside Oxford was gathering momentum. In the pages of the *Edinburgh Review* for 1831 Sir William Hamilton (1788–1856) lashed out at its deficiencies: 'The great interests of the nation, the church and the professions, were sacrificed to the paltry ends of a few contemptible corporations; and the privileges by

OXFORD DIVERSIONS. Rowlandson's print of Mrs Showwell showing some of General Guise's 'dirty' pictures (she is pointing to a painting of Susannah and the elders) to undergraduates for a fee. General Guise, whom Horace Walpole described as a great romancer, bequeathed his collection of pictures to Christ Church, where he may have earlier studied.

STUDENT FROLICS. Christ Church men dance round a bonfire in Tom Quad and haul down the statue of Mercury. A globe and chamber-pots are thrown from windows. The aquatint by Robert Cruikshank is dated 1 May 1824.

In the early nineteenth century undergraduates found time for a variety of amusements. In this drawing by R. W. Buss, dated 1842, one man in casual dress, presumably the tenant of the room, smokes a long pipe, while another, still wearing a cap and gown, plays on a horn.

law accorded to the University of Oxford, as the authorized organ of national education, were by its perfidious governors, transferred to the unauthorized absurdities of their college discipline.' The University, 'of all academical institutions, at once the most imperfect and the most perfectible', could not be trusted to reform itself. 'It is from the State only,' Hamilton concluded, 'and the Crown in particular, that we can reasonably hope for an academical reformation worthy of the name.' In 1837 Lord Radnor (1779–1869), alleging that the colleges misinterpreted their statutes and misused their endowments, demanded the setting up of a Royal Commission, but his proposal was rejected.

Public opinion was, however, increasingly convinced that the University had to be forced to put its house in order, and even in Oxford there was a group of liberal reformers who argued for radical change in the University's government and teaching. A Royal Commission was appointed on 31 August 1850 to inquire into the discipline, studies, and revenue of the University. The die-hards were evasive and hostile in their response, but the Commissioners persevered in their inquiries, and in July 1852 presented their report, the main recommendations of which were to be embedded in the University Reform Act of 1854.

This Act may seem, with hindsight, a somewhat half-hearted attempt at restructuring the administration and curriculum to bring them more in line with national requirements. But it broke the Anglican monopoly, and opened the way for dissenters to matriculate and proceed to Bachelor's degrees. In other ways too it gave a greater voice to liberal tendencies than had before been possible. The Hebdomadal Board, hitherto confined to heads of colleges, was replaced by an elected Hebdomadal Council. The basic representative body of the dons, Congregation, was remodelled. The Vice-Chancellor was authorized to open private halls. In the wake of legislation other significant changes were made. Outmoded college statutes were reformed, non-resident clerical sinecures were weeded out, and provision was made for more effective tutorial supervision. The honours examinations, hitherto restricted to Literae Humaniores and Mathematics, were expanded to include Schools of Modern History and Law, and in due course Natural Science, English, and other faculty subjects were added to the syllabus.

In spite of these changes, there continued to exist a powerful body of opinion in the nation as well as a small though growing body of Oxford residents who felt that the Act had not gone far enough. It had not, for instance, touched the ark of the colleges' strength, their endowments. Moreover, liberal fears were increased by a resurgence of conservative opinion in the University itself; of this the foundation in 1868 of Keble College, commemorating the Tractarian leader, was itself a symbol. The Tories and the High Churchmen had never fully forgiven the University's Member of Parliament, Gladstone, for his promotion and management of the Act of 1854. Although he was returned unopposed in 1857, in 1865 he was defeated by Gathorne Gathorne-Hardy (1814–1906), later Lord Cranbrook, a defeat largely made possible by the postal vote,

THE MASTER OF BALLIOL, Benjamin Jowett, was Vice-Chancellor when the foundation-stone of the new Indian Institute was laid on 2 May 1883. Below the names of the statesmen entered in his Visitors' Book (*right*) come those of the architect, Basil Champneys, and his wife, and Sir Thomas Brassey, son of the famous contractor, and Lady Brassey.

EXTRAMURAL STUDIES AT OXFORD (*below*). Students attending a Workers' Educational Association summer school in 1912 relax in the Fellows' Garden at Balliol with A. L. Smith, the historian and future Master of the college.

May 2   Marquess & Marchioness of Tavisto
Robert Browning.
Marquis of Lansdowne
Salisbury
Kimberley
B___ ___ Basil Champneys
Sir Thomas and Lady Brassey

May 6th   Mr & Mrs Albert Dicey
Mr and Mrs Lionel Tennyson
S. Brearley.
S Nerbrooke
Louis Mallet & Lady Mallet.

which enfranchised the clerical backwoodsmen. From the cloistered quads Gladstone, a devoted spokesman for the University, retired sadly to the tougher surroundings of South Lancashire. 'Young Oxford is all with you,' Goldwin Smith (1823–1910) had told him in 1859, 'Every year more men obtain the reward of their industry through your legislation. But old Oxford takes a long time a-dying.'

This was profoundly true, but pressure outside and to a growing extent inside Oxford was insisting on the University's accountability to the nation. Of this argument a leading spokesman was Mark Pattison (1813–84), the learned if caustic Rector of Lincoln College, who in his *Suggestions on Academical Organization* (1869) put forward far-reaching and radical proposals for making the University a more effective home of scholarship and research. There were other positive signs of the times. It was agreed for the first time in 1868 that students without college attachment should be admitted to the University, so enabling men who could not afford college fees to avail themselves of a University education. Three years later Parliament passed a bill abolishing religious tests for all degrees save those in divinity, still further weakening the Anglican monopoly over the University which die-hards like Dr Pusey (1800–82) sought to retain. The University showed more signs of responding to the widening spectrum of national education. On the initiative of Benjamin Jowett (1817–93) his college, Balliol, and New College allocated £300 a year to the newly established university college at Bristol. In 1878 the University, following Cambridge's lead, agreed to give its support to a scheme by which lectures and tuition under the supervision of the Delegates of Local

UNIVERSITY REFORM. A cartoon by John Tenniel in *Punch* refers to the setting up of a University Commission in 1872, one object of which was to investigate the finances of the University. W. E. Gladstone is opening the chest while a University dignitary looks on.

THE ADMISSION OF WOMEN. The movement for the admission of women to Oxford took place in the 1870s and 1880s, evoking strong feelings from both its proponents and its critics. This drawing from a scrapbook in the Bodleian Library is dated 1882–3.

Examinations should be arranged in the large towns of England and Wales. Later, through the work of the University Local Examinations Delegacy, and by examining through the Oxford and Cambridge Examinations Board, the University indirectly exercised great influence over the curriculum of British schools.

Meanwhile, in 1872, a Royal Commission was appointed to 'obtain the fullest information respecting all matters of fact connected with the property and income either of the universities themselves or of the colleges and halls therein'. In their report, issued in 1874, the Commissioners showed that while the colleges had an annual income of £830,000 the University had only £32,000. These findings resulted in an Act designed to redistribute college revenues in the interests of both colleges and university, leading, for instance, to the creation of a common University fund for the provision of lecturers and to the foundation of new academic posts.

That such changes accorded with current public opinion can hardly be doubted. In the nation at large there had been a resurgence of interest in education, largely stimulated by the affluent middle classes, resulting not only in the provision of compulsory primary education but in the reform of the older independent schools and the foundation of new ones, many of whose pupils studied at Oxford and Cambridge. While a high proportion of Oxford's graduates still proceeded to holy orders, a great many more were to follow a secular career, in the civil and colonial service, in law, teaching, and medicine, and, though still to a smaller extent, in commerce and industry. To meet the needs of the sons of a successful middle class new subjects were added to the curriculum while, in spite of the retention until the twentieth century of compulsory chapel, the Established Church's influence was further diluted. A new generation of private halls, denominational in character, appeared. A further sign of the changing times was the provision which began to be made for the higher education of women. It was stoutly resisted by the more conservative dons. 'Sound learning and the midnight lamp', Thomas Case (1844–1925), the President of Corpus, told *The Times* on 27 April 1884, 'will be succeeded by light literature and the art of conversation at tea-parties. Young men will play at what young women like; the University Park will become a huge tennis-ground, and the river a series of expeditions to Nuneham.'

From the mid-nineteenth century onwards Oxford became news in a way which it had never been in the past. The boat race against Cambridge, initiated in 1829 and an annual event from 1836, attracted a wide interest among thousands who had no association with either university. The University debating-club, the Union Society, became the seed-bed of future leaders of the nation, its past Presidents including such a prominent religious figure as Archbishop William Temple (1881–1944) in 1904, the writers Ronald Knox (1888–1957) and Beverley Nichols (1898–1983) (1909 and 1920 respectively), and such important political personalities as Quintin Hogg, Lord Hailsham (b. 1907), in 1929, Michael Foot (b. 1913) in 1933, Edward Heath (b. 1916) in 1939, Tony Benn (b. 1925) in 1947, and Jeremy Thorpe (b. 1929) in 1951. Oxford became the fictional setting for numerous novels, from *The Adventures of Mr. Verdant Green* (1853–7) by Edward Bradley, a graduate of Durham University, to Max Beerbohm's *Zuleika Dobson* (1911) and Evelyn Waugh's *Brideshead Revisited* (1945). The name 'Oxford' was to be attached to articles which had only a minimal connection with either the city or the University, such as 'Oxford bags', the wide trousers worn by young men in the 1920s, or Frank Buchman's Moral Rearmament movement, which in the 1930s was unjustifiably known as the Oxford Group. Standard English was christened 'Oxford English', which, though it may grate upon northern ears, was the English ambitious foreigners most wanted to learn.

The short- and long-term effects of the First World War on Oxford were a significant landmark in the University's relations with the nation. The majority of Oxford's young dons immediately volunteered for war service and its colleges emptied of undergraduates, who joined the armed forces with patriotic fervour and naïve enthusiasm. In

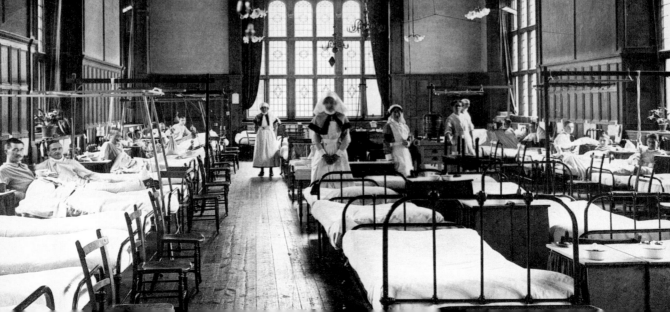

1913–14 there had been 1,400 undergraduates in residence, in 1916 there were 550, in 1917 there were 460, and in 1918 there were 369; those who were left behind were men unfit for military service, Oriental and other foreign students, and women. Some 14,561 members of the University served in the armed forces, 16 received the Victoria Cross, and 2,708 Oxford men were killed in action. Since many of the recruits became young officers, the carnage was especially high, and in terms of potential service to the nation the loss was incalculable.

The University's physical as well as human resources were geared to the war effort. The Examination Schools became a military hospital, and schools of military instruction and aeronautics were set up. Port Meadow served as an aerodrome and huts were erected in the Parks to house the Royal Flying Corps. Scientists directed their research towards the war effort. The pathologist Georges Dreyer (1873–1934), who served with the army in France, worked on the provision of oxygen for high flyers and on the diagnosis of enteric fever; J. S. Haldane (1860–1936) and Bertram Lambert (1881–1963) developed the respirator for use against chlorine gas.

An incidental but ultimately very significant by-product of the war was the decision to set up a Committee of Advanced Studies to promote graduate studies for the newly instituted D.Phil. degree, which was aimed to attract American research students in particular to Oxford and keep them out of the arms of German universities. This paved the way for a major shift towards research which was to occur in subsequent decades.

THE EXAMINATION SCHOOLS (*left*) set out for an examination in 1885, and as the surgical ward of a general hospital during the First World War.

OXFORD HONOURS THE VICTORS. Encaenia 1919 (*below*): *front row*, Admiral Sir Rosslyn Wemyss, Lieut.-Gen. Sir John Monash, General Pershing, General Joffre, the Chancellor Lord Curzon, Field Marshal Sir Douglas Haig, Admiral Sir David Beatty, Herbert Hoover, Sir Henry Wilson; *back row*, the Belgian historian Henri Pirenne, Rear-Admiral Sir William Hall, Rt. Hon. J. R. Clynes, and Lord Robert Cecil.

The ending of the war left Oxford, like Cambridge, with grave financial problems which could not be resolved out of its own resources. College incomes remained depressed by the agrarian recession. The University's revenues, in spite of many generous benefactions, were wholly insufficient to pay for the steadily expanding needs of scientific research. On 6 June 1919 the University reluctantly accepted a decree authorizing the Vice-Chancellor to apply for assistance from the Government. Many dons were very suspicious of a proposal which seemed to threaten the University's cherished independence. 'We do not want Oxford', as one critic put it, 'to voice the views of Whitehall as Berlin once did the views of Potsdam. Oxford stands for freedom; and if she is to fulfil her freedom as the inspirer and guide of the higher national life and thought, she must be free to determine her own curriculum and her own life.' But those who supported the motion not only realized that such freedom was largely an illusion but that without Government help the University could not effectively survive as a centre of excellence. The decree was carried by 126 votes to 88, and henceforth the Treasury was to become a principal paymaster of the University, acting through the medium of the University Grants Committee. The first annual grant was no more than £30,000, increased to £60,000 in 1923–4 but still no more than £110,000 in 1937–8. Thenceforth it was to spiral upwards as increased expenditure and later inflation affected the University's budget.

The Government grant was dependent upon the University's readiness to collaborate with an inquiry into its resources. The first Royal Commission of 1850 had been concerned with the termination of religious discrimination. The second, of 1872, had attempted to make sure that the colleges made efficient, educational use of their endowments. In the very different circumstances of the twentieth century this third inquiry, under the chairmanship of H. H. Asquith (1852–1928), reminded the public of the extraordinary history and nature of the ancient English universities. Contrary to most European practice, undergraduates came into residence for a fixed period of years. They were treated as gentlemen and looked after by servants. Thanks to the invention of the system of individual or paired tutorials, England possessed in Oxford, by the end of the nineteenth century (though not, as is frequently and mistakenly supposed, much before then), the finest teaching university in the world. Not surprisingly, the undergraduates enjoyed themselves in the intimate, relaxed, often boisterous and seldom wholly unintellectual atmosphere at the varsity, and when they went down they formed a homogeneous and active governing élite. By means of scholarships some new blood, at least, had been recruited to that élite in every generation.

But England also possessed in Oxford an exceptionally expensive and exclusive system of undergraduate teaching. The Asquith Commission was confronted with the demands of organized labour for a place in the university sun, and for an end to the monopoly of higher education by purchase. The commissioners spent a great deal of time discussing ways and means of lowering the costs of a college education, before deciding, in effect, that it could not be done. If the State wanted to send working-class

THE INSTALLATION OF LORD GRENVILLE AS CHANCELLOR in 1810 as seen by James Gillray. Grenville was a Whig. He was in favour of Catholic emancipation, and is shown rising in a balloon, wearing a papal tiara and a Chancellor's gown with a large cross on his posterior. In the background the towers of Oxford exhibit Popish emblems.

students to Oxford it would have to pay the going middle- and upper-class rate. Consequently, the findings of the Commission were conservative in tone. But it did express the view that the nation had a duty to maintain Oxford as a world-class university, and endorsed the new system of Treasury grants. It provided, *inter alia*, for a University pension scheme (to promote retirement), and made entry to the University (matriculation) dependent upon a minimum level of attainment (thus excluding the worst class of 'good college men', who were no better than moneyed layabouts). In doing even this much the Commission inevitably incurred the wrath of those who feared for the independence of the colleges (and Asquith was not elected to succeed Lord Curzon, 1859–1925, as Chancellor in 1925). But, significantly, it was the last Royal Commission. Between them, the three Commissions had done just enough to free the University from the stranglehold of the colleges, and to establish parity between the two. It was almost as if successive Governments concluded that Oxford then had sufficient institutional and emotional flexibility to reform itself in the future.

With the ending of the First World War colleges were soon filled to capacity—largely by demobilized warriors, some of whom found it difficult to adjust to the paternalistic college and Proctorial discipline. There were already 1,357 undergraduates in residence by February 1919; the following October there were 2,659. There were 5,689 undergraduates in residence by 1920, including 687 women; 2,892 matriculated in 1919. Although the majority still came from independent schools, there was a small but perceptible change in the social mix, in part made possible by the award for the first time of State scholarships, a system introduced by Lloyd George's President of the Board of Education, H. A. L. Fisher (1865–1940), who became Warden of New College in 1925.

Although, with a few notable exceptions, undergraduates rushed enthusiastically to help break the General Strike in 1926, the immediate postwar generation of students was largely apolitical, if conservative in dress and attitudes. The University remained very much a male-dominated society. Nationally, women had been given the right to vote in elections to Parliament in 1918, but in the face of Oxford's deeply entrenched male chauvinism the women's colleges were still unable to achieve parity of esteem. In May 1920 women students were at last given the right to matriculate and to take all degrees except those in theology, a disqualification removed only in 1935; but in many respects women dons and their students remained second-class citizens. In 1926, in spite of a vigorous defence by a guest speaker, Lucy Sutherland (1903–80, future Principal of Lady Margaret Hall), the Oxford Union, which did not allow women to become members until 1964, voted that the women's colleges ought to be levelled to the ground. This was not, of course, a serious proposal but it pointed to a continuing suspicion of female education which was to persist through the 1930s and 1940s. The only

MATRICULATION is the act of presenting students to the Vice-Chancellor and admitting them into membership of the University. It takes place in the Sheldonian Theatre and is a formal ceremony which demands dark clothing (subfusc) but does not require the participants to fall into step.

significant reforms of the interwar period were the abolition of compulsory Greek in spite of strong opposition from the clerical backwoodsmen, the establishment of the joint school of PPE (Politics, Philosophy, and Economics), which was at least a practical indication of Oxford's growing concern to train minds to meet the future needs of the nation state, and the doubling of the numbers reading Natural Science. There were now fewer ordinands, and an increasing number of Oxford's graduates were finding a career in the law, in the civil service, and in banking, commerce, and industry. Willy-nilly the University had entered a broader secular world, casting behind it the clerical coat in which it had for long been swathed.

The world of the 1930s witnessed a further movement in University and national opinion which external events—the advance of Nazism, Mussolini's Ethiopian adventure, and the Spanish Civil War—served to stimulate and excite. While the composition of the student body did not greatly change, though the slow process of greater democratization continued, undergraduate opinion became decidedly more political and radical in tone. Undergraduates of liberal sympathies, such as the poet W. H. Auden (1907–73) and the future Labour leader Hugh Gaitskell (1906–63), were drawn to the weekly discussions on political matters which had been instituted by the socialist G. D. H. Cole (1889–1959), the Reader in Economics from 1925 and later Chichele Professor, whose appointment had been publicly criticized (if in Latin) by the then Vice-Chancellor. Under the enthusiastic lead of the classical scholar Gilbert Murray (1866–1957), the League of Nations Union attracted a strong following. Philip Toynbee (1916–81), President of the Oxford Union in 1938, was a member of the left-wing October Club, strongly opposed to the Mosleyites; the club was banned by the Proctors, in part for sponsoring an anti-war group meeting at Ruskin College (which had been set up in 1899 to provide educational opportunities for the working man and had in 1913 been approved by the University as a society for higher education, though not a part of the University).

The Oxford Union, if only a partial index to Oxford opinion, had in 1932 been persuaded by George Lansbury to agree by 316 to 247 votes that socialism was the real answer to Britain's problems. Its Presidents in the 1930s included, in addition to Michael Foot and Edward Heath, the politicians J. P. W. Mallalieu (1908–80), Arthur Irvine (1909–78), and Anthony Greenwood (1911–82), the Indian journalist and writer Dooso Karaka (1911–74), and David Lewis (1909–81), who was to become the leader of the Canadian New Democratic Party. The Union attracted national attention, in the main unfavourable, when in 1935 it voted by 275 votes to 153 that its members 'would in no circumstances fight for its King and country'. Subsequently it questioned conventional morality, voted for the abolition of capital punishment, and agreed that British rule in the Empire operated to the detriment of the native peoples.

The climax to the growing political groundswell at Oxford was a by-election for the city in which the Master of Balliol, A. D. Lindsay (1879–1952), stood against Quintin Hogg as an anti-Munich agreement candidate, reducing Hogg's Conservative majority

A TEA PARTY IN LADY MARGARET HALL. In 1934 undergraduate rooms were still heated by open coal fires, and the smoking of cigarettes was a mark of liberation.

by half. Hogg, later Lord Hailsham and Lord Chancellor, was a fellow of All Souls, where there was a group of mainly non-resident fellows, including Geoffrey Dawson (1874–1944), editor of *The Times*, Lord Simon (1873–1954), and Lord Halifax (1881–1959), who were closely associated in the public mind with the policy of appeasement.

The Second World War was probably as much a landmark in Oxford's relationship with the nation as the first had proved to be. Whatever the view they had expressed as students, the majority of the University's members went unquestioning into the armed forces, albeit without the innocent enthusiasm with which their predecessors had greeted the First World War. Student numbers did not decline quite so precipitately, and though many colleges were taken over, Oxford, exempt from enemy air raids, suffered less disorientation than might have been expected. Some of its dons found comparatively comfortable niches in the somewhat ramshackle Ministry of Information or in deciphering enemy codes at Bletchley, among them the future historian and Provost of Worcester, J. C. Masterman (1891–1977). Scientifically significant contributions to the war effort were made by Sir Henry Tizard (1885–1959) and his critic, the arrogant but able adviser of Winston Churchill, F. A. Lindemann (1886–1957), later Lord

Cherwell. More positively, the development of penicillin by Howard (later Lord) Florey (1898–1968) and his associates at the Sir William Dunn School was to prove of inestimable value in the treatment of war wounds.

The ending of the Second World War, even more than that of the first, foreshadowed a social and in some ways an academic revolution. Refugee scholars who had been welcomed at Oxford—such as the classicist Eduard Fraenkel (1888–1970), the musicologist Egon Wellesz (1885–1974), and the physicist Sir Francis Simon (1893–1956)—had strengthened the University's reputation for scholarship, but there was growing pressure to widen the curriculum by the provision of new honour schools and to promote graduate research, more especially in the sciences, on an infinitely greater scale than ever before. Many new graduate societies were founded, of which Nuffield College, which specialized in social studies, was the first. In 1948 the French Levantine businessman, Antonin Besse (1877–1951), gave the University £1,250,000 to set up St Antony's College in order to promote research in international relations. Foundations specializing in a particular area of study were themselves a departure from the traditional function of an Oxford college, where the whole spectrum of academic disciplines was normally covered. The generosity of the Wolfson Trustees enabled the conversion of Iffley College into Wolfson College, with a fine site by the River Cherwell, as a cosmopolitan research centre. Other graduate societies included Linacre, St Cross, which acquired the greater part of the former Pusey House in 1981, and Green College, founded in 1979 by the Texan millionaire Cecil Green (b. 1900) for medical and scientific studies. Other centres of higher education and research which became a part of the University included Templeton College for business studies and Rewley House, generously endowed by the Kellogg foundation in 1982, for continuing education. In 1971–2 there were 2,782 graduates by comparison with 7,976 undergraduates, and 240 registered adult students.

As significant as the increase in the postgraduate population was the campaign for the further democratization of the entry and so for a change in the social composition of the student body. The 1944 Education Act had in effect made the University open to all who could win admission to a college, but the admissions procedure seemed still heavily weighted in favour of the public and grammar school as against boys from secondary and comprehensive schools, while, though the fixed limit on the number of women to be admitted was removed in 1956, women students still formed only a small fraction of the University.

The student mood of the 1960s and 1970s was infected by external influences, more especially by the demands originating in American and some Continental universities for student participation in college and university government. While there were occasional threatening demonstrations and a number of sit-ins, Oxford was far less the victim of student violence than most other British universities, probably because its collegiate structure helped to diminish the possibility of militant action. Yet though the student radicalism seemed to evaporate relatively soon, dons and undergraduates alike realized that if the University was to fulfil its purpose in the nation, it must become fully comprehensive in its intake and more fully stretched in terms of teaching and research.

The University's reaction to these problems was cautious and to some seemed unduly slow. In an introspective mood in 1964 it instituted a commission under the chairmanship of Lord Franks (b. 1905), which advocated a significant modification of the University's cabinet, the Hebdomadal Council, and a change in the method of appointing the Vice-Chancellor. While the Franks Commission did something to make the University more efficient by strengthening its central authority—some thought at the cost of college autonomy—there was some criticism that the Commission's recommendations did not go far enough to make the University sufficiently accountable to the nation which in part subsidized it.

In the closing years of the twentieth century much was in fact done to seal the gap. A maths or science subject was made an acceptable alternative to Greek or Latin as an entrance requirement in 1960, and nine years later the requirement of two languages was ended for scientists. A committee under the chairmanship of Sir Kenneth Dover

SIR OLIVER FRANKS. This photograph was taken in 1948, when the Provost of Queen's College was appointed British ambassador in Washington. In 1962 Lord Franks returned to Oxford as the Provost of Worcester College, and may be remembered for the important and thorough investigation into the University which he chaired in 1964–6.

SUSAN BROWN of Wadham College was the first woman to cox the University VIII. She is seen here in training in December 1980 for the Boat Race of 1981.

(b. 1920) restructured the admissions system with the object of providing for candidates from a wider range of schools, including the comprehensive schools, and consequentially for a broader social grouping.

As importantly, the remaining discrimination against the entry of women was removed by the introduction of co-residence in the great majority of colleges. It had taken some time for the women's colleges to achieve parity with the male societies, and even longer to shatter what Evelyn Waugh (1903–66) described as the 'hard bachelor-dom of English adolescence'. In 1972 five men's colleges—Brasenose, Hertford, Jesus, St Catherine's, and Wadham—changed their statutes to allow the admission of women as graduates and undergraduates. The University requested other colleges to postpone their decisions until it had had sufficient opportunity to scrutinize what was then regarded as an experiment. University and national opinion shifted rapidly against any form of sexual discrimination, so preparing the way for most of the colleges, with Oriel in the rear, to follow suit in 1979, leaving only two single-sex colleges in existence, Somerville and St Hilda's (both women's colleges), at the beginning of the last decade of the twentieth century.

Oxford had so come into line with other British universities that it might have appeared to be just one of the forty-eight, if highly reputed as an international centre of excellence. But a survey of twentieth-century history shows that its contribution to a meritocratic society was actually greater than it had ever been. If there was a very pronounced drop in the number of their ordinands, the two older universities still maintained their hold over the episcopate. Of seven Archbishops of Canterbury since 1928, four had been Oxford graduates. In 43 English dioceses, of 69 bishops appointed between 1940 and 1960 36 were Oxford graduates (and 27 from Cambridge); between 1960 and 1980, of some 74 bishops appointed 30 were educated at Oxford (and 31 at Cambridge). In the House of Commons there was still a substantial, indeed a marginally increasing, number of Oxford graduates. Of 1,758 Members of Parliament elected between 1919 and 1945, 249 had been educated at Oxford (and 210 at Cambridge); between 1945 and 1979, of 1,790 Members of Parliament 345 came from Oxford (and 239 from Cambridge). Of 15 British Prime Ministers since 1914, five of whom were not university graduates, more than half—Asquith, Attlee (1883–1967), Eden (1897–1977), Macmillan (1894–1986), Douglas-Home (b. 1903), Wilson (b. 1916), Heath, and Thatcher (b. 1925)—were Oxford graduates. In 1960 Macmillan, in spite of strong disapproval from his Cabinet colleagues, agreed to be a candidate for the Chancellorship of the University in succession to Lord Halifax, and proved to be a highly successful and popular Chancellor until his death. His successor after a disputed election was the former Labour minister and leader of the soi-disant SDP party, Lord Jenkins (b. 1920).

SIR WILLIAM BEVERIDGE, a distinguished economist, who became Master of University College, was best known for his report on social security, which he is seen discussing at a press conference at the Ministry of Information in 1942.

LADY THATCHER (b. 1925). Margaret Thatcher, née Roberts, read Chemistry at Somerville and became an honorary fellow in 1970. The illustration shows her first visit to the college after becoming Prime Minister in 1979.

There were in fact few aspects of the national life, leaving aside the academic and literary world, in which Oxford graduates did not leave their mark. Raymond Massey (1896–1983), Terence Rattigan (b. 1911), John Schlesinger (b. 1926), Kenneth Tynan (b. 1927), Dudley Moore (b. 1935), Michael Palin (b. 1943), Rowan Atkinson (b. 1955) on stage and screen; William Rees Mogg (b. 1928) and Rupert Murdoch (b. 1931) in the media; Lord Sainsbury (b. 1902), Sir Maurice Hodgson (b. 1919), Sir Peter Parker (b. 1924), Robin Leigh-Pemberton (b. 1927), and Garfield Weston (b. 1927) in big business; Lord Feather (1908–76), Len Murray (b. 1922), and Norman Willis (b. 1933) in trade unionism. Funding from commerce, banking, and industry helped to strengthen the University's relations with the economic life of the country.

Throughout the twentieth century there were, as there still are, those who have questioned whether Oxford had taken adequate measures to meet the political and economic needs of the age, given that to a greater extent than ever before the University and its students were paid for out of public funds. Historically, outside criticism has always been part and parcel of Oxford's long history: by the townsfolk of the city, by Protestant reformers, by Whig politicians, by Nonconformists and radicals in the nineteenth century, by feminists and by socialists in the twentieth. Nor, admittedly, have their criticisms been without some foundation.

In the last analysis, however, if Oxford (like its sister Cambridge) has been on occasions slow to take note of its critics in amending its constitution, its curriculum and admissions system, and its social and academic structure, it has undoubtedly contributed positively, even massively, to the national life throughout the centuries of its existence. Its cultural heritage, in terms of scholarship and research, from the scholastic writers of the medieval University to the scientists and mathematicians of modern times, has been enormous in its range and depth. Throughout its history it has been essentially a teaching university. As a residential and collegiate society it has housed the bodies and sharpened the minds of youth, providing an intellectual and social milieu in which men and more recently women have passed from adolescence to adulthood. From it have sprung a high proportion of the nation's clergy and schoolteachers, and in more recent years the teaching staff, lecturers, and professors for other British universities and for the universities of the Commonwealth. It has trained many of the bishops and leaders of the Established Church (and more recently of other churches as well), and from its graduates the Crown has drawn its ministers and the public offices their personnel.

Once an Oxford man always an Oxford man. Students depart when they have completed their courses, but a very large number of them remain connected by golden memories of their undergraduate years to the continuing life of the University. Headmasters and journalists, politicians and permanent secretaries have all been known to speak, and often without affectation or reservation, of the debts they owe to their colleges and to their college tutors. The depth of this inspired loyalty enables the University—however artificial this may at times appear—to lay claim to the achievement of every successful Oxford man as if it were the achievement of Oxford itself.

But there is more to it than that. Over the centuries Oxford has thrived on the oxygen drawn through its links, via old members, to the life of the nation. As an ivory tower it is nothing: as a part of the world of affairs it is everything. When, in the first half of the eighteenth century, High Tory Oxford distanced itself from the Whig supremacy, the University decayed. Fortunate indeed for the provincial Oxford of port and prejudice that London University was founded not in 1726 but in 1826. By that time Oxford itself was recovering. It could boast of its reformers as well as its reactionaries (and even the reactionaries were colourful and interesting). In the 1850s changes imposed from outside, by the State, were both preceded and assisted by movement from within. In the middle of the nineteenth century the State, thanks largely to Gladstone, began once again to look with favour upon the University. Consciously or unconsciously, the new system of competitive examination for the civil service was tailored to reward the attainments of Oxford—and especially classics—graduates. In keeping with this special relationship, a new printed University *Gazette* was founded in 1870, modelled upon the London one with its lists of official appointments and commissions, and 'Published by Authority'. Beyond the gates of the Oxford colleges lay a carpet leading straight to the corridors of power. The colleges cultivated their old members, and they, in turn, sought

out talented and promising young men who could be taken on to the staff and groomed to succeed them in due course. It was no longer called patronage, but that, with a new nineteenth-century rinse of merit, was what it was.

British statesmen of the late nineteenth and early twentieth centuries continued to put their faith in the ancient universities, whose products they were. When the Great War revealed that the future of the State was bound up with an expansion of the universities, and especially of the natural sciences, Governments began to channel public money towards them. Taking their tone from Asquith, ministers of the Crown refused to interfere with the vital academic freedoms—freedom to pursue knowledge for its own sake, and freedom to select one's own subject of enquiry. This enlightened policy brought a rich dividend. Oxford offered a favourable environment to scholars fleeing from Hitler's Germany, and the University received the largest intellectual blood transfusion in its history. Post-1945 Governments then had all the more reason to smile upon the fruitful relationship between the University and the nation, and to take a relaxed and not altogether ledger-bound view of the expenditure of public money. Departments of State continued to seek out the expertise of university teachers, and Oxford academics, unlike their counterparts in other countries, were in no danger of becoming alienated from the institutional structures of the nation and the exercise of State authority.

FINAL EXAMINATIONS (*facing*). Undergraduates outside the Examination Schools in the High Street in May 1989. Candidates for examinations are obliged to wear subfusc (dark clothes and white tie). Runaway celebrations outside the Examination Schools after the end of the ordeal have often led to the intervention of the Proctors and of the police.

3

The Architecture of the University and the Colleges

GEOFFREY TYACK

THE most tangible of Oxford University's contributions to civilization is Oxford itself. Over a period of seven hundred years this moderately sized provincial town has acquired, through innumerable acts of individual and corporate munificence, a collection of magnificent buildings whose visual effect is hard to match in any place of comparable size in Europe. Yet, viewed in a European or even in an English context, the architecture of Oxford is highly idiosyncratic. The University first acquired a distinctive architectural character in the later Middle Ages, and while from time to time it has successfully assimilated new styles, notably in the late seventeenth and early eighteenth centuries and after the Second World War, it has repeatedly fallen back on a retrospec-

TACKLEY'S INN, 107 High Street, was 'newly built' in 1324, and ceased to be an academic hall in the fifteenth century. This drawing of c.1750 shows the traceried window lighting the communal dining-hall to the left, and the entrance to the 'screens passage' leading from the garden plot to the High Street on the right; beyond this were chambers where students lived five to a room.

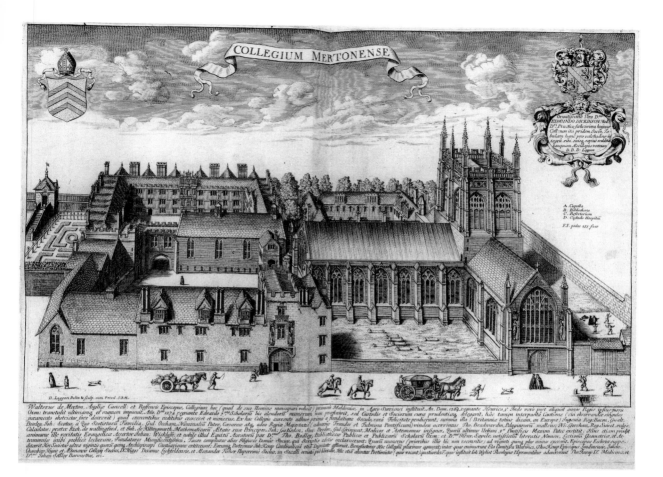

MERTON COLLEGE in the late seventeenth century. The original late-thirteenth-century buildings are in the foreground. The gatehouse dates from 1418, and the range to the left was altered in the sixteenth century. The chapel, with its tower of 1448–51, is on the right, and behind it is Mob Quad, completed in 1378. To its left is the much larger Fellows' Quad of 1610.

tive and intellectually undemanding medievalism which is both a strength—few university cities in the world are more seductively beautiful—and a weakness. In this respect the buildings of Oxford both reflect and help perpetuate the extraordinary institutional and emotional continuity represented by the University and its colleges.

A medieval university was a chartered corporation of scholars, not a set of buildings, and for more than a century Oxford University had no buildings of its own. Teaching took place in rented premises, and students occupied rooms in private houses. Ceremonies were held in St Mary's Church in the High Street, and here an unpretentious two-storeyed Congregation House was built in about 1320, with a meeting-room below and a library above. During the thirteenth century private individuals and religious institutions began leasing houses as academic halls where undergraduates could live communally under the supervision of Masters of Arts. The dining-hall of Tackley's Inn, an academic hall of c.1320, can still be found behind a row of shops on the south side of High Street, and Beam Hall, a smaller late-fifteenth-century building, survives intact in Merton Street. But the academic halls were essentially domestic in character, and made little architectural impact on the town.

The first impressive buildings were erected by the colleges. Oxford colleges have always possessed a strong sense of corporate identity, and their often generous endowments allowed them to build more substantially than the academic halls, whose functions they eventually usurped. The earliest surviving collegiate buildings are at Merton. They are irregularly arranged around a courtyard—a pattern also found in contemporary bishops' palaces and in some of the grander houses of the nobility and gentry—with a dining-hall (much rebuilt in 1872–4) on one side, a house for the Warden (also much altered) on another, and the chapel on a third, where work was in progress in 1290–4. By far the largest and grandest of these buildings is the tall aisleless

NEW COLLEGE, elevation and ground-floor plan of a typical staircase before 1674. The doorway led into a lobby, with the staircase in front and bedrooms shared by four students on each side, lit by large windows, originally unglazed. Each student had his own study-cubicle, leading off from the bedroom and lit by a smaller window. The walls are of durable local stone, probably from Wheatley.

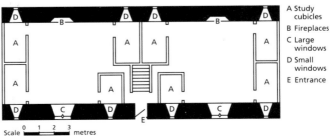

A Study cubicles

B Fireplaces

C Large windows

D Small windows

E Entrance

Scale 0 1 2 3 metres

chapel, lit by large traceried windows which still retain much of their original stained glass, and with the seating facing inwards as in a monastic or cathedral choir. It was built, like the rest of the college, of a rough, tawny-coloured local limestone, with the 'freestone' employed in the elaborate carved detail of the windows coming from Taynton, near Burford, some twenty miles to the west. Limestone is in abundant supply near Oxford, and it remained by far the most common material for the buildings of the colleges and University—but not for the town—down to the mid-twentieth century.

The building of Merton College proceeded piecemeal, as funds permitted, and no attempt was made to impose any kind of architectural unity. Purpose-built accommodation for the small numbers of fellows came with the building of Mob Quad to the south of the chapel, starting in 1287–9 but not completed until nearly a century later. This homely collection of buildings—Oxford's first collegiate quadrangle composed of four ranges of roughly equal length and height—also housed the college's treasury and library, where single-light windows illuminated the stalls in which the books were kept chained. The fellows shared bedrooms, but each had, at least from the 1370s, his own partitioned-off study-cubicle. These sets of rooms, like the 'lodgings' of noblemen's

THE HALL OF LINCOLN
COLLEGE dates from 1437. The
original timber roof survives intact,
but the open fireplace in the middle
of the floor was removed in 1699
and the oak panelling introduced
two years later. The doors in the
screen lead into a passage, beyond
which were the buttery (for serving
drink), the pantry (for serving
food), and the kitchen.

houses which they resemble, were approached directly from the quadrangle through
pointed-arched doorways leading into a lobby and staircase, an arrangement which
was universally adopted in later colleges.

The first consistently magnificent set of collegiate buildings were those of New College, begun in 1380. With seventy members and a Warden, the foundation of William
of Wykeham (1324–1404) was larger than all the other existing colleges put together.
The site, mostly made up of deserted tenements just inside the city wall, was unprecedentedly spacious. And for the first time in Oxford all the buildings were conceived as a
coherent whole. Wykeham's earlier career as an ecclesiastical administrator had familiarized him with large-scale building operations and introduced him to capable and
imaginative master masons, and one of these men, William Wynford (*fl.* 1360–1405),
was almost certainly responsible for the design.

The main buildings of New College were laid out around a quadrangle nearly four
times the size of Merton's Mob Quad. The entrance was through a tall gatehouse—

a mark of exclusiveness and authority in late-medieval England—with niches containing figures of Wykeham, the angel of the Annunciation, and the Virgin Mary, to whom the college is dedicated. The Warden's lodgings were over the gateway, and the fellows and junior members lived in two-storeyed buildings (unfortunately heightened in 1674) around the quadrangle, with the library on the upper floor of the east range. The chapel and hall were placed next to each other in a taller block on the north side, with a Muniment Tower at the north-east corner. This range of buildings was the secular and spiritual heart of the college, and its importance is reflected in the architecture, with an array of tall mullioned windows separated by boldly projecting buttresses surmounted by crocketed pinnacles—the first appearance of 'Perpendicular' Gothic in Oxford. The largest windows light the T-shaped chapel—a plan unique to Oxford—and in the tall and empty antechapel, with much of its stained glass still *in situ*, the grandeur of the original conception can still be experienced. The hall, approached by a flight of steps in the Muniment Tower, is arranged like that of a late-medieval nobleman's or gentleman's house, with an exposed timber roof, a raised dais for the high table at one end,

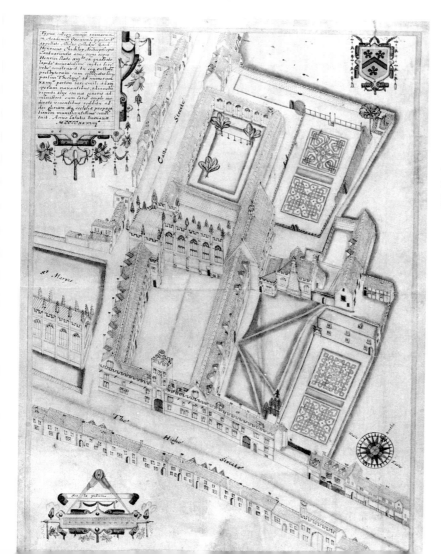

ALL SOULS COLLEGE, with a tower over the gatehouse and the chapel on the opposite side of the front quadrangle. These buildings of 1438–43 survive, but the hall and the cloister beyond were replaced in 1715–34. This is the earliest accurate view of an Oxford college, and comes from one of the maps of college properties commissioned by the Warden, Robert Hovenden, in 1598.

THE GREAT QUADRANGLE OF MAGDALEN COLLEGE, showing the hall and chapel on the left, with the bell tower behind, and the original gatehouse to the right. An unglazed cloister runs round the whole building at ground level. The quadrangle was built of Headington stone. With its Perpendicular Gothic detailing it remains the definitive embodiment of the medieval collegiate ideal.

and a carved wooden screen at the other hiding the entrances to the kitchen, buttery, and pantry. A block of latrines (the Long Room) was placed outside the quadrangle to the east, and to the west of the chapel a cloister was built enclosing a burial-ground, with a bell tower—the first in any Oxford college (1396–7)—to the north against the town wall. When complete, the college possessed the most impressive set of educational buildings in England.

The architecture of New College influenced that of all the larger late-medieval foundations. All Souls (begun in 1438) was laid out along the same general lines, but with the chapel placed opposite the gatehouse. The presence of a long frontage to the High Street gave the master mason Richard Chevynton (*fl.* 1437–43) an opportunity to provide a more impressive façade, the main feature of which is the battlemented gate tower rising up from the centre. Here the collegiate façade achieved its classic form.

The layout of Magdalen (1474–*c.*1480) also owes much to New College, where the founder, William Waynflete (1395?–1486), had been educated. But now the cloister was incorporated within the quadrangle, thus integrating two formerly separate elements of the design and reinforcing the quasi-monastic atmosphere. The master mason responsible for the main buildings was a local man, William Orchard (*fl.* 1468–1504), who supplied the stone from his own quarries at Headington, two miles away, and agreed in 1475 to model the architectural detailing on that of All Souls. The ensemble was completed with the building of the beautifully proportioned bell tower, begun to the designs of another mason in 1492. As in the earlier tower built over the west end of Merton chapel by Robert Janyns (*fl.* 1438–64) in 1448–51, every effort was made to reduce the massiveness of the structure by breaking up the wall surfaces with buttresses and large traceried windows and crowning the skyline with an array of tall pinnacles rising above a pierced parapet. The result is one of the triumphs of English late-medieval architecture.

The first major building erected by the University was the Divinity School. As first conceived in 1423, this was to be a single-storeyed structure comprising one large room for the teaching of theology adorned with elaborate carving and lit by large Perpendicular Gothic windows. Lack of funds made progress painfully slow, and in 1440 the master mason was ordered to dispense with 'frivolous and irrelevant elaborations'. Further changes came when an extra storey was added to house the books given to the University by Humphrey, Duke of Gloucester (1391–1447), in 1444. Finally, in 1479–83, the ori-

THE DIVINITY SCHOOL, from the Oxford Almanack of 1816. This lecture-room, the most ambitious building undertaken by the University in the Middle Ages, was begun in 1423. The most striking feature is the stone vault added fifty-six years later. A comparison with the antechapel of New College shows the increased surface elaboration employed by the master masons of the fifteenth century.

ginal plans for the Divinity School were completed by the building of the stone vault, a *tour de force* of late-Gothic ingenuity, with its net-like pattern of clustered ribs sprouting from pendants of stone hanging from the transverse arches. So extravagant a piece of display could not have been financed by the University alone, and the elaborately carved roof bosses pay tribute to benefactors, of whom the most generous was Thomas Kemp, Bishop of London from 1450 to 1489. Not for the last time, private generosity had enabled the University to act as a patron of bold and magnificent architecture.

The last great architectural enterprise in pre-Reformation Oxford was the building of Cardinal College for Thomas Wolsey (1475?–1530) on the site of the suppressed Priory of St Frideswide, just south of the city wall. The plan was to follow that of Magdalen, where Wolsey had been a fellow in the 1490s, and work began in 1525 under the supervision of two master masons from Henry VIII's Office of Works, Henry Redman (*fl.* 1495–1528) and John Lubyns (*fl.* 1506–29). The main survivals from the original project are the lower parts of the gatehouse, flanked by polygonal turrets encrusted

CHRIST CHURCH FROM THE AIR, looking north-east. On the left is Tom Quad, as laid out in 1525, with the hall in the foreground and the neo-Gothic gate tower added by Wren in 1681–2. The largely late-twelfth-century priory church of St Frideswide (now the cathedral) is to the right. In the distance is the eighteenth-century Peckwater Quad and library.

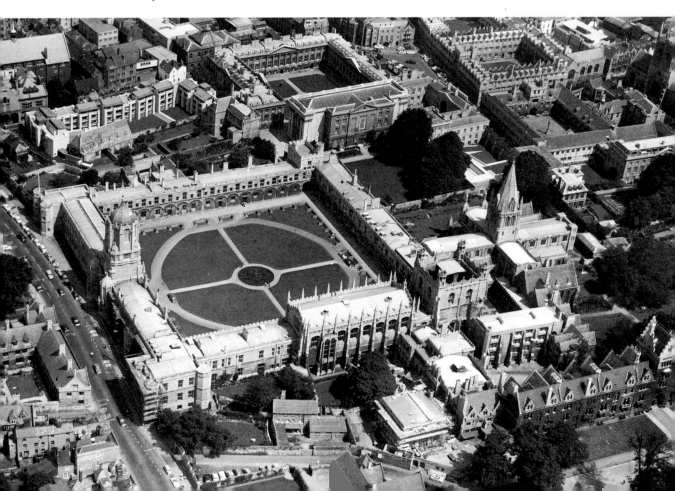

with blind arcading, the huge detached kitchen, and the vast hall—the largest in Oxford—covered by a superb hammer-beam roof designed by another Office of Works craftsman, Henry Coke (*fl.* 1506–29). In the carving of an oriel window at the southern end of the street front there is even a hint of the Renaissance wafted from Hampton Court. But work stopped when the cardinal fell from favour, and the proposed gate-house tower, chapel, and cloister remained unbuilt, though the springing of the cloister vault can still be seen. What remained of the priory church was reprieved to serve both as the chapel of Henry VIII's new foundation, Christ Church, and as the cathedral of the new diocese of Oxford, and the completion of what is now called Tom Quad was postponed for more than a century.

The Reformation marked a major hiatus in the architectural history of Oxford. Chapels were denuded of their statuary and fittings, and some of the libraries of their books. Religious and political uncertainty stifled the wish to build. When the University recovered its confidence towards the end of the sixteenth century there was an urgent need to accommodate the growing numbers of undergraduates. The first response of the by now more powerful colleges was to adapt existing buildings rather than construct expensive new ones. Extra space could easily be found by creating 'cocklofts' in the attics of the older buildings, a practice first recorded at New College in 1539. The fellows of St John's, who had taken over the premises of the suppressed St Bernard's College, recorded in 1573 that they were 'partly through coldness, partly for want of room, constrained to overloft all the chambers in the whole college'. Here and elsewhere the newly created attic rooms were heated by wall fireplaces (a rarity in medieval Oxford) and lit by glazed windows set in gables, the effect of which can be seen in the Old Quadrangle at Brasenose, where the transformation was begun in 1605. Thus the skyline of Oxford, already punctuated with towers and pinnacles, was further enriched by ranks of gables and tall chimneys.

Some internal remodelling also took place. Wood panelling was introduced into college halls, starting at New College (1533–5) and Magdalen (1541). As the number of printed books grew, it became necessary to enlarge college libraries. At Merton the books were transferred in 1589–90 to cases containing stacks of shelves and placed at right angles to the walls, and in due course the other colleges followed suit. Heads of Houses were now allowed to marry, and some colleges, like Jesus, created spacious and comfortable lodgings embellished with wood panelling, elaborately carved chimney-pieces, and moulded plaster ceilings.

Private donors did not resume the pre-Reformation practice of contributing to ambitious building schemes until the beginning of the seventeenth century. The first college to expand substantially was Merton, where a new set of buildings (the Fellows' Quadrangle) was erected in 1610. The buildings represented a new departure for Oxford, both in their unprecedented height—there are three storeys and, in addition, more rooms in the attics—and in the introduction of the orders of classical architecture perched one above the other in a 'frontispiece' in the centre of the south range. This *jeu*

d'esprit must have been the brainchild of the Warden, Henry Savile (1549–1622), who was the chief promoter of the new building, and it was he who introduced the two master masons from his native Yorkshire, John Akroyd (1556–1613) and John Bentley (*c.*1573–1613), both of whom came from Halifax.

There is a similar classical frontispiece between the hall and chapel at Wadham (1610–13), the most complete and most impressive of the new post-Reformation colleges. Here too an outsider, the Somerset-born William Arnold (*fl.* 1600–37), was employed to design and construct the buildings, but again, despite an overall symmetry which the medieval colleges had not possessed, the classicism is no more than an emblematic allusion to a style of architecture which had as yet failed to make substantial inroads into the thinking either of the dons or of the master masons they employed. The richly furnished chapel is lit by Gothic windows filled with painted glass by the Dutchman Bernard van Linge (*fl.* 1622–41) and others—an eloquent evocation of the 'beauty of holiness' sought by an Anglican Church which was increasingly stressing its roots in the past. And in the hall, also lit by pointed windows, there is an open hammer-beam roof of a type which was already obsolescent in domestic architecture. A similar approach was adopted in the rebuilding of two of the oldest colleges, Oriel (*c.*1620–42) and University (1634–77).

Oxford's long attachment to Gothic architecture stemmed not so much from ignorance or conservatism as from a deliberate wish to emphasize institutional continuity. This very powerful urge explains the decision to build the spectacular fan vault of 1638 over the staircase leading to the hall at Christ Church. Few if any vaults of this kind had been built since the Reformation, but there were still masons capable of designing them, and in doing so the mason responsible for the Christ Church vault—probably a Londoner, William Smith—expressed the link between the seventeenth-century college and Wolsey's foundation in the most eloquent way possible.

The most ambitious architectural project of the early seventeenth century was the expansion of the University library and the building of the adjacent Schools Quadrangle. The prime mover, Sir Thomas Bodley (1545–1613), was a fellow of Merton, and in 1610 he made an agreement with Henry Savile's masons Ackroyd and Bentley to build an eastern extension (Arts End) on to the fifteenth-century Duke Humfrey's Library, with a lierne-vaulted passageway (the Proscholium) in front of the Divinity School underneath. Following recent Continental precedent, the bookcases in Arts

THE PRINCIPAL'S DRAWING-ROOM AT JESUS (*above, left*), the first new college to be founded after the Reformation. Its buildings were erected piecemeal on the site of former academic halls, starting around 1571. The lavish internal woodwork (*c.*1630) shows an increased concern for domestic comfort among heads of colleges, which spread in time to fellows and even undergraduates.

THE HALL AND ANTECHAPEL OF WADHAM COLLEGE (*below, left*) are juxtaposed in the range opposite the gateway. The tracery of the windows is of a type unknown to medieval masons, while the 'frontispiece' is a crude attempt to introduce the classical orders into a collegiate setting. The figures over the doorway are the founders, Sir Nicholas Wadham and his wife, and above them is James I.

End were placed against the walls, with the upper shelves reached from galleries. But architecturally the building is even more conservative than Wadham or Merton. The skyline is profusely pinnacled and crenellated, and the façade is covered with blind late-Gothic arcading imitating that of the fifteenth-century building which lies behind—an obvious sign of reverence for the medieval past.

Bodley was also involved in the decision to build a quadrangle to the east of the library containing 'better built scholes' (lecture-rooms), and in his will he left money to add a third storey as a 'very large supplement for stowage of books'. Until the mid-nineteenth century this upper storey housed the University's collection of portraits, thus becoming Britain's first public art gallery; it is now the Upper Reading Room of the library. The quadrangle was begun in 1613 in the same essentially late-Gothic style as the library extension, but the inner face of the gate tower—built to house the University's muniments—is incongruously adorned with the most extravagant of Oxford's architectural 'frontispieces', made up of no fewer than five superimposed orders of columns. A western extension of Duke Humfrey's Library (Selden End) followed in 1632–7, with a new Convocation House underneath, and with its completion the University possessed, for the first time in its history, a complex of impressive buildings of its own.

The Schools Quadrangle, like most of the other buildings in seventeenth-century Oxford, was faced with ashlar from Headington, a stone which, according to Robert Plot (1640–96), was 'very soft and easy . . . but hardening continually as it lies to the weather'. It was therefore well suited to supply the smooth external finish that the promoters of seventeenth- and eighteenth-century buildings admired. But it was less resistant to the atmosphere than the tough rubble stone used in most of Oxford's medieval buildings, and by the end of the eighteenth century it had already begun to fail. The consequences have plagued both the colleges and the University down to modern times.

With medievalism in the ascendant during the first half of the seventeenth century, Oxford was slow to adopt Renaissance architecture. The problem of introducing classical decoration into the fabric of an Oxford college was first solved in an intellectually satisfying and visually pleasing manner in the Canterbury Quadrangle at St John's (1631–6). Here the chief benefactor was Archbishop Laud (1573–1645), a former President of the college and one of the chief ministers of Charles I. The proportions, and to some extent the detailing, were dictated by the need to incorporate the already existing

SIR THOMAS BODLEY chose Perpendicular Gothic for the façade of his library (*above, right*) to emphasize its continuity with the medieval University. The detailing (much of it now replaced in Clipsham stone) is copied from the fifteenth-century Divinity School and Duke Humfrey's Library. The pictorial character of Bodley's Gothic is shown by the way the pinnacles, which pierce the skyline, have no buttresses beneath them.

SELDEN END was built on to the west end of Duke Humfrey's Library in 1632–7 (*below, right*). The books are stacked in cases which take up the whole wall-surface, the upper shelves being reached by galleries—a contrast to the older system of bookcases projecting from the walls, which can be glimpsed in the background in Duke Humfrey's Library.

late-sixteenth-century library block. But in the new east and west ranges the ground floor was treated, for the first time in Oxford, as an open loggia, with monolithic Tuscan columns supporting round arches, and busts of the Virtues and the Liberal Arts in the spandrels. The central arch on each side forms part of a copiously carved two-storeyed frontispiece under a curved pediment, with lead statues by Hubert le Sueur (*c*.1580–*c*.1670) paying tribute to the King and Queen. Thus Laud's craftsmen celebrated Oxford's traditionally close ties to the Crown.

Meanwhile, in the three pedimented gateways to the new Botanic Garden (1632–3) Oxford acquired its first consistently classical structures. The builder, and probably also the designer, was Nicholas Stone (1587–1647), who had been master mason at the new Banqueting House in Whitehall Palace, where he had worked under the supervision of the 'British Vitruvius', Inigo Jones (1573–1652). Like the façades of the Canterbury Quadrangle, the gateways lack the rigorous logic that pervades Jones's buildings, but they nevertheless pave the way for the transformation of Oxford's architecture that took place after the Restoration.

In the century after 1660 Oxford acquired a collection of monumental classical buildings second to none in England. Architecture was now deemed a subject worthy of the attention of gentlemen and scholars, so architectural books were bought for libraries and master masons gradually placed under the supervision of architects (often amateurs) versed in the principles of Renaissance design. The Sheldonian Theatre (1664–9) epitomizes the new approach (see pp. 58–9). It was built, as a setting for academic ceremonial, to the designs of the thirty-three-year-old Christopher Wren (1632–1723), fellow of Wadham and Savilian Professor of Astronomy. This was his first public building, and he took his inspiration directly from a structure of classical antiquity: the U-shaped

CANTERBURY QUADRANGLE, ST JOHN'S COLLEGE (*left*). The 'frontispiece' of the east range encloses a lead statue of Charles I by Hubert Le Sueur, with the royal coat of arms above and that of William Laud below. The arcades on either side reflect the architecture of Renaissance France and Italy, but the windows above, lighting an extension of the late-sixteenth-century library, are still Gothic.

SIR CHRISTOPHER WREN (*right*) introduced a more scholarly version of classical architecture into Oxford. This portrait bust of *c.*1673, by Edward Pierce, who worked for Wren on St Paul's Cathedral in London, captures the spirit of a man of whom Robert Hooke wrote 'there scarce ever met in one man, in so great perfection, such a Mechanical Head, and so Philosophical a Mind'.

Theatre of Marcellus in Rome, illustrated in the third volume of Sebastiano Serlio's *Architettura* (1540). Greek and Roman theatres were open to the elements, but a tarpaulin or *velarium* was sometimes hauled across to protect the spectators from the rain or sun, and in the Sheldonian Wren's ingenious seventy-foot-wide timber roof is hidden from view by an allegorical painting by Charles II's sergeant-painter Robert Streater (1624–80), showing the canvas drawn back to reveal Religion, Art, and Science triumphing over Envy, Hatred, and Malice—an apt summary of Oxford's attitude to the return of Church and King. The superb woodwork reinforces the effect of classical splendour. Externally the building is less of a success, partly because Wren was obliged to make the upper storey lower than originally intended, partly because the main façade was built close to the Divinity School, where no one can see it. 'It resembles a man with his trousers pulled up to his neck', as Sir John Summerson (b. 1904) observed in a lecture. But in its uncompromising classicism the Sheldonian set a standard for Oxford's public architecture which remained unchallenged for nearly two centuries.

The building of the Sheldonian enabled a new generation of Oxford masons to be trained in the art of carving classical detail. Their skills were put to good use in the adjacent three-storeyed building now known as the Old Ashmolean (1679–83). This dignified structure, with its richly carved porch flanked by Corinthian columns, was

THE SENIOR COMMON ROOM OF ST JOHN'S COLLEGE, one of the first purpose-built common rooms, is in a detached building to the north of the chapel designed by the local mason Bartholomew Peisley in 1676. The oak panelling and plaster ceiling (the latter by Thomas Roberts, 1742) created a comfortable and dignified meeting-place for the fellows of the college.

COLLEGIUM S^T TRINITATIS

COLLEGIUM DUNELMENSE, ab antiquo Monasterii Dunelmensis Seminarium, Bibliotheca Aungervillana, in publicos Academicorum usus extructa, olim celebre, post Cœnobiorum strragem sub Henrico VIII. aliquandiu derelictum & incultum jacens THOMAS POPE Miles, ÆD^m MDLV. doctrinæ & religioni redemit: parietes antiquos refarsit & Præsidenti, Duodecim Sociis, totidemque Scholaribus inibi alendis accommodatos reddidit. Cum vero pauperculæ Societas diu ingloria latuisset, tandem sub Kettello Præsidente vigilantissimo caput extulit, sub Bathurfto Patrono munificentissimo doctrinâ, disciplinâ & Convictorum frequentiâ cum primis extitit conspicua: in hoc autem præcipuè celebranda, quod publicum incolarum beneficium magis quam lucrum privatum continuo mediata fuerit; id quod testantur (præter antiqua mœnia ferè universa instaurata, præter Capellam, eximia elegantiæ opus, Refectorium, Culinam) tum Arbustum novâ & elegantiori formâ donatum, tum Hospitia etiam, Benefactorum Symbolis undique impetrata, de novo penitus condita; quæque Collegii limites antiquos duplo ferè ampliores constituant; quin quod & plura adhuc, nec inauspicato uti sperandum est, moliatur.

THE GARDENS OF TRINITY COLLEGE were laid out in the formal French-inspired manner popular in the later seventeenth century. Wren's Garden Quadrangle can be seen in the distance, with the remodelled buildings of the former Durham College to the left, overlooked by the chapel of 1691–4. Post-Restoration colleges echo contemporary country houses both in the design of their gardens and in their internal decoration.

built and probably designed by a local mason, Thomas Wood (c.1644–95), to house the collection of 'rarities' given to the University by Elias Ashmole (1617–92; see below, pp. 245–46). It is therefore England's oldest public museum. It also contained a School of Natural History, and a chemistry laboratory in the vaulted and supposedly fireproof basement, thus serving as Oxford's first purpose-built premises for scientific teaching.

The number of students in Oxford levelled off in the post-Restoration years, and it actually fell in the eighteenth century. But while the University ceased to expand there was an increase in the numbers of gentlemen-commoners, or even, at Christ Church, sons of noblemen. Such privileged youths could not be expected to conform to the old custom of sharing rooms. The fellows of the colleges also expected to be housed as

THE QUEEN'S COLLEGE. The medieval buildings were demolished to make way for the Front Quadrangle, begun in 1709 and completed with the building of the screen wall to the High Street in 1733–6. On the far right is the Williamson building of 1671–2 designed by Wren: facing it is the library of 1692–5. Queen's is now the most consistently classical of all Oxford colleges.

comfortably as their wealthier students. When Celia Fiennes (1662–1741) visited New College in the 1690s she was entertained by a fellow who had 'a very pretty appartment of dineing roome bed chamber and studdy and a room for a Servant'. Similar considerations led to the custom of setting aside a room as a Senior Common Room 'to the end', as Anthony Wood (1632–95) remarked, 'that the Fellows might meet together (chiefly in the evenings after refection) partly about business, but mostly for society's sake, which before was at each chamber by turns'. So the colleges took on more and more of the characteristics of the country houses from whose sons an increasing proportion of their membership was drawn.

The most striking development in collegiate planning was the appearance of the open-ended courtyard. The first Oxford college to build a 'quadrangle' of this sort was Trinity, where the north range of the Garden Quadrangle, with spacious rooms for gentlemen-commoners, was begun to Wren's designs in 1668. The new open-ended arrangement allowed a college's buildings to be visually integrated with the gardens. Both at Trinity and at New College, where the Garden Quadrangle was begun in 1682–4 by William Byrd (b. 1624), one of the masons at the Sheldonian, the new buildings looked out on to elaborate French-inspired formal parterres, swept away alas at the end of the eighteenth century to make way for the present featureless lawns. So the quasi-monastic seclusion which had characterized collegiate planning since the Middle Ages was decisively rejected.

The rebuilding of Trinity continued with the construction of a new chapel in 1691–4. With its attenuated antechapel, large round-headed windows (originally filled with clear glass), and exuberant craftsmanship in wood and plaster, this was the first college chapel to break with the medieval tradition. The new library at Queen's (1692–5) likewise set a precedent for college libraries. Though it was conventional in layout, the lightness of the richly plastered interior and the solemn gravity of the exterior, with its superimposed rows of arched openings, were quite new to Oxford.

Before work began on Trinity chapel the college consulted several 'able judges in architecture', amongst whom was Henry Aldrich (1648–1710), Dean of Christ Church. He had travelled in Italy, where he associated with 'the eminent in architecture', and shortly before his death he began writing an architectural treatise. His own tastes are best revealed in Peckwater Quadrangle at Christ Church (1707–14), where he designed the north, east, and west ranges himself. As in an Italian Renaissance *palazzo*, the largest rooms are placed on a suitably impressive first-floor *piano nobile*, and the upper storeys are articulated by Ionic columns and pilasters over a rusticated base, with a pediment to crown the roof-line on each side—an arrangement which anticipates later urban devel-

THE CLARENDON PRESS BUILDING, which dominates the northern approach to the central University area, was designed by Nicholas Hawksmoor. The curved front of the Sheldonian Theatre and the old Ashmolean Museum can be seen to the right. The walled garden beyond gave way to a new range of buildings for Exeter College in 1833–4.

opments like Queen Square, Bath, begun in 1729. The south side of the quadrangle is occupied by a library begun in 1717, and here a new note of majestic heaviness was introduced through the use of a giant order of Corinthian columns enfolding an Ionic order on the ground floor, as in Michelangelo's Palazzo dei Conservatori on the Capitoline in Rome. This impressive building was designed by another amateur, George Clarke (1661–1736), a fellow of All Souls and former Secretary to the Admiralty. He stepped into Aldrich's shoes as unofficial architectural adviser to Oxford and, in collaboration with the mason-contractor William Townesend (c.1668–1739), had a hand in most of the University's architectural projects of the early eighteenth century.

The first product of the Clarke–Townesend partnership was the rebuilding of Queen's. Starting in 1710, the medieval front quadrangle was replaced by a three-sided courtyard with two massive residential wings stretching forward from a new chapel and hall—the first in Oxford to be given a consistently classical treatment. The centre of this range is emphasized by an engaged Tuscan temple front surmounted by a cupola on the roof—an idea borrowed from Wren's Chelsea Hospital—and the college is closed off from the High Street by one of the most masterly strokes of architectural legerdemain in Oxford: a heavily rusticated screen wall built in 1733–6, with a circular domed 'temple' over the porter's lodge in the centre sheltering a statue of Queen Caroline. Oxford's main street was thus given a compelling classical focus.

In its final form the entrance to Queen's owes much to Christopher Wren's gifted pupil Nicholas Hawksmoor (c.1661–1736). He was introduced to Oxford by Clarke, and worked closely with him and Townesend on several projects, including that for a completely new college, Worcester, begun in 1720 at the western edge of the city on the site of the medieval Gloucester Hall. Here for the first time in Oxford the hall, chapel, and library were placed in one range, at the entrance, with wings (only one of which was built) stretching out towards the open country, where an Arcadian landscape garden with a lake was made in the 1790s.

Hawksmoor's first independent Oxford building was a new University printing-press (1712–15), financed out of the profits of the *History of the Great Rebellion* written by the Earl of Clarendon (1609–74). Hawksmoor was fascinated by the architecture of classical antiquity—which, like Wren, he knew only through drawings—and in his hands the Clarendon Building became a gateway or 'Propyleum' to an Acropolis of learning (the Schools and Bodleian Library), its symbolic importance underlined by its temple-like proportions and by the giant Doric portico on the northern side. The passageway running through the building is aligned on the entrance to the schools, and leads into an open space with the Sheldonian Theatre on the western side. Thus an essentially utilitarian structure was made to serve an important rhetorical function.

This creation of a public space to the north of the Schools Quad was followed by the making of another to the south. In his will the fashionable physician John Radcliffe (1650–1714) left £40,000 towards the building and endowment of a new library on the site of a conglomeration of modest houses occupying the space bounded by St Mary's

AT THE CENTRE of this aerial view of the colleges lies Radcliffe Square, which was created in 1737 as a setting for the circular library built to the designs of James Gibbs. Dozens of houses were cleared to make this open space, which is Oxford's finest example of monumental urban planning.

SIR CHRISTOPHER WREN'S TOM TOWER (1681–2) seen from Peckwater Quad, where it appears framed between the Library, designed by George Clarke and built in 1717–72, and the lodgings for gentlemen-commoners built to the designs of Henry Aldrich in 1707–14.

THE RADCLIFFE LIBRARY, interior in 1818. The dome rests on a drum pierced by windows which light the central space, and the bookcases are placed in an ambulatory behind the massive arcade. The rich effect owes much to the plasterwork by the Swiss-Italian Giuseppe Artari, the Dane Charles Stanley, and the local man Thomas Roberts.

Church, Brasenose and All Souls Colleges, and the Schools. The library was to be Radcliffe's memorial, and Hawksmoor mooted the idea of a domed rotunda inspired by the mausoleums of classical antiquity, standing in what he envisaged as a 'Forum Universitatis'. But he died before the site became available, and it fell to the Italian-trained James Gibbs (1682–1754) to design what is now called the Radcliffe Camera (1737–48). In his hands the building was imbued with a Baroque panache which contrasts startlingly with the Gothic turrets and spikes of the surrounding structures. Pairs of Corinthian columns resting on a rusticated ground floor (originally open) lead the eye upwards to the buttressed attic storey and dome. The lofty interior is equally impressive, its grandeur reinforced by the contemporary woodwork, plasterwork, and ironwork. With the completion of this superb building the University finally had a physical setting commensurate with its academic prestige.

For all the allure of classical architecture in the century after the Restoration, Gothic never entirely died out. When Christopher Wren was asked in 1681 to build a tower over Wolsey's gatehouse at Christ Church he 'resolved it ought to be Gothick to agree with the Founder's work', thus giving the Oxford skyline one of its most memorable features. The Radcliffe Quadrangle at University College (1717–19) is a virtual copy of the earlier Front Quadrangle, down even to the provision of a gate tower with a fan vault constructed by the masons Bartholemew Peisley (*c*.1683–1727) and William Townesend. And at All Souls, where Hawksmoor provided both classical and Gothic designs for a large extension on the site of the old cloisters, the fellows opted in 1715 for his idiosyncratic version of Gothic to match the architecture of the surviving fifteenth-century buildings. The new buildings were aligned on what was to become Radcliffe Square, with a pair of pinnacled towers at the centre of the east range and a screen wall to the west. But the interiors of the new Codrington Library, and of the remodelled hall and buttery which followed later, are classical in character. Gothic was acceptable when the context dictated its use, but many years were to pass before it became a moral crusade.

In 1736, the year in which both Hawksmoor and Clarke died, Sir Nathaniel Lloyd (1669–1745), a fellow of All Souls, asserted that 'Hawksmoring, and Townsending, is all out for this Century'. The dilettante don working in conjunction with a talented mason now finally yielded to the professional architect with a nationwide practice. One of the most talented and prolific of the latter, James Wyatt (1746–1813), virtually monopolized commissions in late-eighteenth-century Oxford. His new library at Oriel (1788) is one of the most accomplished Renaissance-inspired buildings in any college, and his Canterbury Gate at Christ Church (1775–8) takes its place alongside the Clarendon

HAWKSMOOR'S DESIGN FOR ALL SOULS COLLEGE, 1715. The North Quadrangle, to the left, is a Baroque building in Gothic dress. The twin towers recall the west front of a medieval cathedral. The Codrington Library takes up the whole of the left-hand range. Hawksmoor envisaged doubling the size of the medieval front quadrangle to the right, but fortunately this was never done.

TWO STAGES IN THE RESTORATION OF MAGDALEN COLLEGE CHAPEL. *Left*, the chapel in 1814, looking west, after James Wyatt had added a plaster Gothic vault. He left the seventeenth-century stalls and organ screen untouched, but they were replaced in the more thorough restoration of 1830–5. *Right*, Cottingham's design for the main body of the chapel, looking east, with new stalls in the Perpendicular Gothic style, and new statues on the reredos in place of those destroyed after the Reformation.

Building and the High Street front of Queen's College as one of the most satisfying eighteenth-century contributions to the Oxford townscape. In the Radcliffe Observatory (1772–94) he transformed an earlier and more pedestrian design (by Henry Keene, 1726–76) into one of the most impressive monuments of English neoclassicism. The lucid, spacious interiors with their rib-like ceilings are Wyatt's, and his also is the octagonal tower in which the telescopes were placed. This was based on the Hellenistic Tower of the Winds in Athens, illustrated in Stuart and Revett's *Antiquities of Athens* (1762). Thus the legacy of classical antiquity was harnessed to the cause of science, and Oxford acquired one of the finest scientific buildings of its time.

Wyatt was also involved in restoring some of Oxford's medieval buildings. Admiration for Gothic architecture grew throughout the eighteenth century, and with it came a new concern for stylistic consistency. At first this meant the removal of post-Reformation fittings and their replacement by new furnishings in the Gothic style, an enterprise carried out by Wyatt in New College chapel in 1788–94 and, to a more

BALLIOL COLLEGE, *c.*1860, showing the deterioration of the Headington freestone used for the main buildings in Oxford between the fifteenth and eighteenth centuries. All the buildings shown here, except for the Fisher Building of 1768, by Henry Keene, on the left, were destroyed to make way for Alfred Waterhouse's Broad Street buildings of 1867–8, with their Gothic detailing and Bath stone walls.

limited extent, in the hall and chapel at Magdalen in 1791. The 'restoration' (or, more appropriately, rebuilding) of Magdalen chapel was completed by the more scholarly Lewis Nockalls Cottingham (1787–1847) in 1830–5 as the culmination of a systematic programme of repairing the older parts of the college, including the replacement of the entire upper floor of the north range of the fifteenth-century quadrangle in 1822–8. So the love of Gothic architecture led paradoxically to the removal of the last vestiges of genuinely medieval craftsmanship from parts of Oxford's finest medieval buildings.

The cause of restoration was advanced by the shocking state of Oxford's stonework. Early photographs show even quite recent buildings ravaged by decay, their walls blackened by smoke from coal fires. Nathaniel Hawthorne (1804–64) found the effect picturesque when he visited Oxford in 1856, but noted that 'the Oxford people . . . are tired of this crumbly stone, and when repairs are necessary, they use a more durable material'. By this time Bath stone, made easily available after the opening of the Kennet and

Avon Canal, had already been used to reface the frontages of Lincoln (1824), All Souls (1826–8), Pembroke (1829–30), and Exeter (1834–5). These 'restorations' involved far more than the replacement of worn stonework. At All Souls and Lincoln sash windows introduced in the eighteenth century were replaced by new ones with mullions, and at Pembroke and Exeter interesting seventeenth-century features were swept away to give the façades a bland neo-Tudor uniformity they had never possessed. The transformation of Turl Street was completed when the largely eighteenth-century front of Jesus was subjected to a drastic rebuilding at the hands of J. C. Buckler (1793–1894) in 1854–6. Here character, texture, and variety were all sacrificed in favour of a monotonous and repetitive 'collegiate Gothic' whose dead hand blighted countless educational establishments for the rest of the nineteenth century.

The University, unlike the colleges, remained attached to classical architecture throughout the first half of the nineteenth century. For the new University Press in Walton Street (1826–7) a dignified design by Daniel Robertson (*fl.* 1812–43) was chosen, with the entrance in the form of a Roman triumphal arch. And in 1841, following a competition—the first for a major university building—England's most creative and scholarly classical architect, Charles Robert Cockerell (1788–1863), was commissioned to build a new structure housing the University Galleries (now part of the Ashmolean Museum) and the Taylor Institution for the study of modern languages. The building stands on a massive rock-like plinth, like a Grecian temple, and the façades to St Giles' and to the newly created Beaumont Street are a masterly distillation of motifs taken from ancient Greek and Roman architecture and from that of Renaissance Italy. Cockerell had, in his youth, excavated the temple of Apollo at Bassae in the Peloponnese, and the Ionic order used in the Portland stone columns is derived from that building, as is the frieze running around the top of the staircase hall. Thus architecture and decoration complement the works of art on display and pay tribute to the enduring power of the classical ideal.

The University Galleries and Taylor Institution comprised Oxford's last important classical building. When, after an inconclusive competition, Convocation came to vote in 1854 on a design for a museum for the University's scientific exhibits which would be built, along with laboratories and lecture-rooms for the new Honour School of Natural Science, on an open site adjoining the Parks, it plumped for a Gothic scheme by the little-known Benjamin Woodward (1815–61), co-architect of the museum at Trinity College, Dublin. Gothic, it was widely believed, was more 'natural' than classical architecture, and was therefore especially appropriate for a building designed to display the wonders of the natural world. Gothic had been used by the young George Gilbert Scott (1811–78) in the Martyrs' Memorial (1841) and, but for the obstinate anti-Catholicism of the head of the college Richard Jenkyns (1782–1854), Balliol might have been rebuilt to designs prepared two years later by that most eloquent apostle of the Gothic Revival, A. W. N. Pugin (1812–52), whose zeal for the revival of medieval architecture was matched by the fervour of his Roman Catholic faith. Woodward's bold, symmetrical façade for the University Museum draws on the civic buildings of Flanders, and much of the internal detailing derives from Italian Gothic, recently celebrated at great length in John Ruskin's *Stones of Venice* (1851–3). Ruskin (1819–1900), a friend of the chief promoter of the museum, Henry Acland (1815–1900), thought that 'all art employed in decoration should be informative, conveying truthful statements about actual facts', and the University Museum (1855–60) is an eloquent expression of that ideal. It abounds in naturalistic carved ornament, and the columns on the first floor of the courtyard are composed of different forms of stone from the British Isles, with the name of each carved at the base. But the most startling feature of the interior is the roof, entirely of glass, supported on pointed arches of cast iron which rest on clustered Gothic columns, again of iron, with wrought-iron foliage patterns on the capitals, all carried out by Francis Skidmore (1816–96) of Coventry (see p. 281). The attempt to reconcile nineteenth-century technology with Gothic truth to nature could go no further.

The University Museum was the first of several highly original mid-Victorian Gothic buildings in Oxford. Echoes of its naturalistic detailing can be found in the leafy streets of St John's College's North Oxford estate, whose development began in the 1850s. George Gilbert Scott's new chapel at Exeter (1856–9) draws upon the architecture of thirteenth-century France in its apsidal shape, its height, and its rib-vaulted construction, and the interior glows with stained glass dimly illuminating carved work in stone, wood, and iron—a powerful assertion of Tractarian values. But the most thorough rebuilding of an older college took place at Balliol, starting with the chapel built by William Butterfield (1814–1900) in 1856–7, where the outside walls are made up of bands of stone in contrasting colours like geological strata—a daring exercise in 'constructional polychromy'. Alfred Waterhouse (1830–1905) was responsible for both the dour Bath stone front to Broad Street which followed in 1867–8 and the new hall in 1875–7. So the college which had pioneered academic reform acquired a set of buildings which evoke the medieval collegiate ideal.

In 1868–82 Butterfield was entrusted with the design of the first college to be built on a completely new site for over two hundred years. Keble College was intended to be a living memorial to the Oxford Movement, aiming to attract 'diligent students living simply', many of whom would go into the Anglican ministry, and the choice of Butterfield as architect stemmed from his reputation as a builder of Tractarian churches and educational establishments. Though steeped in Gothic architecture, Butterfield believed that it had to be adapted for modern use. He broke with Oxford precedent by arranging the seating of the dazzlingly colourful chapel in rows facing towards the altar (see p. 148), and by placing the undergraduates' rooms along corridors. Most important of all, he used brick as the main building material, arranging it in polychromatic pat-

TAYLOR INSTITUTION (*facing*). The centre of the façade, echoing a Roman triumphal arch, is marked by four freestanding Ionic columns whose capitals were modelled on those inside the Temple of Apollo at Bassae (Greece) excavated by the architect C. R. Cockerell. The design of the attic storey, with arches pushing up between the columns, was suggested by late-Roman models in the Middle East.

terns of extraordinary virtuosity—a decision which, though sanctioned by medieval precedent, has never been forgiven by those who equate good architecture with 'good taste'. The buildings exude a sense of creative energy, and, more than any others of their date in Oxford, succeed in capturing the restless, striving, dynamic spirit of medieval architecture.

The completion of Keble College marks the end of the heroic phase of the Gothic Revival in Oxford. In the new St Swithin's Quadrangle at Magdalen (1881–5) the architects, G. F. Bodley (1827–1907) and Thomas Garner (1839–1906), deliberately chose a restrained, undemonstrative style matching that of the older parts of the college. An equally craftsmanlike version of Gothic was employed by Basil Champneys (1842–1935) at Mansfield College (1887–9), a Congregationalist theological establishment. And in the shadowy incense-laden chapel of the Anglo-Catholic Pusey House, begun in 1911, 'the last enchantments of the Middle Ages' were evoked with poignant sensitivity by Bodley's pupil Temple Moore (1856–1920).

A more worldly strain is represented by the work of Thomas Graham Jackson (1835–1924). A member (and subsequently fellow) of Wadham and a pupil of Gilbert Scott, Jackson soon shed his early commitment to secular Gothic in favour of an eclectic style based on that of the early seventeenth century, which was, he believed, 'eminently suitable to modern usage'. The first and most important of his many Oxford commissions was for a new Examination Schools (1876–82) on the site of the Angel Inn in the High Street (see p. 175). With the number of students doubling between 1820 and

THE NORHAM MANOR ESTATE IN NORTH OXFORD was laid out for St John's College in 1860 by William Wilkinson, as a leafy suburb of detached and semi-detached villas. The houses were occupied by wealthy tradespeople and also (after the relaxation of the statute forbidding them to marry) by dons and their families.

1900, and with all of them now taking written examinations (and even attending lectures), the old Schools were inadequate, and the University decided to hand them over finally to the Bodleian Library. Jackson aimed to give his new building 'a collegiate character which would harmonize with the buildings of Oxford', and it is this undemanding visual charm and deference to the *genius loci* which explains his appeal to those dons of Walter Pater's (1839–94) generation who increasingly valued 'sweetness and light' over passionate religious commitment. Jackson was no purist, and in his new buildings at Brasenose (1882–1911)—Pater's own college—and Hertford (1887–1914), a revived foundation incorporating a disparate collection of buildings belonging to defunct academic halls, he cheerfully mixed together styles as different as Tudor-Gothic and neo-Georgian in a way which anticipates the 'post-modernism' of our own times.

Jackson was unusually sensitive to the texture of buildings. The Examination Schools are faced with a durable limestone ashlar from Clipsham (Lincolnshire)—also used in his refacing of the upper storey of the old Schools—and this stone has subse-

BASIL CHAMPNEYS was the most widely employed architect in late-Victorian Oxford after T. G. Jackson (whose buildings for Hertford College can be seen on the right). The Indian Institute, 1882–4, which closed the eastward vista from Broad Street, is an example of the eclectic 'free style' which was widely employed in Oxford at that time.

quently been used to reface many of Oxford's most famous older buildings. In many of his collegiate buildings, like the new High Street front of Brasenose and the new buildings at Trinity (1883–7), he returned to medieval practice by using coursed rubble (from Bladon, near Woodstock) for the walls and Clipsham stone for the dressings. This combination was used again and again in Oxford down to the mid-twentieth century.

The late nineteenth century saw the building of the first women's colleges. They all grew up outside the central University area, and in time they evolved a distinctive architectural identity of their own which owed little to traditional ideas of style, materials, and planning. The most satisfying of the earlier buildings are at Lady Margaret Hall, where the Wordsworth, Talbot, and Toynbee blocks (1896 and 1909–15) were designed by Sir Reginald Blomfield (1856–1942) in a domestic neo-Georgian style, with red-brick walls, hipped roofs, and long internal corridors, and placed in a silvan setting among lawns stretching to the River Cherwell. Giles Gilbert Scott (1880–1960) added an impressive neo-Byzantine chapel next to his neo-Georgian Deneke Building in 1931, and in 1959–66 Raymond Erith (1904–73) built the massive red-brick Wolfson Quad in front of Blomfield's buildings—a striking profession of faith in the virtues of classical architecture in an unsympathetic era.

More buildings have been built by Oxford University in the twentieth century than in any other. One reason has been the vast increase in scientific activity. Towards the end of the nineteenth century the University Museum became the focus for a cluster of architecturally undistinguished buildings for scientific teaching, but as research came into its own after the turn of the century larger and more impressive buildings were required, like the red-brick neo-Georgian Dyson Perrins Laboratory for organic chemistry in South Parks Road, built to the designs of Paul Waterhouse (1861–1924) in 1913–16 (see p. 314). So what is now called the Science Area came into being, and has continued to grow in a piecemeal manner ever since.

New accommodation was also needed for the University's libraries. In 1933–4 Hubert Worthington (1886–1963) extended T. G. Jackson's Radcliffe Science Library. His work epitomizes the architecture of interwar Oxford in its flat roofs, its rugged walling of Bladon rubble stone, its spacious and well-crafted interiors, and its mannered detailing, echoing the much-admired Dutch and Scandinavian architecture of the time. Giles Gilbert Scott's New Bodleian (1937–40) was a more ambitious project designed to provide new reading-rooms and storage space for five million books on a site opposite the Clarendon Building, but linked to the existing Bodleian Library by an underground tunnel. In its layout and construction the new library broke completely with earlier traditions. Its central core is a steel-framed book-stack—an idea taken from American libraries—but reading-rooms and offices were wrapped around it, and encased in rubble masonry. Despite this use of local stone, the massive building fails to blend into its surroundings, and the predominant impression is one of ponderous shapelessness. The ceremonial key broke in the lock at the royal opening.

THE DENEKE BUILDING OF LADY MARGARET HALL of 1931–2 maintains the ladylike neo-Georgian tone of the earlier parts of the college, but the chapel is Byzantine in inspiration. The architect, Giles Gilbert Scott, was responsible, *inter alia*, for the design of Liverpool Anglican Cathedral, the red telephone box, the street lamps of Oxford, and the New Bodleian Library.

RHODES HOUSE was designed as the headquarters of the Rhodes Trust and completed in 1929. The domed rotunda, a memorial to Alfred Milner, the first High Commissioner of the Union of South Africa, represents the architect Herbert Baker's commitment to classicism. The buildings which envelop the rotunda belong to the cosier Arts and Crafts tradition, with walls of Bladon rubble stone.

The finest of Oxford's interwar buildings were commissioned not by the University, nor by the highly unadventurous colleges, but by more marginal institutions. Edwin Lutyens (1869–1944) designed Campion Hall for the Jesuits on a cramped site to the south of Pembroke College in 1934–6, and in 1929 the Trustees of Cecil Rhodes (1853–1902) commissioned Herbert Baker (1862–1946) to build Rhodes House, an altogether more lavish structure, in South Parks Road. Like the Radcliffe Camera, Rhodes House was designed both to commemorate a benefactor and to benefit the University. Baker had been influenced in his youth by the doctrines of the Arts and Crafts movement, and had later worked closely with Rhodes in South Africa. He wanted to make the Oxford building 'as styleless and elementary as possible', and much of it has the simple, unadorned character of the Cotswold manor houses so admired by architects of his generation. Yet this earthy quality goes hand in hand with a classical sophistication displayed in the domed entrance rotunda—a miniature temple with a bird from what was then Rhodesia on the summit—and in the logical, axial planning of the whole building, with its generous provision of spaces for circulation. Thus two seemingly contradictory traditions are successfully merged.

Conservatism remained a hallmark of Oxford's patronage of new architecture until well after the Second World War. At Nuffield, the first of Oxford's all-graduate colleges, the ennobled car-manufacturer Lord Nuffield (1877–1963) turned down the stark flat-roofed design prepared in 1939 by Austen Harrison (1901–76), the former Government

WOLFSON COLLEGE, 1969–72, lies in North Oxford on the banks of the Cherwell. The architects, Powell and Moya, drew inspiration from International Modernism, and the ubiquitous use of concrete for the walls was a sharp break with local building traditions. The college was designed to house 124 graduate students, and was the first in Oxford to contain flats for families.

architect in Palestine, on the grounds that it was 'un-English', and insisted that the architect prepare 'something on the lines of Cotswold domestic architecture'. And it was in this vein that the college was built on a reduced scale in 1949–62, its timid ashlar-faced elevations interrupted by the lumpish, unbuttressed tower, surmounted by an absurd spike—a parody of the towers and spires of medieval Oxford.

To a handful of architecturally minded dons in the 1950s, deliverance from such parochialism could only come from the 'international style' of Gropius (1883–1969), Mies van der Rohe (1886–1969), and Le Corbusier (1887–1965). Like the Gothic Revivalists of the 1850s and 1860s, many of the younger architects of this period saw a virtue in bold experimentation and took a positive delight in the use of forms and materials which they believed would express the spirit of the age. Student numbers were again expanding (they doubled between 1939 and 1985), and the volume of research, especially in the sciences, was growing. Funds were now available from central Government to augment those supplied by private benefactors and the colleges' own endowments. The stage was thus set for another period of adventurous patronage of new buildings.

The first college to commission a self-consciously Modern Movement building was St John's, where the 'Beehive' block (so named because of its hexagonal rooms) was built in the North Quadrangle in 1958–60 to the designs of Michael Powers (b. 1915) of the Architects' Co-Partnership. Here the staircase plan was retained, but the conven-

THE DINING-HALL OF ST CATHERINE'S COLLEGE, 1960–4. The massive roof-beams are supported on slim piers of polished concrete, while the walls are of plain yellow brick made to the architect's own specification. Arne Jacobsen also designed the fittings and furnishings, down even to the knives and forks used on high table.

tional appearance of collegiate buildings was totally abandoned in favour of a jagged geometrical form determined by the internal layout. The pairs of rooms thought appropriate for 'young gentlemen' in the nineteenth and early twentieth centuries gave way to single study-bedrooms like those in the women's colleges. And instead of Cotswold stone and mullioned windows there were now broad expanses of Portland ashlar walling and large plate-glass windows in metal frames.

Similar principles inspired the partnership of A. J. Powell (b. 1920) and J. H. Moya (b. 1921) in their design for a four-storeyed block on a very confined site behind T. G. Jackson's New Quadrangle at Brasenose in 1959. They later went on to design the cunningly contrived Christ Church Picture Gallery and Blue Boar Quadrangle (1964–8), a new building for Corpus Christi in Magpie Lane (1969), and finally, in 1969–72, a complete new college for graduates, Wolfson. These buildings are all notable for their careful choice of materials, and in their different ways they all effect a subtle compromise between the ideals of modernism and the more pragmatic, picturesque virtues of much earlier English architecture.

A more uncompromising vision of modernism inspired the Danish architect Arne Jacobsen (1902–71) when he designed St Catherine's College on a site among the water meadows of the Cherwell in 1960–4. Both in its layout and in its architectural character St Catherine's represents as sharp a break from tradition as Keble a century earlier. The plan is strictly geometrical, almost classical in its strict rationality, with two long low ranges of residential blocks facing an open space broken up by detached buildings housing a cavernous hall, a library, and a large lecture-room (there is no chapel). The upper floors of the residential blocks are cantilevered out, their plate-glass curtain-walls interrupted only by concrete beams. The ubiquitous yellow brick is as alien to Oxford's traditions as the red brick of Keble, and the skyline is broken only by a perfunctory bell tower. Relief comes mainly from sensitive planting and a pervasive feeling—rare in the older colleges—of unenclosed space. Nowhere in Oxford is there a stronger sense of a modern university as a secular, essentially utilitarian, institution.

The first University buildings to embrace the Modern Movement were in the Science Area and to the north of Keble College, where the obtrusive Department of Engineering building was erected to the designs of Ramsey, Murrey, White, and Ward in 1960–3. A more subtle approach was adopted in the St Cross Building (1961–5), where the architects Leslie Martin (b. 1908) and Colin Wilson (b. 1922) fitted a complex of libraries and lecture-rooms demanded by the rapidly expanding Faculties of English,

THE ZOOLOGY AND PSYCHOLOGY BUILDINGS of 1966–70 were designed by Leslie Martin, who concentrated a large amount of laboratory and teaching space on to the site without raising the buildings to a great height. He employed several 'brutalist' mannerisms derived from the later work of Le Corbusier, notably the use of unornamented precast concrete panels for cladding the walls.

Law, and Economics into a highly ingenious agglomeration of cuboidal blocks faced in buff brick, reminiscent of the avant-garde European sculpture of the 1920s. But in the ziggurat-like Zoology and Psychology building in South Parks Road (1966–70) Martin went on to espouse the then fashionable 'brutalist' idiom, with the laboratories arranged in a series of massive steps, the services placed in towers, and the concrete walls deliberately left rough to show the wooden shuttering—a favourite Corbusian mannerism—and in his University Offices in Wellington Square (1969–73) he imposed a numbingly insensitive concrete structure on to what had been an inoffensive residential area.

The late 1960s and early 1970s mark the climax of Oxford's experimentation with unusual plans, materials, and shapes. Sometimes the form of a new building grew naturally out of the exigencies of the commission, as with the fan-shaped concrete superstructure to the linear accelerator of the Nuclear Physics Department (1970) by Philip Dowson (b. 1924) of Arup Associates. More often it was determined by the structural method used. Arup Associates' Sir Thomas White Building at St John's (1971–6) was built within a clearly expressed concrete frame, and the walls of the disquietingly futuristic hall and common-room block at St Antony's (Howell, Killick, Partridge, and Amis, 1968–70) are made of huge rectangular panels of pre-cast concrete interrupted only by canted window-frames. In Ahrends, Burton, and Koralek's masterly extension to Keble (1969–77) the massive fortress-like external elevations are of yellow brick, but the internal walls are a sinuous sheet of glass complementing, but not competing with, Butterfield's earlier buildings. And in the extraordinary Florey Building for Queen's (1968–71), designed by James Stirling (b. 1926), four levels of glass-walled study-bedrooms are arranged within a semicircular amphitheatre-like structure raised on concrete stilts to command a tree-girt pastoral view over the River Cherwell, with the almost windowless rear walls clad throughout in bright red tiles—one of the most spectacular statements of the so-called functionalist ethic in postwar Britain.

The financial difficulties of the 1970s brought Oxford's flirtation with the Modern Movement to an end. By the 1980s a widespread revulsion against the cultural legacy of modernism had set in, as demonstrated in the Sainsbury Building at Worcester (MacCormac, Jamieson and Pritchard, 1983). Here geometrical assertiveness gives way to a modest, understated reticence harking back to the vernacular tradition which had inspired Oxford's pre-war architects, and making good use of the picturesque lakeside situation. The *genius loci* could not have reasserted itself more ingratiatingly.

It is a paradox that the heyday of modernism in Oxford should have coincided with a growth in knowledge about, and concern for, the architecture of the past. Since the Second World War the history of Oxford's buildings has been chronicled more accurately

THE FLOREY BUILDING OF QUEEN'S COLLEGE, 1968–71. James Stirling shocked public opinion when he chose bright-red bricks and tiles for the outer walls of this block of undergraduate rooms placed well away from the rest of the college on the east bank of the Cherwell. The building is an isolated monument dominating its surroundings, and, like Keble College a century earlier, it flouts the *genius loci*.

than ever before. The redundant churches of St Peter-in-the-East and All Saints have acquired a new lease of life as the libraries of St Edmund Hall and Lincoln College. And in a massive programme of 'systematic refacing', starting in 1957, the last decaying traces of Headington ashlar have been removed from the fronts of the main buildings, to be replaced by pristine stonework, much of it from the Clipsham quarries. The recarved details can now be seen clearly, in some cases for the first time for generations. So, in a university whose character is inextricably linked to its architectural inheritance, the sentimental appeal of crumbling stonework has been sacrificed in favour of a reproduction of vanished excellence.

4

The University's Contribution to Religion

GEOFFREY ROWELL

OXFORD has made a significant contribution to religion because Oxford was cradled in the Church. The early colleges and halls were religious foundations, founded for such objects as 'the profit of the holy church of God', or to the honour of 'our Lord Jesus Christ and of his glorious mother Mary and of all the saints'. Provision was made in early collegiate statutes for the celebration of mass and the regular saying of the canonical hours. Frequently there were particular obligations on the fellows of a college to pray for their founder and his kin after their decease. The common life of colleges had much of a monastic character.

Round about the year 1200 a young man, Edmund Rich, was, according to Roger Bacon (1220?–92), the first to lecture on Aristotle's *Sophistici elenchi*. He went on to teach theology, urging his pupils with the maxim 'Study as if you were to live for ever: live as if you were to die tomorrow.' Rich became Oxford's first Archbishop of Canterbury in 1233, holding the primatial see for seven years until his death in 1240. The University wrote to support his canonization a year later, and Pope Innocent IV declared him a saint (St Edmund of Abingdon) in 1247. So very early on Oxford had its own saint.

Edmund Rich had lectured on logic, one of the liberal arts, and later on theology, which in the medieval period was one of Oxford's primary contributions to religion. Robert Grosseteste (1175–1253), John Duns Scotus (*c.*1264–1308), Robert Kilwardby (d. 1279), Archbishop of Canterbury, Thomas Bradwardine (1290?–1349)—also briefly Archbishop of Canterbury—and the 'nominalist' William of Ockham (1300?–49?) were amongst the most illustrious in a galaxy of scholastic luminaries.

Robert Grosseteste came from humble origins in Suffolk and is first known in Oxford about the year 1208 as a 'Master' in theology. From 1229 to 1235 he was Reader in Theology at the Franciscan house situated 'outside the city wall'. He was later to leave some of his books to the Oxford Franciscans, and some eight or nine of these have

FORMAL, PUBLIC DISPUTATION was characteristic of the medieval university. In this illuminated initial from Averroes' commentary on Aristotle's *Metaphysics*, two philosophers are shown discussing Aristotle's treatment of non-perceptible substances that are always in the same state and suffer no change, here represented by Christ and two angels. The iconography reflects the influence of Aristotelian philosophy on theology in the second half of the thirteenth century.

onlıd
cꝛauo
qıuð
em eſt
ðe lõa

survived. Grosseteste went on from Oxford to be bishop of the unwieldy diocese of Lincoln, to which Oxford at that date belonged. Grosseteste's works include commentaries on Aristotle and on the Scriptures, the most notable being the *Hexaemeron*, in which he shows considerable knowledge not only of the Latin Fathers of the Church but also of the Greek. This was doubly remarkable in that few of his contemporaries were acquainted with the writings of the Greek Fathers in translation, and even fewer were able, as Grosseteste was, to read them in the original Greek. Although Grosseteste knew Aristotle, he did not use Aristotle's metaphysical framework to solve theological problems. His preferred starting-point was mathematical physics and optics, and his mathematical concerns drew him in a Neoplatonist direction. Grosseteste's scientific interests were powerful in shaping the contrasting approaches of the Universities of Paris and Oxford, Paris having a prime interest in metaphysics and Oxford in mathematics, logic, and physics. Grosseteste's Christocentric theology was combined with an interest in knowledge by illumination and revelation, following in the footsteps of St Augustine. Roger Bacon, another famous Oxford Franciscan, shared Grosseteste's scientific interests and his interest in mathematics. Although he emphasized the freedom of scientific research for its own sake, he was also convinced that the rationale for such study was to glorify God. Absolute certainty was grounded in God and came only through the divine light illuminating the human mind.

The links between the Universities of Paris and Oxford as great centres of learning can be seen in the career of John Duns Scotus, the 'subtle doctor', who moved back and forth between Oxford and Paris from 1291 until his death in 1308. Scotus's most important work was the *Ordinatio*, which was based on his Oxford lectures on the *Sentences* of Peter Lombard (*c*.1100–60). As a theologian he attempted to mediate between a theology inspired by Aristotle and the Augustinian tradition, represented by his main opponent, Henry of Ghent (*c*.1235–93). He stressed that all contingent events were dependent upon the divine will, distinguishing between the absolute power of God (i.e. all the possibilities which God could actualize) and the ordained power of God (those possibilities which God has in fact actualized). The created universe was radically contingent. Psychologically and metaphysically the will had primacy over the intellect, and the value ascribed to created actions depended entirely on the value given to those actions by the divine will. In Scotus we see the beginnings of a retreat from the view that theology was a science. In the history of Christian doctrine it was Scotus who produced the first defence by a major theologian of the doctrine of the Immaculate Conception of the Blessed Virgin Mary, a dogma formally defined for the Roman Catholic Church by Pope Pius IX in 1854. Six centuries after Duns Scotus lectured in Oxford another Oxford man, the Jesuit poet Gerard Manley Hopkins (1844–89), found in Scotus's theory of knowing and his emphasis on the unique individuality of things a stimulus to the working out of his original poetic conceptions of 'inscape' and 'pitch'. Hopkins's appreciation is expressed in his poem *Duns Scotus's Oxford*:

> Yet ah! this air I gather and I release
> He lived on; these weeds and waters, these walls are what
> He haunted who of all men most sways my spirits to peace;
> Of realty the rarest-veinèd unraveller; a not
> Rivalled insight, be rival Italy or Greece;
> Who fired France for Mary without spot.

The great nominalist William of Ockham, a little later than Scotus, followed Scotus in his theological writing. An Oxford student, Ockham lectured on Lombard's *Sentences* in the University from 1317 to 1319. In the controversies concerning free will, justification, grace, and predestination Ockham ascribed merit to human actions in the gaining of God's favour. Scotus had claimed that predestination *preceded* the good actions that God knew people would perform; Ockham maintained that God predestined people to grace on the basis of their merits that he had already foreseen. In the field of ethics Ockham claimed that actions were to be accounted as morally good simply on the basis that God had ordained these rules—so that it was conceivable, for instance, that God might have created a universe in which murder was good. Ockham's denial of the existence of abstract universals (nominalism) contributed powerfully to the emergence of individualism. God himself is viewed as 'the most single being', and we have no direct knowledge of him, merely indirect reflections which never lead to certainty, only to probability. Faith, in subjection to authority, is what must guide the believer.

Scotus and Ockham concentrated on an Augustinian view of God's freedom. By contrast Thomas Bradwardine, student and lecturer at Merton in the early fourteenth century, reduced all created actions to an extension of God's activity. In human activity humanity was an 'instrument of God', not God's partner, and Bradwardine reacted strongly against what he believed to be a recrudescence in the teaching of the schools of the old Pelagian heresy, which exalted human will and effort as necessary to salvation, and reduced God's grace to knowledge of the good rather than a gift enabling the doing of good. His strongly Augustinian emphasis makes him in some ways a forerunner of the Reformation, as his interest in mathematics and physics foreshadows Galileo and the seventeenth-century physicists. Bradwardine went on to become Archbishop of Canterbury in 1349, but died in the same year from the Black Death, which carried off many of the foremost Oxford thinkers of the day.

Amongst the many fourteenth-century luminaries that Oxford nurtured John Wyclif (1329?–84) occupies a notable place. A secular priest rather than a member of a religious order, Wyclif became Master of Balliol *c*.1360. In his theological and philosophical stance he was strongly opposed to the nominalism of Ockham.

In his philosophical writings he used the same types of logical analysis as had become popular in Oxford in the earlier part of the fourteenth century, but they were worked out in the context of his metaphysical realism. For him the truth of propositions depended solely on their conformity to the intelligible being and the universal reality that were known by and identical with the divine mind. Many of Wyclif's theological teachings found their origin in his philosophy. In particular he was concerned with the nature of the Church, the authority of the Bible, and the theology of the Eucharist. Unlike St Augustine (and almost every medieval thinker), who had thought of the Church as a mixed body of believers, some of whom will be saved and some damned, Wyclif maintained that the Church consisted only of those who would be saved. Who those will be is known only to God, and the Church is therefore defined in terms of God's conception of it and not in terms of the visibly existing, temporal institution. Since it is impossible for us to know who belongs to the Church, the proper Christian authority is the Bible. Scripture is self-sufficient and its truth is based directly on the eternal true reality existing in the divine mind. In his teaching on the Eucharist Wyclif denied transubstantiation, maintaining that God cannot destroy any existing substance, and that when the Eucharistic change is defined in terms of the doctrine of tran-

substantiation it involves precisely that. In the Eucharist, he argued, the substance of bread and wine remained, yet Christ was really present, contained within the bread and wine. Drawing on the scientific approach of Bacon and Grosseteste, particularly their interest in optics, he suggested that in the Eucharist the eye sees the substance of bread, under which Christ lies hidden, but that Christ is present as an image is present in a mirror. The body of Christ is not multiplied in the Eucharist, but is reflected.

Because of his unorthodox teachings Wyclif was condemned by a University Commission in 1381 and left Oxford to take up residence on his Leicestershire living at Lutterworth, to which he had been presented by the Crown in 1374. His theological influence was significant, even if the more recent recognition that he is to be seen in terms of contemporary medieval debate means that earlier Protestant presentations of him as 'the morning star of the Reformation' must now be qualified. He was critical of papal power and the manifest abuses of the Church hierarchy, going so far as to refer to the Pope as Antichrist, and his adherents as the 'twelve daughters of the diabolical leech'. Wyclif also attacked the worship of saints and superstitious pilgrimages, as well as the ecclesiastical abuses of pluralities (the aggregation of ecclesiastical offices) and the non-residence of absentee parish priests and Church dignitaries. He appealed powerfully for the Church to be recalled to its original apostolic state, abandoning temporal possessions and claims to jurisdiction. His theological teaching and concern for Church reform gained him a number of followers, who were given the name of Lollards and were included in Archbishop Courtenay's (c.1342–96) condemnation of Wyclif in 1381. (It is suggested that the term 'Lollard' may derive from a word meaning 'chanter' or a 'mumbler of prayers', or that it may be linked with the Latin *lollium*, 'tare'.) The Lollards based their teaching on personal faith, divine election, and the Bible, and maintained that everyone had the right to read and interpret Scripture for himself. Wyclif himself began a translation of the Bible into English, which was completed by two of his followers. From early academic beginnings the Lollard movement became more diffuse and socially critical, remaining active until the middle of the fifteenth century.

Wyclif's influence was not confined to England, but was also significant for the Hussite movement in Bohemia. Hus (c.1370–1415) himself, already alerted to similar ideas through the writings of his Czech fellow countrymen, became acquainted with Wyclif's writings at the time of Richard II's marriage to Anne of Bohemia. Hus translated Wyclif's *Trialogue* and incorporated large portions of Wyclif's writings into his major work, *De ecclesia* (1413), written after his excommunication by the Pope in 1411. Hus was tried and condemned at the Council of Constance in 1415—which also condemned two hundred Wycliffite propositions—and was burnt at the stake.

By the late fifteenth century Renaissance influences were impinging on the medieval University. William Grocyn (1446?–1519) was first a fellow of New College and then Reader in Theology at Magdalen, and he lectured at Exeter College. From 1488 to 1490 he was in Italy, principally Florence, and on his return contributed to the revival of Greek in the University. Grocyn's example encouraged John Colet (1466?–1519) likewise to go abroad to learn Greek. On his return to Oxford in 1497 Colet delivered a series of lectures on the Pauline epistles, reflecting the new critical approaches to the biblical text rather than the traditional scholastic interpretations. These lectures, which in 1499 won the plaudits of Erasmus (c.1466–1536) when on a visit to Oxford, continued until Colet's appointment to the deanery of St Paul's in 1504. Magdalen in particular became a centre of the new learning, and Thomas Wolsey (1475?–1530) was elected a fellow there, going on to become under Henry VIII Archbishop of York, a cardinal, and Lord Chancellor. Oxford owes to him the founding of Cardinal College, converted by the King after Wolsey's disgrace into Christ Church (1532).

The downfall of Wolsey marked the beginning of the English Reformation, and led to changes which inevitably had a significant impact on Oxford, the University being so closely linked with the Church. Thomas Cromwell (1485?–1540), appointed Vicar-General in 1535, not only presided over the dissolution of the monasteries, but was also responsible for the visitation of the universities. His Commission was carried out at Oxford by Richard Layton (1500?–44), a Cambridge-trained lawyer, assisted by John London (1486?–1543), the vacillating and somewhat unscrupulous Warden of New College. The old courses in scholastic theology, based on the study of Lombard's *Sentences*, were replaced by study of the Bible. There was much destruction of manuscript volumes of medieval theology and philosophy. It was reported that pages from books in New College library were gathered up in the quadrangle for making 'sewelles [scarecrows] or blawnsherres [deer-scarers] to kepe the dere within the wode'. The study of canon law all but ceased. The monastic houses in or near Oxford—Rewley, Eynsham, Godstow, Osney, and Abingdon—were dissolved, and the dependent colleges of the great monasteries of Gloucester, Durham, and Canterbury were suppressed along with their mother houses. Gloucester Hall was to be absorbed into Worcester College, the site of Durham College was acquired by Sir Thomas Pope (c.1507–59) in 1555 to become his new foundation of Trinity College, and Canterbury College was absorbed into Christ Church. The Franciscan and Dominican friars, who had occupied such a prominent place in the medieval University and its theological studies, likewise disappeared.

JOHN TAVERNER was appointed 'informator Choristorum' of Wolsey's Cardinal College (later Christ Church) in 1525. One of the great polyphonic masters of sixteenth-century England, he was the composer of eight masses. This extract, 'Et in terra pax' from his *Missa 'Gloria tibi Trinitas'*, reputedly incorporates a portrait of Taverner.

The accession of Edward VI (1547) had brought further reforms, the Protestant cause in Oxford being supported in particular by Richard Cox (*c*.1500–81), Chancellor of the University from 1547 to 1552 and the first Dean of Christ Church. It was through his influence and that of Archbishop Cranmer (1489–1556) that the Italian reformer Peter Martyr (1500–62) was made Regius Professor of Divinity in 1548. The wives of Cox and Martyr were among the first women to reside in Oxford colleges. Martyr's wife died in 1553 and she was buried in Christ Church, though during the Marian re-action her remains were disinterred, only to be reburied, mingled with the supposed relics of St Frideswide, in 1558. In 1549 it was Martyr who preached the inaugural ser-mon before the Commissioners appointed by the King to visit the University. They were charged with the reallocation of ancient religious endowments, turning funds tra-ditionally expended by the Church to educational ends. The new statutes introduced by the Commissioners established University sermons, laid down rules for chapel ser-vices, the reading of Scripture, and the celebration of communion, and ordered the removal of unnecessary altars, superstitious monuments, and noisy chapel bells.

In 1549, the year which saw the issuing of the the first Prayer Book, there was a major disputation on the Eucharist between Peter Martyr and leading Catholic protagonists. University disputations of this kind were paralleled by disputes and feuds in colleges between conservatives and reformers. At Magdalen the President, Owen Oglethorpe (d. 1559), felt compelled to resign in 1552, only to return to office a year later following the accession of the Catholic Mary. The reversal of religious policy meant that colleges received royal letters abolishing all injunctions and ordinances made since the death of Henry VIII which were contrary to college statutes. Some Oxford figures went into exile on the Continent, but far fewer than the seventy-six exiles from Cambridge. Peter Martyr, after a period of six months in prison, was allowed to leave for Strasburg, where he was reappointed Professor of Theology. The small group of Oxford exiles included most notably Richard Cox, Dean of Christ Church, who was to become known for his part in the disputes with John Knox (*c*.1514–72) at Frankfurt, a battle between the 'Cox-ians' and 'Knoxians'. John Jewel (1522–71) of Corpus Christi, having at first signed the Marian articles recanting his Protestantism, fled eventually to Frankfurt and Zurich. On his return with the accession of Elizabeth he was to become one of the leading Anglican apologists. Jewel owed much to his experience on the Continent, but his ideas were in many respects already shaped by the end of Edward's reign in 1553. In a sermon of 1552 he was inveighing against those who 'broughte in transubstantiations, masses, calling upon saints, sole life, purgatorie, images, vowes, trifles, follies, bables . . . which the scriptures never hearde of . . . O if the worde of the Lorde might be heard, among so many clamours and in so great a hurlye burly.'

For those who remained in England, the leading reforming bishops of Edward's

THOMAS CRANMER became Archbishop of Canterbury in 1533. The author of the English Prayer Books of 1549 and 1552, he suffered from the change of religious policy under Mary Tudor, and in 1556 he was tried and burnt at the stake in Broad Street on 21 March. The portrait, of 1546, is by Gerlach Flicke.

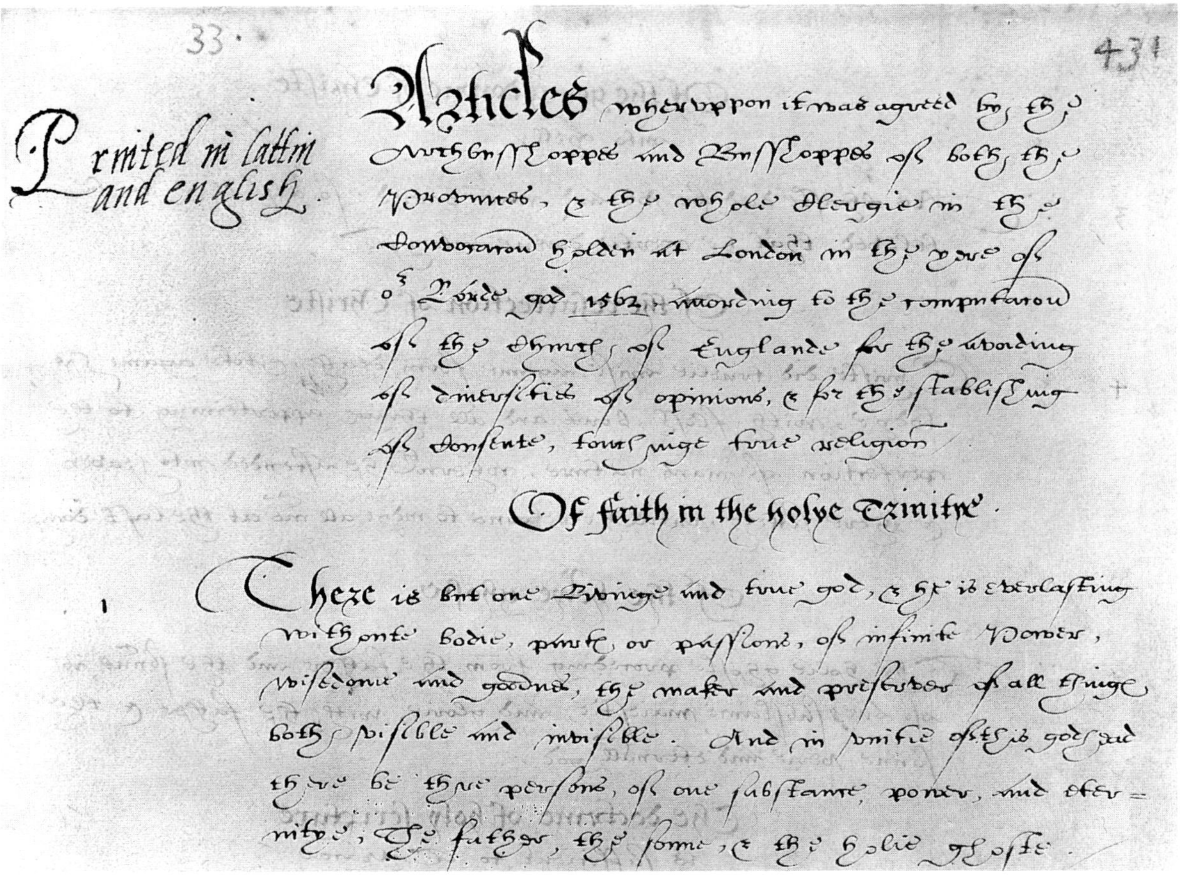

The handwritten manuscript text (in period script) reads:

Printed in Latin and English

Articles whervppon it was agreed by the Archbisshoppes and Bisshoppes of both the provinces, & the whole clergie in the convocation holden at London in the yere of o[ur] Lorde god 1562, according to the computation of the Churche of Englande for the avoiding of diversities of opinions, & for the stablishing of consente, touchinge true religion

Of faith in the holye Trinitie.

There is but one liuinge and true god, & he is everlasting withoute bodie, partes, or passions, of infinite power, wisdome and goodnes, the maker and preseruer of all thinge, both visible and invisible. And in vnitie of this godhead there be thre persons, of one substance, power, and eter= nitie, The father, the sonne, & the holie ghoste.

THE THIRTY-NINE ARTICLES OF RELIGION issued in 1571 set out the Anglican position on Reformation contro- versies. Subscription to the Articles was required of the clergy, and between 1581 and 1854 it was a condition for matriculation at Oxford.

reign, Oxford was to be the scene of martyrdom. In March 1554 Thomas Cranmer, Archbishop of Canterbury, Hugh Latimer (1485?–1555), Bishop of Worcester, and Nicholas Ridley (1500?–55), Bishop of London, were brought from the Tower of Lon- don to Oxford and imprisoned in the Bocardo jail, the prison over the North Gate near St Michael's Church, reserved for 'scholars and other slight offenders of the better class', in preparation for a theological disputation with their Catholic opponents. It was said that Oxford was chosen as the place for the disputation because of the orthodox Catholic loyalty shown by the University during the Protestantism of Edward's reign. On 14 April Cranmer, Latimer, and Ridley were brought before the Commissioners in the University Church, and were given the precise terms of the three questions to be debated—the Real Presence of Christ in the Eucharist, transubstantiation (the manner of the Eucharistic change), and the mass as a sacrifice. Cranmer was ordered to submit a written statement of his beliefs. Two days later the disputation began in the Divinity School. The arguments continued over three days, and on 20 April the three were brought before the Commissioners in St Mary's to be told that they had been proved

The fyrſt Booke

Concerning Lawes, and their ſeuerall kindes
in generall.

The matter conteined in this fyrſt Booke.

1 THE cauſe of writing this generall diſcourſe concerning lawes.
2 Of that law which God from before the beginning hath ſet for himſelfe to doe all things by.
3 The lawe which naturall agents obſerue, & their neceſſarie maner of keeping it.
4 The lawe which the Angels of God obey.
5 The lawe whereby man is in his actions directed to the imitation of God.
6 Mens firſte beginning to vnderſtand that lawe.
7 Of mans will which is the firſt thing that lawes of action are made to guide.
8 Of the naturall finding out of lawes by the light of reaſon to guide the will vnto that which is good.
9 Of the benefit of keeping that lawe which reaſon teacheth.
10 How reaſon doth leade men vnto the making of humane lawes, whereby politique ſocieties are gouerned, and to agreement about lawes whereby the fellowſhip or communion of independent ſocieties ſtandeth.
11 Wherefore God hath by ſcripture further made knowne ſuch ſupernaturall lawes as doe ſerue for mens direction.
12 The cauſe why ſo manie naturall or rationall lawes are ſet downe in holie ſcripture.
13 The benefit of hauing diuine lawes written.
14 The ſufficiencie of ſcripture vnto the end for which it was inſtituted.
15 Of lawes poſitiue conteined in ſcripture, the mutabilitie of certaine of them, and the generall vſe of ſcripture.
16 A concluſion, ſhewing how all this belongeth to the cauſe in queſtion.

HE that goeth about to perſwade a multitude, that they are not ſo well gouerned as they ought to be, ſhall neuer wāt attentiue & fauourable hearers; becauſe they know the manifold defects whereunto euery kind of regiment is ſubiect, but the ſecret lets and difficulties, which in publike proceedings are innumerable & ineuitable, they haue not ordinarily the iudgement to conſider. And becauſe ſuch as openly reproue ſuppoſed diſorders of ſtate are taken for principall friends to the common benefite of all, and for men that carry ſingular freedome of mind; vnder this faire and plauſible coulour whatſoeuer they vtter paſſeth for

The cauſe of writing this generall diſcourſe.

good

RICHARD HOOKER was educated at Corpus Christi College; his *Treatise on the Laws of Ecclesiastical Polity* made him the leading apologist of the Elizabethan religious settlement and one of the most renowned theologians of the Church of England. He defended the retention of episcopacy against Puritan criticism, and provided Anglicans with a formally based philosophical theology.

wrong in the disputation and were therefore asked to recant and express their belief in the Real Presence in the Eucharist. Refusing to do so, they were condemned as heretics and told they were 'no members of the church'. In September 1555 Cranmer, as an archbishop who had been approved by the Pope, had to face a further trial, appearing in St Mary's before the papal commissioners headed by James Brooks (1512–60), Bishop of Gloucester. The proceedings were passed to Rome for judgment. On 1 October Ridley and Latimer were excommunicated after a trial for heresy, and on 16 October were burnt at the stake in the town ditch in front of Balliol, just outside the north walls of Oxford. Cranmer was brought to watch from the roof of the Bocardo prison, and saw Ridley in particular suffer a slow and excruciating death.

Cranmer had occupied himself in prison by attempting to write a reply to Bishop Stephen Gardiner (1490?–1555) on the Eucharist. His Catholic sister used her influence to have him removed from the Bocardo to the house of the Dean of Christ Church. On 4 December 1555 in Rome Paul IV, having received the transcript of the trial, excommunicated Cranmer for heresy and commanded him to be degraded from holy orders and handed over to the secular power for punishment. When the sentence reached Oxford Cranmer was returned to the Bocardo prison. Woodson, the governor of the prison, whom Cranmer had come to regard as a friend, urged him to recant. Pressed, it would seem, by the psychological pressure and loneliness of his imprisonment, Cranmer gave way, and in January 1556 signed two recantations. Despite these he was destined to be burnt, but was first publicly degraded from his orders, the humiliating ceremony at Christ Church being presided over by Edmund Bonner (*c*.1500–69), Bishop of London. Other recantations followed, but when on 21 March he was taken to St Mary's prior to being burnt, he responded to the sermon by Henry Cole (1500?–80), Provost of Eton, by repudiating his recantations and declaring that 'as for the Pope, I refuse him as Christ's enemy and Antichrist, with all his false doctrine, and as for the Sacrament, I believe as I have taught in my book against the bishop of Winchester'. So he followed Latimer and Ridley to the stake, holding out to the flames the hand which had signed the recantations. Not quite three hundred years later the commemoration of the Reformation martyrs by the erection of the Martyrs' Memorial was marked by further religious controversy, the scheme being set on foot by those concerned for the Protestant identity of the Church of England, who hoped that such a proposal would embarrass John Henry Newman (1801–90), Edward Bouverie Pusey (1800–82), and the supporters of the Oxford Movement.

The burning of Cranmer, Latimer, and Ridley and the other Reformation martyrs was to be paralleled in the next reign by the sufferings of loyal Catholics, some of whom were Oxford men. Notable among them were the Jesuits Edmund Campion (1540–81) and Robert Parsons (or Persons) (1546–1610). Campion, who was a junior fellow of St John's in 1557, was executed at Tyburn in 1581. Parsons was a fellow of Balliol from 1568 to 1574 and joined with Campion in the Jesuit Mission to promote Catholicism in England, but was forced to flee to the Continent after Campion's arrest and execution.

THE VIRGIN'S PORCH, with its 'barley-sugar' columns of the kind widely supposed to have been used in Solomon's Temple, is a notable seventeenth-century addition to the medieval University Church. It was finished in 1637 at the expense of Morgan Owen, chaplain to Archbishop Laud, and the statue of the Virgin marked Oxford's seventeenth-century High Churchmanship.

When Elizabeth succeeded her half-sister Mary, with a consequent further change in religious policy, those who had gone into exile returned. Of those from Oxford few returned to the University, which they viewed as a centre of reaction: John Parkhurst (1512?–75), the future Bishop of Norwich, described it to the Swiss Reformer Heinrich Bullinger (1504–75) as being 'as yet a den of thieves, and of those who hate the light . . . There are few gospellers there, and many papists.' John Jewel was of the same opinion, telling Bullinger in 1559 that the universities were 'depressed and ruined . . . At Oxford there are scarcely two individuals who think with us; and even they are so dejected and broken in spirit, that they can do nothing.' All that Peter Martyr had planted had, in Jewel's view, been 'torn up by the roots', reducing the vineyard of the Lord to a wilderness. A year later he was complaining to Peter Martyr that Oxford was 'without learning, without lectures, without any regard to religion'. The colleges were filled with 'mere boys and empty of learning'. Many of the colleges were staunchly conservative, with the notable exception of Magdalen, where Lawrence Humphrey (1527?–90), exiled under Mary, was reinstated as President. Humphrey was to provide a warm welcome in Oxford for many Swiss students, remembering with gratitude the hospitality that he and Jewel had been accorded in Zurich. 'In mind and inclination', he wrote, 'I shall always be a Zuricher.' As the Elizabethan settlement took hold, the religious discipline of the University was forwarded by college catechists, appointed for the instruction of the undergraduates, and by a notable increase in preaching. The latter was not always welcomed: it was a matter of concern to John Howson (1557?–1632), who became Vice-Chancellor in 1602, that there had been too much running up and down to hear preachers so that *oratoria* (houses of prayer) had been turned into *auditoria* (places of hearing), in which the people desired to be 'knowers, then *Seraphim*, hot and zealous'. Preaching, so often at the centre of Puritan concern, needed to be set firmly within the context of the corporate worship of the Prayer Book liturgy.

It is notable that the two greatest apologists for Anglicanism, and defenders of the Elizabethan settlement of religion, were both Oxford men—John Jewel, whose *Apologia Ecclesiae Anglicanae* appeared in 1562, and another fellow of Corpus Christi, Richard Hooker (c.1554–1600), the first five books of whose *Treatise on the Laws of Ecclesiastical Polity* were published in 1594. In both instances, though the authors were Oxford men, their works were published when they were no longer resident in the city, Jewel being Bishop of Salisbury and Hooker Master of the Temple in London and later rector of Boscombe in Wiltshire.

Elizabethan Oxford came to provide a home, concentrated in particular colleges, for a theology within a broad Continental Reformed tradition, though it in general 'remained less rigid, less insistent [and] less precise than that hammered out in Cambridge'. Oxford became a strong defender of the Anglican tradition, as befitted the uni-

WILLIAM BUTTERFIELD favoured the use of materials which 'this locality and this age supply', and the bricks for Keble College were manufactured in Wheatley. There was medieval precedent for the colourful treatment of wall surfaces, and Butterfield believed that his startling polychromy would add gaiety to the buildings.

IN MOST COLLEGE CHAPELS the seating is arranged longitudinally. Choristers and scholars face each other across the aisle and can chant antiphonally. This is the chapel of Oriel College, which was completed in the 1640s.

versity of Jewel and Hooker. In the seventeenth century William Laud (1573–1645), whose zealous and authoritarian attempt to enforce ecclesiastical discipline, order, and sacramental practice led to conflict with Puritan divines and his eventual downfall as Archbishop of Canterbury, had a significant impact on Oxford. As a fellow of St John's from 1593 and President from 1611, he endeavoured to maintain High Church principles, emphasizing against the Puritans the visibility and continuity of the Church of Christ, the reverent ordering of the liturgy, and the setting of the study of Scripture within a knowledge of the theology of the Church Fathers and the teaching of the early Councils.

In 1629, a year after Laud was appointed Bishop of London, he became Chancellor of the University. He enforced discipline, revised the statutes, founded academic posts, and enriched the libraries. In religious matters he encouraged 'seemly gestures', enjoining the fellows of Merton to bow towards the altar and giving his support to the adornment of college chapels with hangings and painted windows. His chaplain, Morgan Owen (1585?–1645) of Jesus College, later Bishop of Llandaff, presented the south porch at St Mary's, with the statue of the Virgin over it which gave considerable offence to the extreme Protestants, and he endeavoured to secure orthodox Anglicanism in the Channel Islands by persuading Charles I to found fellowships at Jesus, Pembroke, and Exeter for Channel Islands boys. As archbishop he overrode the objections of the Warden and fellows of All Souls to secure a fellowship for Jeremy Taylor (1613–67), one of the most learned of the seventeenth-century Anglican divines. In many ways Laud himself was 'a sad little man, emotional and tactless', who tended to look to the early Church not for principles but for a fixed model to be copied in detail. Yet he had a profound influence on Oxford and on the Church of England, not least through his disciples, who, after the marginalization and exile of the Commonwealth period, came into their own at the Restoration. To an extent he forged within Oxford—even when the existence of many different opinions in the University has been recognized—its continuing link with the High Church tradition in Anglicanism.

Of a different temper from Laud's was one who may be taken as representative of Oxford's contribution to the English tradition of spirituality, Thomas Traherne (*c.*1636–74). Coming up to Brasenose from his native Hereford in the early 1650s, during the period of the Commonwealth, he was disappointed in his search for a tutor who would teach him 'felicity'. 'Drawn with the Expectation and Desire of some Great Thing', Traherne stood in the tradition of Augustinian spirituality of the restless heart that found its peace in God. Our wants at the deepest level are 'the ligatures that bind us to God': 'It was the infinit Wisdom of God, that did implant by Instinct so strong a Desire of felicity in the Soul, that we might be excited to labour after it, tho we know it not, the very force wherewith we covet it supplying the place of the Understanding.' As a child Traherne had seen 'all in the Peace of Eden': 'Eternity was Manifest in the Light of the Day, and something infinit Behind every thing appeared: which talked with my Expectation and moved my Desire.' For Traherne, as later on for Gerard Manley Hop-

WILLIAM LAUD's 'fencing of altars' and restoration of traditional ceremonies in worship earned him the enmity of the Puritans, as seen in this woodcut of 1641, in which the Puritan is portrayed as the man of God, and Laud, in episcopal robes, is of Man (holding the Service Book) and of the Devil (holding a book of superstition).

Of God,   Of Man,   Of the Divell.

kins, the world was 'charged with the grandeur of God'. His spirituality was affirmative, not negative, suffused with a sense of the divine glory transfiguring creation, and reflecting a Christian Platonism more typical of Cambridge than of Oxford. In both his *Centuries of Meditation* and his poetry Traherne's spirituality speaks powerfully. This spirituality is also to be found in the poetry of Henry Vaughan (1622–95), who was at Jesus some fifteen years before Traherne came to Brasenose, though he left without taking his degree.

In September 1641 Parliament directed that the Laudian reordering of churches, whereby the Communion table had been moved back to the east end of the church and fenced with rails, be discontinued. All 'crucifixes, scandalous pictures of any one or more persons of the Trinities, and all Images of the Virgin Mary shall be taken away and abolished, and . . . all Tapers, Candlesticks, and Basins, [shall] be removed from the Communion Table.' Bowing at the name of Jesus or towards the east end of the church were also forbidden. The Vice-Chancellors of Oxford and Cambridge and the heads of colleges were ordered to enforce this directive in college chapels, and also to ensure that the Lord's Day was duly observed by the restraint of 'all Dancing, or other Sports' and by the encouraging of preaching. So the character of Oxford religion was changed during the Commonwealth period, and the Book of Common Prayer ceased to be used after royalist Oxford's surrender to the Parliamentary forces in 1647. Four years earlier Lent had been discontinued, and meat was eaten in college halls throughout what had previously been a time of fasting and abstinence. The diarist Anthony Wood (1632–95), the self-proclaimed 'historiographer and antiquarie' of the University, observed that those who attacked the Anglican Establishment also attacked the universities, lambasting them as 'the nurseries of wickedness, the nests of mutton tuggers, the dens of formal droanes'. Colleges and halls were 'cages of unclean birds'. During this time, Wood noted, discipline was 'strict and severe', disputations and lectures and catechizing were frequent, 'preaching and praying too much'. ''Twas "scandalous" to have a short and quaint sermon', or 'to have a formall starcht prayer before it; and "verie ridiculous" to conclude with the Lord's prayer on bended knees'.

The restoration of Charles II in 1660 again altered the religious character of Oxford. The tables were turned and those restored to their former positions 'put themselves in the most prelaticall garbe that could be'. The Book of Common Prayer, organs (dismissed by the Puritans as the 'whining of pigs'), sung services, and surplices were restored. At Christ Church unknown opponents of the Restoration changes thrust all the surplices into the Peckwater privy, provoking a vulgar verse, supposedly a lamentation of Edward Lowe (d. 1682), the organist:

> Have pity on us all, good Lairds,
> For surely we are all uncleane;
> Our surplices are daub'd with tirds,
> And aye we have a shitten Deane.

All flesh is Grass, the best men vanity;
This, but a shadow, here before thine eye,
Of him, whose wondrous changes clearly show,
That GOD, not men, swayes all things here below.

WILLIAM PRYNNE was an undergraduate at Oriel. He became prominent as a Puritan opponent of Charles I and Archbishop Laud, and suffered imprisonment and had his ears cut off. Liberated by the Long Parliament, he took a leading part in the prosecution of Laud. This portrait is taken from *Canterburie's Doome* (1646), the first part of Prynne's *Compleat History* of Laud's trial and execution.

New marble floors, pinnacles, and an organ were provided for St Mary's, many college chapels were renovated, and new chapels were built at St Edmund Hall and Brasenose.

The accession of James II provoked yet another religious crisis in Oxford, which, as a bastion of Anglicanism, now had to engage with a Roman Catholic on the throne (see above, pp. 53–55). Obadiah Walker (1616–99), the Master of University College, declared himself a Roman Catholic. In 1686 James appointed the Roman Catholic John Massey (1651–1715) Dean of Christ Church on the death of Dr Fell, and it was not long before Massey set up a Roman Catholic chapel in the college. In 1687 a vacancy in the Presidency of Magdalen led to the most acrimonious and sustained crisis, when James nominated the Roman Catholic Anthony Farmer (b. 1658) as the new President. The fellows refused to accept him and elected another candidate, John Hough (1651–1743). In the ensuing dispute Farmer, who was accused of numerous misdemeanours, was dropped, and the Bishop of Oxford, Samuel Parker (1640–88), who was thought to be sympathetic to the Popish cause, was nominated in his stead (though actually ineligible under the college statutes, not having been a fellow). Again the fellows refused, petitioning the King on his visit to Oxford, but in vain. Parker was installed and the King's Commissioners expelled the twenty-five fellows who refused to accept him. Roman Catholics were nominated in their place, but they were there for less than a year before being ejected in their turn when William of Orange was preparing to invade England. In October 1688 Dr Hough and his colleagues were reinstated.

The character of Oxford as a 'confessional' university in which all members had to assent to the Anglican formularies made it peculiarly vulnerable to the vicissitudes of religious and political change. Although a limited toleration was granted to dissenters in 1689, Oxford remained an Anglican university and subscription to the Thirty-nine Articles of Religion was required from all who matriculated (at Cambridge subscription was at graduation, thus permitting dissenters to attend the university though not to take degrees). Oxford remained a bastion of Toryism. Although there were few who refused to take the oath to William, the University threw out the King's scheme for widening the doctrinal comprehensiveness of the Church (and so of the University). After 1689 Oxford, which had been such a close ally of personal monarchy, found itself in opposition, 'dedicated to defending the status and authority of church and clergy in a world of politics which had suddenly grown cold and hostile'.

The eighteenth century saw the University still solidly Anglican, the bulk of college fellows being ordained unmarried clergymen; both college and University provided a regular round of preaching, teaching, and liturgical prayer. More than 120 University sermons of various kinds were preached in the course of a year, and in the mid-eighteenth century a bequest by John Bampton (d. 1751), a Canon of Salisbury, enabled the

A SCULLION AT CHRIST CHURCH who is said to have excelled himself by singing Protestant and patriotic ballads against James II even before the Revolution of 1688 took place. The portrait was painted by John Riley.

THE UNIVERSITY COMMUNION PLATE, two chalices and patens, two flagons and an alms-dish, all dating from the early seventeenth century. Now in the Ashmolean Museum, they were used regularly until very recently at the one surviving Latin Communion Service celebrated in the University Church before the beginning of each term.

establishment of eight lecture-sermons, the first course of which was delivered in 1780. The lecturer was bidden to defend the orthodox doctrines of the Trinity and the Incarnation, and the authority of Scripture and of the early Fathers of the Church, treating of the articles of the Christian faith in the Apostles' or Nicene Creed. The lectures on this foundation were to provide an apologia for orthodox Christianity at a time when the theological temperature was reduced and deist and rationalist ideas were abroad. In colleges the compulsory worship was often merely formal, one Christ Church undergraduate commenting that 'prayers are nothing more than a muster, and do not last more than ten minutes'. Communion was celebrated on the great festivals and generally on the first Sunday in every term. The well-known early-nineteenth-century engraving by George Cruickshank (1792–1878), 'Black Matins, or the effect of late drinking upon early rising', represents a characteristic disarray at college worship which had long prevailed.

If there was a widespread lukewarmness and formality in religion, it is not surprising that there were those who reacted against this and strove for a deeper piety and more vigorous faith. One such was John Wesley (1703–91), fellow of Lincoln, who found in what was known by the end of 1730 as the 'Holy Club', first gathered by his brother Charles (1707–88), a pattern of devotion and religious life. Charles wrote: 'Diligence led me into serious thinking. I went to the weekly sacrament, and persuaded two or three young students to accompany me, and to observe the method of study prescribed by the Statutes of the University. This gained me the harmless name of Methodist.' Writing in his journal in 1740, John looked back to the beginnings of the Club: 'In November 1729, my brother, and myself and one more agreed to spend three or four evenings a week together. Our design was to read over the classics, which we had before read in private, on common nights, and on Sunday some books in divinity.'

The Club soon extended its membership and its programme, adding social work, prison-visiting, and observance of fast-days. The pattern remained, however, loose and flexible, small groups meeting in different colleges for a mixture of mutual academic help and devotional purposes. Wesley was encouraged in living as a 'Primitive Christian' by a new recruit to the Club, John Clayton of Brasenose (1709–73), who had links with the Manchester Nonjurors. He also read a number of writings in the Christian mystical tradition, particularly after his encounter with William Law (1686–1761) in July 1732. The pattern of corporate devotion, good works, fasting, and self-examination parallels contemporary movements in Continental pietism, which encouraged the meeting of small groups for edification and growth in holiness and the nurturing of a religion of the heart. Wesley endeavoured to encourage his pupils in the same way and, like Newman a century later, was criticized for his particular understanding of his tutorial responsibility. A young man, Richard Morgan (matriculated 1733), complained to his father about the devotional exercises Wesley was forcing upon him, leading him to be mocked as a 'Methodist'. Wesley defended himself, writing to the father that religion was 'a constant ruling habit of soul; a renewal of our minds in the image of God; a recovery of the divine likeness'.

The 'Holy Club' proved to be the seed-bed of a movement of religious revival which

JOHN AND CHARLES WESLEY, the leaders of the Methodist revival, at the first Methodist Conference in London in 1779. They are depicted in the pulpit and stall of a typical 'three-decker' pulpit.

spread far beyond Oxford, though there are many other and later influences which shaped Methodism. One of the other leading figures of the eighteenth-century Evangelical Revival of which Methodism was a significant part was George Whitefield (1714–70), who was later to represent the Calvinist wing of the revival. A servitor of Pembroke College, with few resources—'never a poor creature set up with so small a stock'—he was converted through the influence of the Wesleys. Whitefield had been attracted by the Methodist group and had observed them 'go through a ridiculing crowd to receive the Holy Eucharist at St. Mary's'. Charles Wesley befriended him and introduced him to the group. 'They built me up daily in the knowledge and fear of God . . . I now began, like them, to live by rule, and to pick up the very fragments of my time, that not a moment of it might be lost . . . Their hearts glowed with love for God.' When Whitefield attended a weekday celebration of communion at St Mary's 'they knewe I was commenced Methodist'.

At the end of 1735 the Wesleys left Oxford to engage in missionary work in Georgia—a venture which proved both more difficult and less successful than they had envisaged. John Wesley retained his fellowship at Lincoln, which at least provided him with some income until he had to vacate it on his marriage in 1751. (After the Reformation Heads of Houses were allowed to marry, but college fellows were required to be celibate—a rule included in the Laudian statutes of 1636.) He remained ambivalent towards Oxford, critical of its laxity and lukewarm or formal religion, yet recognizing how much his own earlier piety had been nourished and informed by its society and ideals. In August 1744 he returned to give a University sermon, which William Blackstone (1723–80) described in the following terms:

We were last Friday entertained at St. Mary's by a curious Sermon from Wesley the Methodist. Among other equally modest Particulars, he informed us, 1st That there was not one Christian among all the Heads of Houses, 2ndly that Pride Gluttony, Avarice, Sensuality, and Drunkenness were the general Characteristicks of all Fellows of Colleges who were useless to a proverbial Uselessness. Lastly, that the younger Part of the University were a Generation of Triflers, all of them perjured, and not one of them of any Religion at all.

It was Wesley's last significant formal connection with Oxford. What began with the spiritual searchings in Wesley's room in Lincoln and elsewhere in Oxford had an impact not only in England but throughout the world, yet, as Wesley's most recent biographer has reminded us, 'Methodism was not in anything like the sense of the later Tractarians an "Oxford Movement" at all.'

The constitutional changes of the early nineteenth century, following the upheaval of the revolutionary and Napoleonic wars, signalled the end of the confessional State and were the harbinger of similar changes in Oxford as an Anglican confessional university. The repeal of legislation disabling dissenters and Roman Catholics, and the political changes of the 1832 Reform Bill, altered the constitutional position of the Church of England and raised the question of Anglican identity—nowhere more so than in Oxford, the centre of Anglican High Churchmanship and the nursery of a large percentage of the Anglican clergy. The interference of the secular power in the episcopal order of the Church of Ireland pointed to similar legislation to reform the Church of England. This was the catalyst for the Assize Sermon on 14 July 1833 preached by John Keble (1792–1866), fellow of Oriel and Professor of Poetry, on the theme of 'National Apostasy'. In that sermon, and in the subsequent *Tracts for the Times*, the theological emphases of the Anglican apologists of the seventeenth century were brought out: the apostolic succession of the Christian ministry of bishops, priests, and deacons; the importance of tradition—the Fathers of the Church, the early councils, and the liturgy; the corporate character of Christian faith as opposed to the individualist religion of private judgement, be it Evangelical pietism or donnish rationalism; a sense, against those who would have their religion cut and squared to an all too human clarity, that faith was mysterious, and God was awesome, and that it was holiness rather than mental power which led to the knowledge of God.

The Oxford Movement had deeper roots than contemporary Romanticism, yet the Romantic reaction against eighteenth-century rationalism was a seed-bed in which it flourished. And it flourished not least because of the genius of those who were its leaders, the reserved yet attractive John Keble, whose religion of the heart was not worn on

JOHN HENRY NEWMAN, a fellow of Oriel and Vicar of the University Church, was one of the leaders of the Oxford Movement until he became a Roman Catholic in 1845. His friend and fellow convert, William Lockhart (1820–92), wrote: 'It was when Newman read the Scriptures from the lectern in St Mary's Church ... that one felt ... that his words were those of a seer who saw God.'

ESSAYS AND REVIEWS was published in 1860 and provoked a strong orthodox reaction. In 1869 Gladstone appointed one of the contributors, Frederick Temple, Bishop of Exeter. Here two High Churchmen, J. W. Burgon and G. A. Denison, are imagined burning the new bishop on the very spot outside his own college, Balliol, where three centuries earlier Ridley, Latimer, and Cranmer had been martyred.

his sleeve; the learning and mystical piety of Edward Pusey; and the subtle mind and moral power of John Henry Newman.

'On what ground do you stand, O presbyter of the Church of England?', asked Newman in the first of the *Tracts*. It was no use relying on the privileges and status of State recognition, only apostolic authority would suffice. In controversy with the French Abbé Jager (1790–1868) and in his subsequent *Lectures on the Prophetical Office of the Church* (1837) Newman set out an apologia for the *via media* of the Church of England between the Church of Rome and 'Popular Protestantism', as it is called in Newman's subtitle. Rome was criticized for over-systematization of doctrine and for placing reliance on contemporary Church authority rather than the controlling inheritance of Christian antiquity. Protestantism, by appealing to the Bible only, in practice made every man his own interpreter, thus denying the authority of Church, creeds, and tradition in favour of unfettered private judgement.

In his sermons, preached to growing congregations during his time as Vicar of St Mary's, Newman maintained the overriding imperative of holiness, and as much as Wesley before him criticized the undemanding, lukewarm religion that was socially acceptable. In an important series of University sermons he engaged with some of the challenges of contemporary rationalism, and attacked the accommodating rationalist and liberal theologies which seemed to him to have forgotten that Christianity claimed to be divine revelation, not the 'painful inductions from existing phenomena' of philosophical thinkers. His exploration of the relationship between faith and reason, begun in the University sermons, built on the work of an earlier Oxford (and Oriel) apologist for Christianity, Joseph Butler (1692–1752), and found particularly vivid expression in his attack on utilitarian principles in the *Tamworth Reading Room Letters* (1841), in which he reminded his readers that many a man would 'live and die upon a dogma', but no man would be 'a martyr for a conclusion'. *An Essay in Aid of a Grammar of Assent* (1870) was to provide a sustained exposition of the 'real' and 'notional' ways in which assent is given in questions of religious truth.

The years between John Keble's Assize Sermon of 1833 and Newman's move to the Church of Rome in 1845 were heady years of religious controversy in Oxford. The conflict was considerably sharpened by Oxford's own Anglican identity. If the Tractarians recalled the Church of England to a sense of catholic continuity, then Newman's arguments in Tract Ninety, endeavouring to reconcile the Thirty-nine Articles and the teaching of the Council of Trent, seemed to make nonsense of the University's religious tests. After 1845 Pusey, as Canon of Christ Church and Regius Professor of Hebrew, was viewed as the acknowledged leader of the catholic revival in Anglicanism, and fought to preserve the Anglican confessional character of the University in a society of increasing religious pluralism. A man of ascetic life, great learning, and personal holiness, he was much sought after as a confessor and spiritual director, and contributed significantly to the revival of religious orders within the Church of England. In Oxford Richard Meux Benson (1824–1915), a Student (i.e. fellow) of Christ Church, founded the Society of St John the Evangelist, commonly known as the Cowley Fathers, in 1866.

If Oxford was at the heart of the catholic revival in Anglicanism in the nineteenth century, it also increasingly felt the impact of the critical study of the Bible. The controversial collection *Essays and Reviews*, published in 1860, contained essays by Frederick Temple (1821–1902), a former undergraduate of Balliol, later to be Archbishop of Canterbury, and Benjamin Jowett (1817–93), Regius Professor of Greek, who was to be Master of Balliol from 1870 to 1893, as well as by Mark Pattison (1813–84), Rector of Lincoln, who increasingly repudiated the Tractarianism of his earlier years. Although it was other contributors who were prosecuted in the ecclesiastical courts, Jowett in particular remained under suspicion for his liberal views on the interpretation of Scripture.

The passing of the Universities' Tests Act in 1871 brought to an end Oxford's exclus-

ively Anglican character, while at the same time preserving provision for religious instruction and worship according to the use of the Church of England in the college chapels. John Keble's death in 1866 provided the occasion for High Churchmen to respond to the new religious pluralism by founding a new college in Keble's memory. This was to have the dual purpose of providing an Oxford education on Anglican principles and of widening access to Oxford. Edward Stuart Talbot (1844–1934) was appointed as the first Warden when the college opened in 1870, and he was later to be numbered among the group known as the 'Holy Party', which inluded Henry Scott Holland (1847–1918) and Charles Gore (1853–1932) the first Principal of Pusey House, founded as a memorial to E. B. Pusey, to house his library, and be a centre of Christian teaching and pastoral work in the University. It was this younger group of Oxford High Churchmen who in 1889 produced a major book of essays, *Lux Mundi*, which attempted to bring the Tractarian inheritance into a creative relationship with contem-

THE CHAPEL OF KEBLE COLLEGE (*left*), designed by William Butterfield, was opened on 25 April 1876, when Dr Pusey preached at the service. The arrangement of seats facing the altar (and not as in other chapels facing each other) marked the sacramental focus of the Oxford Movement, as was appropriate in a college founded as a memorial to John Keble.

'HIGH' AND 'LOW' IN OXFORD CHURCHMANSHIP, and the tensions between them, are depicted in the cartoon of 1878 showing the Anglo-Catholic Father Noel dragging his church of St Barnabas off to Rome, while the Evangelical Rector of St Aldate's, Canon Christopher, tries in vain to restrain him.

porary thought. From the same group came the inspiration for the founding in Oxford in 1892 of what became one of the most significant of Anglican religious communities, the Community of the Resurrection, which was to find its home at Mirfield in Yorkshire. Scott Holland became a leading member of the Christian Social Union, and these later decades of the nineteenth century saw new social ventures promoted from Oxford, notably Toynbee Hall in Whitechapel, which had close links with Balliol, and Oxford House in Bethnal Green, which began after a meeting held in Keble.

Although the religious tradition of the University remained predominantly High Anglican, there were also Evangelical stirrings, marked by the foundation in 1879 of the Oxford Inter-collegiate Christian Union (OICCU), two years after the foundation of CICCU, the parallel society at Cambridge. For more than a century OICCU has been the focus of much undergraduate Christian life and commitment, and has brought to Christian faith many who have gone on to serve the Churches, both within its own distinctively Evangelical tradition and beyond. From the time of a notable mission by the American evangelists Moody and Sankey (Dwight L. Moody, 1837–1899, and Ira D. Sankey, 1849–1908) in 1882, which culminated in a meeting in the Corn Exchange attended by over a third of the undergraduates in the University, the Christian Union has organized and supported regular missions to the University.

Oxford's historic links with the Church meant that theological questions were always a major concern of the University. It is therefore at first sight surprising that in the Oxford education which a large percentage of Anglican clergy received, theology as

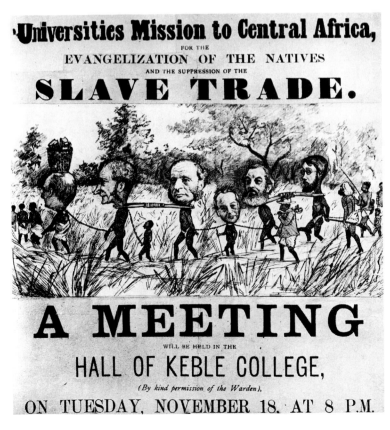

THE UNIVERSITIES MISSION TO CENTRAL AFRICA, founded in response to an appeal made by David Livingstone in 1857, was High Church in character. Edward Stuart Talbot, the first Warden of Keble College, which supplied many clergy for the Church overseas, is seen here in 1882–3 as the last in a line of notable Oxford churchmen who are depicted as victims of the slave trade.

MISSIONARY ENTHUSIASM was no less apparent at the Evangelical end of the ecclesiastical scale, as this photograph, taken in 1899, of a missionary breakfast filling the Town Hall shows.

such featured hardly at all as part of the undergraduate course, let alone training in pastoral and liturgical skills. The most ancient chairs in Theology—the Lady Margaret (1502), and the Regius Professorships of Hebrew and Divinity (1546)—were sixteenth-century foundations. Not until the nineteenth century were other theological chairs established—the Regius Chairs of Ecclesiastical History and Moral and Pastoral Theology in 1842, and the two biblical professorships, the Dean Ireland (1847) and the Oriel (1877), followed in the twentieth century by the Nolloth Professorship of the Philosophy of the Christian Religion in 1920. The 1842 chairs were annexed to canonries of Christ Church. One of the notable holders of the Chair of Pastoral Theology was Edward King (1829–1910), later Bishop of Lincoln, whose saintly life made a strong impression on his contemporaries. Of the fifteen post-Reformation commemorations in the calendar of the *Alternative Service Book 1980*, King joins seven other Oxford figures, James Hannington (1847–85), the martyred Bishop of Eastern Equatorial Africa, Richard Hooker, John Keble, Thomas Ken (1637–1711), the non-juring Bishop of Bath and Wells, William Tyndale (d. 1536), the bible translator, and the Wesleys.

The establishment of more professorial posts in Theology was symptomatic of the growing concern in the Victorian Church, and in Oxford in particular, for a more professional and trained clergy. Increasingly it came to be felt that an academic training in classics and mathematics, without any specific theological input, was grossly insufficient as training for the ordained ministry. Remedies were sought in the found-

THE GHOSTS OF KING HENRY VIII AND CARDINAL WOLSEY haunt members of the Cathedral Chapter as they play at cards in Christ Church Hall. Dr Pusey lays a card on the table watched by Canons H. P. Liddon and C. A. Heurtley, and Archdeacon C. Clerke. Canons E. King and W. Bright engage in conversation.

ing of theological colleges to provide for specifically priestly formation and theological training, and in the emergence first of college and then of University lectures in Theology for those proceeding to ordination, leading eventually to the establishment of the Honour School of Theology in 1868. The syllabus was closely tied to the ordination requirements of the Church of England—hence the stress on the study of Scripture and the history of the early centuries of the Church. The examinations were set by clergy of the Church of England, and, although the passing of the Universities' Tests Act in 1871 meant that the University was no longer Anglican, the assumption remained that the Theology degrees were still closely linked to the theological training of Anglican clergy. A memorandum of 1904 maintained that the time was not yet ripe to admit non-Anglicans to the conduct of this examination.

It was indeed the case that the University continued to supply a large number of Anglican clergy, the new foundation of Keble playing a particularly significant part. Many of these went to serve in the Church overseas, where Oxford had particular links through missionary ventures such as the Oxford Mission to Calcutta. The ecclesiastical tradition of Oxford continued to be maintained after the Anglican monopoly was ended, but was enriched by the founding or transfer to Oxford of colleges and private halls of other Christian traditions—Campion Hall (Jesuit), Mansfield (Congregationalist), Regent's Park (Baptist), and others. Of twentieth-century Archbishops of Canterbury, Randall Davidson (1848–1930), Cosmo Gordon Lang (1864–1945), William Temple (1881–1944), Geoffrey Fisher (1887–1972), and Robert Runcie (b. 1921) were all Oxford men. Arthur Foley Winnington-Ingram (1858–1946), Bishop of London from 1901 to 1939, and Cyril Garbett (1875–1955), an excellent pastor who was Archbishop of York from 1942 to 1955, were perhaps the most outstanding of the many leading churchmen produced by the new Anglican foundation of Keble. In 1920 the award of honorary Doctorates of Divinity to a Congregationalist, Dr Selbie (1862–1944), Principal of Mansfield, and a Roman Catholic, Baron von Hügel (1852–1925), signalled a further broadening of Oxford's religious tradition. C. H. Dodd (1884–1973) at Mansfield was later to become the most distinguished British biblical scholar of his age, serving as Director of the New English Bible translation in the late 1940s and 1950s.

Compulsory chapel began to languish in Oxford after the First World War. The climate became more secular. College chaplains and other concerned Christians in the University attempted to counter this by sponsoring regular university missions, teaching-weeks on the Christian faith with devotional and expository addresses. In 1931

WILLIAM TEMPLE, an exhibitioner at Balliol and a fellow of Queen's College, was one of the most notable churchmen of the mid-twentieth century, becoming Archbishop first of York and then of Canterbury. His concern with social and economic problems gained him considerable prominence.

William Temple's Mission to the University was remembered by many as a powerful exposition of the Christian faith. Oxford also produced, in the interwar years and after, a notable group of Christian thinkers and apologists, Anglo-Catholic theologians like N. P. Williams (1883–1943), E. L. Mascall (b. 1905), and Austin Farrer (1904–68), and the 'Inklings', J. R. R. Tolkien (1892–1973), Charles Williams (1886–1945), and C. S. Lewis (1898–1963), whose *Mere Christianity* and other writings continue to be widely influential and acceptable across a broad spectrum of Christian traditions. During and after the Second World War Oxford saw the beginnings of two significant movements of Christian social concern, Christian Action and the more broadly based Oxford Committee for Famine Relief, which was to grow into the major relief organization Oxfam.

In the Theology Faculty the Anglican monopoly ended, with non-Anglicans coming to share in the work of both examining and teaching, though the syllabus remained strongly focused on biblical and historical studies until the end of the 1960s. In the early years of that decade it was still possible to assert that the majority of those reading

THE MASSAI HEALTH SERVICES PROJECT (*right*) founded by the Evangelical Lutheran Church of Tanzania brought women into the management of community affairs. Women asked for a cattle-dip and Oxfam supplied the materials; the dip came into operation in October 1989, and when it began to generate a profit the women opened a bank account. Here, Mrs Kisota receives instruction in bookkeeping from Paulina Natema of MHSP.

OXFAM was founded at a meeting in the Old Library of the University Church in 1942 under the auspices of the vicar, Canon Theodore Richard Milford (*below*). The objective was the relief of famine and sickness arising as a result of the war. Oxfam has since grown to become the leading British charity dealing with relief work, spending up to £50,000,000 a year.

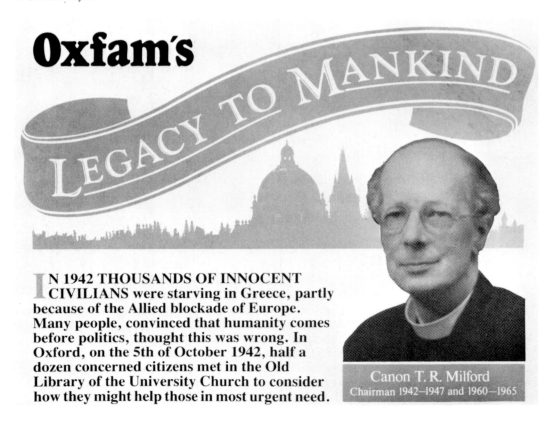

Oxfam's

LEGACY TO MANKIND

IN 1942 THOUSANDS OF INNOCENT CIVILIANS were starving in Greece, partly because of the Allied blockade of Europe. Many people, convinced that humanity comes before politics, thought this was wrong. In Oxford, on the 5th of October 1942, half a dozen concerned citizens met in the Old Library of the University Church to consider how they might help those in most urgent need.

Canon T. R. Milford
Chairman 1942–1947 and 1960–1965

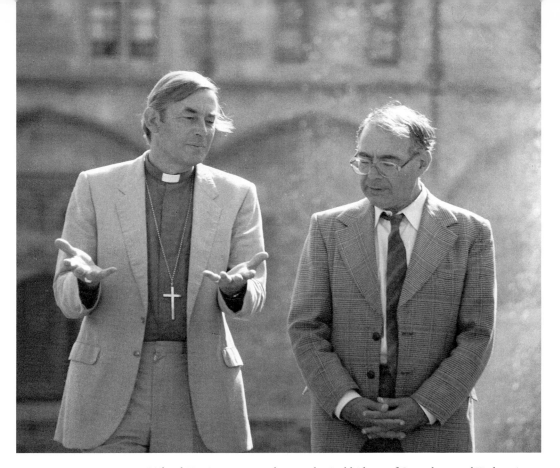

THE BISHOP OF OXFORD, Richard Harries, was consultant to the Archbishops of Canterbury and York on inter-faith relations, at the same time that Lionel Blue was vice-chairman of the Standing Conference of Jews, Christians, and Moslems in Europe. They are seen here in August 1989 at Christ Church during the making of the television film *In Search of Holy England*.

Theology were ordinands, and also that they would have had a classical education, and for many of them theology would be a second degree.

Much has now changed. The introduction of a joint School of Philosophy and Theology in the 1970s and the broadening of the Theology syllabus reflects a wider interest in theological study than the older ordinand constituency. Historical and doctrinal studies have expanded, and there have been some small moves in the direction of the study of other world religions, but Oxford has, probably wisely, built on its strengths, and the Theology school is still at its core concerned with the Judaeo-Christian tradition rather than with the phenomenology of religion. The undergraduates are now of all denominations or none, and amongst them there is a high percentage of women. The older constituency is represented by the entitlement of the denominational theological colleges to matriculate a limited number of qualified ordinands each year to read Theology as a second degree as part of their ministerial training.

The development of the Oxford Faculty of Theology contrasts with the pattern in European universities. Although Anglicans are, not surprisingly, well represented in the faculty, the Oxford faculty is ecumenical, unlike the separate Catholic and Protestant faculties found, for historical reasons, in German universities. A Jesuit and a Baptist have both chaired the Faculty Board in Oxford in recent years. Although the canon-professorships at Christ Church remain, recent decisions to separate University teaching posts in Theology and college chaplaincies point further along the road travelled since the nineteenth century of an increasing separation between the roles of priest, pastor, and theologian in the formal structures of the University.

Over the last century and a half one of the most significant alterations in the religious map of England has been the growth of the Roman Catholic Church. In the nineteenth century the Oxford Movement converts, most notably Newman and Manning, contributed importantly to this. Ronald Arbuthnot Knox (1888–1957), a convert of a later generation, played a significant role as Catholic chaplain at Oxford together with notable Jesuits such as C. C. Martindale (1879–1963) and Martin d'Arcy (1888–1976), and there were a number of other intellectual converts. Oxford, for all the increase of secularism and the virtual disappearance of clerical Heads of House and ordained teachers (with the exception of a few colleges with academic chaplains and the canon-professors of Christ Church), still continues to be a powerful centre of Christian activity, where the level of participation in worship by young people is still significantly higher than the national average. Oxford's traditional High Churchmanship has made it more concerned with questions of Church polity than Cambridge. It remains the only city in England with three Anglican theological colleges: St Stephen's House, Wycliffe Hall and Ripon College Cuddesdon. The presence in Oxford of the Catholic

DR SARAH COAKLEY was the first woman to be appointed to a tutorial fellowship in Theology—at Oriel College in 1990.

halls, the Dominican *studium* ('study-centre') at Blackfriars, and the three colleges in the Free Church tradition—Mansfield, Regent's Park, and Manchester—alongside the vigorous life of some of the city churches, is a sign that this is likely to continue. The Orthodox tradition is also represented by the double Russian and Greek parish and the ecumenical centre of the House of St Gregory and St Macrina, founded by Nicolas Zernov (1898–1980) together with his wife Militza. As a result of a conversation with Zernov Norman Spalding (1877–1953) founded a lecturership in Oxford in Orthodox studies (a post unique in British universities), to which first Zernov himself, and later Kallistos Ware (b. 1934) (an English convert to, and subsequently a bishop in, the Greek Orthodox Church), were appointed.

Debates affecting the Church at large are certain to be reflected in Oxford, even when they do not begin there. In a cold climate for faith Oxford may no longer be the training-ground for the clergy it once was, yet it remains enmeshed in its religious past. It was scarcely surprising that the trenchant analysis of the Anglican Establishment published as the anonymous preface to the 1987–8 edition of *Crockford's Clerical Directory* issued from the pen of an Oxford ecclesiastical historian, Gareth Vaughan Bennett (1929–87), whose tragic suicide as the newspaper press tried to identify the author shocked the Church of England. Although college chapels remain constitutionally Anglican (apart from the Catholic and Free Church foundations), Christian co-operation has grown significantly, as has the role of town churches in relation to college chapels. In 1977 Cardinal Suenens (b. 1904), Archbishop of Malines-Brussels, became the first Roman Catholic to be invited to lead the University Mission sponsored by the college chaplains. This was followed by another mission in 1981, when Roman Catholic, Anglican, Orthodox, and Free Church speakers led a mission in which Cardinal Basil Hume (b. 1923) and Archbishop Robert Runcie were the joint speakers on the opening night. In 1990 the celebration of the centenary of the death of John Henry Newman was a major academic and ecumenical occasion.

For almost eight centuries Oxford has been a powerful Christian influence in the nation and overseas through its theology, learning, and publications (the University Press is one of the major publishers of Bible and Prayer Books); through its institutional links with the Church of England, from the Christ Church canon-professors to the exercise of ecclesiastical patronage by many of the colleges; and through movements of religious revival—the Franciscan schools, Wyclif, the Laudians, Wesley and the Methodists, and the Oxford Movement, to name the most significant. That influence is likely to continue, though in a quieter way, in a society that is both more religiously pluralist and more secular than ever before and in which Christians now face new challenges and new opportunities in dialogue with those of other faiths and secular ideologies.

DESMOND TUTU became Bishop of Lesotho in 1976 and of Johannesburg in 1984. Up to the time he was elected Archbishop of Cape Town in 1986 he was prominent in political protest. As soon as black leaders became free to play an active role in shaping South Africa's future he withdrew into the background. He was awarded an Honorary Doctorate of Divinity by the University in 1990.

5

The University's Contribution to Classical Studies

H. D. JOCELYN

No secular libraries or schools survived the departure of the Roman army from Britain in AD 409. Latin went out of use very quickly as a language of ordinary discourse. It is doubtful whether Greek had ever been much studied on the island. The architectural and artistic monuments of classical civilization disappeared or became unrecognizable. The Christian clergy eventually established a new educational system, but one designed to suit their own needs. Continuing loyalty to the Bishop of Rome ensured the preservation of a species of Latin in the English Church's ritual and in its Government. This was a sclerotic medium of communication, only occasionally loosened up by study of the pagan literary classics. It tended more to conceal than to make plain the user's meaning.

The University of Oxford was from its beginning an instrument of the Church, and its members used the Church's Latin to communicate with each other. In the late twelfth century, and through the thirteenth, grammatical theory, logic, and natural philosophy dominated the curriculum of the Faculty of Arts, as they did in the same faculty of other medieval universities. The texts read came either from late antiquity or from the twelfth and thirteenth centuries themselves. The chief skill acquired by a student of the Arts was in general disputation. Poetry and artistic prose—any kind of work written to charm rather than to instruct—laboured under ecclesiastical suspicion. The higher Faculties of Medicine and Law remained very small in comparison with that of Theology. Most students and teachers were either already in the service of the Church or destined to be so. Few men stayed very long in Oxford, and those who did rarely pursued a particular set of interests at all profoundly. An exception was Robert Grosseteste (1175–1253), who devoted himself to scientific as well as theological speculation and even learnt Greek in order to get behind the Latinized traditions of the subjects which interested him.

ROBERT GROSSETESTE'S GREEK. The variant readings in the left-hand margin of this page of a thirteenth-century codex of the works attributed to Dionysius the Areopagite were added by Grosseteste, who translated and commented on 'Dionysius'. The codex was probably among those bequeathed to the Grey Friars of Oxford, neglected, and finally dispersed. It returned to Oxford in the Canonici collection in 1817.

In Italy secular culture never suffered as much damage at Christian and barbarian hands as it did elsewhere in Europe. The early Italian universities attracted the laity. They concentrated on medicine and law rather than on theology. Growing accumulations of economic wealth and new forms of civil government stimulated in the fourteenth and fifteenth centuries a demand for an education significantly different from one appropriate to a priest or a monk. Texts of ancient works in verse and prose, long unread, were disinterred from libraries. Cicero's orations and Quintilian's treatise on the education of the orator revealed a variety of Latin unquestionably superior to any used in later times. It was realized, furthermore, that such works came from a form of society with a small governing élite similar to that of many Italian cities of the new age, and that they embodied a system of civilized values fit to rival or even replace the medieval ideal. They centred on man and the human, not on God and the divine.

Many of those who taught in Italian Arts faculties were not clerics. Declamation challenged disputation as the chief academic exercise. A form of Latin aiming at classical standards replaced the barbarized medieval type. Bishops, cardinals, and popes became as anxious as secular princes to recruit to their service writers of elegant Latin. A desire to know at first hand the Greek authors admired by Cicero and Quintilian grew strong. The language of the Byzantine Church and bureaucracy was believed not to differ from the Greek used by Plato and Demosthenes, and many men from the Greek-speaking areas of the Mediterranean were recruited as teachers.

Those who went from Oxford to an Italian university in the course of the fifteenth century to further their studies in law or medicine could not fail to be affected by the humanistic ferment in the arts, but none returned to teach or hold office in Oxford. On the other hand, diplomatic visitors from the papal Curia educated in the new way impressed the London Court, and some English aristocrats began to patronize scholars of the new learning, to collect books, sometimes even themselves to attend the more famous Italian schools. The youngest son of Henry IV, Humphrey, Duke of Gloucester (1391–1447), was the most remarkable of the early English Italophiles. He presented to

DUKE HUMPHREY meant his books to be read. The sketch endeavours to represent the original appearance of the library built in the second half of the fifteenth century as the upper storey of the Divinity School. The Duke contributed to the building expenses.

RICHARD FOXE, Lord Privy Seal to Henry VII and Henry VIII, founder of Corpus Christi College. He encouraged the study of Greek and the classical form of Latin but thought it 'a sacrifice for a man to tarry any longer at Oxford than he had a desire to profit'. Johannes Corvus [Jan Rave] made the portrait in *c*.1520 after Foxe had become blind.

the University many books of a theological character and some which contained classical texts. Significantly, the latter went unread.

The period of Tudor rule saw bigger changes elsewhere in England than in Oxford. The monastic colleges closed, but the rest escaped confiscation of their wealth and more were founded. The medieval form of Latin remained the language of the liturgy of college chapels and the University Church, as of the University statutes. Humanistic Latin found a readier welcome in the grammar schools, as did Greek. Students arriving from the grammar schools were eventually, through their very presence, to have some effect on the medieval atmosphere of the University. When Richard Foxe (1448?–1528) drew up statutes for the new Corpus Christi College in 1517, he demanded that there should be readers both of the arts of *humanitas* (i.e. of classical Latin and the literature of this language) and of the Greek language. Of the professorships instituted for the University in 1540 by Henry VIII, the so-called 'Regius Chairs', one was in Greek; the King ignored Latin. Two related aims motivated the learning of Greek in the Tudor period: one was to read the more important source-books of medieval medicine and astronomy, the other to study the New Testament in its original language. Nevertheless,

SCENE OF TERENCE'S *EUNUCHUS* (III. ii) redrawn at the Benedictine Abbey of St Albans in the twelfth century after the style of the time. The original artist had the classical theatre in mind (note the masks). Those who performed the text of the *Eunuchus* in Merton College in 1567 would have dressed in the sixteenth-century theatrical manner. The codex was given to the Bodleian Library in 1704.

in Oxford no drastic reform of the Arts Faculty curriculum, of the kind initiated in German universities at the beginning of the sixteenth century and carried further after the reformation of the German Church, was attempted.

More important for the future than efforts to humanize Oxford from outside was the usurpation in the late sixteenth century by college fellows, all men in Anglican orders, of the teaching role earlier exercised by the University's Regent Masters. Efforts to establish a salaried University professoriate had not got very far; intellectual instruction thus came to be combined with moral and religious supervision. In many colleges a tutor would deal with the whole curriculum. This militated as strongly against the health of the traditional Arts as against the development of new subjects like Greek. No very visible boundary was placed between school and university studies where the literary classics were concerned, and the student from a good school made little further progress with Latin when he got to Oxford. Successive Professors of Greek found less and less to do, and began to treat their post as merely a step to a higher one in the Church or State; they were always products of Oxford itself.

In the second half of the sixteenth century the increasing presence in some colleges of men of wealthy family uninterested in a clerical career affected the curriculum little. Undergraduate performances on festive occasions of the scripts of the classical Latin dramatists made only a superficial concession to the humanism of the secondary schools: interestingly, no Greek script was ever tried. The traditional curriculum, with its emphasis on Latin books and above all on Aristotle in Latin translation, seemed to provide a basic sufficiency both for the intending priest and for the intending statesman. It is thus not surprising if classical erudition did not blossom in sixteenth-century Oxford in the way it did in Paris and even in Medicean Florence and papal Rome. The demand made in 1576 that only those who subscribed to the Thirty-nine Articles of the national Church should be matriculated, and the series of measures which followed against the Romanist recusants, drove a number of established teachers to leave Oxford, but these took little in the way of classical learning with them. Few of the great Continental Protestant scholars who suffered Catholic persecution sought refuge in Oxford. Isaac Casaubon (1559–1614), King Henry IV of France's erudite librarian and Europe's finest Greek scholar, did receive a personal welcome in Merton College in 1610 from this college's most untypical head, Henry Savile (1549–1622). The University had no position, however, that it could offer him, suited to his talents.

In 1615 Savile presented the University with a set of Greek types, and one of the most cherished schemes of William Laud (1573–1645) was the establishment of a University printing-house capable of issuing erudite editions of Greek and Latin texts. The early years of the seventeenth century saw a number of new chairs created, plainly with the

WILLIAM CAMDEN as portrayed by Marcus Ghearaerts the younger, 1622. Camden added this note to the section on the University of Oxford in the Bodleian copy of his topographical and historical account of Britain: 'Remember there also that William Camden ... gave ... £140 yearly to a historical lecture, and instituted thereto Mr. Degory Wheare for the first lecturer.' He gave the portrait, now at Worcester College, to Wheare.

ΧΡΥΣΟ.ΟΣΑΝΛΕΘΙΤΟΛΙΤΟΙ ΡΑΔΗΘΝΤΕΣ ΚΑΤΑΣ ΑΙ ΝΗ
ΙΣ ΣΜΥΡΝΑΙΟΝΑΕΧΗΣΟΛΟΣ ΑΝΛΕ ΚΑΙΕΜΜΑΤΝΙΔΙΑΙΤΟΝΟ
..Γ ΚΑΕΙΑ. ΛΝ ΡΑΙΕΧΟΜΕΝΟΜ ΕΠΙΤΗΣ ΨΥΛΑΞΙΣ ΤΗΣ ΤΟΛΙ
..Ο.Σ ΑΝΛΕ ΣΜΥΡΝΑΙ ΟΙΣ ΑΙΕΙΣ ΚΑΤΑΣ ΚΗΝ.ΣΙΝ ΤΟΙΣ ΑΤΤΟ.ΧΕΙ
ΙΑΣ ΥΝ ΦΡΑΤ Χ ΟΙΠΙΣ Ε ΑΜΗΝΟΝΜΙΣΟ ΥΣ ΟΛΛΕ ΟΤΑΜΙΑΣ
ΤΟ ΛΕ.Ο ΠΡΟΣΟΛ. ΝΟΜ ΟΣΔΙΑΕ Τ ΟΥ ΜΕΝΕΜΜΑΤ ΝΗ ΣΙΑΙ ΚΑ Τ
ΟΥΣ ΑΛΛΟΥΣ ΤΟΥΣ ΚΑΤΑΧΩ.ΡΙΖΟΜ ΕΝΟΥΣ ΕΙΣ ΤΟ ΠΟΛΙ ΤΕ
ΜΗΤΕΡΑ ΤΗΝ ΣΙ ΠΥΛΗΝΗΝΚΑΙ ΑΤΘΟΛΛΟ.ΤΟΝΕΜΙΤΑΝΛΟΙΣ ΚΑΤ
ΤΑΙΣ ΣΥΝ ΘΗΚΑΙΣ ΑΙΣ ΣΥΝΤΕΘΕΙΜΑΙ ΠΡΟΣ ΣΜΥΡΝΑΙΟΥ ΣΕΙΣ
ΚΑΙ ΤΗΣ ΜΥ ΡΝΑΙΩΝ ΠΟΛΕΙ ΚΑΙ ΑΤΤΑΡΕΙΛΗ ΘΑΠΑΡΑΤΟΥΒΑΣΙΛΕΩΣ
ΠΑΡΑΒΗΣ ΟΜΑΙΤΟΙ ΚΑΤΑΤΗΝΟΜΟΛΟΓΙΑΝΟΥ ΑΡΜΕ ΤΑΘΗΣΩ ΕΠΙ
.ΟΝΟΙ ΑΣ ΑΣ ΤΑΣΙΑΣ ΤΟ ΥΣ ΚΑΤΑΤΟΥΣ ΣΜΥΡΝΑΙΩ ΝΝΟΜΟΥΣ ΚΑΙ
ΤΗΙ. Α Χ ΦΡ ΙΜΕΝΑ Σ ΜΥ ΡΝΑΙΟΙΣ ΥΠΟΤΟ. ΒΑΣΙΛΕΩΣ ΣΕΛΕΥΚΟΥ

INSCRIPTION recording a treaty of the third century BC between Smyrna and a neighbouring city, which John Selden published in 1629. The name of King Seleucus II appears at the bottom of this section (*far right*). The stone arrived in Oxford in 1667. The study of such stones, 'epigraphy', became important in the University only in the twentieth century.

idea of modernizing Oxford's studies. Two pertained to classical antiquity, those of Thomas White (1550?–1624) in Moral Philosophy (1621) and William Camden (1551–1623) in History (1622). These chairs, however, soon went the way of the Regius Chair of Greek, the incumbents rarely doing anything to further their subjects in a scientific way.

The statutes which Chancellor Laud promulgated in 1636 and which determined the University's general constitution for two and a half centuries confirmed for Greek its formal position among the Arts and for Aristotle his authority in science and philosophy. An addendum of 1662 emphasized the importance of 'Literae Humaniores' (so spelt) as a complement to the study of divinity. The Laudian constitution fixed the colleges as the centres of the University's teaching and gave supreme power in the University to a 'Hebdomadal Council' consisting of the college heads. Little was left for the professors to do except bear honorific titles. Most college fellows had to enter holy orders promptly. Marriage compelled the resignation of a fellowship. Some stayed in Oxford until a church living presented itself, others all their lives. They guided the morals of the young and based what they taught on what they themselves had learnt. The headship of a college offered a man the leisure to extend his learning by independent study. Mostly, however, it encouraged intellectual idleness or served merely as a stage in an ecclesiastical career to be completed outside Oxford. Any depth of learning a college head possessed tended in any case to be theological rather than classical. The fact that the serious teaching of medicine and law took place in London rather than in Oxford severely constricted the character of the University's classical scholarship.

The most important centre of classical studies in the seventeenth century was the Dutch University of Leiden, an institution managed by laymen who recruited professors from outside as well as inside Holland, paying more attention to their grasp of the subjects they had to teach than to the character of their religious convictions and encouraging them to enhance their own learning. In this century clerically managed Oxford added little to the stock of European scholarship. The case of John Selden (1584–1654) demonstrates rather than contradicts the point. There came from Selden's

LADY POMFRET'S GIFT. A Roman copy of a third century BC representation of a Muse; the most interesting of the sculptures from Lord Arundel's collection which the Countess of Pomfret purchased and presented to the University in 1755. Before the Muse with crossed legs came into the hands of Arundel she had inspired Michelangelo and Tintoretto to fresh creations.

hand in 1629 an account of the inscribed stones procured in Smyrna by an agent of the famous collector of antiquities Thomas Howard, second Earl of Arundel (1586–1646); this exposition won the respect of contemporary students of Greek antiquities. But, significantly, Selden had left Oxford immediately upon graduating to pursue a career in law and politics in the capital. There he found a better milieu for scholarly research than he would have in Oxford.

The victors in the civil wars of the seventeenth century made no attempt to alter the pattern of Oxford's studies, although there were men among them who wondered, like William Walwyn (*fl.* 1649), why it was necessary to train priests in Hebrew, Greek, and Latin at a time when the Scriptures were in English. A much more subtle and thoroughgoing critique of the way the English gentry were by then having their sons educated was developed by John Locke (1632–1704), a product of Christ Church itself. This did not persuade the Government of William III or any of its eighteenth-century successors to push reform on to the grammar schools or the universities.

Through most of the eighteenth century Oxford slept. Progress made elsewhere in mathematics and natural philosophy did not affect the curriculum or the intellectual tone of the University. Of the seven men whom Charles Burney (1726–1814) selected in 1809 as the bright stars of eighteenth-century English classical scholarship only two, Jonathan Toup (1713–85) and Thomas Tyrwhitt (1730–86), were educated at Oxford. Toup, who made important advances in the study of the Greek lexicographers, passed most of his life as a parish priest in Cornwall. Tyrwhitt, who applied eighteenth-century method with some success not only to a range of Greek authors but also to the English poets Chaucer and Shakespeare, resided for a time after graduation in Merton College, but occupied himself in civil-service posts in London rather than in college teaching.

Some of the inscribed pieces of marble once owned by the second Earl of Arundel came into the possession of the University in 1667, some of his sculptures in 1755 (see below, p. 170). These and other gifts of antiquities did not rival the treasures that were to accumulate in London in the British Museum, but they had potential value for the student who wanted more than a merely literary understanding of ancient society. R. Chandler (1738–1810) of Magdalen College catalogued them soon after graduating. While maintaining his connection with Magdalen, Chandler travelled extensively in Turkey, inspecting and recording what had survived of that country's ancient Greek cities. The great majority, however, of those who in the course of the eighteenth century laid the foundations of England's enduring interest in the material remains of the classical world were wealthy amateurs, artists, and architects, men untouched by university education.

Around the end of the eighteenth century higher education underwent drastic change in France and in the princedoms of Northern Germany. The study of Latin and Greek literature continued in the schools, and those of Germany cultivated Greek more intensively than they had done before. Anyone, however, who continued with classical studies at university henceforth usually did so with a view to a career as a

RICHARD FOXE, Bishop of Winchester, founded Corpus Christi College and bequeathed to it his English silver-gilt crozier of *c.*1487. St Peter is seated in the crook, and the pelican feeding its young (in medieval tradition with blood from its own breast) is a symbol of the sacrament of the body of Christ.

teacher at secondary or higher level in the service of the State. In the 'seminarium philo-logicum' which J. M. Gesner (1679–1761) established at the University of Göttingen (founded in 1753) there developed a form of teaching and learning which was to spread through every German university in the next century and to give German classical scholarship one of its special characteristics. From Göttingen too, and the climate created by its scientific and technical departments, came the major impulse towards making the regular publication of the results of original research the prime duty of a university classics teacher. The supremacy in classical scholarship which The Netherlands took from France in the late sixteenth century passed in the early nineteenth to Germany.

The excitement generated in German literary circles by the archaeological discoveries being made in the old classical lands spread quickly to the universities. Their secular character enabled them to take in without difficulty the study of ancient art, with its emphasis on the naked human form. The versions of Greek and Roman history left by the classical historians underwent sceptical criticism, and efforts were made to utilize the fast-growing mass of inscriptional evidence in the study of ancient social and political institutions. The discovery of how Greek and Latin related to the old languages of the Celts, Germans, and Indians revolutionized grammar. Archaeology and comparative linguistics combined to feed a burgeoning interest in the early form of Greek religion. A notion that the ancient Germans were more closely related to the ancient Greeks than to any of the other Indo-European peoples took hold, and the humanism of the fifteenth and sixteenth centuries, with its emphasis on Christian Rome, gave way to enthusiasm for a classical civilization imagined to be essentially Greek and essentially pagan. Nevertheless, Latin remained the language of the seminar and of scholarly publication.

England arrogated to itself the credit for the defeat of Napoleonic France's imperial ambitions and, although it was undergoing transformation at the economic base, delayed taking steps to renovate its ancient institutions. For most of the nineteenth century the Anglican Church kept control of the universities and the secondary schools which fed them. The position of classical studies in the Oxford curriculum remained much as it had been in Laud's day: likewise the way these studies were pursued. What blocked radical change for so long was in large measure the prestige won by the public examination which at the beginning of the century had replaced the old disputations as the climax of the exercises for the Baccalaureate in Arts. The candidate had to offer himself for an 'ordinary' test or for a more 'solemn' one held in the Easter Term, at which 'honours' were awarded. By 1809 there were separate special tests in the 'Literae Humaniores'—defined as 'the Greek and Latin Languages, rhetoric and moral philo-

BANNER OF THE BLESSED VIRGIN MARY, crowned and adored by angels, painted on damask silk, and presented to St John's College by the father of Edmund Campion. A potent symbol of the old order. A fellow of St John's, Edmund entered the Society of Jesus in 1573, and was executed at Tyburn on 1 December 1581.

THE ARUNDEL ANTIQUITIES as the Vice-Chancellor of 1757 perceived them. The copper engraving for the University Almanack sought to exhibit 'the connexion of the studies of antiquity, sculpture and architecture, with what is usually called academical learning . . . The University, attended by her three Faculties, is introduced from her gothic retirement by Minerva to the knowledge of these arts'.

sophy in so far as they are derived from the ancient authors'—and in the 'Disciplinae Mathematicae et Physicae'. Either test or both could be taken by the man who wanted an honours degree. The names of successful candidates were posted in classes of descending merit for all to see. This form of the final examination was by 1820 known as the 'Great-go'; the preliminary examination—officially 'Responsions' after the ancient *responsio*—as the 'Little-go'. Few attempted the mathematical test, but the one in Literae Humaniores attracted more and more candidates each year. It was otherwise in Cambridge, where a parallel development in the mode of examining maintained the primacy of mathematics.

In 1830 the scope of Oxford's Literae Humaniores was redefined as comprising 'the histories of Greece and Rome, rhetoric and poetry and moral and political science in so far as they may be derived from the ancient Greek and Roman writers, and illustrated, if need be, from modern authors, with Logic and with Composition (in Latin)'. Philosophy soon came to dominate the examination, Joseph Butler's *Analogy of Religion* (first published in 1736) being the first 'modern' text to enter the syllabus. In 1850 the examination was split into two: the first, controlled by so-called 'Moderators' and called 'Moderations', comprised 'pure' scholarship; the second demanded composition in Greek and Latin prose and translation from prescribed books, but the main emphasis lay on philosophy, modern as well as classical, and on ancient history and antiquities. By 1853 'Smalls' and 'Greats' had replaced 'Little-go' and 'Great-go' in common parlance. The official term 'Moderations' soon came to be abbreviated to 'Mods'.

Written papers began very early in the century to take up the major part of the honours examination in Literae Humaniores. The position of University Examiner acquired great prestige, the powers of appointment being jealously guarded by the heads of the colleges. Ambitious men sought honours in the way such had once sought patrons. Among those ranked in the first class between 1801 and 1850 were two future Prime Ministers, Robert Peel (1788–1850) and W. E. Gladstone (1809–98)—both, it may be noted, men from outside the old aristocracy—and a considerable number of others destined to become Parliamentarians of distinction. As college fellowships became more competitive and the manner of election more objective, a ranking in Literae Humaniores below the first class proved ever more of a handicap. Many of the older tutors found the task of preparing their men for the ordeal too much for them, and there came into existence the private coach, who, in return for a fee, imparted skill in handling a particular area of the examination. It did not escape remark that the new competitiveness reflected more the ethos of the rising commercial classes than that of the landed aristocracy and gentry, with their reliance on networks of patronage. Few of the Oxford-educated aristocrats who gained Parliamentary prominence in the nineteenth century had accepted the honours challenge. On the other hand, no man ranked in the first class by the examiners between 1801 and 1850 achieved through his later efforts in the world of learning a parallel ranking in the opinion of Continental classical scholars.

A conscious effort was made to keep the Literae Humaniores curriculum a plausible preparation both for the Anglican clergyman, whose assimilation of the values of the landed classes set him apart from the priests of other lands and other forms of Christian cult, and for the man of affairs. Hence, no doubt, the prominence of philosophy and the low profile of the more exact forms of scholarship. The University had many critics in regard both to the absence of non-classical subjects and to the restricted nature of the actual classical instruction provided. To some it appeared to offer a peculiarly unsatisfactory training for priests. In their eyes Aristotle, 'that uncircumcised and unbaptized Philistine of the schools', played an excessive role. To others the University's studies seemed good enough for priests but not for men of affairs in a much-changed world. Many looked to the German universities as offering a pattern for reform. A tutor of the old type and at the same time one of the most successful of the new examiners, Edward Copleston (1776–1849), defended vigorously and confidently what went on, arguing that 'the cultivation of literature raised men above an illiberal absorption in their

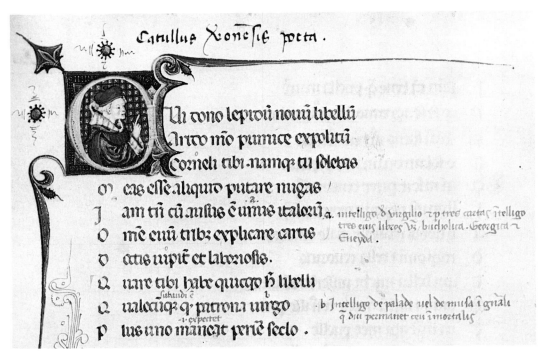

Catullus Veronensis poeta.

Un dono lepidum nouum libellum
Unico mio pumice expliciti
Corneli tibi namque tu solebas

o eas esse aliquid putare nugas
i am tū cū ausus ē uniuus italorū   a. intelligo d virgilio tp tres cartas intelligo
o me eum tibz explicare cartis   tres eius libros vz. bucholica. Georgica z
o atis iupit et laboriosis.   Eneydd.
a uute tibi habe quicqd h libelli
a ualecūq quod patrona uirgo   b Intelligo de palade uel de musa ī gnāli
p lus uno maneat perne seclo.   q diu permanet ceu ī mortālis

A GAISFORD PURCHASE. Catullus' first poem as it appears in a codex of the Canonici collection purchased for the Bodleian Library in 1817 on Gaisford's initiative. The illuminator of the codex, made in Italy c.1400, has depicted the ancient poet as a Master of Arts taking part in a disputation. Robinson Ellis (see pp. 179, 180) consulted the codex but failed to realize its importance.

specialised pursuits and strengthened the basic qualities of the mind', and that 'no literature fulfilled this office better than that of the classical authors'. For Copleston the University's task was to turn out leaders, not critics; research of the German type had no place in it.

Scholarship of a quality at least comparable with that to be found in Cambridge and on the Continent was not entirely absent from early-nineteenth-century Oxford. Of the ten Englishmen who in 1820 seemed to Samuel Parr (1747–1825) to be the luminaries of the time, two had been educated there: Peter Elmsley (1773–1825) and Thomas Gaisford (1799–1855). Elmsley was an extremely wealthy man, and after graduation travelled widely in France and Italy studying manuscripts of the Attic tragedians. He was elected Camden Professor of Ancient History in 1823. What he published won admiration from the Cambridge disciples of Richard Porson (1759–1808). He could not, however, be ranked as a scholar anywhere near the University of Leipzig's Gottfried Hermann (1772–1848). Gaisford became a Student of Christ Church on graduation but regularly sought intellectual companionship among studious men in Holland and Germany. He was appointed the Regius Professor of Greek in 1812. Although he did not possess the acuity of an Immanuel Bekker (1785–1871) or a Wilhelm Dindorf (1802–83), he equalled these scholars in industry and fertility of publication, making intelligent use of the resources he had himself as a curator helped to gather in the Bodleian Library. His editions of treatises on grammar, of lexica, and of scholia preserving remnants of ancient literary commentaries were little read in Oxford but found appreciative users on the Continent.

During Gaisford's long occupancy of the Regius Chair few younger men pursued his kind of scholarship with any zeal. H. G. Liddell (1811–98) and Robert Scott (1811–87) produced in 1843 a Greek dictionary largely based on the work of J. G. Schneider (1750–1822) as extended by Franz Passow (1786–1833). Like the two Germans, they abandoned Latin as the medium of explicating the vocabulary of Greek. They received encouragement from Gaisford and continued to supplement their work as it went through successive editions. Its purpose, however—this needs to be stressed—was to assist the schoolboy and undergraduate rather than to establish Greek lexicography on a sound scientific basis. It did not bear comparison with the revision of Henri Estienne's *Thesaurus Linguae Graecae* brought out by K. B. Hase (1780–1864) and the brothers Dindorf in Paris between 1831 and 1865. Nevertheless, its success signalized the growing importance of Greek in English classical studies.

Those who reported to Queen Victoria in 1853 'on the organisation of the permanent civil service' stated their admiration of the way Oxford and Cambridge tested 'the staple of classics and mathematics'. The committee which reported to the President of the Board of Control in 1854 'on the reform of the public admission to the civil service of the East India Company' recommended a competitive test clearly modelled on those operated by the two universities. A subtly different rationale for classical studies from the one defended by Copleston can be discerned in this committee's statement: 'skill in Greek and Latin versification has indeed no direct tendency to form a judge, a financier, or a diplomatist. But the youth who does best what all the ablest and most ambitious youths about him are trying to do well will generally prove a superior man.' Enormous changes ensued in the composition of the top levels of the two services. 'Greats' men soon dominated both—the guardians of Platonic Republics, so to speak—and their success helped to keep the form of 'Mods' and 'Greats' steady and their results respected through more than a century of change in the general pattern of Oxford's studies.

Not everybody at Oxford approved wholeheartedly of the kind of regime which produced a first-class Greats man. Mark Pattison (1813–84) frequently complained that Oxford treated the pagan classics merely as a propaedeutic to the Christian Gospel and that its curriculum no longer provided an adequate mental culture for the young. Outside Oxford criticism of the classicist monopoly grew intense. It is noteworthy how much those who reported on the two civil services, despite their respect for English educational tradition, stressed the value of some of the newer studies. Separate 'Schools' of Mathematics and Natural Sciences and a new one of Jurisprudence and Modern History were created in 1850, but for a long time it was necessary for a man interested in one of these schools also to be examined in Literae Humaniores. Although five further schools had been created before the outbreak of war with Germany in 1914,

Literae Humaniores remained the largest; it attracted the best candidates and could shrug off criticism made from both within and without. A young man of academic ambitions still frequently took Greats before he submitted to examination in the school of his real interest. The Professors of History, Law, and Theology continued to be Greats men until far into the twentieth century. The sustained effort begun in 1890 by the growing contingent of University teachers in the natural sciences to have Greek removed from Responsions was still short of its goal in 1914.

The Reform Act of 1854 struck down the religious tests for matriculation. It gave Congregation a large role in the government of the University and permission to use English rather than Latin in debate. New statutes were henceforth to be drafted in English. The term 'Literae Humaniores' stayed less out of respect for tradition than because the emphasis on Ancient History and Philosophy and the inclusion in the syllabus

VESTIBULE OF THE EXAMINATION SCHOOLS (*right*), a building conceived in 1858 and constructed between 1876 and 1882 to the design of T. G. Jackson. The principal purpose was to provide space for the growing amount of University examining. In a speech deploring the state of Oxford's archaeological collections A. J. Evans (1851–1941) remarked on 'the scandalous way in which the University has been impoverished in order to build its Marble Palace of Examinations'.

THE TERROR OF THE EXAMINERS (*below*). A cartoon drawn around 1870. 'Adolphus' wanted only a pass degree. The 'ordinary' final examination still consisted of mathematics, classics, and divinity. Private 'coaches' did the bulk of the actual teaching. Represented here are C. J. C. Price, a fellow of Exeter College, M. J. Turrell, a well-known professional coach, and R. Gandell, the Laudian Professor of Arabic.

of English philosophical texts ruled out a literal translation like 'Classics' or 'Classical Literature'. The abolition in 1871 of the remaining University and college religious tests foreshadowed the dissolution of the curious Oxford alliance between Anglicanism and classical studies. Much more immediate were the effects of the Reform Act of 1876: the abolition of celibacy as a requirement for the tenure of a college fellowship; the creation of short-term fellowships for the specific purpose of carrying out research; the setting up of Boards of Studies with powers in regard to the design of the syllabuses; and the consequent restructuring of the faculties of the University.

If in the third quarter of the century the still much-touted unity of Oxford classical studies had any reality, the new structure of faculties, based rather more on the pattern of examining than on intellectual considerations, maimed it severely. The Regius Professor of Civil Law went into the Faculty of Jurisprudence and took Roman law with him. Palaeography went into the Faculty of History. Philosophy, on the other hand, accompanied Greek, Latin, and Graeco-Roman history into the Faculty of Literae Humaniores. Poetry came in, although the Professor of this subject had ceased to lecture in Latin and did not restrict himself to the Greek and Latin classics. So too did comparative philology, although the practitioners of this subject gave no special status to Greek and Latin among the so-called 'Indo-Germanic' or 'Indo-European' languages. Archaeology could of its nature have little to do with literature, and was to be defined in such a way as not to exclude barbarian antiquities; nevertheless, when a professor finally came to be appointed he was assigned to the Faculty of Literae Humaniores.

From 1855 candidates for 'Mods' and 'Greats' who did not belong to the Anglican Church were permitted to substitute pagan Greek books for the Gospels and the Acts of the Apostles. Men in holy orders nevertheless still dictated the tone of the colleges and continued to do so even after 1871. Among the several factors in Oxford's unwillingness to accept archaeological studies was the ancient Judaic dislike of the representations of the naked male and female form beloved of Greek artists and their patrons. The clerical spirit took on various new guises. Women were grudgingly permitted to offer themselves for the classical Mods examination in 1884, but not for Greats until several more years had passed. As late as the 1890s many college tutors were denouncing a proposal to remove Greek from Responsions as a veiled attack on the Christian religion.

The teaching of the classical curriculum remained effectively in the hands of the colleges. Many of these treated research quite openly as an activity which could only divert a tutorial fellow from proper attention to his pupils and the social obligations of college life. Specialization went no further than separating instruction in the subjects constituting Mods from instruction in ancient history and philosophy, the principal constituents of Greats. The classical professoriate had difficulty in defining a role for itself, and made no open resistance to the pressures of collegiate tradition.

The insularity and backwardness of Oxonian classical scholarship in the middle of the nineteenth century resulted to some extent from the narrowness of the base of recruitment into the colleges and of appointment to teaching positions. The graduates of the University of Glasgow who came into Balliol College with a Snell Exhibition to read for a second bachelor's degree were for long almost the only foreign leavening to the southern English and Welsh dough. The affiliation statutes passed from 1880 onwards made it easier for other Scottish universities and for the new English and colonial institutions to send men to Oxford. The Scottish universities had by the second half of the nineteenth century lost confidence in themselves, and the more recent foundations were still seeking an identity. They tried as far as they could to recruit their classical teachers from the ancient colleges of Oxford, Cambridge, and Dublin. Believing their own graduates to need a finishing elsewhere, they sent the more linguistically able to Cambridge and those with interests in philosophy and history to Oxford. The Rhodes Scholars who started to arrive in quite large numbers from the colonies and the

AN APHRODITE WITHOUT HER CLOTHES copied in the imperial period from a well-known Hellenistic original. The statue had excited Francis Bacon and other visitors to Lord Arundel's London home. The Oxford authorities kept it well hidden between 1755, when they acquired it, and the end of the nineteenth century. Not, of course, for aesthetic reasons.

United States in 1902 rarely had the grounding to cope with Mods or Greats. It could be that a desire to cater for the obvious talent of these men had more effect on the general pattern of Oxford's curricula that any pressure for change which had come or was to come from British Governments.

On Gaisford's death in 1855, the Regius Chair of Greek went to Benjamin Jowett (1817–93), a somewhat unorthodox clergyman who had made a name for himself as a Balliol tutor and as a University examiner. Unlike Gaisford, Jowett delivered lectures, lectures which are now famous for the scorn they provoked from the young A. E. Housman (1859–1936). Jowett despised the 'pamphlets, periodicals and programmes' of the Germans and saw his main professorial duty as making known to a wide public the most important Greek authors. He retained the chair even after being elected Master of Balliol. In the latter capacity he encouraged the revival of dramatic activity in the University, permitting the hall of Balliol to be used for a performance of Aeschylus' *Agamemnon* in 1880. Jowett was succeeded in 1893 by a protégé of Pattison's, the layman Ingram Bywater (1840–1914). Bywater lacked Pattison's rebellious spirit and penetrating hindsight, but possessed in abundance both political shrewdness and diplomatic tact. He was admired in Germany itself for the precise scholarship of his 1877 collection of the fragments of the early Ionian philosopher Heraclitus. In 1908 the Regius Chair was awarded to Gilbert Murray (1866–1957), who had spent ten years in the chair of Greek at Glasgow and had translated some of Euripides' tragedies for performance on the London stage. Although hostile to clerics as a class, Murray possessed a vague religiosity extracted from his reading of the Greek classics. He chased after intellectual fashions, admiring the literary criticism of A. W. Verrall (1851–1912) and the anthropology of J. E. Harrison (1850–1928). In the tradition of Jowett, he wanted to introduce to a wider public something which he called the Greek 'spirit' and which he thought he could distinguish from the Greek language. He excited undergraduates with his Glasgow-style lectures as much as he irritated some of their elderly tutors with his opinions. Housman, who was a friend of Murray's, thought he could have been a first-rate scholar if he had not preferred to be a second-rate man of letters.

In the course of the first half of the nineteenth century serious-minded undergraduates, the so-called 'reading men', came to study the logical, rhetorical, metaphysical, and ethical writings of Aristotle in the original Greek rather than in Latin or English. Some of the dialogues of Plato took a place near the centre of the syllabus. English philosophical works crept in gradually at the edges. The college tutors felt themselves to be the spiritual heirs of Plato (as much perhaps as of Jesus Christ) and struggled against the empiricist lines of thought which had developed among secular-minded men in London, Cambridge, and Edinburgh since the seventeenth-century civil wars. However, the major influence on their own thinking in fact came more from the writings of the Germans Immanuel Kant and G. W. F. Hegel than from Plato. In the years between 1854 and 1914 little changed. Few college tutors or professors, the most distinguished of whom was T. H. Green (1836–82), left much in writing behind them.

ROBINSON ELLIS as sketched by Giovanni Casanova in 1902. The archetypal eccentric professor, a joy to caricaturists and to story-tellers.

History entered the syllabus for the final examination in Literae Humaniores in 1830, and was given greater importance by the reform of 1850 (see above, p. 171). When George Rawlinson (1812–1902), a clerical professor of the old style, retired in 1889, the Camden Chair went to H. F. Pelham (1846–1907), who admired the kind of historical research pursued and promoted in Berlin by Theodor Mommsen (1817–1903). The chair passed from Pelham to F. J. Haverfield (1860–1919), in whose epigraphical studies Mommsen had taken a benevolent interest. Mommsen also exercised a strong influence through his pupil the Russian P. G. Vinogradoff (1854–1925); on arrival in Oxford in 1903 the latter established within the Faculty of Law a seminar of the Berlin type.

It may seem strange today that Oxford had no professor of Latin literature before 1854. To most college tutors of that time, however, Latin was just something one picked up at school and polished a little at university; they felt they could themselves do everything needed. The readership in the arts of *humanitas* established by Richard Foxe (see above, p. 163) was resurrected as the 'Corpus Christi Professorship of the Latin Language and Literature'. The first two holders of the new chair, John Conington (1825–69) and Edwin Palmer (1824–95), did not quite know what to do with it. Conington, who had avoided holy orders and shown other signs of independence in his youth, abandoned himself in middle age, in Pattison's bitter words, 'to the laziest of all occupations with the classics, namely of translating them into English'. Henry Nettleship (1839–93), who had been an undergraduate at Lincoln College and on Pattison's advice had gone in 1864 to hear the lectures of Moriz Haupt (1808–74) in Berlin, spent fifteen years in the chair. An attempt to construct a new Latin dictionary proved too much for his physical constitution and the resources available. His successor, Robinson Ellis (1834–1913), possessed a genuinely scholarly interest in various Latin poets not much read in clerical Oxford and an urge to study the medieval manuscripts which carried their works. His intellect did not, however, match his industry. The work of his successor, A. C. Clarke (1859–1937), enjoyed more respect abroad, but Clarke's career ran its course under the shadow cast by the two great men of late-nineteenth-century British Latin scholarship, A. E. Housman, who failed Greats in 1881 but became Professor of Latin at Cambridge thirty years later, and W. M. Lindsay (1858–1937), who exchanged a tutorship of Jesus College in 1899 for a professorial chair in his native Scotland.

The polyglot German immigrant Max Müller (1823–1900), who had studied in Berlin under the comparativist Franz Bopp (1791–1867), secured in 1869 a transfer from his Chair of Modern Languages to a new Chair of Comparative Philology. Müller's friend A. H. Sayce (1845–1933), who had been to Leipzig to hear Georg Curtius (1820–85), acted as his deputy from 1876 to 1890. The extra-linguistic theorizings of Müller and Sayce served to confirm the comfortable belief of the mass of the college tutors that the study of Greek and Latin could derive no real benefit from that of the cognate languages.

There had been several attempts over the centuries, mostly from outside or from the academic margin, to interest Oxford in the material remains of the classical past. An archaeologist had been proposed from inside for the Regius Chair of Greek in 1855, namely C. T. Newton (1816–94), the excavator of Halicarnassus. W. H. Pater (1839–94), a tutor in philosophy at Brasenose College, had constructed out of the writings of Plato, Winckelmann, and Ruskin a view of Greek art and architecture which Greats men could at least entertain. The 1877–81 Commissioners recommended the establishment of a chair devoted specifically to archaeology. An acrimonious debate ensued about the definition of the professor's duties. Some felt that all places and all periods ought to fall within his purview. Those who held that only Greece and Italy should be covered and that time should stop not long after the beginning of the Christian era got most of their way.

ART AND THE GREEK HEROES. The decorator of a Theban skyphos of the late fifth century BC, purchased for the Ashmolean Museum in 1892, has represented, perhaps on the basis of a local farce, Odysseus' escape from shipwreck and his encounter with Circe. The drawings contrast interestingly with the way the epic poet Homer handled the story.

The first man appointed to the new 'Lincoln Chair of Classical Archaeology and Art' was W. M. Ramsay (1851–1939), who found he could not live in Oxford on the salary provided. His continuing interest in topography and epigraphy did not in any case appeal either to the traditionalists or to those who wanted to change the whole direction of Oxford's studies. He was replaced in 1887 by Percy Gardner (1846–1937), a Cambridge graduate who had made his name as a numismatist at the British Museum and looked down his nose at the cultures which preceded and followed that of the classical era. Gardner agitated to have archaeology made an integral part of the Greats syllabus. He believed that the bookish kind of classical studies begun in the English public schools and continued at Oxford caused the natural love of the beautiful to dry up in the young and made them blind to the physical details of their environment. Optional papers with an archaeological link were added at his urging to the Mods and Greats examinations in 1890. More ambitious proposals failed in the face of an opposition which included men not hostile to archaeological research as such but sceptical of the educational value claimed for it by enthusiasts.

COLUMN OF A PAPYRUS ROLL. The roll, which originally contained the first two books of the *Iliad*, was found by Flinders Petrie in 1887 propping up the head of a mummified corpse in the cemetery of Hawara. It was presented to the Bodleian Library by Jesse Haworth, a wealthy Manchester textile merchant who financed Petrie's excavations.

The intensive archaeological investigations which commenced in Egypt when Napoleon ended the rule of the Mamelukes in 1798 continued through the nineteenth century. From the 1870s onwards remnants of papyrus books of the Ptolemaic (332–30 BC) and Romano-Byzantine (30 BC–AD 642) periods began to be found in large numbers and to make their way to libraries in the more prosperous centres of European culture. Sayce, who retired from a fellowship at Queen's in 1890 to reside in Egypt, played an important role in acquiring material for the Bodleian Library as well as for the British Museum. Clarke spotted the talent of two of his Queen's pupils, B. P. Grenfell (1869–1926) and A. S. Hunt (1871–1934), and encouraged them to go to Egypt, learn the techniques of excavation from the likes of W. M. Flinders Petrie (1853–1942), and look specifically for papyri. The new kinds of University and college research fellowships helped to maintain the two men abroad for many years. They found much and distinguished themselves by the manner in which they published their finds. Grenfell was appointed Professor of Papyrology in 1905, but little attempt was made to organize teaching of the new science. The Balliol tutors of Edgar Lobel (1889–1982) sent him after a first in Greats (1911) to teach Latin prose composition for the Professor of Humanity in Edinburgh. Murray and Hunt saw that he was capable of better things, and on their advice he went to Berlin to study with the eminent German papyrologist

Wilhelm Schubart (1873–1960) and to listen to the by then almost legendary Ulrich von Wilamowitz-Moellendorff (1848–1931).

The effects on Oxford's studies of Britain's losses in the 1914–18 war, of the decisions announced in 1917 concerning the future administration of India, and of the economic depression which hit the country in the 1920s, to say nothing of the syllabuses followed in the State-supported secondary schools after the 1902 Education Act, were ultimately profound, but they took a long time to manifest themselves clearly. Greats men still headed most of the colleges when the war ended. Those who had struggled so long to do away with the compulsion upon all undergraduates to study Greek finally succeeded in 1920. Latin, however, continued to be demanded in Responsions. The absolute numbers enrolling each year for Literae Humaniores stayed steady, and the calibre of the best seemed to be as good as ever. The classical teachers who returned from civil and military postings in 1918 were in no mood to change anything, those who had been in actual combat being the most conservative of all. The war and its result seemed to confirm early-nineteenth-century feelings about the direction of German university

GREEK'S SHORT-LIVED VICTORY. This card accompanied a reproduction of a bronze head of a young athletic victor, presented to Thomas Case, the President of Corpus Christi College, by those who helped him to persuade Convocation to vote down in 1911 a proposal to make Greek no longer compulsory for Responsions. Case was a man better known for his sporting than for his intellectual powers.

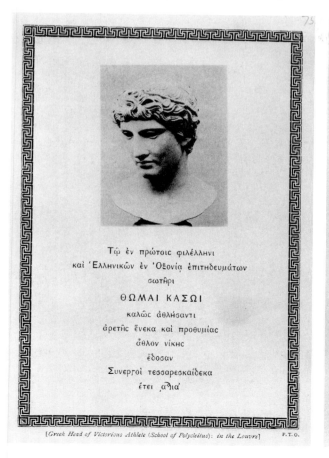

Τῷ ἐν πρώτοις φιλέλληνι
καὶ Ἑλληνικῶν ἐν Ὀξονίᾳ ἐπιτηδευμάτων
σωτῆρι
ΘΩΜΑΙ ΚΑΣΩΙ
καλῶς ἀθλήσαντι
ἀρετῆς ἕνεκα καὶ προθυμίας
ἄθλον νίκης
ἔδοσαν
Συνεργοὶ τεσσαρεσκαίδεκα
ἔτει ͵αϠια´

[*Greek Head of Victorious Athlete (School of Polycleitus): in the Louvre*]   P.T.O.

Preservation of Greek at Oxford

Date.				For Greek.	Against.
CONGREGATION.					
Nov. 11, 1902	...	...	...	189	166
Feb. 9, 1904	...	...	...	164	162
				131	102
Nov. 29, 1904	...	...	...	200	164
Nov. 22, 1910	...	...	...	188	152
May 16, 1911	...	...	...	79	156
CONVOCATION.					
Nov. 28, 1911	...	...	...	595	360

The Six
Oct. 23, 1911

T. CASE, Pres. of C.C.C.
G. DICKINS, St. John's.
F. A. DIXEY. Wadham.
F. MADAN, B. N. C.
T. C. SNOW, St. John's.
W. H. STEVENSON, St. John's.

A. W. CAVE, Magd.   H. LE B. LIGHTFOOT, C.C.C.
C. D. FISHER, Ch. Ch.   J. MURRAY, Ch. Ch.
R. W. T. GÜNTHER, Magd.   C. PLUMMER, C. C. C.
A. HASSALL, Ch. Ch.   F. C. S. SCHILLER, C C C.
          A. K. SLESSOR, Ch. Ch.
Christ Church]   [*Jan. 24, 1912*

P.T.O.

education. The exercises of composition in verse and prose continued to dominate the Mods examination. Some tutors treated these as an activity with its own internal justification; others believed that there was no better way in which to acquaint serious students with the particular literary qualities of the best Greek and Latin authors. On the other hand, the philosophical half of Greats took in more and more modern logic as the years passed, and the historical half more and more argument arising from non-literary evidence.

Oxford as a whole was in fact gradually losing its classicist character. The Schools of Modern History, Jurisprudence, English, and Modern Languages competed more and more successfully with that of Literae Humaniores for entrants. Several more new schools were created between 1918 and 1939. That of Philosophy, Politics, and Economics (dubbed 'Modern Greats' before it became 'PPE') gave the philosophers a second constituency and moved their interests even further from what the ancient thinkers had written. It became a magnet for men of the kind of ambition Greats had once satisfied.

The professoriate of the Faculty of Literae Humaniores was externally little touched by the war. It is possible, however, to detect something of a loss of heart. No one

GILBERT MURRAY in the company of three actresses, Mary Newcomb (*left*), Vivienne Bennett (*front*), and Evelyn Hall, at the Old Vic in 1935. The translation of Euripides' *Hippolytus* made in 1901 and first staged in 1904 at the Lyric Theatre was undergoing yet another revival.

LEKYTHOS ADMIRED BY J. D.
BEAZLEY. The figure represented is
the goddess Victory. Beazley put the
vase, made and decorated at Athens in
the early fifth century BC, together with
forty others as the work of the 'Master
of the Boston Pan-Krater' in 1912. It
had been obtained in 1890 in Gela by
A. J. Evans, who thought it was of local
Sicilian origin.

V. 312.

occupied himself seriously with the subject of his chair. Murray gave most of his energy to preaching on international affairs and what remained to writing books addressed as much to the general public as to scholars.

The Chair of Classical Archaeology and Art went on Gardner's retirement in 1925 to a local product, one of Gardner's own pupils, J. D. Beazley (1885–1970), who had already made a European and transatlantic name for himself through applying to Attic painted pottery, in a strikingly systematic way, the methods which Giovanni Morelli (1816–91) developed to distinguish the painters of the Italian Renaissance. The memory of Beazley's brilliance as an undergraduate, the competence in Greek and Latin he showed as a Mods tutor in Christ Church, and the obvious quality of his intellect made him generally acceptable within a Faculty of Literae Humaniores somewhat different from the one with which Gardner did battle. Beazley for his part showed himself aware of the limitations of archaeological studies in a way most enthusiasts were not. He did not take part in efforts to extend the role of such studies in either Mods or Greats.

When Clarke retired in 1935 the only man in Oxford of any standing in Latin studies was E. A. Barber (1888–1965). Although both Housman and Lindsay had continued to labour productively in other places, neither succeeded in finding a pupil of any great promise. There had, however, just arrived in Cambridge a refugee from the National Socialist regime in Germany, Eduard Fraenkel (1888–1970), a pupil of Wilamowitz who had held chairs in Kiel, Göttingen, and Freiburg. A comparison of what Fraenkel and Barber had published by 1935 shows the enormous gap which still existed between Germany's Latin and Oxford's. Oxford swallowed its pride and elected an alien for the first time to the Corpus Christi Chair.

If Greek scholarship had been the criterion, the best man to have succeeded Murray was Edgar Lobel, who on Hunt's death in 1934 had been entrusted with those literary papyri from Oxyrhynchus that remained unpublished. Lobel made obvious his total lack of interest in holding the Regius Chair, and Murray found it easy to impose on the Prime Minister a man of his own stamp, E. R. Dodds (1893–1979).

GREEK STATER (x2) struck in Tarsus early in the fourth century BC for a Persian satrap (note the obverse) needing to pay Greek mercenary troops (note the reverse). The coin was presented, like many, to supplement the Ashmolean Museum's Greek collection by E. S. G. Robinson, a pupil of Percy Gardner's who became a University Reader in Greek Numismatics.

Inscriptions on stone, papyrus documents, and numismatic data won increasing attention from Oxford's ancient historians in the period between the wars. A change in the intellectual climate, as much as the bequest of C. B. Heberden (1849–1921), enabled the University's scattered collections of Greek and Roman coins to be brought together in the Ashmolean Museum in 1922.

The results of the revision of Liddell and Scott's Greek dictionary, which Henry Stuart Jones (1867–1939) had commenced in 1911, saw the light of day between 1925 and 1940 in ten successive fascicles. Stuart Jones had the assistance from 1920 to 1937 of the philologically expert Roderick McKenzie (1887–1937). The revised dictionary was a considerable achievement. Work on a much more ambitious revision of Passow's lexicon began around the same time in Germany under the management of Wilhelm Crönert (1874–1942), but had failed to get going again after 1918.

Between Adolf Hitler's assumption of power in Germany in 1933 and the outbreak of the Second World War many refugee scholars received a welcome in Oxford. Among them were classical philologists, like the above-mentioned Eduard Fraenkel, classical archaeologists, students of classical philosophy, ancient historians, and Roman lawyers. Oxford gave these men and others something more than physical shelter. The development in the University in the late nineteenth and early twentieth centuries of certain specialized branches of study—epigraphy, codicology, papyrology, art history, and numismatics in particular—the continuing strength of the traditional form of classical education in the schools which fed the colleges, and the tolerance of the southern English for erudite eccentricity had created an environment in which the marvellous talents of the refugees could continue to bear fruit; it was otherwise with most of those who ended up in the United States or in one of Britain's more recent overseas colonies. The ways in which undergraduates were prepared for Mods and Greats underwent little change as a result of the immigrant presence. Nevertheless, by 1945 Oxford was spoken of by many Continental classicists as 'the best German University in Europe', and many of their pupils came to further their studies there.

ROMAN DENARIUS (x2) struck in a Greek mint in 42 BC by M. Junius Brutus, who had engineered the assassination of Julius Caesar allegedly in the interest of republican liberty. The reverse has the cap of liberty between two daggers and the inscription EID[IBVS] MAR[TIIS] 'on the Ides of March'. The obverse with Brutus' own head prompts another view of historical reality.

EDUARD FRAENKEL amid his books. Two railway wagons were required to remove them from Germany in 1934. When Fraenkel retired from the Chair of Latin in 1953, such was his standing that Corpus Christi College permitted him to retain a set of rooms where 'the symbiosis between him and his books might continue'.

The Second World War did not depress the spirit of the University in the way the First had done. Most of the pre-war members of the Faculty of Literae Humaniores survived. The posts which they had filled in the service of the State stretched their talents in new ways and increased that peculiar form of self-confidence which success in the Mods and Greats examinations conferred. Bright young men returned to complete their studies. Others equally bright began, most of them from the old public schools with their powerful systems of classical instruction still intact; an increasing number, however, came from State-maintained grammar schools, making up in intelligence, industry, and ambition what they lacked in linguistic preparation. The universities of Scotland and the former colonies continued to send a proportion of their best graduates in classics to sit the Greats examination. Literae Humaniores radiated a glow none of the newer schools could quite match. Most of the colleges still had Greats men at the top. The tutors picked up the threads of their pre-war careers and went on as if nothing had changed. A remarkable number of those who had been appointed to readerships and professorships before 1939 resumed a vigorously productive way of life and continued long after formal retirement to exercise an influence on younger scholars. The new professors had a style about them which drew attention to their subjects outside the faculty.

The White Chair of Moral Philosophy (see above, p. 166), the Waynflete Chair of Moral and Metaphysical Philosophy, and the Wykeham Chair of Logic (the latter two were founded during the period of reform in the second half of the nineteenth century) had long been occupied by Greats men who taught an amalgam of Plato, Aristotle, and the German idealists. Gilbert Ryle (1900–76), who had proceeded from Mods and Greats to the newly established 'PPE' and had then as a Christ Church tutor gained notoriety for a highly unclassical, highly un-Oxonian view of the relationship of mind and body, was elected to the Waynflete Chair in 1945. Ryle's kind of thinking already had its own momentum in Oxford when F. Waismann (1896–1959), the chief organizer of the famous 'Vienna Circle', took up residence there in 1938 after Austria was absorbed into the Third Reich. Two other Greats men, A. J. Ayer (1910–89) and J. L. Austin (1911–60), helped Ryle complete the divorce of Oxford philosophy from the classical tradition. Thenceforth it was hard to hold that Plato and Aristotle could make a contribution to debate about live issues. Austin was elected to the White Chair in 1952 and Ayer to the Wykeham Chair in 1959.

On the resignation of H. M. Last (1895–1957) in 1948 a man of very different cast succeeded to the Camden Chair of Ancient History. Ronald Syme (1903–89) had come to Oxford from New Zealand in 1925 to do Greats. His abiding interest proved to be in the men, particularly those from the provinces, who made the Roman system of government and administration work. The new techniques of prosopography attracted him more than the intricate abstractions of constitutional law. A book published on the eve of the war, which presented a portrait of the Emperor Augustus, one of Last's heroes, coloured by what Syme had observed of the dictators of Russia, Italy, Germany, and Spain, was the source of his public reputation.

In 1952 G. E. K. Braunholtz (1887–1967), who listed no publications in *Who's Who*, was replaced in the Chair of Comparative Philology by L. R. Palmer (1906–84), a man trained in Cambridge and Vienna whose pen never lay still. The latter's election coincided with the claim by Michael Ventris (1922–56) to have deciphered the language of the so-called Linear B tablets found at Cnossos on the island of Crete in 1900 by A. J. Evans (1851–1941), then Keeper of the Ashmolean Museum. Palmer had no doubt that Ventris was right, that the language was a second-millennium form of Greek, and threw himself both into interpreting the new texts and into discussing their significance for the history of the early Aegean states. Excursions into archaeology and use of the *Observer* newspaper and the BBC to propagate his views scandalized many of Palmer's colleagues.

Fraenkel retired from the Corpus Christi Chair of the Latin Language and Literature in 1953, to be succeeded by R. A. B. Mynors (1903–89), a Balliol Greats man more like Fraenkel's predecessors. The German philologist had practically annexed Greek literature to the Latin chair. He was permitted after retirement to continue the seminar he had instituted on the model of those of Göttingen and Berlin. Here he applied to a simultaneous textual and literary interpretation of a range of traditionally admired works of poetry a vast acquaintance with every aspect of Greek and Roman life. The concept of a single science of antiquity which Fraenkel had imbibed from Wilamowitz came in the course of time to merge in the general consciousness with Oxford's willingness to cover everything from modern logic to archaeological stratification under the now almost magical term 'Literae Humaniores'. Fraenkel's spiritual home lay in the library of Ptolemaic Alexandria. Mynors, on the other hand, would have been more at his ease in the scriptorium of a medieval monastery.

In 1956 Beazley was followed in the Lincoln Chair of Classical Archaeology and Art by Bernard Ashmole (1894–1984) of the British Museum, an art historian and an organizer of the stamp of Gardner. The importance of other areas of archaeology was recognized with the creation in the same year of a Chair of the Archaeology of the Roman Empire. The first holder, I. A. Richmond (1902–65), had won distinction as a field excavator with techniques that in 1885 were only in their infancy.

The post-war professors all took their teaching role very seriously. Some even made themselves comfortable in the new media of mass communication. The ghost of Jowett still haunted Oxford. Significantly, Lobel, who scheduled for 1.00 p.m. on Saturdays the classes forced upon him by an increasingly influential Faculty Board, retired (1958) still a reader.

Not only the senior appointments made during the 1950s but also those at the level of college tutorships seemed to betoken continued life in Literae Humaniores. Roman law retained the same degree of importance in the programme of the School of Jurisprudence which James Bryce (1838–1922) had given it during his tenure of the Regius Chair of Civil Law. Outside Oxford, however, the study of Greek and Latin faced a crisis. The failure of the Egyptian expedition of 1956 marked the end of Britain's imperial pretensions. All areas of British life were eventually affected, not least education and the role played therein by classical studies. Discontent with what was perceived as élitism in the educational tradition became more and more vocal. The number of leading men with anything of a classical education even in the Church, to say nothing of Government and the civil service or the medical and legal professions, had already declined noticeably. A growth of admiration for Greats men in the upper reaches of banking and commerce could only be temporary.

L. C. Robbins (1898–1984) did not feel obliged, as nineteenth-century educational reformers had, to criticize an excessive attention to the classics on the part of Oxford and the other British universities. The view of the function of universities which permeated the 1963 report of his Commissioners did not, however, easily accommodate the way in which Oxford's classical teachers and their pupils had been accustomed since the early nineteenth century to think of what they were doing. None of the universities established in Britain between 1961 and 1966 acquired a classical department of the kind thought essential to the late-nineteenth- and early-twentieth-century foundations and even to those of the immediate postwar years. Most ignored classical antiquity completely. The new kind of secondary school so vigorously promoted by the Labour Government of 1964–70 had little room for subjects like Greek and Latin. Even in the old-style State-maintained grammar school, with its highly selective entry,

I. A. RICHMOND in 1964 at an excavation of the Roman fort at Birrens in the company of A. S. Robertson, director of the excavation. Richmond had himself dug at the site in 1937. His encyclopaedic knowledge of Roman military practice made his advice on what to look for on the ground much sought after by fellow archaeologists.

the proportion of pupils studying Latin had already dropped in a question-raising way (Greek having long been thoroughly marginalized). The morale of the classical departments of the old civic universities, never very high, had been reduced by two developments: on the one hand departments of English, History, and French ceased to insist that their students have at least some acquaintance with Latin, and the remedial courses to which the classicists had devoted so much of their energies went into terminal decay; on the other, State assistance enabled more and more of the cleverer classical products of the grammar schools to go straight to a Cambridge or Oxford college. The decision of the Universities of Cambridge and Oxford in 1961 no longer to demand a knowledge of Latin from their matriculants, even from those wishing to study English or European literature, history, or law, removed a vital prop from beneath the classical tradition of the English schools. The manner in which the 1966–8 Committee on the Civil Service chaired by J. S. Fulton (1902–86) criticized the predominance in the administrative class of the service of the philosophy of the 'generalist' or 'all-rounder' struck hard at the ideological claims so long made for Literae Humaniores.

Oxford's now disproportionately large classical establishment could not insulate itself from what was happening throughout the country and indeed within the University itself. Good young men and women were, it is true, still offering themselves for the school of Literae Humaniores. The best-regarded public schools held tenaciously to their classical foundations. The establishment in 1957 of State assistance for candidates for research degrees led to the production through the 1960s of a number of impressive dissertations by men and women who had passed through Mods and Greats and, more importantly, to a marked change in the ethos of the college classical tutor. The publications of the Clarendon Press were helping to give Oxford the primacy in classical studies once enjoyed by Göttingen and Berlin. Nevertheless, many observers saw through what had become little more than an elegant façade. General linguistic competence had declined dramatically. The new generation did not accept the validity of the traditional exercise of composition. T. F. Higham (1890–1975) and others similarly skilled at composition retired, and fewer and fewer had enough faith in their own mastery of the exercise to be able to inspire confidence in their pupils. Tutors in other subjects were beginning to ask awkward questions about the overall quality of the classical matriculants. Dodds, ever painfully sensitive, shook his head about the classical tutor who, he heard, had discouraged a pupil from contemplating research and an academic career on the ground that the subject would not outlast the pupil's lifetime. He did not, however, feel able to dismiss the tutor's prediction.

The structure and content of the Literae Humaniores curriculum had engendered debate from 1850 onwards, but had undergone little substantial change. By 1966 the dominance of composition in Mods and of epigraphy and modern logic in Greats was arousing bitter criticism. Worry about the likely quantity and calibre of future recruits led all factions within the faculty to agree that some kind of radical change to the inherited system was necessary. The collegiate base of instruction for the honour school fixed certain boundaries in advance. Not for nothing were the classical tutors the strongest opponents of Franks's proposals to strengthen the Faculty Boards and to extend the instructional role of the University at the expense of that of the colleges.

When serious discussion of the Literae Humaniores curriculum began, some of the considerable number of archaeologists now lodged in Oxford wanted to give their subject a structural place in it, on the same level as that occupied by literature, history, and philosophy; but others, as in the 1880s, saw archaeology in a much wider context than that offered by the classical world. A deep scepticism about archaeology's larger educational pretensions still affected those whose major interest lay in the older disciplines.

Some feared that full acceptance of the demands from archaeology would encourage similar demands from comparative philology, a subject with more relevance to the older disciplines, more intellectual clout, and less attractiveness to the young. There was no way, of course, in which either of these subjects could be effectively taught except through the University. Despite the transformation which Oxford philosophy had undergone since 1850 and the tenuousness of its remaining links with Plato and Aristotle, neither the philosophers nor the exponents of literature and history wanted the subject to take up its official abode elsewhere. One result of the discussion was to remove compulsory prose and verse composition from Mods and to inject a considerable amount of Greek philosophy. Greats on the other hand acquired a third leg: it became possible to combine literature with either history or philosophy, as well as history with philosophy in the traditional way. New schools which joined Latin with English and with various Romance languages, and Greek with Byzantine studies, were approved not long after.

The system inaugurated in 1969 has now lasted over two decades. Rhetoric about the unity of classical studies is still strong. Nevertheless the outsider can often see little but a conglomeration of discrete bits interchangeable with bits of other dissolving unities. The proud claims made for the early-seventeenth-century Anglican amalgam of

THERMOLUMINESCENCE-MEASURING INSTRUMENT in use at the Oxford Research Laboratory for Archaeology and the History of Art. The intensity of the glow of a heated sample of powder from a ceramic object is proportional to its age.

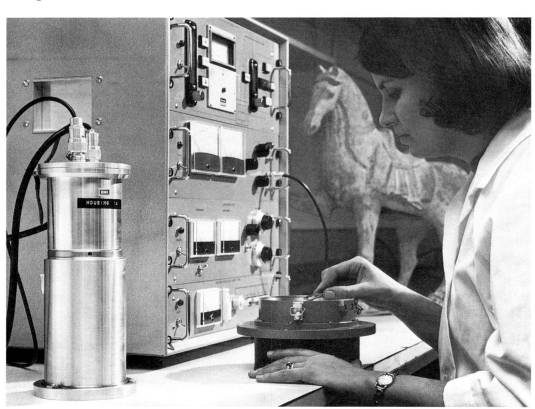

BOGUS POTTERY MOULD depicting a couple about to perform a sexual act. Acquired for the Ashmolean Museum by J. D. Beazley through E. P. Warren, an American gentleman scholar much interested in ancient erotica. A thermoluminescence test revealed that it could not have been manufactured, as Warren and Beazley believed, in the first century BC.

medieval Christianity and Renaissance humanism were repeated and accepted for a remarkably long time. The conservative and the liberal nineteenth-century restatements of those claims are now, however, usually applied to other subjects. The development of new theoretical models of non-literate societies, the shifts of class sympathies among practitioners, and the application of scientific technology to the dating of material objects take archaeology each day further away from what the subject was in the time of Percy Gardner. The imposition on the schools maintained by the State of a single curriculum with little place even for Latin will have consequences at present hard to calculate. Oxford is unlikely to lose all the classical part of its inheritance, but this may become increasingly difficult to disentangle from patterns of study orientated towards the present and constantly changing.

6

Oxford's Contribution to Modern Studies in the Arts

ALAN BELL

MODERNITY of study has never been foreign to Oxford: even in the Middle Ages the University's logicians were prominent exponents of philosophical systems which were modern at the time. But for the purposes of this chapter 'modern studies' is used to embrace those schools of secular, non-classical, non-scientific study that were established following the university reforms of the mid-nineteenth century. The Royal Commissioners of 1850 had noted severely that 'the fact that so few books of profound research emanate from the University of Oxford materially impairs its character as a seat of learning'. This was to change dramatically during the second half of the century, with the professoriate leading in research. The contribution of the teaching staff of the colleges followed later. The balance of higher study and undergraduate teaching varied from faculty to faculty, but scholarly standards were gradually raised in parallel with tutorial needs.

The Victorian innovations were not systematized into a 'School of Literae Recentiores', more up to date but by no means less polite than the Literae Humaniores they complemented. Modern History, Law, English, Modern and Oriental Languages, the mixed 'Modern Greats' School of Philosophy, Politics, and Economics, and Music: these are here taken in turn as representing 'modern studies'. In addition, Oxford's special contribution to learned publishing through its own University Press is included, partly as a reminder that Oxford's contribution to the modern humanities is not confined to the scholarly output of its teaching faculty.

The administrative structure of undergraduate teaching and examination forms a chronological framework as the schools were successively established, though it may seem rather compartmentalized for the history of scholarship. There has been a good deal of cross-fertilization, for example between Modern History and Social Studies, especially in that area where past politics blends into contemporary history, and inter-

MARK PATTISON, Rector of Lincoln, a gaunt but not unattractive misanthrope, famous in his day for an encyclopaedic but unproductive learning in the history of classical scholarship, and as a champion of specialized higher study within the increasingly tutorial university system.

national relations into diplomatic history. The boundaries of examinable curricula cannot confine polymaths whose varied interests ventilate several disciplines. How can one classify Friedrich Max Müller (1823–1900), the University's Professor of Comparative Philology? As Sanskrit scholar, or (with less enduring reputation) as student of mythology and comparative religion, or as the learned editor of over fifty volumes of the Oxford University Press series Sacred Books of the East? Such typically Victorian virtuosity embraces several mere academic schools. And in the twentieth century another considerable Oxford figure eludes simple classification: R. G. Collingwood (1889–1943), with his twin careers as a philosopher of unusual breadth of interest and as an authority on the inscriptions of Roman Britain, with the first volume of the *Oxford History of England* to his credit, along with a substantial list of archaeological writings. The learned life of Oxford is refreshed by such versatilities.

The twin functions of teaching and research, forever at the centre of discussions of the role of the University, should be complementary, though it was a long time before the tension between the two became a fruitful one. The tutorial process of essay-reading and discussion, repetitious and time-consuming though it is, had shown itself to be an adaptable and exportable Oxford ideal (though in fact it originated not with the college tutors but in the 'cramming' work of early-nineteenth-century private coaches who set up in business at a time of educational negligence among the dons). The incrustations of the tutorial grind can sap scholarly energy, and in the past led all too easily to an indifference, even a hostility, to the duty of learned research. College preoccupation with undergraduate teaching, and the developing professional identity of the growing tutorial cadre, led to a long-standing antagonism between the tutors and the professors, with much party strife in Victorian times and resonances heard even in recent years. The problem of balancing teaching and research commitments recurs, not least in recent discussions of whether, in the interests of an elusive national academic 'efficiency', Oxford ought not to become more of a 'research' university or designated graduate school, leaving teaching at Bachelors' level to others.

In Victorian Oxford such issues were polarized in the views of two outspoken heads of colleges: Mark Pattison (1813–84), Rector of Lincoln, and Benjamin Jowett (1817–93), Regius Professor of Greek and Master of Balliol. In spite of their intellectual differences, these contemporaries had much in common, and they both, though clergymen, sat at an angle to the prevailing religious orthodoxies. Pattison, a historian of Renaissance classical scholarship, wrote proudly in his posthumously published

BENJAMIN JOWETT, Master of Balliol and Regius Professor of Greek, pictured reflecting upon his achievements as Vice-Chancellor between 1882 and 1886. At Balliol the tutorial work of the college was emphasized, not least as training a new generation of proconsular administrators. The appointment of Balliol men as heads of other colleges spread Jowett's influence across the University.

MUTAT TERRA VICES: VICISTI, BALLIOLENSIS!

Memoirs of having 'lived wholly for study'. He had been a college tutor, and a conscientious one, and had hoped for good things from the reforms of the 1850s. His attitude changed, however, when he saw that the pursuit of examination honours had become an end in itself. He wrote that 'education among us has sunk into a trade', and that 'all the aspirations of a liberal curiosity' had been stifled by the 'school-keeping' of 'arid shop-dons'. He believed that Oxford should be an institute of higher study, dedicated to the high cultivation of the mind, rather than a vocational school for public life. This was not an ivory-tower yearning founded on his own unachieved ambitions in historical scholarship. It was soundly based on a knowledge of German academic systems, with a dominant professoriate and a stated duty to pursue higher learning. Pattison's was a noble aspiration which helps to redeem his crabbed and self-pitying reputation.

In contrast, Jowett stood for the importance of the tutorial function, and at Balliol the tutorial work of the college was greatly strengthened during his long period as a reforming Master. He aimed at an ideal of liberal education that would train in civil virtue and moral duty the young men needed for the upper reaches of public administration, not least in the Indian Empire (see below, p. 345). Jowett was a productive writer (though his classical work achieved more of literary reputation than of scholarly respect), but in his life the higher achievements of scholarship always lost out to tutorial imperatives. His Balliol ideal predominated in late Victorian times, and was emulated by most other colleges.

Since then much has changed, and research is rarely if ever seen at such a discount. Oxford has many college tutors who are scholars of international reputation, and many scholars who within the University have an enviable local renown as tutors. After the Second World War, for example, the history undergraduates of Magdalen had the privilege of being taught by two complementary but very different scholars: K. B. McFarlane (1903–66), a medievalist whose researches (many of which were published only posthumously) altered general conceptions of the social structure of England in the later Middle Ages, and A. J. P. Taylor (1906–90), who was not only well known professionally as a nineteenth-century diplomatic historian but was nationally famous as a journalist and publicist.

The problem of balancing teaching and research interests is a personal rather than an institutional one, and many may share the view of a Balliol tutor who became Regius Professor of Modern History, H. W. C. Davis (1874–1928). He said that 'Study and research were valueless unless accompanied by teaching; teaching of history was bound to be uninspiring, empty of all genuine content and even definitely mischievous, unless accompanied by study and research.'

A major factor in the change in tutorial attitudes to scholarship, and to the development of higher studies, was the introduction of the D.Phil. degree in 1917. At a time when the rapid growth of scientific research was reformulating the topography of knowledge, Oxford had shown undue reluctance to introduce 'research' degrees. It was thus failing to meet an international demand for appropriate doctoral qualifications, and putting itself in danger of lapsing into the curricular cosiness of a liberal arts college. A B.Litt. had been introduced in 1895 (at the same time as the B.Sc.), and graduate work in some areas (seventeenth- and eighteenth-century English literature, for example) enjoyed a reputation well beyond the formal standing of the actual degree. But in so examination-orientated a university, in which colleges then made most of their appointments to teaching fellowships from among those who had done well in their BA finals, formal qualifications in 'research', in the form of a book-length dissertation incorporating original work, seemed a foreign notion to be treated warily.

When eventually the doctorate of philosophy was made available at Oxford, it was a

IN 1758 SIR WILLIAM BLACKSTONE became the first holder of the Vinerian Chair of English Law, which is attached to All Souls College. In this portrait by Tilly Kettle his hand rests on his influential *Commentaries on the Laws of England*, published between 1765 and 1769.

long time before the degree established itself in the collective mind as being wholly respectable. Some continued, even after the Second World War, to regard it as a German–American intrusion, unnecessary as a *rite de passage* for the best of students and meriting only rather perfunctory supervision for lesser candidates. Such attitudes, now obsolete, initially prevented the growth of co-ordinated graduate instruction in the humanities. This was likewise seen as another alien practice, threatening with seminars long-established traditions of personal study. That too has now greatly changed.

Formalization of study by the award of doctorates took a long time to win acceptance. Institutionalization by the construction of premises took even longer. Some subjects had from the start been served by designated research institutes, as with Modern Languages at the Taylor Institution. Others, like the Oriental Institute, came later to provide for a wide range of linguistic needs. The undergraduate colleges remained in general practice, but All Souls, restricted to graduates, had from its foundation a concentration on history and law, and made its library facilities at the Codrington, specialized since the mid-nineteenth century, available to the University at large. The principal change came with the foundation of Nuffield College just before the Second World War, with its stated commitment to research in the social sciences. After the war came St Antony's, dedicated to modern history and international relations.

St Antony's has gathered round itself a congeries of regional 'centres', under a partly collegiate, partly University umbrella. This is an effective solution to the problem of how to provide for specialist research in a deliberately universalist academic framework, and of how to match in the Arts the centralization that laboratories provide in the Sciences. The University itself is sponsor of the Institute of Economics and Statistics, and there are now many smaller centres, such as a Transport Studies Unit or a Centre for Criminological Research, which seem to proliferate in the red-brick villas of North Oxford. Such a concept of the institutionalization of research was (like the villas themselves) unthought of at the start of the period of 'modern studies', when the foundation of a School of Modern History led the way for many similar developments in the humanities.

A joint Honour School of Law and Modern History was established in 1850. It was something of a marriage of convenience, which endured only until 1872. Modern History had had a professor since 1724 (see above, p. 55). Up to the time Thomas Arnold (1795–1842) was appointed to the chair in 1841 the incumbents had been dull sinecurists, virtually negligible in historical writing. Regius appointments were highly susceptible to political influence. They produced, for example, Goldwin Smith (1823–1910), a busy controversialist (Disraeli called him 'the wild man of the cloisters'), who held the chair during the early years of the joint School but had little influence on his professorial subject.

QUEEN'S COLLEGE LIBRARY (1692–5) (*left*) has one of the finest and least altered interiors in Oxford. It is chiefly notable for its woodwork, and for the plasterwork of the ceiling. Nearly a century after it was built the books were at last unchained in 1780.

Smith resigned in 1866. On this occasion Government patronage worked excellently, and provided from an Essex parsonage the Revd William Stubbs (1825–1901), already a notable editor of medieval texts, to which he had applied the developing scientific methods of Continental scholarship. His main concern as a scholar was with English constitutional development in the Middle Ages, a characteristically Victorian preoccupation in an era when parliamentary government appeared to be the distinctive achievement of the English nation. Stubbs was a firm Tory, but his strong sense of the ordered development of Parliament gave his extended narratives a Whiggish, teleological view of constitutional development. Not that there was anything easy or concise in such an approach: the three volumes of *The Constitutional History of England in its Origin and Development* (1874–8) are declaredly tough going. 'The History of Institutions cannot be mastered,' he announced, 'can scarcely be approached, without an effort.' By stressing the rigour of his investigations, Stubbs was clearly on guard against allegations that Modern History could not of itself provide a tough enough course of study to bear comparison with Greats.

WILLIAM STUBBS (shown here in Sir Hubert von Herkomer's portrait) was the first Regius Professor of Modern History to have a decisive influence on the shaping of the School. His inaugural lecture of 1866 was a milestone in English historiography. In it he introduced himself 'not as a philosopher, not as a politician, but as a *worker* at history'.

Stubbs's own *History* was a solid replacement for the loose literary narratives that had been all that was previously available for set reading, and his *Select Charters and Other Illustrations of English Constitutional History, from the Earliest Times to the Reign of Edward I* (1870, and eight editions to 1913) provided just the text to match in examinability the classical set books of the Greats syllabus. Expository lectures on Stubbs's *Charters* were long a backbone of undergraduate instruction. Stubbs's example held sway in Oxford for generations. His authority confirmed the Faculty in a concentration on English history, and on medieval studies, that prevailed well into the twentieth century. This historiographical influence, though profound, was not wholly salutary. There was an insularity of approach, and research was constricted by the boundaries Stubbs had set. It would be long before medieval history at Oxford was broadened by economic, cultural, and intellectual themes.

At the research level, Stubbs's influence showed itself more prominently elsewhere, notably at the new Victoria University of Manchester, where under T. F. Tout (1855–1929), a Stubbs pupil, and his successors there arose something more like a concentrated school of historical studies than anything that existed elsewhere in Britain. In Oxford, although the *Charters* and *History* became the staple of the curriculum (and were followed by volumes of Tudor and Stuart documents from other hands), the great man's influence was much less. Not even his authoritative professorial lectures and masterful narratives could begin to found a research school for historical study.

Within the Arts faculties—it was to be a very different story in the Sciences—the professors established too little power in directing the way in which studies developed. Stubbs and his successors were to find their strategic aspirations frustrated because their research interests were felt by the already entrenched tutorial body not to match closely enough the needs of college pupils. 'The historical teaching of history', Stubbs wrote to his successor, 'has been practically left out in favour of the class-getting system of training.' Stubbs became Bishop of Chester in 1884, and was later to be Bishop of Oxford. He was succeeded in his chair by the historian of the Normans, Edward Augustus Freeman (1823–92), a combative polemicist for his subject, whose reciprocated admiration for the Bishop was commemorated in the couplet by the economic historian Thorold Rogers (1823–90):

> While ladling butter from alternate tubs,
> Stubbs butters Freeman, Freeman butters Stubbs.

Freeman, who throughout his professorship continued the production of his immense narratives, was a doughty advocate of higher study, but suffered even more than his predecessor from the antipathy of an increasingly professionalized lumpentutoriate. He was in turn succeeded by James Anthony Froude (1818–94), the Tudor historian against whom Freeman had conducted a prolonged campaign for his inaccuracies. Froude was a superannuated littérateur who was regarded with derision by contemporary specialists: 'the methods of a patent-medicine man and the mind of a

SIR CHARLES HARDING FIRTH, Regius Professor of Modern History and a leading British historian of the seventeenth century. His strong views on the duty of the School of Modern History to train historians in research provoked the animosity of the college tutors, and led to administrative strains throughout his professorship.

party hack' was one Oxford judgement of *English Seamen of the Sixteenth Century*, Froude's published course of lectures from his two years in the chair. He had little influence on the development of the subject. Neither did his successor Frederick York Powell (1850–1904), a Christ Church don specializing in Icelandic saga literature, whimsically promoted to a chair which he held for a decade.

Sir Charles Firth (1857–1936), Regius Professor from 1904 to 1925, was a very different historical personality, well established by the time of his elevation as the leading British historian of the seventeenth century, continuing in much of his work the tradition of studying English constitutional history. When he took up his chair, History at Oxford was in a weak and divided state. Firth, who sought to lead by precept as well as by the example of his own industrious scholarship, delivered as his inaugural lecture *A Plea for the Historical Teaching of History*. He inspired a number of pupils who made distinguished contributions to seventeenth-century studies, and was a vigorous supporter of the movement to establish Schools of English and of Modern Languages. But his plea for well-organized historical research in Oxford provoked the powerful tutorial body into prolonged opposition, and the creation of a research school that might have stood comparison with Continental institutions (the French, for example, had had their École des Chartes since 1821, and their École Pratique des Hautes Études since 1868) was to elude him. Just after the First World War, the foundation of an institute was urged by A. F. Pollard (1869–1948), the Tudor Parliamentary historian, then a fellow of All Souls. The suggestion that it should be based in Oxford was rejected, and in 1921 it was set up under the wing of London University. It was better placed there, as a metropolitan establishment, than tied to a university where—despite the introduction of higher degrees—advanced teaching was still not well organized.

After so many failures in professorial initiatives, the quiet determination of Sir Maurice Powicke (1879–1963) achieved notable success. Powicke was a medievalist whose own Oxford training had received a strong admixture of the history school at

SIR MAURICE POWICKE, the eminent medievalist, who brought to Oxford on his appointment as Regius Professor of Modern History in 1928 the experience of collaborative enterprise and a knowledge of Continental scholarship, which broadened the study of his subject from too great a concentration on English constitutional history.

Manchester University, to which the Stubbs tradition had migrated and expanded. On returning to Oxford in 1928 he broadened the Stubbsian institutional range to embrace the intellectual history of the Middle Ages, making good use of the fine manuscript resources of the Bodleian and the college libraries. Under Powicke's aegis there was a flowering of medieval studies, which moved out of a constitutional furrow—and incidentally prepared the way for a thorough reassessment of the history of the University itself. Though the School as a whole has moved gradually towards more modern periods of study, the innovations of Powicke's period are an important legacy linking it with the days of Stubbs and the founders.

Much of what Firth advocated came to pass, but gradually and informally. Within the tutorial body there was a growing recognition of a parallel duty of research, and achievement in (or aptitude for) research began to weigh with committees appointing to tutorships. Many of the tutors showed themselves to be productive scholars of recognized standing, even without the D.Phil. as a near-mandatory initial requirement, and even without the stimulus of an externally imposed 'publish or perish' policy. The professorial body was also much expanded. In 1862 All Souls had founded a Chichele Chair, which was to have but two holders in its first eighty-four years. First there was Montagu Burrows (1819–1905), originally a naval officer; he was succeeded by the versatile and energetic Sir Charles Oman (1860–1946), writer on medieval warfare and numismatics, who was best known for his seven-volume *History of the Peninsular War* (1902–30). Oman also found time to be the University's Member of Parliament for many years. More recently this Chichele Chair has been assigned to the medieval period. Imperial (later Commonwealth) History has had its chair since 1905, thanks to the benefaction of Alfred Beit (1853–1906), a business associate of Cecil Rhodes (1853–1902) in South Africa. The History of War gained a professorship (another All Souls foundation) in 1909, with a series of holders much concerned with warfare in the twentieth century, and with strategic studies and international relations.

Oxford has had a long-standing interest in American history. James Bryce (1838–1922), who published *The American Commonwealth* in 1888, was a Regius Professor of Civil Law, and the Rhodes Scholarships have incidentally helped to emphasize Anglo-American historical links. The Harmsworth Professorship, founded in 1922 by the first Viscount Rothermere (1868–1940), the newspaper magnate, provided a prestigious appointment for visiting American scholars; its first holder was Samuel Eliot Morison (1887–1976). The annual Harmsworth appointment was eventually supplemented, thanks to an endowment by the Rhodes Trustees, by a permanent Rhodes Chair from 1969. A Professorship of Economic History was inaugurated in 1931, and one in the History of Science followed in 1973. Other professorships with a regional speciality have included those in Russian and Balkan History (1961) and in the History of Latin America (1967).

The number of chairs is but one index of the growth of the subject, and it would be misleading to see Oxford's contribution to historical studies only at professorial level.

The constituency of Oxford-trained scholars working elsewhere is a very large one, though their achievements may not always be easy to attribute to their undergraduate or postgraduate training. This wider group includes influential figures as different as R. H. Tawney (1880–1962) and Sir Lewis Namier (1888–1960), both of them undergraduates (and later both briefly fellows) of Balliol. Tawney read Greats before turning to economic history, from which he branched out into socialist commentary on education, poverty, and society at large. His *The Acquisitive Society* was published in 1921 at the end of his Balliol fellowship. In later life he showed a strong dislike of Oxford, but it is clear that he owed to his career there more than he cared to admit.

Namier, more gratefully inclined, read Modern History before the First World War, and afterwards returned for a short while to teach it at Balliol. This was at a time when he was settling into his prolonged study of the structure of English politics at the time of the American Revolution, which occupied him for the rest of his academic career at Manchester and London. Oxford made an important contribution to the development of his thought, not least in supporting his private researches for some years during the 1920s.

It is difficult to select works representative of the large but discrete output of Oxford historians over the last half-century, when most research reflected 'a variety of taste rather than the unity of an academic tradition'. Spirited intra-University discussions of the social composition of Civil War England have had a wider historiographical importance than the location of their principal participants, and other themes—such as Oxford's belated but eventually enthusiastic academic acceptance of social history—belong more to the general history of historical study than in a specifically Oxford context. Nor should Oxford historical scholarship be assessed solely through the publications of its History Faculty. For example, the great critical edition of Erasmus's letters, *Opus Epistolarum Des. Erasmi Roterodami* in eleven volumes (1906–47), was the product of a lifetime's dedicated work by P. S. Allen (1869–1933), President of Corpus Christi College. It is a text fundamental to the history of the Renaissance and Reformation, yet its editor was not formally a historian.

Law, which had originally been twinned with Modern History in the joint Honour School, had always seemed the minority partner in that unsatisfactory combination. The structure of the combined course reflected the supposed requirements of the educated country gentleman, and in addition to providing some mental preparation for the magistracy, its elements of politics and economics gave it something of a 'Modern Studies' air. It was not until 1872, however, when the Honour School of Jurisprudence achieved independence, that the academic study of law began to develop satisfactorily in Oxford.

Although set texts such as Justinian's *Institutes* and Blackstone's *Commentaries* provided an examinable base to match that customary in classical studies, the new School, like other newly established subjects, faced a serious problem of inadequate textbooks, and at the outset had only outmoded manuals for practitioners as its set books. This

W. R. ANSON, Warden and reformer (he has been called 'second founder') of All Souls, from Sir Hubert von Herkomer's portrait at the college. His textbooks set new standards for the systematic coverage of legal subjects, and provided the teaching material urgently needed by the new Honour School of Jurisprudence.

was changed by the arrival of clear, systematic texts such as *Principles of the English Law of Contract* (1879) by Sir William Anson (1843–1914), whose *The Law and Custom of the Constitution* (1888–94) was another influential treatise.

In contrast to administrative developments in Modern History, the late-Victorian Professors of Law were from the start influential in giving their School a prominent professorial presence, at a time when the tutors in the subject were few and undistinguished. The Vinerian Professorship (founded in 1758 with the great William Blackstone, 1723–80, as first incumbent) was occupied between 1882 and 1909 by A.V. Dicey (1835–1922), author of *The Law of the Constitution* (1885), *Law and Public Opinion in England* (1905), and an important study of *The Conflict of Laws* (1896). The first holder of the Corpus Professorship of Jurisprudence was Sir Henry Maine (1822–88), who as a young man, before several years of legal work in India, had been Regius Professor of Civil Law at Cambridge. In 1861 he had published *Ancient Law, its Connection with the Early History of Society, and its Relation to Modern Ideas*, a historical study of the evolution of institutions, written soon after Darwin's *Origin of Species*. Maine was succeeded by Sir Frederick Pollock (1845–1937), well known not only as jurist and legal historian but as a founding editor (from 1883) of one of the most eminent of academic journals, the *Law Quarterly Review*, an office of which A. L. Goodhart (1891–1978), later Master of University College, was to be a very influential Oxford incumbent. Pollock's own successor in the chair, Sir Paul Vinogradoff (1854–1925), the historian of medieval law and society, came to Oxford as a self-exiled liberal, after holding a professorship in Moscow. Vinogradoff introduced to Oxford the hitherto unfamiliar method of teaching by seminar, with a group of advanced students concentrating on different aspects of a text or problem, and publishing the results.

James Bryce was Regius Professor of Civil Law from 1870 to 1893, though his reputation was to be based not on his work in Roman law but on his career as a statesman and diplomatist. All Souls, from its foundation very much a lawyers' college, also founded a Chichele Chair in International Law, held from 1859 to 1874 by Mountague Bernard (1820–82), well known to his contemporaries as an authority, with a practice in arbitration that has been characteristic of his successors. The Chichele Chair's holders have included Sir Humphrey Waldock (1904–81), who was later President of the International Court of Justice.

The Law School was thus well established, in its historical and philosophical tendencies as well as in its tradition of systematic exposition in textbook form, under its founding professors. They prepared the way for a further generation in which their pupils rose to prominence, first as tutors and later on succeeding to the chairs themselves. Among this generation were men like Sir William Holdsworth (1871–1944), whose twelve-volume *History of English Law* (1903–38) was begun while he was a tutorial fellow of St John's and completed when he eventually became Vinerian Professor. G. C. Cheshire (1886–1978), who held the Vinerian chair from 1944 to 1949, is another example of the tutor (in this case of Exeter College) turned professor, productive and influential throughout his career. Cheshire's *The Modern Law of Real Property* (1925), *Private International Law* (1935), and—with his pupil C. H. S. Fifoot (1899–1975)—*The Law of Contract* (1945) formed a trio of textbooks that rapidly established, and in many successive revisions consolidated, their status as authorities. Judicial recognition has in England been only guardedly accorded to academic law, but Cheshire was recognized as one who came to enjoy a greater authority than many judges: Lord Denning (b. 1899) called him 'the most outstanding academic lawyer of his time'.

Though most of the research achievement of the School has been related to its teaching needs, it has proved adaptable. In recent years criminological and socio-legal studies have found their place in the Oxford legal curriculum. The characteristic philosophical cross-fertilizations of Oxford have added to the expository traditions of the School of Jurisprudence another element, in which scholars like H. L. A. Hart (b. 1907) have been prominent, both through works like *Causation in the Law* (1959) and *The Concept of Law* (1961), and through long-continued and influential seminar discussions in legal theory and analysis. The Law Faculty's research capability and its teaching facilities were both much enhanced by the new faculty premises, including the

THE BODLEIAN LAW LIBRARY, opened in 1964 in the new building on the St Cross site, provided space and light, and open-access facilities which had not been available in the old buildings, and enabled the collections to grow rapidly to meet the needs of the faculty. The architect was Sir Leslie Martin, the Professor of Architecture at Cambridge.

SIR WALTER RALEIGH, seen here in fancy dress as his (unrelated) namesake, energized the nascent study of English literature during his tenure of the Merton chair. He aimed to build up 'a school of half a dozen that could make things buzz', and recruited a teaching staff of high calibre.

Bodleian Law Library, opened in 1964 as the principal constituent of the St Cross Building.

There had been a suggestion that a Professorship in English Literature should be established as an adjunct to the new Modern History School, but Stubbs had decisively rejected it. The foundation of an English School was to be a prolonged and sometimes bellicose process. Underlying the discussions there was an anxiety about the intellectual rigour of a subject which tended to be judged by the critical standards of late-nineteenth-century journalism. In the 1890s Professor Freeman had sought in debate an assurance that 'by literature was intended the study of great books, and not mere chatter about Shelley'. The possibility of dilettantism had earlier been avoided by awarding the Merton Professorship of English Language and Literature, on its foundation in 1885, not to a discursive critic but to a severe Anglo-Saxonist, A. S. Napier (1853–1916), thus guaranteeing from the outset that there would be a demonstrably scholarly approach.

C. S. LEWIS, widely known for his contributions to children's literature and to Christian apologetics, was influential in the development of Middle English studies at Oxford, which through his initiative lost much of their excessively linguistic concentration. His *The Allegory of Love* (1936), a study of the literary tradition of courtierly love, has a range and freshness that continue to enliven the subject.

The Honour School began in 1894. It was a favourite with women candidates, but because of a lack of adequate teaching provision on the literary side it remained under-developed. This changed in 1904, when there arrived from Glasgow (the Scottish universities having long ordered literary teaching better) a lively young professor, Walter Raleigh (1861–1922). 'Raleigh', a colleague wrote, 'was never subdued to the purely academic', and his breezy teaching manner was very stimulating, though his reputation as a critic has not worn equally well. Raleigh recognized the need for literary scholarship within the School, and in 1908 brought in as his Reader the Edinburgh-trained David Nichol Smith (1875–1962). Nichol Smith was influential as a research supervisor, and as a scholar and critic assisted the general revival of eighteenth-century literary studies. Percy Simpson (1865–1962) was another of the early generation of lecturers, who not only sustained a huge teaching load at all levels but helped to introduce into the B.Litt. course the demands of the 'new bibliography', which revolutionized the

study of Elizabethan dramatic texts, aiming to treat them as precisely and thoroughly as the ancient classics.

With such exponents, the School was dominated by the literary historians. For the earlier period an emphasis on Old and Middle English texts ensured a stiff enough approach; they long formed a compulsory segment of the undergraduate course, and movements to make them optional provoked strong opposition. It was the great philologist Joseph Wright (1855–1930) who succeeded to Napier's role on the linguistic side. His career, from a childhood as donkey-boy in a Yorkshire woollen mill to the Corpus Chair of Comparative Philology, is a marvellous tale of Victorian self-improvement. His enduring monument is the six volumes of the *English Dialect Dictionary* (1896–1905), which he published successfully at his own expense when no other backing could be secured for the venture.

Raleigh died in 1922, leaving a School which in the words of its historian 'demonstrated that literary study is itself a demanding and complex subject, and that academic rigour is not the peculiar prerogative of less alluring disciplines'. Its development after the First World War is usually contrasted with that of the English Faculty at Cambridge. In Cambridge, alongside the contextual, philosophical courses of teachers like E. M. W. Tillyard (1889–1962) and Basil Willey (1897–1978), the 'practical criticism' of I. A. Richards (1893–1979) and the severely judgemental approach of F. R. Leavis (1895–1978) took firm root. Leavis's high moral stance has much in its intellectual ancestry of Matthew Arnold (1822–88) and *Culture and Anarchy*, but such critical orthodoxies were never to establish themselves so firmly in Arnold's own university: Oxford was to remain much more diversified in its approaches to literature. Arnold himself, and the other great Victorians, long remained out of bounds. A cut-off date of 1830 for

RICHARD ELLMANN, Goldsmiths' Professor of English Literature 1970–84 and author of studies of Joyce, Yeats, and Wilde, came to Oxford with a wide experience of American literary teaching behind him. His arrival marked the beginnings of a radical overhaul of the syllabus, which was strikingly modernized during his tenure of the Goldsmiths' chair. This photograph was taken in 1982.

SIR ROBERT TAYLOR, the architect, died in 1788, leaving his fortune to found an institution in Oxford for teaching modern European languages. Legal complications prevented the estate from falling to the University until 1835. Ten years later the Taylorian (*facing*) was opened in a wing of C. R. Cockerell's new University Galleries. It provides a substantial, and very handsomely housed, library for its subject.

the special periods examined in Schools, which was abandoned only in the 1960s, ensured a determined historicism in undergraduate studies and beyond.

As time passed, the earlier part of the syllabus (and in consequence more advanced studies) took on a less narrowly linguistic complexion in the hands of teachers like J. R. R. Tolkien (1892–1973) and C. S. Lewis (1898–1963), both of them even better known outside Oxford than within the confines of their learned specialities. Tudor studies continued under the direction of scholars like F. P. Wilson (1889–1963), not least as a research supervisor, whose learning balanced the work of colleagues better known to the public, such as Nevill Coghill (1899–1980), the translator into modern English of Chaucer's *Canterbury Tales* (1951), or the literary biographer Professor Lord David Cecil (1908–86). Early jokes concerning 'chatter about Shelley' were proved misguided by pioneering textual work on Wordsworth (by Ernest de Selincourt, 1870–1943, Helen

Darbishire, 1881–1961, and others), which with work on other poets established a local tradition of Romantic scholarship. Especially prominent among students of seventeenth-century literature was Helen Gardner (1908–86), Merton Professor of English Literature 1965–75, whose editions of Donne's *Divine Poems* (1952) and *Elegies, Songs and Sonnets* (1965) replaced with new authority the earlier Oxford edition. Here was a historical approach that was not anti-modernist: Dame Helen, critically a traditionalist, was also a pioneering textual analyst of the poetry of T. S. Eliot.

As in History, there was in English a gradual move forward in the period covered by the undergraduate courses, and consequently a modernization of the range of graduate study. During the 1960s there was a major reconstruction of the syllabus, which reduced the amount of compulsory language work and brought the subject forward first to 1945, before abandoning even this constraint. Among the professors during this period was the American Richard Ellmann (1918–87), biographer of Joyce and Wilde. The subject acquired a much more modern appearance than it had previously enjoyed. It seems, too, to be possible for the School to maintain a 'fruitful diversity' which avoids the strait-jacketing of critical theory without unduly neglecting its significance.

Sir Charles Firth had been a staunch advocate of an English School. He was even more outspoken in his promotion of Modern European Languages, with which he had some statutory connection as part of the original duties of the Regius Chair of Modern History. There was some activity in the subject even before the formal establishment of a School. Max Müller's versatility seemed well suited to his holding (from 1854) a Taylorian Chair of Modern European Literature, and subsequently (from 1868) the new Professorship of Comparative Philology. There was a fair amount of individual scholarly work, shown for example in the *Icelandic Dictionary* compiled by Richard Cleasby (1797–1847) and Gúdbrandr Vígfússon (1828–89) and published in 1873, and in Vígfússon and Powell's *Corpus Poeticum Boreale* (1883), works of importance though not closely related to courses of study. Corporately there was a vigorous and learned local Dante Society, founded in 1876, as evidence of a general interest in Italian studies. Above all, to help pave the way for such developments, there was the Taylor Institution, opened in 1845 as 'a foundation for the teaching and improving of the European languages'.

A proposal to set up a School of Modern European Languages (including English) had failed in 1887, in the face of objections that may already have become familiar in this chapter. 'The real question', an opponent wrote, 'is whether [Modern Languages] are worthy of being treated as a serious subject of University study: of a study, that is, as thorough and well organised as the study of Greek and Latin languages is at present.' Inevitably in the Oxford of the time there was a feeling that European languages were more suitable for women than fitted to the robuster needs of the masculine mind; it was noticed that such lectures as were held appeared to attract a largely female audience. It was not until 1903 that an Honour School was set up, nine years later than for English and 179 years since the first teaching provision had been made at the time of the foundation of the Regius Chair of Modern History. It took some time for an innovation derided as 'the Honour School for intending schoolmistresses' to establish itself in scholarship. Chairs came in German (1907), Romance Languages (1909), Italian and French (both in 1918), and Spanish (1927), and in due course the many other specialities in which teaching was needed were provided for at professorial or readership level. Special excellences showed themselves, for example in a florescence of medieval French studies, and of French philology, in the 1920s and 1930s.

Throughout this expansion the Taylorian, complemented by the Bodleian, provided central facilities for teaching and research. The Taylorian has attracted substantial research collections, so that, for example, it is one of the three or four best research libraries in the world for the study of Voltaire and the French Enlightenment, and its holdings are well attuned to the research needs of its faculty. The range of individual scholarly achievement has been very wide—from the folk-tales of the Dodecanese published by R. M. Dawkins (1871–1955) to the distinctive contribution to comparative Slavonic philology made by Boris Ungebaun (1898–1973), or the edition of the *Salons* (1957–67) and other work on Diderot by Jean Seznec (1905–85), one of the most distinguished of the holders of the Marshal Foch Professorship of French Literature.

The Oxford tradition in the study of Oriental languages runs back to Laudian times—even earlier if the Chair of Hebrew (1546) is taken into account—and to the foundation of the Laudian Chair of Arabic in 1636. Among the most celebrated of all Laudian Professors was the revered D. S. Margoliouth (1858–1940), whose polyglot output of editorial and expository work was fully equal to his now unsurpassable record of tenure of a chair, which he held from 1889 to 1937. Sanskrit had been provided for by the endowment of the Boden Professorship in 1832 (it was intended by its founder to assist 'the Conversion of the Natives of India to the Christian Religion'). A Professorship of Chinese was established in 1876, and other linguistic and historical professorships and lecturerships have followed in the present century, culminating in the notable endowment in 1979 of a Nissan Institute for Japanese Studies, a joint venture of the University and St Antony's College.

Each of these linguistic developments required specialized library resources. Archbishop Laud (1573–1645) himself had recognized this, and his own benefactions to the University included many Arabic and other Oriental manuscripts, along with his gifts of Western material. Printed Chinese volumes were among the earliest collections formed by Sir Thomas Bodley (1545–1613) for his library, to be the foundation of a major collection of classical Chinese literature. The Indian Institute was founded in 1875, as both library and museum and as a centre for Indian studies. It had a role in the instruction of cadets for imperial service, very much in line with Jowett's vision of Oxford as a special training-ground for the Anglo-Indian administrative cadre. Its library, strong in Sanskrit manuscripts, now forms part of the New Bodleian. Institutionalization was completed in 1960 by the formation of the Oriental Institute, which brought together teaching accommodation, administrative headquarters, and the library of the Faculty of Oriental Studies in a single building to the rear of the Ashmolean Museum.

There had long been a need for a new School that would offer the varied curriculum and intellectual challenge of Greats, but without its requirement of classical languages. In 1920 a three-year 'Modern Greats' course was introduced, combining Philosophy, Politics, and Economics; its original colloquial name has long since been abandoned in favour of 'PPE'. Predictably enough, the innovation was seen as a further nail in the coffin of the classical course, but Literae Humaniores has proved surprisingly resilient. Non-classical philosophy, up to the introduction of the new School, had, for want of a more suitable curricular slot, found its way into an extension of the Greats syllabus; there was now an opportunity to free the subject from its tie with Ancient History.

The modern-studies mixture decided on for Oxford was very different from the greater undergraduate specialization of Cambridge, where an Economics Tripos had been established as early as 1903. At that stage Oxford had gone only so far as to provide a lowly Diploma in Social Studies, and there was a strong feeling that Economics, in any proposed Honours course, should be studied alongside other subjects. It was not until 1970 that greater specialization was allowed within the PPE framework, with candidates required to take any two of the three constituents of Philosophy, Politics, or Economics. Other subject combinations became available as examination options around that time, for example mixing Philosophy with Physics, or Economics with Modern History.

Changes of this kind at BA level were a reflection of the varying prominence of Philosophy in the Oxford academic firmament. Before and during the First World War the philosophical climate of Oxford had been distinctly lukewarm. The prevailing doctrine had been a Hegelian idealism which had percolated through earlier eminences like T. H. Green (1836–82) and F. H. Bradley (1846–1924). Their successors were inbred, and were isolated even (perhaps especially) from Cambridge, where with G. E. Moore (1873–1958), Bertrand Russell (1872–1970), and others there was much astir in the Edwardian period. 'I do not think that anyone would come to Oxford to seek for anything very original or subtle in philosophy,' T. S. Eliot, then a young American graduate student at Merton, wrote in 1914. He also noted that the historical approach, so characteristic of Oxford's attitude to the humanities, prevailed in philosophical work: this could scarcely be a recipe for originality.

The local philosophical scene was to receive a salutary jolt from the younger practitioners of the new School. A leading figure among them was Gilbert Ryle (1900–76), who had added a pace-setting first class in the new PPE finals to his earlier first in Greats. His principal book, *The Concept of Mind*, did not appear until 1949, but it had been preceded by many influential papers, elegant, cautious, and 'philosophically eager', which did much to raise the standard of discussion. Ryle also developed Continental philosophical links for himself, and encouraged others to do so. It was he who sent his pupil A. J. Ayer (1910–89) to study in Austria, and the result was Ayer's sprightly

GILBERT RYLE was a formidable presence in Oxford philosophy, first as a Christ Church tutor and later as Waynflete Professor of Metaphysical Philosophy. He was mainly responsible for devising the Bachelor of Philosophy course, which provided advanced teaching for graduates and the best-known qualification of its time for academic philosophers in Britain and beyond.

and iconoclastic *Language, Truth and Logic* (1936), which imported a freshening, but to traditional circles unwelcome, injection of Continental positivism from the Vienna Circle. Any lingering attachments to the Greats-led tradition were soon smartly terminated by academic generations that included Sir Isaiah Berlin (b. 1909) and Sir Stuart Hampshire (b. 1914). After the Second World War Cambridge, where in the 1930s Ludwig Wittgenstein (1889–1951) had extended the work of Russell and Moore, was to see the centre of gravity in analytical philosophy moving towards Oxford.

One very important administrative change was introduced by Ryle after he became Waynflete Professor of Metaphysical Philosophy in 1945. He and his colleagues knew that a D.Phil., involving at least three years of concentration on a single problem, was too narrowing a preparation for a career in the academic teaching of philosophy. A new advanced course was therefore devised, leading to the degree of Bachelor of Philosophy, which combined some dissertation work with a series of written papers in taught subjects covering a range of problems much wider than a doctoral thesis could embrace. The new degree, introduced in 1946 and first examined in 1948, proved very successful; as the philosophy departments of British universities expanded, they were largely staffed by holders of the new Oxford B.Phil.

As well as initiating a new degree course, post-war Oxford philosophy took on a distinctive tone, due very largely to the penetrating influence of J. L. Austin (1911–60). Austin published relatively little, but worked orally, both in his lectures (there was a famous series called 'Sense and Sensibilia') and with invited groups of younger dons, attempting to unravel the 'ordinary language' of professional argument. In these seminars technical terms were refined, and then refined again. Austin's awesome critical intelligence demolished many a treatise and stifled many an imperfectly considered intended publication. Philosophical discussion, so appropriately nurtured by Oxford's established tutorial practice, a Socratic ideal, seemed to its participants to be enhanced by this intense communal pursuit of linguistic accuracy. Influential though the technique was in Oxford, some outsiders saw it as trivial and excessively self-centred, as 'a pursuit of linguistic distinctions for linguistic distinctions' sake'. Others were puzzled by its apparent restriction to English vocabulary and English usage. Notwithstanding such reservations, there was undoubtedly a feeling of intellectual buoyancy in Oxford philosophy of the time. The phase was stimulated by Austin's astringent guidance, but it did not long survive his early death.

A change was needed, which was provided in 1959 by the return to Oxford, as Wykeham Professor of Logic, of A. J. Ayer, after the experience of a dozen years in a London

A. J. AYER was Wykeham Professor of Logic from 1959 to 1978, an animating spirit in his subject. Sociable and spry, amorous and acute, and never disdaining the limelight, he—in succession to Bertrand Russell—came to represent philosophy for a general audience.

SIR JOHN HICKS, from the portrait by Mark Wickham now at All Souls, where he was a fellow from 1952, as Drummond Professor of Political Economy. His substantial contributions to economic theory led to his being awarded the Nobel Prize for economics in 1972.

University chair. The reputation of his early *Language, Truth and Logic* had endured, though he himself became increasingly critical of many of its positions. Some of his later writings, particularly *The Problem of Knowledge* (1956), were acts of retrenchment from earlier arguments. Ayer enjoyed a substantial popular reputation through his broadcasting and public work, but in Oxford he developed the professorial 'informal instruction' into an incisive graduate seminar of wide range, which avoided the sectarianism of Austinian analysis.

In contrast with Philosophy, where the development of the subject owed much to traditional discussion, Politics and Economics, its partners in the 'Modern Greats' troika, demanded much more of an institutional framework. There have of course been many individual practitioners, some of them occupying chairs attached to All Souls: the Drummond Chair of Political Economy, founded in 1825, whose holders have included the Nobel Prizewinner Sir John Hicks (1904–89); the Gladstone Chair of Political Theory and Institutions, founded in 1912; and the Chichele Chair of

Government and Public Administration, dating from 1944. In International Relations the tailoring magnate Sir Montague Burton (1885–1952) founded a chair in 1930; it has proved the focus for a lively postgraduate following. But in addition to the writings and teachings of individuals, many branches of both Politics and Economics were seen to need the physical reality of a research school. The subjects thus came to disrupt the traditions of collegiate Oxford, and eventually to make academically specialized foundations in the humanities much more acceptable.

The major institutional provision for both Economics and Politics came about through Lord Nuffield (1877–1963). In 1937, when he offered to found a 'college' specializing in engineering and accountancy, A. D. Lindsay (1879–1952), then Master of Balliol, and Douglas Veale (1891–1973), the Registrar, managed to steer this determined benefactor towards objectives better suited to the University's own development plans. Oxford had by a recent concordat left Engineering to Cambridge, but Social Studies were in special need of support. Nuffield's proposition was deftly transmuted: 'Engineering' into Physical Chemistry (a new laboratory was built), and 'Accountancy' into a 'research' college mainly for the social sciences. Lord Nuffield was apparently convinced by Lindsay's advocacy of the need to form a bridge between the theoreticians and the practitioners, and indeed the college that bears his name makes

G. D. H. COLE, Reader in Economics and one of the most prominent of the early fellows of Nuffield College (shown here in a photograph of 1952). Cole was widely known as a writer on social history and on Labour policy, though his socialist connections did not endear him to Lord Nuffield, the founder of his college.

DAME MARGERY PERHAM, an imposing monitrix of overseas government, was one of the best-known figures of her day in the field of colonial administration. A tireless publicist and analyst of African affairs, she was no mere desk-bound academic: this photograph shows her in the Sudan in 1939, on the last of a series of research visits undertaken between the wars.

special provision for the attachment of politicians and industrialists for discussion and investigative projects.

The planning of Nuffield College was interrupted by the outbreak of war, and its buildings were not completed until the mid-1950s. Enough of a start had been made by 1939, however, for the college—still under University tutelage and not yet an independent foundation—to undertake social and economic surveys. Some of these were commissioned by Government and intended for use in post-war planning; G. D. H. Cole (1889–1959), Reader in Economics, was prominent in their organization.

After the war, as the college achieved greater cohesion and won the full favour and further endowments of its founder, it gained a high reputation for its research work. Among subjects in which it achieved fame were studies in trade unionism and industrial relations, and in colonial administration, the latter under the direction of Dame Margery Perham (1895–1982), one of Nuffield's first fellows and well known as a commentator on colonial affairs. The college established a special place for itself, too, in psephological studies, deriving from a series that began with a detailed analysis of *The British General Election of 1945* (1947). It was one of the co-authors of this inaugural volume, R. B. McCallum (1898–1973), later Master of Pembroke, who invented the word

SIR ROY HARROD, from a photograph taken in 1955. Harrod was both a respected economic theorist and well known as a commentator on economic affairs, combining this work with a dedicated tutorial career at Christ Church, where he was a considerable social and cultural presence for many generations of undergraduates.

'psephology', an Oxonian coinage derived from the Greek *psēphos*, the pebble which Athenians dropped into an urn to record their vote.

When PPE was set up as a joint School in the 1920s it necessarily relied for teaching on modern historians and philosophers. It was some time before a new generation of economists showed itself a force among the tutors. At Christ Church the first tutor in Economics was appointed on the strength of his first classes in Greats and Modern History, and the college then sent him off to Cambridge to learn enough of the subject to be able to teach it. The appointment was a very successful one, and the training had important results: Sir Roy Harrod (1900–78) became one of the most influential of Oxford economists. He published, particularly in the 1940s and 1950s, much seminal work on the trade cycle, dynamic theory, and international monetary theory; and his brief attachment at Cambridge introduced him to John Maynard Keynes (1883–1946), with whom he kept closely in touch and whose biography he was later to write with notable success. Oxford economists did not display the orthodoxy of a school, Keynesian or otherwise; the practitioners had a much more varied approach. Many have been not merely theoreticians but practical advisers as well. Harrod himself, for example, was much consulted during the Macmillan Government (1957–63), and in the Wilson administration that succeeded it Thomas Balogh (1905–85) served as a Cabinet Office adviser on economic affairs. Balogh, a fellow of Balliol and later a life peer, was one of a group of *émigré* Hungarian economists who had considerable influence on Labour Party thinking after the war. In contrast to the Liberal (and later Conservative) Harrod, he was a man of the far Left. He became a specialist in the economics of underdeveloped countries and was for some years an adviser to the United Nations Food and Agriculture Organization.

The Oxford academic economists of the 1930s found themselves ill served by the existing libraries. A movement gained force for the foundation of an institute to provide facilities that would match laboratory developments in the sciences. The Institute of Economics and Statistics was set up in 1935; it gathered a substantial library and provided a research centre for statistical approaches to economic and social problems, in developing countries as well as in the United Kingdom. After many moves, the institute settled in the 1960s as part of the new library buildings at St Cross.

Finally, in a university in which the theoretical influence of T. H. Green continued strong, and where the practical example of social reformers like the elder Arnold Toynbee (1852–83) and Canon Samuel Barnett (1844–1913) was treasured, the long Oxford tradition of the study of social problems should also be mentioned. Toynbee Hall, a mission station in Whitechapel, was balanced by Barnett House (founded 1913) as a study centre in Oxford, and for many years a Certificate in Social Training was offered by the University. This was to prove a remote ancestor of the M.Sc. degree in Applied Social Studies, a course offered from 1972 onwards, which took account of the growth, and rather reluctant acceptance, of sociology as an academic discipline. Mistrust of this new subject was by no means confined to Oxford, though the University has been no stranger to sociological research, more widely defined—not least in investigations by the Institute of Economics and Statistics into the distribution of income and wealth in Britain. In Oxford, too, much sociological enquiry has remained with anthropology, in which the University has long-established interests.

Among the range of 'modern studies' subjects there is one with a long University history behind it before it became formally adopted as a School. A Professorship of Music was founded by William Heather (1563?–1627) in 1626, but the organization of the subject as a faculty dates only from 1944. It was not until 1950 that Music was accepted as an examination subject for Arts degrees, though the D.Mus. and B.Mus. (which were then reorganized) were both of considerable antiquity. Between the foundation of the chair and the introduction of the Honours course, the record is a mixed one. The professorship, a non-resident appointment for much of its existence, had originally been combined with the duties of the Choragus, a University functionary supervising

SIR HUGH ALLEN, Heather Professor of Music from 1918 until 1946, enjoyed a special reputation as the energetic and authoritarian conductor of the Bach Choir, regarding his performing duties as professor as more important than musicological research work.

musical exercises. When the two positions were split, the professor had as his main duty that of composing an ode for the installation of the Chancellor.

There were some distinguished names associated with the Heather Chair, including that of the organist William Crotch (1775–1847), who held the position for half a century, and eminent Victorians such as Sir Henry Bishop (1786–1855), composer of 'Home, Sweet Home', and Sir Frederick Gore Ouseley (1825–89), the reviver of English choral training, as well as Sir John Stainer (1840–1901) and Sir Charles Hubert Hastings Parry (1848–1918) later in the century. Their professorial contribution, confined to occasional lecturing and intermittent attendance, was not equal to their eminence as national musical figures.

The Oxford musical tradition developed otherwise, in the larger college chapels and in musical societies culminating in the famous Oxford Bach Choir (founded in 1896, but incorporating Crotch's Oxford Choral Society of 1819 and other organizations). The elegant and acoustically congenial Holywell Music Room of 1748 was only one of a range of differently sized venues that Oxford offered for performances. Sir Hugh Allen (1869–1946), Heather Professor from 1918 until his death, was very much of this choral tradition, more of a conductor-professor than scholar, though he did much to revise the existing academic courses.

Full reorganization took place under Allen's successor Sir Jack Westrup (1904–75), who held the chair from 1947 to 1971. He continued active in University operatic productions, and devoted much scholarly energy to editing new texts for them; and his special interest in the history of English music had resulted in the definitive *Purcell* (1937) and many subsequent studies. The tradition of operatic scholarship was continued under Westrup's successor Denis Arnold (1926–86), with his research interest in Venetian music of the High Renaissance—again displaying musicological scholarship that was in no danger of losing touch with practical musicianship.

Among other recent scholars based in Oxford have been Frank Harrison (1905–87),

SIR JACK WESTRUP, Allen's successor, had an interest both in operatic production and in ensuring that his performances were soundly based in scholarship. Monteverdi's *Orfeo* was revived by him as an Oxford undergraduate in 1925, with *L'incoronazione di Poppea* two years later; he continued to work on Monteverdi and other operatic composers throughout his life.

DR J. A. H. MURRAY, patriarchally bearded and wearing as usual his cherished academic cap, in the 'Scriptorium', the iron shed that provided the workshop for the editor of *The New English Dictionary* and his team. Originally erected at Mill Hill School when he was still teaching there, it was moved to Banbury Road, Oxford, to improve communications with the University Press.

sometime Reader in Music, whose studies began in pre-Reformation British music and later embraced the comparative ethnographic study of instruments, and the distinguished Viennese Byzantinist Egon Wellesz (1885–1974). Wellesz, an exile of the 1930s, was both a composer in the tradition of Schoenberg (whose pupil he had been) and an expert decipherer of Byzantine musical notation, a subject in which Oxford became, through the presence of this eminent scholar, a centre for study. Wellesz's research extended Oxford's range of scholarly expertise, which has otherwise been more closely related to the fine library resources of the University, notably the books and manuscripts of the Bodleian itself, and to historic instruments in the Bate Collection at the Faculty of Music, and in many college and museum collections.

Professor York Powell maintained that a university consisted of a library and a press. Each is of central importance to the propagation of sound learning. The University's good fortune in having at its centre the Bodleian Library, with its privilege of British statutory deposit dating back to 1610 and its tradition of wide-ranging supplementary acquisition of foreign publications, lies at the foundation of much of the scholarship in 'modern studies' discussed in this chapter. The Bodleian's position as the major 'public' academic library of the nation was established long before the Library Department of the British Museum was formed. This early primacy has given the Bodleian a special position in the world of libraries, which is enhanced by the availability nearby of well over a hundred college, faculty, and departmental libraries. The phrase 'Oxford library system' may seem a misnomer to those whose research is founded on more unified and systematized resources; yet, like so much in Oxford that at first sight seems antiquated and anomalous, the libraries often prove themselves flexible and workable. Recent advances in automation will eventually confirm this, but even with the aids available to previous generations the massive concentration of libraries in central Oxford fully met the first of York Powell's 'university' requirements.

As for the stipulated need for a press, the local tradition is equally ancient and prominent. It affects all areas of study, and the Oxford University Press is of obvious importance in theology, classics, and (more recently) the sciences, as well as in the 'modern studies' mentioned in this chapter. The year 1478, the date when the itinerant printer Theodoric Rood, from Cologne, produced at Oxford the first of a handful of minor works, marks the beginning of University printing, though the trade in manuscript books had made Oxford an important publishing centre long before that. For a long time the history of Oxford publishing lacked continuity. The Bible trade, in which the University shared the English privilege with Cambridge and with the King's Printer in London, was profitable enough to sustain the 'learned' side. Academic publishing was ready to play its part in the development of 'modern studies' as soon as the University enlarged its curriculum. This occurred at a time when the national educational system came to demand an unprecedented supply of new and authoritative textbooks. Both the Oxford-based Clarendon Press and the London-based general publishing business (the two branches are now amalgamated) made significant contributions to the great commercial expansion of the Press in the mid-Victorian period. Oxford's established place in theological and classical publishing was maintained, but its publishing arm was soon able to meet local, and national, teaching needs in the newly recognized fields of study, for example with Stubbs's *Constitutional History* or Anson's *English Law of Contract*. With such titles, and innumerable schoolbooks, on the list, the Press grew rapidly from being 'a somnolent self-contained attachment of a large printing house to become the greatest academic publishing business in the world'.

The Press as a whole was particularly important in the development of English studies, building on the experience and reputation of editions like the six-volume *Boswell's Life of Johnson* (1887) by G. Birkbeck Hill (1835–1903) or the *Complete Works of Geoffrey Chaucer* in seven volumes (1894–7) by W. W. Skeat (1835–1912), as the foundation of a series of English texts that have collectively made a major contribution to the textual codification of the national literature. Knowledge of the requirements of classical scholarship had made the publishers editorially responsive to the needs of the 'new bibliography' in English studies, even if the prolongation of projects because of more stringent standards of editing must sometimes have severely tried their patience. C. H. Herford (1853–1931) and Percy Simpson's edition of Ben Jonson, commissioned in

1902, was not completed until the publication of its eleventh volume in 1951—but it is one of the great editions of its age. The editions of Donne (1912) by H. J. C. Grierson (1866–1960) and Gerard Manley Hopkins (1918) by Robert Bridges (1844–1930) were two Oxford publications that had a special impact on twentieth-century English literature. Malory, Milton, Samuel Johnson, Jane Austen, Wordsworth, and Dickens are among the authors for whom the Press has provided texts that are authoritative for their time, and the scholarly editing of English correspondence that has enjoyed an extraordinary florescence in this century is very much a phenomenon of Oxford publishing. Shakespeare has proved much more elusive, editorially speaking, with a series of false starts throughout the century, until the Oxford Shakespeare, edited by Stanley Wells (b. 1930), appeared in 1986, in both old-spelling and modern editions, accompanied by textual commentary and a set of supporting editions of individual plays.

Though many of the Press's chief executives, who bear the title 'Secretary to the Delegates' (that of 'academic publisher' came late in the annals of Oxford academic publishing), had special interests in English literature, the Oxford name was to be almost as strong in history. There were broad surveys such as *A Study of History* in ten volumes (1934–54) by Arnold Toynbee (1889–1975), which enjoyed an extraordinary postwar vogue, and famous textbooks like that of S. E. Morison and H. S. Commager (b. 1902), *The Growth of the American Republic* (1930 and many subsequent revisions), the latter a production of the Press's large branch office in New York. Once the Delegates, the managing committee of senior members of the University, brought themselves to admit that the best of dissertations, thoroughly revised, might be admissible as OUP publications, the list of historical monographs expanded rapidly.

Most prominent of all was the fourteen-volume *Oxford History of England*, under the general editorship of G. N. Clark (1890–1979), published between 1934 and 1961. Each volume was assigned to a single authority, unlike the *Cambridge Modern History* (1902–12) and the other Cambridge University Press series which were made up of chapters by experts. With its one-man-one-period approach, the Oxford *History* was less consistent than some differently planned sets, but most of its volumes provided an authoritative statement of English history as assessed by the scholarship of its (rather prolonged) generation. There were some very distinguished contributions, notably *England 1870–1914* by R. C. K. Ensor (1877–1958), and the whole project was eventually rounded off by a sparkling addendum, A. J. P. Taylor's *England 1914–1945*, which came out in 1965. A *New Oxford History of England* is now under way, again with volumes assigned to single specialists; no doubt it will as a whole reflect a further shift away from the older conventions of political narrative.

In more general publishing, the Oxford name became attached to substantial anthologies, beginning with the *Oxford Book of English Verse, 1250–1900* (1900), edited by (Sir) Arthur Quiller-Couch (1863–1944), and to compilations like the *Oxford Companion to English Literature* (1932) by Sir Paul Harvey (1869–1948). The *Oxford Dictionary of Quotations* (1941) and the *Oxford Dictionary of the Christian Church* (1958) are representative

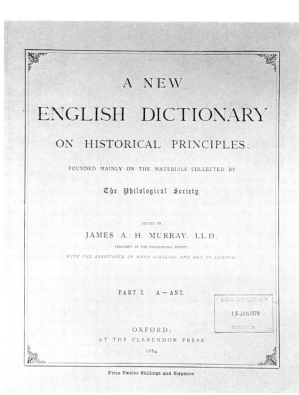

THE NEW ENGLISH DICTIONARY, later *The Oxford English Dictionary*, in various forms: the cover of the first fascicule, A–ant, published in 1884 as the opening instalment of the dictionary 'on a historical basis'; and the second edition of the OED on CD-ROM, which transforms the way in which scholars use the dictionary. Questions that could take months of research using the printed book can now be answered in seconds.

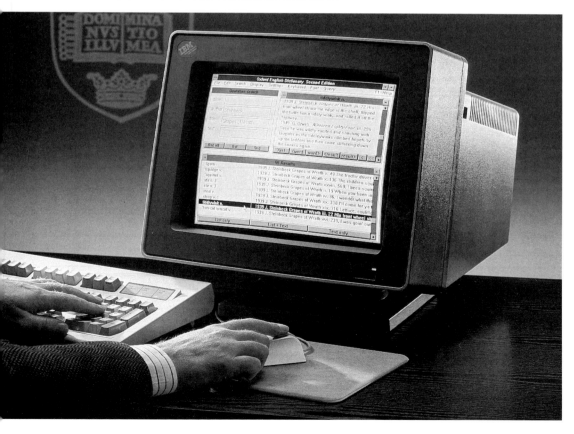

of a whole library of single-volume reference works whose solid blue bindings provide weighty assurance of concise and authoritative information.

The Press also fell heir to one of the greatest of Victorian literary enterprises, the *Dictionary of National Biography*, that grand project in sixty-three volumes (1885–1901), devised by George Smith (1824–1901), head of the publishing house of Smith Elder & Co., and edited by Sir Leslie Stephen (1832–1904) and Sir Sidney Lee (1859–1926). George Smith's family presented it, as a national treasure, to the University in 1917. It was not then seen as a wholly welcome gift, bringing with it as it did the twin obligations of keeping the main work in print, and of providing periodic supplementation to cover the eminent deceased of the twentieth century. The decennial—and most recently quinquennial—Supplements have, however, proved their worth as a continuing reference work in twentieth-century history, though the challenge of a general revision of the main work still remains to be taken up. Much, perhaps most, of it remains valuable, but a further century of historical scholarship has to be taken into account since the biographies were first compiled. The problems of financing and staffing such an enterprise are indeed huge; perhaps one day they will be solved in a way that matches the spirit of the Victorian projectors of the original *Dictionary*.

'Oxford' in a title had become a warranty, but the publication which more than any other placed the University's name before the world as an accepted lexical authority began life without 'Oxford' in its name. *A New English Dictionary on Historical Principles; Founded Mainly on The Materials Collected by The Philological Society* commenced publication, from the Clarendon Press, in 1888, but it was not until 1895 that 'Oxford' appeared on the title-pages of its periodically issued parts. What is now known familiarly as 'the *OED*' was to earlier generations of scholars 'the *NED*'. It was originally the project, launched in 1857, of the London-based Philological Society, and was taken over by the Press, after careful assessment, in 1879.

The involvement of Dr J. A. H. (later Sir James) Murray (1837–1915), a self-taught philologist from the Scottish Borders and later a schoolmaster at Mill Hill in North London, in the great dictionary project is one of the epics of the history of scholarship. His thoroughness, his analytical flair in selecting, ordering, and concisely and precisely defining from the mass of word-slips that had been assembled by the Society, and later much amplified by his own better-instructed volunteer readers, were all legendary. These traits were equalled by his determined defence of the project against limitations threatened by the Delegates of the Press, who were increasingly alarmed by the growth in length, time, and financial involvement that the project incurred. It took the Delegates many years to understand that the frugal and self-sacrificing editors were not fools, and that 'it was the language itself that was insane'. Dictionary-making on this

DAVID AS PROPHET AND MUSICIAN, manuscript illumination from Psalm I of a twelfth-century Bible sent by the Chapter of Winchester Cathedral as a foundation-gift to the Bodleian Library at the instance of the Warden of New College, George Ryves.

B E A T V S

B E A T G V S

VIR

VIR Q NON ABIIT IN CONSI-
LIO IMPIORV ET IN VIA PEC
CATORV NSTETIT ET IN CATHEDRA
PESTILENTIE NON SEDIT.

Sed in lege domini uoluntas ei: & in le
ge eius meditabitur die ac nocte.
Et erit tanquam lignum qd plantatum
est secus decursus aquarum: quod
fructum suum dabit intempore suo:
Et folium eius non defluet: & omnia
quecunque faciet prosperabuntur.
Non sic impii non sic: sed tanquam puluis
quem proicit uentus afacie terre.
Ideo non resurgunt impii iniudicio:
neque peccatores inconsilio iustorum.
Qm nouit dominus uiam iustorum:
& iter impiorum pibit.

Psalmus dauid .II.
QVARE fremuerunt gentes:
& popli meditati sunt mania:

Q NON ABIIT IN CONSLO IMPI
ORV ET IN VIA PECCATORV
NON SE DET IN CATHEDRA
DERISORV NON SEDIT.

Sed in lege domini uoluntas eius. & in
lege eius meditabitur die ac nocte.
Et erit tanquam lignum transplantatu
iuxta riuulos aquarum. quod fru
ctum suum dabit intempore suo.
Et folium eius non defluet. & omne
quod fecerit prosperabitur.
Non sic impii. sed tanquam puluis
quem proicit uentus.
Propterea non resurgent impii iniudicio.
neq; peccatores incongregatione iustoiz
Qm nouit dominus uiam iustorum
& iter impiorum pibit.

Psalmus dauid .II.
QVARE turbabuntur gentes:
& tribus meditabuntur inania

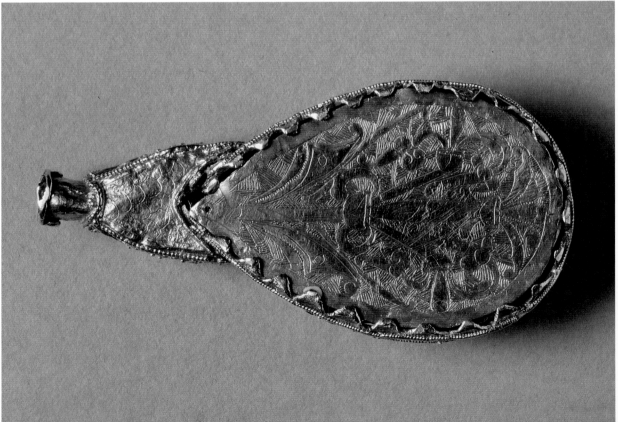

unprecedented scale and to such exacting editorial standards gave rise to production problems previously unknown. The Press only gradually realized that it had a quite exceptional undertaking on its hands, and one in which it could take a justifiable pride.

The first fascicle, A–Ant, was published in February 1884, and Murray soon afterwards moved to Oxford to supervise the work there. He found himself 'caught in the web of words', though he was by no means unwillingly entrapped, whatever the difficulties he experienced with the publishers and whatever the social and academic slights he felt the University offered to the distinguished but unattached resident in its midst. Murray himself was responsible for the text of about half the entire *Dictionary*, but he had the skilled assistance of Henry Bradley (1845–1923), W. A. (later Sir William) Craigie (1867–1957), and C. T. Onions (1873–1965), each a philologist of the first rank—and each, like Murray, *Oxoniensis* only by adoption. But it was James Murray whom the public identified as the great man of the whole enterprise. The General Post Office installed a special pillar-box outside his Banbury Road workshop, and they recognized 'Dr Murray, Oxford' as a sufficient address for the vast correspondence the *Dictionary* generated. Murray died in 1915, and it was left to Bradley and his younger colleagues to bring the work to a conclusion. The last volume came out in 1928, ending with 'Zyxt', a form which gave a brand-name to 'the last word in soaps'. This was seventy years after the Philological Society had set out on a project that then seemed simply and promptly realizable. A further volume of supplementary material, with the bibliography, followed in 1933, completing the main work. The overall cost to the Press was then estimated at well over £300,000; but recognized lexical authority, under an Oxford imprint, outweighed mere financial calculations.

Many years before the *Oxford English Dictionary* was finished, it was used as a quarry by the brothers H. W. Fowler (1858–1933) and F. G. Fowler (1870–1918) to produce the *Concise Oxford Dictionary* (1911) and later the *Pocket Oxford Dictionary* (1925). With the Fowlers' individual but authoritative manuals on *The King's English* (1907) and *Modern English Usage* (1926), these smaller dictionaries reinforced the notion of 'Oxford English' not just as a variety of the received pronunciation but as an international standard, reinforced by the two-volume *Shorter Oxford Dictionary*, closely based on the main work. And to meet the needs of the Overseas Education division of the Press, which perceptively foresaw the huge expansion of teaching needs in English as a foreign language, there was soon to follow from A. S. Hornby (1898–1979) the *Oxford Advanced Learner's Dictionary of Current English*, the proofs of which arrived from Japan just before Pearl Harbor. It was to become the Press's best-selling book after the Bible, and consolidated its publisher's position in the world market.

As for the *Oxford English Dictionary* itself, the language could not be expected to pause in its development to suit the phasing of learned compilation. The duty of further

THE ALFRED JEWEL, rock crystal, *cloisonné* enamel and gold, ninth century, given to the Ashmolean Museum in 1718. One of the greatest treasures of Anglo-Saxon art, it bears an inscription which reads 'Alfred had me made'.

supplementation, apparent even by 1933, was even more obvious after the Second World War, and by the mid-1950s the Press had reconstituted its Dictionary Department, aiming to produce a single large additional *OED* volume within seven years. In 1986 this phase of activity was completed in four volumes, in a little over four times the period originally assigned to it. The *Supplement*, mainly concerned with twentieth-century addenda and thus taking into account 'a spectacular increase in technical language', is based on a coherence of source material that makes it a particularly satisfactory set to use. It has a value of its own, but even before it was completed a further project was under way to merge the main *Dictionary* and its published addenda into a single alphabetical sequence.

The 'second edition', an important stage in the *Dictionary*'s progress, came out in 1989. In it the entire text was reset in one alphabetical sequence, typographically handsome and phonetically regularized. It is a considerable achievement—especially in data-processing—and a convenient one to use. The entire text of OED^2 is also available on a compact disc, with all the speed and power of access that the technology commands. The next stage, a more thoroughly revised third edition, compiled from its inception with electronic assistance, is already in preparation with a view to publication in the first decades of the next century. Its physical form may be very different, but its methods must be those of Murray himself, and it will be very much an Oxford University Press product.

The words 'On Historical Principles' in the *Dictionary*'s title define a technique of lexicographical arrangement. But in more general terms the phrase might be taken as providing a unifying theme for the humane studies discussed in this chapter. A 'historical' approach can be discerned in many disciplines—particularly, for many years, in English literary studies—that would have pleased both Stubbs as a 'worker at history' and Firth as an advocate of professional historical training. Schools had been established, not merely as examination units but as schools of thinking; and they could prove their value alongside, and not in opposition to, the Classics. The fears of those who had seen Greats threatened by every succeeding development in 'modern studies' were shown to have been greatly exaggerated. Above all, the 'school-keeping' that Mark Pattison had castigated—the mere cramming for examinations and the neglect of the organization and prosecution of research—has been reduced to a point at which even he might have been able to take some pleasure in Oxford's wide-ranging and distinctive contribution.

The Collections of the University

OLIVER IMPEY

THE way in which the University has collected, displayed, neglected, disposed of, housed, catalogued, studied with, and taught from its varied accumulations of eight hundred-odd years is the subject of this chapter. The University today owns Museums of Art and Archaeology, of Ethnography, of Natural History, and of the History of Science, as well as smaller more specialist collections that are kept separately, such as the Bate Collection of Musical Instruments or the Herbarium. There is a large number of libraries, many of which are subordinate to the great Bodleian Library, a Botanic Garden, an Arboretum, and a nature reserve. There is no zoo; in this respect the University falls short of the seventeenth-century ideal of universality.

We are concerned here with the many collections of objects acquired by the University for their own sake rather than with such things as early charters, important though these may be. The University acquired books or objects because someone at Oxford, often a curator or a professor, thought them useful or desirable, or because a donor

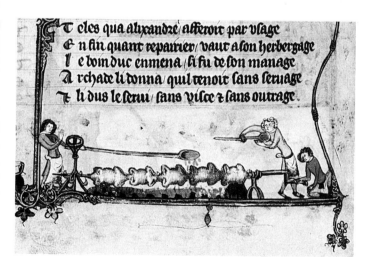

SPIT-ROASTING, illuminated marginal detail from the 'Romance of Alexander', mid- and late-fourteenth-century manuscript, Flemish and English, 'undeniably one of the great picture books of the Middle Ages'. First recorded in London in 1466, it was given to the library, almost certainly by Sir Thomas Bodley himself, in 1603–4.

thought that the University ought to own them. Wherever possible, notice will be taken of the purpose for which things were acquired as well as of the methods of storage, use, or display employed by the University, which may tell us much of how the relevant authorities perceived these things.

Acquisitions had to be kept in a place thought appropriate at the time and in a manner which allowed them to be available for use. Books were housed in purpose-built libraries; but initially, and indeed into the nineteenth century, libraries did not only hold collections of books. They also contained the objects, the *artificialia* (man-made objects) and the *naturalia* (natural specimens), that were essential for the study of man and of the natural world; little distinction was drawn between these objects and books, the products of learning. As thinking and knowledge progressed, so did the perception change of how each subject was related to another, with consequent need for changes in classification. This in turn led to the need to rehouse many of the objects, eventually in purpose-built museums. This is a process to which there can never be an end.

The quasi-monastic nature of the colleges ensured that students based their work in and offered their loyalty to their college. It was therefore the colleges that housed the first books kept in the University, with Merton leading the way. The first recorded gift of books to the University was that of several copies of the Bible from Rogerus de Insula (d. 1235), Chancellor of the Diocese of Lincoln (which then included Oxford) between 1217 and 1220.

In the 1320s Thomas Cobham, Bishop of Worcester (d. 1327), presented some books and the money needed to house them in a room to be built over the old Congregation House attached to the University Church; owing to legal disputes, this was not completed until 1410. The librarian was to be the University Chaplain. In 1439 Humphrey, Duke of Gloucester (1391–1447), a major donor of money towards the building of the new Divinity School, gave the University 129 books, valued at over £1,000. By the time of his death he had given over six hundred volumes. In 1444 the University, recognizing that Cobham's room was too small, appealed to the Duke for assistance in building a library over the Divinity School. Duke Humfrey's Library was opened in 1458, eleven years after the Duke's death. The books from Cobham's library were transferred and considerable further donations of books immediately came in.

How the library was fitted is not known for certain, but in all probability it resembled that of Magdalen College (of about the same date), with tall bookcases at right angles to the long walls and with narrow reading-benches and desks on which to rest the chained books. In 1550 the library was emptied and virtually destroyed by the Commissioners of Edward VI for reformation of the University; even the book-shelves and desks were torn out and sold.

It was thus an empty room that Sir Thomas Bodley (1545–1613) determined to refound as a library; his first offer to the University is dated 23 February 1598. The new 'public' Library of the University was opened on 8 November 1602, already holding some 2,500 volumes, many of which would have contained more than one book. The

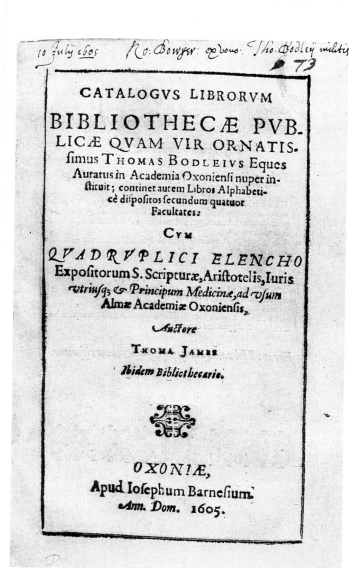

CATALOGVS LIBRORVM

BIBLIOTHECÆ PVB-
LICÆ QVAM VIR ORNATIS-
simus THOMAS BODLEIVS Eques
Auratus in Academia Oxoniensi nuper in-
stituit; continet autem Libros Alphabeti-
cè dispositos secundum quatuor
Facultates:

CVM

QVADRVPLICI ELENCHO
Expositorum S. Scripturæ, Aristotelis, Iuris
vtriusq; & Principum Medicinæ, ad vsum
Almæ Academiæ Oxoniensis.

Auctore

THOMA JAMES

Ibidem Bibliothecario.

OXONIÆ,
Apud Iosephum Barnesium.
Ann. Dom. 1605.

THE FIRST PRINTED CATALOGUE of the Bodleian Library, 1605, compiled by Thomas James. About 8,600 entries, with an author index between the main part and the appendix, made this the most advanced catalogue of any European library. The necessity for the appendix indicates the speed at which the library was growing.

first Librarian was Thomas James (1573?–1629), and the first printed catalogues appeared in 1604, 1605, and 1620. (Cambridge University Library had published its first catalogue, of 451 books and some manuscripts, in 1582.)

The physical appearance of the library has been altered by the building of the 'Arts End' in 1612, but the arrangement of the bookcases and desks was much as it is today. The books and manuscripts were kept together, both on the shelves and in the catalogues, and the volumes stood upright on the shelves, edges facing outwards (the spines were unmarked) and chained to a loop running on a lockable rod. The method of cataloguing in 1620 was by the arrangement still in use even in this age of the computer, with books classified alphabetically by author's name followed by a full transcription of the title.

The 1620 catalogue was the first alphabetically arranged catalogue of any public library since ancient times, and it consisted of some 675 pages. As in the earlier catalogues, most books were in Latin; Bodley himself always doubted the value of books in English, and the first large group of works in English arrived only in 1640 with the library of Robert Burton (1577–1640). The first Folio of Shakespeare was received in 1623, but was not catalogued until the 1635 appendix to the 1620 catalogue.

Catalogues themselves had been made necessary by the presence of unchained books in the library. There was no provision either for the expense of the preparation of catalogues or for their publication; this was met by the ingenious regulation of 1621, that all readers had to buy a catalogue as part of their admission procedure and had to buy new catalogues as they appeared. This was rescinded only in 1692. A two-part catalogue of books, costing 19s., was published in 1674; by 1692 stocks of this were low and the compulsory purchase of a catalogue by readers was ended. A catalogue of manuscripts was published in 1698.

PARTHENIA, frontispiece of the first engraved book of music in England, containing compositions by William Byrd, John Bull, and Orlando Gibbons. A copy was presented to Princess Elizabeth, the daughter of James I, in 1611, and this copy was received by the Bodleian Library under the agreement with the Stationers' Company of 1610.

In 1610 the library was granted by the Stationers' Company of London the right to the gift of a copy of every new book published in England. Unfortunately, more often than not individual publishers failed to supply books. In 1614, for example, only 15–20 per cent of the works that should have come were received, and virtually no works were received during the Interregnum (1649–60). Many of the books which were supplied were rejected—Bodley referred to some of these as 'idle books and riffe raffes'. Naturally enough, successive librarians sought to compel the stationers to carry out their obligation, and the provision was given statutory force in an Act of Parliament of 1710. Even then it remained a source of quarrels and litigation, because it was easily evaded by publishers. Eventually, in 1814, a new Act was passed, which was so much more effective that in 1836 Oxford rejected an offer of a grant of £500 per annum in lieu of the rights. But even this legislation proved insufficiently strong, and it was not until it was amended in 1842 that Bodley finally began to receive its due. This meant that the library no longer had to buy new books published in England, but could concentrate on the purchase of foreign books and of old collections. Attempts were later made to rescind or restrict the Act, or to 'buy out' the rights. Fortunately none succeeded, and the University today receives a vast number of valuable and essential publications.

Bodley's legacy produced an income of £62. 15s. per annum, though this was greatly reduced later in the 1640s, as it was based on rents no longer collectable. In 1642–3 only £12 was spent on books and in 1645 only £2. 16s. Relatively unmolested during the Civil War (though bankrupt in 1647), the library remained open. Few books were purchased for some years thereafter. On the other hand, the first of the great benefactions of manuscripts that were to enrich the library over the centuries began to come in during the 1620s: those of Sir Thomas Roe (1581?–1644) in 1628, of the third Earl of Pembroke (1580–1630) (including that of Barocci, c.1535–1612) in 1629, and of Sir Kenelm Digby (1603–65) in 1634. The extensive series of gifts of Archbishop Laud (1573–1645) began in 1635; these included coins, Egyptian antiquities, and an album of Mogul miniature paintings, the first identifiable examples in a European collection. (Until well into the nineteenth century the Bodleian collections were of objects as well as of books and manuscripts. In particular, the Picture Gallery and the Anatomy School were to hold large collections, while the coins and medals were to become among the most important in Britain.)

Before 1628 there had been about a thousand volumes of manuscripts; the collections of Roe, Barocci, and Digby added 600 and that of Laud another 1,250. Many of Laud's were Arabic and Greek, and the Bodleian hence became a centre for the study of these cultures. Collections were still coming in; on the death of John Selden (1584–1654), one of the greatest of the library's benefactors, some 8,000 of his books came to the library. The University could also rise to an occasion. Such was the opportunity to buy the collection of manuscripts of Sir Christopher Hatton (1540–91), famous for its Anglo-Saxon material, in 1671. To this were added, by bequests, the Anglo-Saxon collections of Francis Junius (1589–1677) and of Bishop John Fell

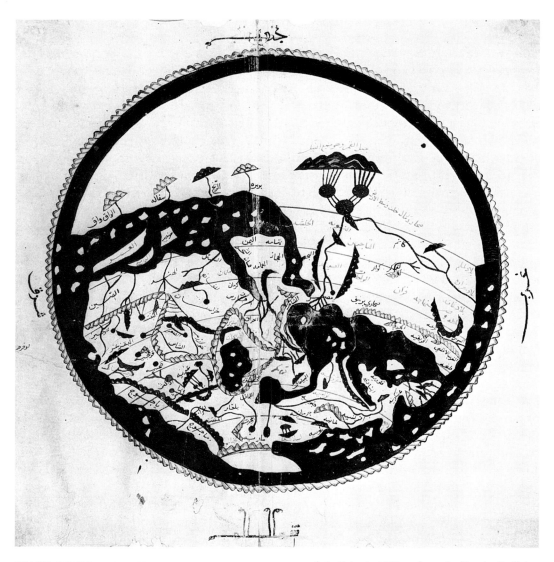

ARABIC WORLD MAP OF THE TWELFTH CENTURY, copy, made in Cairo in 1533, and acquired by the Bodleian in the purchase of the library of the great orientalist Edward Pococke in 1692. Note that south is at the top of the map.

(1625–86). Thus in fifteen years the Bodleian became a major centre for Anglo-Saxon studies. This was to be a pattern thereafter: a collection of books or manuscripts attracted scholars, who later left their own books to the library.

The disposal of duplicates, often first editions where a later one had been received, was commonplace. In 1676 so many were sold that £248 was raised (one of the casualties was the First Folio Shakespeare of 1623: it was repurchased by the University in 1905 for £3,000). The £248 was borrowed by the University for use in the building of the Ashmolean Museum and only repaid some ten years later. The librarian complained of an annual income of only £10, and yet money was raised to buy one collection of 420 Oriental manuscripts formed by Edward Pococke (1604–91) for £800 and another of 600 formed by Robert Huntington (1637–1701) for £1,000; these greatly strengthened the Laud bequest. An abortive attempt was even made to buy the library of Vossius (1577–1649), the Dutch Renaissance scholar, for the enormous sum of £3,000 (the books went to Leiden).

The early eighteenth century was not a great age for the library, nor were many benefactions received; from 1700 to 1703 there is no record of any expenditure on books. And yet the Bodleian was one of the few public libraries in Europe to which a scholar or connoisseur with no affiliation could gain access. Many foreign readers were admitted, mostly from the German States, and visitors even complained about overcrowding. Undergraduates were admitted only exceptionally.

The will of Dr John Radcliffe (1650–1714) left to a group of trustees the sum needed for the purchase of land and erection thereon of a new library. Radcliffe was under the mistaken impression that the 1710 Copyright Act would make it unnecessary to purchase English books and determined that his Camera would house foreign publications. By the time the Radcliffe Library was opened, in 1749, its purpose had changed and it was to house an ill-assorted and heterogeneous collection of books throughout the eighteenth century. It was, in spite of its handsome building and endowment, no use to the University, as the first librarian, Francis Wise (c.1685–1767), locked the doors and bought few books. One of his successors, Thomas Hornsby (1733–1810), librarian from 1783 to 1810, bought not a single book, as he was too busy being Radcliffe Observer, Savilian Professor of Astronomy, and Sedleian Professor of Natural Philosophy at the same time. It was not until the appointment of George Williams (1762–1834) in 1810 that the library began to serve some purpose, buying books on medicine and natural history (Williams was a physician and Professor of Botany) to the value of £500–700 per annum. The first printed catalogue appeared in 1835. From 1841 to 1862, however, the annual expenditure on books fell back to only £200. Henry Acland (1815–1900), Radcliffe Librarian from 1851, was charged with the removal of the scientific books from the Camera to the new University Museum in August 1861; Acland had been one of the museum's leading proponents. The Camera became a reading-room for the Bodleian and the ground floor was enclosed (see p. 105). Eventually—as late as 1927—the Radcliffe Camera was transferred to the possession of the University.

The Bodleian undertook a major rearrangement of books in 1719, when folio and quarto volumes were separated for the first time. In 1720 a proposal for a 'Union catalogue' of the University and college libraries was put forward but came to nothing: it gives some indication, however, of the importance of the college Libraries. A two-volume catalogue of printed books was published in 1738, the first since 1695. It was to remain the only general catalogue of the Bodleian books until 1843, and became a standard work: other libraries, such as that of Cambridge University (in 1752), bought it for use as the basis for their own catalogues, annotated and interleaved.

The library, as we have seen, held more than books. The Laudian curiosities arrived in the 1630s and the first part of the Arundel Marbles in 1667. These were part of the collection formed by Thomas Howard, Earl of Arundel (1586–1646), between 1602 and 1646, and consisted of inscriptions, sarcophagi, and bas-reliefs; it was John Evelyn (1620–1706) who persuaded Arundel's grandson to give them. The statues were to follow in 1755, gift of the Dowager Countess Pomfret (d. 1761). The 1667 gifts were built into the wall between the Sheldonian and the Ashmolean, remaining there until the mid-nineteenth century, when they were placed first in the Ashmolean basement (the old chemistry laboratory) and then moved to the new University Galleries.

The Picture Gallery, now the south and east wings of the Upper Reading Room of the Bodleian Library, held the University's collection of paintings, then mostly portraits, and cabinets of coins and medals. The huge medal cabinet given by Ralph Freke (1595/6–1684) in 1657 stood in the south-east corner of the room, probably next to one of the five given by Laud. It was still there in 1710. The Picture Gallery was not used to hold books until 1824.

The Anatomy School on the first floor of the south wing of the Bodleian Quadrangle was the recipient of the many specimens of natural history that flowed into the Bodleian along with books, coins, medals, pictures, and other artefacts. Much of the collection was of medical interest, such as bladder-stones (there was one in the library at least as early as 1593), or was made up of abnormalities from the natural world; there were specimens on view in 1630. John Evelyn (1620–1706), the virtuoso and diarist, visited the school in 1654, commenting on the natural-history specimens ('nothing extraordinary, save the Skin of a Jaccal, a rarely Colour'd Jacatroo, or prodigious large Parot'), and again in 1664. *Artificialia* were kept in the tower at the Bodleian, where Evelyn saw 'Josephs parti colourd Coate', now regrettably no longer in the University's possession. Many of these curiosities, including Guy Fawkes's (1570–1606) lantern, were to be transferred to the University Galleries in 1887. Such collections were also to be found in London in the Royal College of Physicians, in the Royal Society, and in the Tradescant collection, which was to come to Oxford in 1683. A list of curiosities of about 1675 comprises much medical material as well as '2 Doadoes' among many birds, mammals, and reptiles. Among later oddities was the 'Dragon' faked up in 1704 from the body of a dead rat by Jacob Bobart the Younger (1641–1719), Superintendent of the Physic Garden. The 'young whale found in the River Severn below Glocester' noted by Thomas Hearne (1678–1735) in 1705 had been transported to Oxford at a cost to the University of 14s. 6d. In the early eighteenth century so crowded were the specimens that a contemporary, after commenting on the dirt and disorder (which he also criticized at Cambridge), mentioned that anatomy-teaching could no longer be carried out there but had to be done elsewhere. This was true, and the Anatomy School moved to Christ Church. By the mid-century there seems to have been the greatest confusion, and indeed competition, between the Anatomy School collection and that of the Ashmolean Museum.

Already at the beginning of the seventeenth century it was becoming apparent that

GUY FAWKES'S LANTERN (*left*), metal and glass, supposedly used on the Fifth of November 1605 in the Gunpowder Plot—a typical 'curiosity' acquired by the Bodleian Library for its associations, and later transferred to the Ashmolean.

THE DODO (*right*), attributed to Roelant Savery. Early catalogues of the Bodleian and Tradescant collections indicate that the University once owned three specimens of the dodo, the now extinct flightless bird from Mauritius. Today only a skull, some skin from a head, and a foot remain in the University Museum.

the formation of 'Universal Collections' to encompass all knowledge was impossible. The doubling of the size of the known world in the sixteenth and early seventeenth centuries caused profound changes in the ways of thought of the Western world. Peoples, animals, and plants unknown either to the classical world or from the Bible threw doubts on both these sources. Men were obliged to think for themselves instead of relying on authority and not only to look at the new specimens of God's and man's handiwork arriving in Europe almost daily, but also more critically to examine their own surroundings. It was the beginning of a new natural history that included both *naturalia* and the *artificialia*.

Collections had almost always included a garden, a 'paradise'. The first attempt at a scientific botanic garden was that of Padua in 1545 and the next that of Leiden in 1587.

John Gerard (1545–1612) attempted in 1589 to interest the University of Cambridge in a botanic garden, but failed. The first botanic garden in England, the Physic Garden in Oxford, was founded by the Earl of Danby (then Henry Danvers) (1573–1644) in 1621, with the astonishing gift to the University of £5,000 for the purpose. This was to be specifically for the growing of medicinal plants (a 'physic' garden) and of such plants as would be useful for the teaching of botany by a professor. The name of the garden was changed to its present one, the Botanic Garden, only in 1840.

Much of Danby's money was spent on the arch and on the great walls that still frame the garden. From 1638 the head gardener was Jacob Bobart (1599–1680), who held the post for thirty-seven years, to be followed by his son, who held it for another forty-one

THE DANBY GATE OF THE PHYSIC GARDEN, with Jacob Bobart and his pet goat, copied on to a Chinese export porcelain plate of the mid-eighteenth century from a European print of 1713 which had been used as the frontispiece to *Vertumnus* by Abel Evans. The plate has been purchased recently for the Department of Eastern Art by a college fund.

years. The first Professor of Botany, Robert Morison (1620–83), King Charles I's physician, was not appointed until 1669. Both the Bobarts were energetic men. The first catalogue of the garden, published in 1648, lists some 1,600 plants; the second edition of 1658 gives some 2,000, of which not more than 600 were native to England. Morison, a contemporary of but no friend to John Ray (1627–1705), the systematic botanist and zoologist, was working on a natural system of plant classification (before the time of Linnaeus (Carl von Linné), 1707–78) and was interested in variegated plants, as his successors are today. At the same time Sir Thomas Millington (1628–1704), Professor of Natural Philosophy, was considering the sexuality of plants (ten years before Camerarius, 1665–1721, proved it in experiments published in 1694), an interest followed by the younger Bobart. The Bobarts were both keen collectors of plants and of seeds. The son initiated a practice that is maintained in the garden today, and has spread to botanic gardens all over the world, that of the circulation of a list of seeds available for exchange. The Loggan print of the garden of 1675 shows a large conservatory for the raising of tender plants, possibly the first in England. It also shows the formal arrangement for the systemic beds that has survived, after many vicissitudes, to this day.

The conservatory was enlarged by the gifts of William Sherard (1659–1728) in the 1720s, among which was the establishment of the Sherardian Chair in Botany. John Dillenius (1687–1747), the first to hold the chair, conducted Linnaeus around the garden in 1736. Though he was not entirely convinced by Linnaeus's binomial system of plant classification, he was evidently much impressed, and offered Linnaeus half of his professorial salary to remain in Oxford. Linnaeus, alas, refused: had he accepted, Dillenius would have been remembered for more than his notorious introduction of the Oxford Ragwort, *Senecio squalidus*. (See also p. 275.) From 1747 to 1783 the garden slept under the evasions of the Professor, Humphrey Sibthorp (1713–97). His successor, his son John (1758–96), was a very different man and an enthusiastic collector of plants and seeds, mainly from Greece and the Aegean; this led posthumously to publication of his *Flora Graeca* of 1806–40. The garden flourished during his tenure, but was again neglected for the following thirty-odd years. It was only with the appointment of Charles Daubeny (1795–1867) in 1834 that things improved. Daubeny successfully raised money for the garden and built new greenhouses. A vital resource for a garden that aspires to a wide collection, greenhouses have been a major, though expensive, source of pleasure and interest since.

The foundation of the Physic Garden was, in effect, part of the new approach to learning of the seventeenth century. In 1648 the Oxford Experimental Philosophy Club was founded; although it lasted in its initial form only until 1658, it undoubtedly gave a major impetus to the foundation of the Royal Society in 1660. Many of the 'new men' moved to London, but the time had come for serious study in Oxford of the new experimental sciences. Elias Ashmole (1617–92) was part of this movement (see below, p. 304). In 1644 he had studied mathematics, astronomy, and natural philosophy at Brasenose; he was a founder Fellow of the Royal Society. When, in 1675, he formally offered his collections to the University, the proposed gift comprised not only his own collections of manuscripts, medals, and gold coins, but also the very large and valuable collection of rarities of the Tradescant family. This had been formed by John Tradescant (d. 1637?) and his son John (1608–62), who had both been gardeners, travellers, and collectors of plants, animals, and curiosities. Their collections had been exhibited to the public in Lambeth, at 'Tradescant's Ark', and Ashmole had helped to prepare the catalogue, the first of an English collection to be published, in 1656. He had also catalogued the coins and medals (his major interest in the collections) of the Bodleian, being awarded a doctorate for his pains.

The celebrated Tradescant collection was not untypical of its time, being comparable, for instance, to those of Sir Walter Cope (d. 1614) and of Robert Hubert (*fl.* 1630–70), whose collection became the basis of the Royal Society's. It was also comparable to those housed in the Bodleian. The collection was divided into *Artificialia* and *Naturalia*, the latter comprising minerals as well as specimens of natural history. The most celebrated of those that survive today (at least, in part) was the dodo, probably acquired in 1638. The 'Artificialls' comprised anything made by man, from works of art through coins and medals to ethnographic items. Here again there is a very famous survivor, 'Powhatan's mantle' of deerskin with shell decoration (Powhatan, father of Pocahontas, 1595–1617, was King of Virginia), which was certainly in the collection by 1638. The younger Tradescant had given the collection to Ashmole, allowing his wife a life interest only. There was friction between Mrs Tradescant and Ashmole before the collection was finally his.

MAP OF VIRGINIA (*facing*), drawn by John Smith, 1612, copperplate by William Hole. Smith was one of the original settlers in Jamestown; in 1607 he was captured by the chief, Powhatan, whose 'mantle' is listed in the Tradescant collection in 1656.

TOMAHAWK (*below*), wood, north-east North America, seventeenth century. Of the six 'tamahacks' in the Tradescant collection in 1656, only three survive, the earliest securely recorded examples known. The name derives from an Algonquin word, and later came to be used for the metal axes introduced by Europeans.

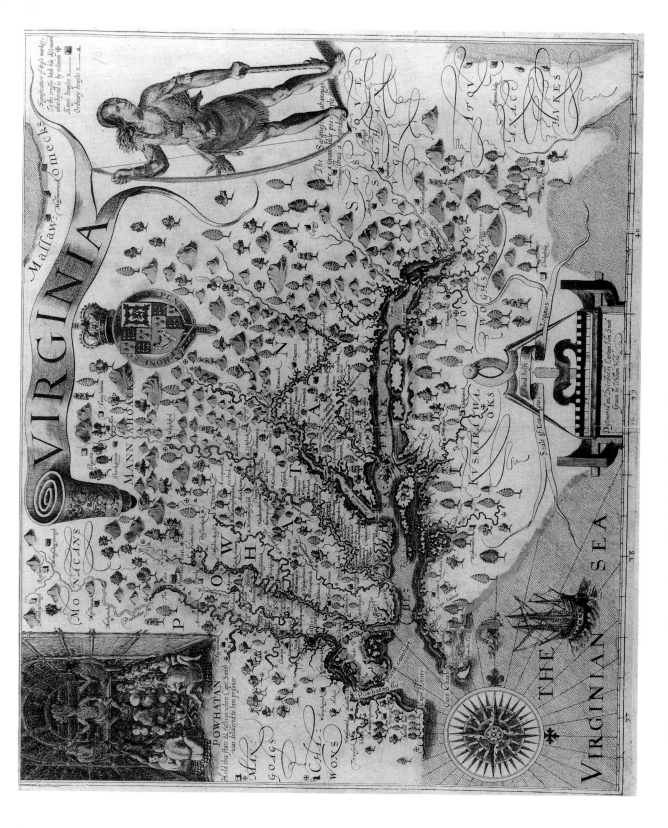

Ashmole's offer of this great collection came at a convenient time for the University. The Experimental Philosophy Club had begun the encouragement of observational and experimental science, and the University determined to set up a lecturership in 'Philosophicall History' to be held by Robert Plot (1640–96), whose *Natural History of Oxfordshire* was with the University Press at that time. The collection was to be housed in 'some large Roome, which may have Chimnies, to keep those things aired that will Stand in need of it'. It was decided by 1677 that a room would have to be built for the purpose, and the opportunity would be taken to build a chemistry laboratory and a lecture-room at the same time. Work began on a site in Broad Street between the Sheldonian Theatre and Exeter College in 1679, using money borrowed from the profits of the sale by the Bodleian of duplicate copies of books. The Ashmolean Museum was formally opened by the Duke and Duchess of York in May 1683.

The institution thus established demonstrates some of the method of empirical study in the University. Chemistry was to be studied with natural history, a subject that was now forced to include the natural history of man. The objects both of natural history and of the work of man were actually to be used for study and not simply as objects of curiosity; if study faltered every now and then during the history of the museum, then this was usually attributable as much to the inertia of individuals concerned with the collection as to a general lack of interest within the University. There had always been some resistance to the museum: in some quarters it was referred to as the 'knick-knackatory'.

Visitors could view the collections, for a fee, only under the guidance of the Keeper or Under-Keeper. The Under-Keeper was paid by the Keeper from his salary of £50 per annum. The first Keeper was, appropriately, Robert Plot, succeeded by his Under-Keeper Edward Lhuyd (1660–1709). Both of these active and forward-looking men added to the collections and enhanced the prestige of the museum. Both made considerable contributions to research and were successful in attracting gifts from others, not only of scientific material but also of works of art and ethnography.

Into both of these categories falls the Pala sculpture of Vishnu given by Sir William Hedges (1632–1701) in 1686–7, the first identifiable acquisition by a Western museum of an Indian sculpture. A major benefactor of the period was Martin Lister (1638?–1712), who gave, *inter alia*, the finest collection of fossil and modern shells in Britain; another was William Borlase (1695–1772), who formed a large collection of metals, minerals, and crystals from Cornwall.

Much acquisition of material was by exchange; duplicates, as at the Bodleian, were ruthlessly given away or exchanged. This was undesirable as it was liable to destroy the integrity of single collections. Thus the collection of fossils accumulated by Edward Lhuyd during his prolonged absences from the museum cannot now be identified. The German traveller and compulsive diarist, Zacharias Conrad von Uffenbach (1683–1734), who visited the museum in 1710, has left a very full account of the contents; he was not much impressed by the collection, though he allowed it to be better than that of the Royal Society at Gresham College. A natural complainer, von Uffenbach was horrified that 'even the women are allowed up here for sixpence'. He did at least admire Lhuyd's fossils.

Under the Keepership of John Whiteside (1679–1729) from 1714 to 1729 the museum received in 1718, by bequest of Nathaniel Palmer (1660/1–1717), one of its greatest treasures, the Alfred Jewel. This rock-crystal and gold object with an enamel image, possibly a personification of the sense of sight, perhaps for use as a reading pointer, bears an inscription which reads 'Alfred had me made'. Certainly dating from the ninth century, it was found in 1693 near Athelney in Somerset. Another unusual gift

VISHNU (*below left*), basalt, a Pala sculpture of the eleventh century, acquired by Sir William Hedges and listed in the first Ashmolean Museum Book of Benefactors in 1695, the earliest recorded Indian sculpture in Britain. Sir Arthur Evans transferred this to the Pitt Rivers Museum as ethnographic; now it is on loan to the Ashmolean.

TAHITIAN CHIEF MOURNER'S DRESS (*below right*), made of fabric, shells, and feathers, collected on Captain Cook's second voyage (1772–5) by Johann Rheinhold Forster, from whom it was acquired by the University. Transferred as ethnology to the Pitt Rivers Museum by Sir Arthur Evans, this collection of Cook material is of vital importance in the dating and origination of such objects.

was the iron-lined hat worn by the regicide John Bradshaw (1602–59) during the trial of King Charles I. So popular was the museum in the early eighteenth century that fees produced an astonishing income of about £80 per annum. Whiteside's major contribution to the museum was his accumulation of a large series of scientific instruments, including the fine clock by George Graham (1673–1751) incorporating the new dead-beat escapement which made it the most accurate and advanced clock in Europe.

George Huddesford (1699–1776), Keeper from 1732, was as slothful as Humphrey Sibthorp in the Physic Garden; and his son William (1732–72), Keeper from 1755, was as energetic as Sibthorp's son John. The most remarkable incident of the elder Huddesford's Keepership was the determination by Sir Hans Sloane (1660–1753) not to leave his collections to Oxford; they became the basis of the British Museum, opened in 1759. Nearly lost also were the vast gifts to the museum and to the Bodleian of Richard Rawlinson (1690–1755), which finally arrived in 1755. William Huddesford rearranged the animal and plant material according to the binomial system of Linnaeus. Much of the early collection of organic material was found to be in a very poor state, and this was ordered to be burnt, without regard to Ashmole's stipulation that if anything decayed to the extent that it had to be destroyed then it should be recorded in a drawing first. Huddesford also tried to acquire archival material for the museum, including Lhuyd's papers. He has been judged one of the most effective Keepers of the eighteenth century, even though public interest in the museum (to judge by the income from fees) dropped considerably. He took little interest in antiquarian studies, though he encouraged gifts of coins. Under his successor William Sheffield (1732–95), Johann Reinhold Forster (1729–98) donated the highly important (but at the time little considered) South Pacific material that had been gathered during the voyages of Captain Cook (1728–79). More than 130 of the original 170 specimens survive in the Pitt Rivers Museum.

Several colleges had collections of curiosities, some of which survive. The John Pointer (1668–1754) collection of about 1740, belonging to St John's College, now on loan to the Museum of the History of Science, contains what may be the earliest surviving collection of birds' eggs. The John Oglander (1736/7–94) collection of *materia medica*, from the second half of the eighteenth century, is on loan from New College. Charles Daubeny's magnificent collection of minerals was sent to the University Museum by Magdalen College as late as the 1940s.

On the whole such collections, even that of the Ashmolean, declined in relevance, especially as aids to teaching, during the eighteenth century. It was only with the totally new approaches to the study of antiquity and of the sciences during the nineteenth century that the collections again became important to the functions of the University.

The foundation by Dr Matthew Lee (1694–1755) of a Readership in Anatomy led to the concentration of the teaching of medicine in the Anatomy School in Christ Church. Lectures and dissections took place in a room in which there was also a considerable collection, popularly known as 'Skeleton corner'. Preparation of specimens took place in an adjoining stable, to the discomfort of nearby coachmen; one day they raided the

JAW OF THE DINOSAUR *MEGALOSAURUS* found a few miles from Oxford at Stonesfield and described by Buckland in 1824. Plot had illustrated a dinosaur bone as that of a giant: the concept of (and name) dinosaur began with Richard Owen in 1842, but Buckland had recognized this specimen, which is in the University Museum, as a giant 'lizard'.

stable and threw into St Aldate's the partly macerated skeleton of a giraffe. A dog ran away with the tail, and the giraffe skeleton, on display today in the University Museum, has some of its caudal vertebrae replaced by leaden imitations. To this collection was soon added the appropriate material from the Anatomy School in the Bodleian; it was to remain there until the foundation of the University Museum in the 1860s. In 1833 the palaeontological and mineralogical specimens, including the newly acquired Richard Simmons (1781/2–1846) collection of minerals, were moved from the Ashmolean to the Clarendon Building, lately vacated by the University Press, under the supervision of William Buckland (1784–1856); some rooms were opened as the Clarendon Museum in 1838. Buckland had been appointed Reader in Mineralogy in 1813 and in Geology in 1819. His lectures, given in the Ashmolean, were immensely popular. He was a great collector of specimens, including the jaw-bone and, later, other parts of the first recognized dinosaur, *Megalosaurus bucklandi*. Later gifts included ichthyosaurs and plesiosaurs from Lyme Regis collected by Miss E. Philpot (1780–1857). These included Types (ideal specimens defining the characteristics of a family) of many of the 'Poissons fossiles' identified by Louis Agassiz (1807–73). The great strength of the Jurassic collection was consolidated by W. J. Arkell (1904–58) in the 1920s and 1930s.

Thus, as they grew, the Ashmolean's collections were being dispersed; the building in Broad Street was soon to hold little save the zoological, archaeological, and ethnographical material. To some extent this negated the efforts of the Duncan brothers John Shute (*fl.* 1831) and Philip Bury (1772–1863), successive Keepers, who published the first general catalogue of the museum in 1836. In 1858 the library of books and manuscripts, catalogued in 1845, was moved to the Bodleian; so, surprisingly, were the coins and medals. The Duncans rearranged the central floor as the main exhibition space, losing the top floor to the examiners (a new body); it was regained by Arthur Evans (1851–1941) only after 1884. There had been some suggestion that room might be found in the museum for another reading-room for the Bodleian.

In the Bodleian the reading-rooms were made more comfortable; the fixed benches were replaced by Windsor chairs in 1753. The books were unchained from 1757: this was late, for many Cambridge libraries had unchained a century previously. Funds for purchases were still sadly lacking, but in these years the Bodleian received some splendid donations: the William Sancroft (1617–93) papers from Thomas Tanner (1674–1735), Bishop of St Asaph; the early English books of Nathaniel Crynes (1685/6–1746); the Russian material of Daniel Dumaresq (1712–1805); and, greatest of all, the vast collections of Richard Rawlinson. This indefatigable collector bequeathed his entire collection of manuscripts (now in 5,205 volumes) to the library, as well as other items to the Ashmolean. This was by far the largest gift the library had ever received; it was not finally sorted and catalogued until 1893.

In the 1780s the finances of the Bodleian were dramatically improved by the imposition of charges even upon members of the University. In one year income from fees rose from £10 to £480. This enabled the library to buy numbers of incunabula (books printed before 1501) at the Pirelli and Crevenna sales, though money also had to be borrowed for the purpose. It was not paid back for five years.

In 1847 Henry Acland, Librarian of the Radcliffe Library, was appointed Dr Lee's Reader in Chemistry; a keen collector of natural-history specimens, he laid out the Christ Church Anatomy School collection after the latest ideas of John Hunter (1728–93). At the same time the Revd F. W. Hope (1797–1862) presented the University with his great collection of insects and other arthropods and his library, including a large collection of engraved portraits. The latter went to the Radcliffe Camera and the natural-history specimens were stored in the Taylor Institution, newly built as part of the University Galleries complex.

Art and classical archaeology were recognized by the University on the building of the University Galleries in 1851–4. Into this neo-Grecian building were moved most of the paintings from the Bodleian (and elsewhere) and the Arundel Marbles, some other classical antiquities, including some of the newly acquired Alessandro Castellani (1823–83) Etruscan material, and a considerable collection of casts from the Antique. Other antiquities remained in the Ashmolean, unregarded until the time of John Parker (1806–84) and of Arthur Evans. Also to the new building came a major part of the unique collection of drawings by Raphael and Michelangelo formed by Sir Thomas Lawrence (1769–1830). These were bought for the University by public subscription, mainly due to the efforts of the Revd Dr Henry Wellesley (1791–1866) in 1846; many Oxford persons subscribed, but most of the money came from one donor, Lord Eldon (1751–1838). Among the hundreds of drawings bought, fifty-four are still accepted as by

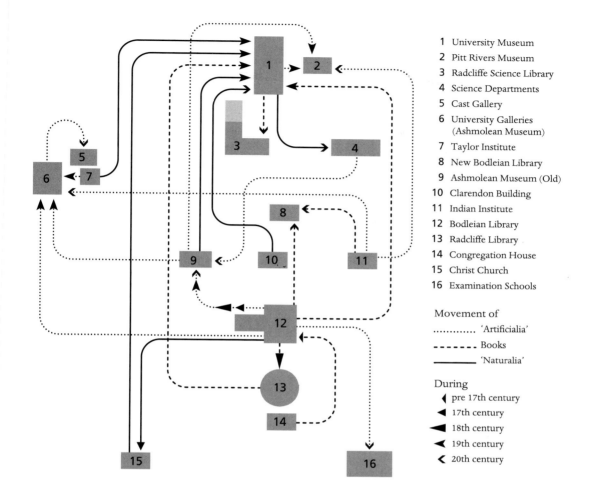

1 University Museum
2 Pitt Rivers Museum
3 Radcliffe Science Library
4 Science Departments
5 Cast Gallery
6 University Galleries
   (Ashmolean Museum)
7 Taylor Institute
8 New Bodleian Library
9 Ashmolean Museum (Old)
10 Clarendon Building
11 Indian Institute
12 Bodleian Library
13 Radcliffe Library
14 Congregation House
15 Christ Church
16 Examination Schools

Movement of
.... 'Artificialia'
- - - - - - - Books
─────────── 'Naturalia'

During
❮ pre 17th century
◀ 17th century
◀ 18th century
◀ 19th century
❮ 20th century

MAJOR MOVEMENTS OF COLLECTED MATERIAL
BETWEEN INSTITUTIONS

Michelangelo and sixty-eight as by Raphael; it is the most important collection of Raphael drawings in existence.

The University Galleries provided a new focus for gifts from old members of the University, who had more usually given to their colleges. Thus, the Hon. W. T. H. Fox-Strangways, later Earl of Ilchester (1795–1865), who had already given two substantial collections of Old Master paintings to Christ Church in 1828 and 1834, gave a third collection to the University Galleries in 1850. During a stay in Italy Fox-Strangways had formed a taste, unusual for its time, for the early Florentines; from him came one of the Galleries' most famous paintings, *A Hunt in a Forest* by Paolo Uccello. This excellent start was continued with the gift by Lord Ellesmere (1800–57) in 1853 of a collection of

TWO HEADS OF APOSTLES, drawing on paper by Raphael. The University, through active fund-raising, purchased in the 1830s a major part of the collection of old-master drawings formed by the painter Sir Thomas Lawrence, at a time when such drawings were only just beginning to be accepted as works of art.

drawings by the Carracci (Agostino, Annibale, and Lodovico) and with the gift by Chambers Hall (1786–1865) in 1855 of drawings by Leonardo, Rubens, Rembrandt, Corregio, Dürer, Adriaen van Ostade, and Claude. The extensive collections of drawings and engravings formed by Francis Douce (1757–1834) were transferred from the Bodleian. Between 1861 and 1871 John Ruskin (1819–1900) gave a collection of drawings and water-colours, especially rich in the works of J. M. W. Turner (1775–1857). The School of Drawing named after Ruskin was established in 1871; this was to lead to the introduction of a Final Honour School in Fine Art in 1978. The study of the History of Art at graduate level has been recognized since 1955 by the establishment of a chair, of which the first holder was Edgar Wind (1900–71), and of a department in 1961.

At the beginning of the nineteenth century the natural-history collections of the University were still widely dispersed. Anatomy was in Christ Church, zoology in the

PORTRAIT, PROBABLY OF GENTILE
BELLINI (*c.*1429–1521), attributed to
Giovanni Bellini (1430–1516). This fine
drawing was part of the collection of paintings and drawings, unusual for its time, left
to his old College, Christ Church, by
General John Guise in 1765. Christ Church
now has its own Picture Gallery. The
drawing was recently exhibited (Royal
Academy, 1992) attributed to Andrea
Mantegna (1431–1506).

Ashmolean, geology in the Clarendon, and the Hope collection of entomology in the
Taylorian. It now became evident that a new building was needed to house these collections. The moving spirits behind this idea were Acland, the Reader in Anatomy, the
younger Duncan, Keeper of the Ashmolean, Daubeny, Professor of Botany (and Chemistry), and John Phillips (1800–74), who had become Reader in Geology in 1853. The
University accepted the proposal in 1855, and four acres of land were bought from Merton College. It was Acland's intention that the new Science Area should include a
botanic garden and a zoo, a scheme which nearly brought an end to the Botanic Garden
on its early site: even Daubeny wished it to move. The University doubted the wisdom
of this idea and sought the advice of Sir Joseph Hooker (1817–1911) of Kew, who firmly
recommended that the garden stay where it was, and is.

Between 1860 and 1866 the collections of geology and natural history were all trans-

THE PITT RIVERS MUSEUM, interior, *c.*1910, showing the Haida Totem pole acquired in 1901. The arrangement of the museum by type of artefact rather than by area of origin stems from General Pitt-Rivers's own work on the evolution of the musket.

ferred to the University Museum. Science books were also brought there from the Radcliffe Camera, to be removed again to an adjacent Radcliffe Science Library in 1902–3. John Phillips, the Reader in Geology, who had become Keeper of the Ashmolean Museum in 1854, was made the first Keeper of the new museum in 1860. This now housed Departments of Experimental Philosophy (Physics), Mineralogy, Chemistry, Anatomy, Physiology, and Zoology; Botany remained at the Garden. The east side of the building was soon to be extended to house the Pitt-Rivers collection of ethnography. Today the collections of mineralogy, geology, zoology, comparative anatomy, and entomology (based on the Hope collection, received in 1849) remain in the University Museum.

The original gift to the University of Lieutenant-General Augustus Henry Lane Fox Pitt-Rivers (1827–1900) in 1883 comprised some 15,000 specimens of ethnological material. Pitt-Rivers was convinced that ethnology and archaeology should be studied together; as the inventor of stratigraphical excavation he is regarded as one of the founding fathers of modern scientific archaeology. The works were to be displayed (as they still are) on a comparative basis, with no geographical or temporal divisions; this is a system, gradually abandoned elsewhere, that is now recognized again as useful. A special building was erected to the east of the University Museum and Edward Tylor (1832–1917) was made Lecturer in Anthropology, the first such appointment in Britain. The collections have grown ever since; Tylor acquired the great Haida Indian totem-pole from Queen Charlotte Island in British Columbia in 1901.

To the Pitt Rivers Museum came much of the remaining Ashmolean ethnological material. There was not much left in the Ashmolean: it was due only to the efforts of John Parker and Arthur Evans (Keepers 1870–84 and 1884–1908 respectively), and to the munificence of the collector Charles Fortnum (1820–99), that it survived. Under the Keepership of John Parker the first intimations of the possibility that Charles Fortnum might leave his great collection of Renaissance paintings, bronzes, and ceramics to the University had been heard. A movement was started to attempt to persuade the University to found a Museum of Art and Archaeology. For a time it seemed that the former Picture Gallery of the Bodleian would suffice, and this was actually set up in 1884. Under Arthur Evans it became clear that this would not do. Evans, like Parker, was an antiquarian, and he was to steer the Ashmolean firmly in the direction of his interests. In 1885–6, as a bargaining-counter in his efforts to prise the coin collections from the Bodleian (in which he failed), Evans reluctantly allowed the transfer of some of the ethnological material from the Ashmolean to the University Museum. Finding it difficult to draw a distinction between archaeology and anthropology, he pragmatically resolved to retain for archaeology the works of all of Europe, as well as the works of Mediterranean and Oriental lands that had contributed to Western civilization; other things, even items as important as the Forster Cook material or the Hedges Vishnu, could go to the anthropologists. It was a workable solution but not an entirely happy one, one that had to be revised in the mid-twentieth century with the recognition of Chinese, Japanese, and Indian works of art as art.

Neither Evans nor Fortnum (remarkably) was to be put off by the snubs of a dilatory University. Fortnum began to lend some of his collection to the Ashmolean, where Evans exhibited it on the upper floor, at last vacated by the examiners. Both Evans and Fortnum pressed for a new museum; the University procrastinated, and in 1891 Fortnum made elaborate proposals for the erection of a new building to the north of the University Galleries. In 1892 this was accepted, and the move to the new building was completed by November 1894. The old Ashmolean building, for the first time in 201 years, lost its function as a museum. The Ashmolean and the University Galleries were to be run as two separate institutions until the resignation of Arthur Evans (now knighted) in 1908, whereupon the two were amalgamated under the name 'Ashmolean Museum' (at the insistence of Fortnum), with David Hogarth (1862–1927) as Keeper.

BLUE AND WHITE JUG, of Medici 'porcelain', given by Charles Fortnum. It is one of only about seventy known pieces made in Venice *c.*1565 in emulation of Chinese porcelain. Fortnum's persistent wish to give his collections of decorative art to the University was one of the major impulses to the expansion of the Galleries.

Material was still arriving in the University that was soon to be housed in the University Museum. Many of the collections of zoological material that were accepted in the nineteenth and early twentieth centuries contained Type specimens. Some of these have only recently been recognized as such: Type specimens of birds have been found in the William Burchell (1782?–1863) collection (1865) and in the Dr George Such (b. 1797/8) collection (1825–6); and of tortoises and the Galapagos Sea Iguana in the Thomas Bell (1792–1880) collection (1861–94). Of the osteological collection a little still remains of Tradescant material; much of the vast collection formed by Professor George Rolleston (1829–81) for his comparative work on human crania (which so interested Pitt-Rivers that it may have helped in his decision to leave his collection to Oxford) was disposed of as recently as the 1940s.

The Department of Botany remained at the Garden until 1951, when it moved into a new building in South Parks Road. In tune with the times, this is now called the

Department of Plant Sciences. In the Garden the systemic beds were rearranged in the 1880s according to the *Genera Plantarum* (1896) of George Bentham (1800–84) and Sir Joseph Hooker, superseding the inaccurate arrangement derived from Linnaeus. The greatest change to come to the Garden was as late as 1943, when an extension of three-quarters of a hectare was made beyond the south wall. This new area now includes a bog garden and an informal pond. In 1962 the Garden acquired the Nuneham Park Arboretum, now run as an outstation. At first only the two-hectare Pinetum, planted by successive Lords Harcourt between 1830 and 1865, was acquired. Later additions have made this up to twenty-three hectares, allowing considerable scope for the collection of larger trees and shrubs, particularly calcifuge species (as much of the Arboretum is on lower greensand), thus freeing space in the Garden.

In 1925 the old Ashmolean building reverted to museum use again, to house the Museum of the History of Science. Here again it was the efforts of a professional and a donor (Arthur Evans's brother Lewis, 1853–1930) that united to persuade the University to agree. The professional was R. T. Gunther (1869–1940), who had for years been searching the University for material evidence of the history of scientific work and discovery at Oxford. The consolidation of the teaching of science within University departments instead of within colleges, where laboratory teaching tapered off and

TORTOISE, *Testudo tentoria*, by John Sowerby and Edward Lear, unpublished plate for Bell's *Monograph of the Testudinae* (1833–5) in the Radcliffe Science Library. Now renamed *Cyclemys orbiculata*, the model for this engraving was only recognized as the Type specimen in the 1950s when the collection of Bell's tortoise material in the University Museum was re-examined.

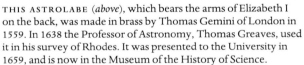

THIS ASTROLABE (*above*), which bears the arms of Elizabeth I on the back, was made in brass by Thomas Gemini of London in 1559. In 1638 the Professor of Astronomy, Thomas Greaves, used it in his survey of Rhodes. It was presented to the University in 1659, and is now in the Museum of the History of Science.

LE MESSIE (*right*), violin by Antonio Stradivari, Cremona, 1716. Widely considered the finest violin in existence, unfortunately this instrument is now too fragile to be played today, unlike some others in the Hill collection, such as the Kirkman harpsichord.

ceased altogether in the 1940s, meant that colleges were prepared to give or lend scientific instruments of great interest. By far the most important of these was the magnificent set of instruments ordered by the Earl of Orrery (1676–1731) from the best makers in the early eighteenth century, a complete Gentleman's Cabinet of instruments, found by Gunther in Christ Church. The Museum of the History of Science is one of the finest anywhere, best known for navigational instruments, astrolabes, and the large collection of microscopes. From the scientific departments it has continued to collect apparatus of significance as it becomes redundant or superseded; acquisitions include such things as some of the ceramic pans used for the first culture of penicillin.

(There has not been the physical space for the retention of evidence of the history and development of the computer.)

In 1894 the ground floor of the new Ashmolean held the Arundel Marbles; in Evans's new wing, directly opposite the front door, stood casts from the Antique. As early as the sixteenth century casts of famous statues were considered essential to learning. P. B. Duncan had bought some (since removed) for the Radcliffe Camera in 1825. There are now some three hundred, though these are rehoused. Above the marbles and the lecture-room were the collections of fine art. The further west of these rooms was subdivided in the 1920s and a mezzanine floor inserted, greatly increasing exhibition space.

Part of this space was taken up by the collection of Pre-Raphaelite paintings bequeathed by Thomas Combe (1797–1872), Printer to the University, who had been a friend of many of the artists and in particular of William Holman Hunt (1827–1910). Mrs Combe gave *The Light of the World* to Keble College. Now much appreciated, these paintings were for some time as out of favour as the contemporary gifts of his own paintings by Sir Hubert von Herkomer (1849–1914), now in the Schools, are at present.

The Department of Fine Art began to benefit from the gifts of Mrs W. F. R. Weldon (d. 1936) in 1915; these continued until 1937 and, in 1926, included the last painting by Claude, *Ascanius Shooting the Stag of Sylvia*. In 1934 (Sir) Karl Parker (b. 1895) became Keeper at the Ashmolean, following Kenneth (later Lord) Clark (1903–83), and began his remarkable series of purchases for the museum of drawings, many by old masters but also others by the then unfashionable Samuel Palmer (1805–81) and the 'orientalists' such as John Frederick Lewis (1805–76).

In 1939 Arthur and Alfred Hill (1860–1939, 1862–1940) presented nineteen stringed instruments, including the most celebrated violin in the world, Le Messie, signed by Stradivarius of Cremona and dated 1716. This formed the basis of the collection of musical instruments. Wind instruments were to follow with the acceptance of the Philip Bate (b. 1909) Collection by the University in 1970, but this and further gifts are housed in the Music Faculty Building.

The Daisy Linda Ward (1883–1937) collection of Dutch still-life painting and the F. Hindley-Smith (d. 1940) collection of Impressionist and Post-Impressionist paintings were both received in 1940. The magnificent collection of silver, especially rich in the work of Paul de Lamerie and of the other Huguenot silversmiths—the finest such collection in the world—was one of the things to come from Gaspard Farrer (d. 1946) through the National Art Collections Fund in 1946, to be followed by the gifts of Francis Mallett (d. 1947), of furniture, Renaissance bronzes, and European and Chinese ceramics. The Pissarro archive, given by the family in 1950, gave the museum its unique holding of drawings by Camille Pissarro. In the H. R. Marshall (1891–1959) collection the museum holds the finest representation of the early periods of coloured Worcester porcelain.

In the twentieth century the Department of Antiquities has continued to receive archaeological material from the Mediterranean world, Egypt, and the Near East, often from excavations partly supported by the department. In this way material was received from Nimrud, given by Sir Max Mallowan (1904–78), from Almina, given by Sir Leonard Woolley (1880–1968), and from Jericho, given by Dame Kathleen Kenyon (1906–78).

The Egyptian collection holds the greatest amount of excavated material in Britain; much of it came from Sir Flinders Petrie (1853–1942), who was working in Egypt mainly from the 1890s to the 1920s. Among this is a unique collection of prehistoric material. The most beautiful of Petrie's gifts is surely the lovely frieze of the Princesses (*c.*1350 BC) from Tell el-Amarna. The work of Professor F. Ll. Griffith (1862–1934) at Kawa was recognized by the Government of the Sudan when it presented to him the shrine built by workers from Memphis for the Nubian King Taharqa, who was also a Pharaoh of the Twenty-fifth Dynasty. Given by Griffith's widow in 1936 and erected by 1942, this is the only example of an Egyptian architectural monument in Britain. The institute for the study of Egyptology that bears Griffith's name was established in 1939, within the Ashmolean.

When Arthur Evans wanted to excavate the Palace of Minos at Knossos in Crete, he bought the site. The finds from Crete brought back by Evans form the basis of the finest collection outside Iraklion. Evans also bought Greek pots; this is a subject much studied in Oxford, particularly by Sir John Beazley (1885–1970), for the attribution of painted decoration to particular workshops.

In 1927 Arthur Evans gave the collections of his father, Sir John Evans (1823–1908), a pioneering student of the early artefacts of man. Flint implements were no new thing to the museum—there had been examples in several early collections, including those of Ashmole (figured by Dugdale in his *Antiquities of Warwickshire* of 1656), Plot, and Borlase; it was the new understanding that the ancestry of man lay much further back in time than had ever been thought possible that mattered. John Evans had been to Abbeville with Sir Joseph Prestwich (1812–96) in 1859 to see for himself the early material found by Boucher de Perthes (1788–1868); he was immediately convinced and col-

'LINEAR B' INSCRIPTION on a clay tablet of the late Minoan period, found at Knossos by Sir Arthur Evans. The script, which here refers to a 'horse-chariot without wheels' (visible top right), was deciphered a decade after Evans's death by an architect, Michael Ventris, who had been inspired by Evans's lectures.

SKETCH BY EDOUARD MANET for *Le Déjeuner sur l'herbe*, the famous and scandalous painting he exhibited in 1863 at the 'Salon des Refusés'. Formerly the property of a resident of Oxford, this picture was allocated to the Ashmolean by the Treasury in lieu of tax in 1979.

lected examples on the spot. This fitted in well with the theories of Charles Darwin, published in *The Origin of Species* in the same year.

After a struggle of forty years, the retired Arthur Evans saw the Bodleian reluctantly hand over its collection of coins to the Ashmolean in 1921. Many of the colleges also deposited their collections over the next few years. The Coin Room became a full department in 1961. The long history of the collections of coins and medals held by the University, reaching back to Archbishop Laud in the 1630s, depends upon the recognition of coins not only as objects of intrinsic worth, of interest and beauty, but also as visible evidence of history: the latter is a more recent development, and is an accolade as yet denied by most historians to other works of art. The collection is now particularly strong in coins of the ancient world, much of the Greek collection being given by Sir Edward Robinson (1887–1976), and in the early Anglo-Saxon coinages, following the purchase of the Crondall Hoard in 1944 as a memorial to Sir Arthur Evans.

A new Department of Eastern Art took over the collections of the Museum of Eastern Art, opened in 1946 under William Cohn (1880–1961) in the Indian Institute. The collection combined that of the Institute, which had itself opened in 1896 to hold books relating to India and Indian arts and crafts, with the Oriental collections that had accumulated in the Department of Fine Art, now called the Department of Western Art. The move to the Ashmolean in 1961 was stimulated by the huge gift of Chinese ceramics by Sir Herbert Ingram (1876–1958). There was no space at the Institute, and room was made at the Ashmolean by removing the casts to a purpose-built gallery behind the museum. The department has continued to grow, mainly by gifts, arguably into the finest collection of Oriental art outside the National Museums in London. The Francis Mallett and A. H. Sayce (1845–1933) collections of Chinese art were transferred from Western Art; the Thomas Barlow (1607–91) gift of Islamic ceramics was followed by the vast gift by Gerald Reitlinger (1900–78) of Chinese, Japanese, and Islamic ceramics. Eric North (1891–1979) and Jeffery Story (d. 1984) left collections and purchase-funds, the latter specifically restricted to the Japanese collection. A large gift of Indian printed

PALAEOLITHIC STONE AXE, given by Boucher de Perthes to John Evans at Abbeville in 1859. Such axes, found in association with animal remains, were just being recognized as evidence of man's antiquity, beyond the dates deduced from biblical 'evidence'.

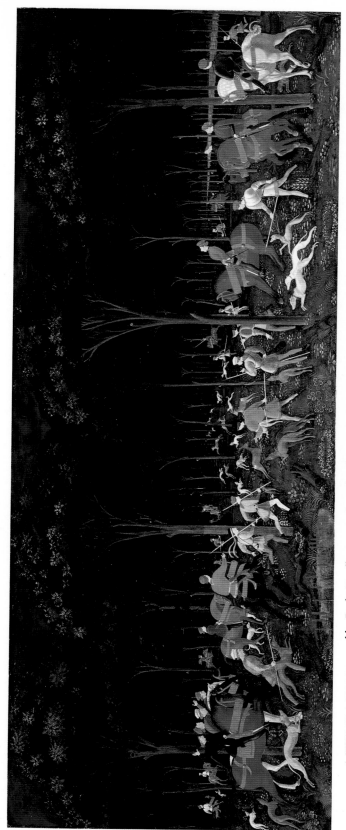

A HUNT IN A FOREST, panel by Paolo Uccello, now in the Ashmolean Museum, which hints at the new interest of the Florentine painters in geometric perspective. Such fifteenth-century paintings were unfashionable at the time of this gift to the University Galleries by Fox-Strangways in 1850.

BLOIS, watercolour painting of *c.*1830 by J. M. W. Turner, given to the University by John Ruskin, Slade Professor of the History of Art in the 1870s and 1880s, as part of the series of paintings, including his own, used for his immensely popular lectures and demonstrations.

cotton fragments of the fourteenth to eighteenth centuries, found outside Cairo, is today being restored and catalogued with the aid of the Foundation established by J. Paul Getty (1892–1976).

In 1968 the Bodleian took the books of the Indian Institute, whose library it had already been administering since 1929. Absorption of whole libraries was no new thing for the Bodleian: as well as the Ashmolean library (1860), in 1884 Bodley had taken over the Savilian library, basically a seventeenth-century collection devoted to books and manuscripts relating to astronomy and mathematics, and in the following year the Music School library. The Bodleian also administers the libraries of Rhodes House and of the Law Faculty. But other collections were to leave Bodley for the Ashmolean: the coins in 1921, the Hope collection of engraved portraits in 1924, the Rawlinson seal matrices in 1927, and the A. H. Sutherland (d. 1820) engravings in 1934. This is a process of redistribution within University collections that will continue.

The nature of the Bodleian had greatly changed in the late nineteenth century, reflecting the readership, which in turn reflected the changing methods of teaching within the University. In mid-century there were few but constant readers: in 1845 only 215 persons used the library, and attendance averaged between eight and ten readers a day. Undergraduates were still taught, not expected to discover for themselves, and even their college libraries were not regularly available to them. By 1909 there were usually about a hundred readers each day in the Radcliffe Camera alone, many of them women; by 1920 there were 500–600 readers each day in the Camera and in 1941 the ground floor was converted to a reading-room. Today there are about 32,000 registered readers; there are 24 reading-rooms and 2,086 seats for readers. On an average day in term there will be about 800 readers at any one time in the afternoon.

The collections were, of course, expanding enormously. In 1885 these were thought to contain 406,159 printed volumes; by the 1930s about 58,000 volumes a year were being added from copyright alone and decisions had to be taken to restrict these numbers. In 1935 advisory committees were set up to consider purchases. The library doubles the size of its collections every 25–30 years.

Gifts were still considerable, but tended to be of smaller numbers of books—at least after the vast Francis Douce bequest in 1834 and the Ingram Bywater (1840–1914) bequest of books relating to the history of classical learning. Gifts today are more usually of the papers of eminent or interesting persons: the papers of William Beckford (1759–1844), for instance, have recently been given in memory of Sir Basil Blackwell (1889–1984). Papers may also be deposited on indefinite loan: the National Trust has deposited the papers of Benjamin Disraeli (1804–81). Large collections could still be bought in the nineteenth century. These included the David ben Abraham Oppenheimer (1667–1735) Hebrew collection in 1829 and in 1844 the Persian and Mogul material of Sir William Ouseley (1767–1842), Sir Gore Ouseley (1770–1844), and J. B. Elliott (d. 1859). In 1887 the Librarian, E. B. Nicholson (1849–1912), bought the eleventh-century Gospel-lectionary of Queen (St) Margaret of Scotland, its identifica-

WILLIAM EDWARD (KITS) VAN HEYNINGEN, oil portrait (1972) by Sir William Coldstream of the first Master of St Cross College, one of the new graduate colleges, founded in 1965.

tion hinging on its involvement in a miracle recorded in the book and elsewhere. Another event was the repurchase in 1905 of the First Folio Shakespeare that had been sold as a duplicate in 1676. Today, although the library spends nearly £1,500,000 on books and periodicals each year, collections are rarely purchased.

The problem of storage became acute. Even with the Upper Reading Room and several of the Schools available, the library was running out of space: the store under Radcliffe Square, finished in 1912, was clearly going to be filled by 1935. Stimulated by a generous offer from the Rockefeller Foundation, the University decided to build a new library to supplement the Bodleian, physically as close as possible, at the corner of Broad Street and Parks Road. A contract was signed with Sir Giles Gilbert Scott (1880–1960) in 1936, and by 1940 the New Bodleian was theoretically ready to hold five million books. Even with the war on, a million and a half books were moved in; Bodley was virtually empty for the duration. Services were maintained from the New Bodleian, and a tunnel for the transfer of books between Old and New was built. There is now a large book depository at Nuneham Courtenay which is obliged to increase in size every three or four years. Access is not allowed to the stacks, and, as ever, no book may be borrowed: in the seventeenth century both King Charles I and Oliver Cromwell were refused permission to take books out of the library.

A large number of the books (about 16½ per cent) is on open shelves. In 1920 the system of cataloguing was altered, leading to a dual catalogue, pre- and post-1920. Since 1985 accessions have been recorded on card and since September 1988 on computer, with on-line search facilities. Work on the transfer of all catalogue information to the computer continues today.

This discussion of the collections of Oxford University has taken little account of the holdings of the colleges. Every college has a library, sometimes utilitarian, for undergraduate use, although many hold important groups of manuscripts or incunabula. Most colleges have portraits of former fellows, and it is probably true to say that all colleges commission such portraits, at least of the Head of House. Some colleges have magnificent accumulations of silver, though much was lost to the Oxford mint at the time of the Civil War, when King Charles I was resident in Oxford. Some colleges, such as Magdalen, have specialist collections of pictures, though none can compete with Christ Church; many have isolated works of art in chapels (El Greco and Epstein in New College) or in Senior Common Rooms (Berckheyde in Brasenose). Other colleges have

BEAKER AND COVER, silver gilt, probably made in London *c.*1460. Purchased by Oriel College in 1493 (for £4. 8*s.* 1*d.*) at a time when members of the college, having no chapel of their own, were bound to attend services in St. Mary's church. Used in the college chapel consecrated in 1642, and still in possession of the college.

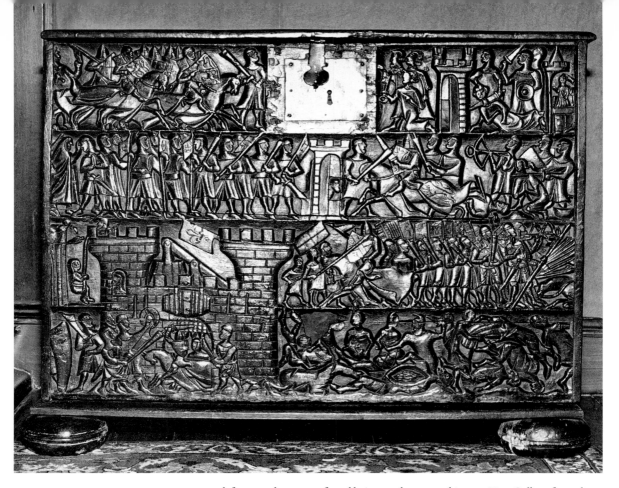

THE COURTROI CHEST, wood, fourteenth century, found being used as a corn-bin.on a New College farm about 1905. The front panels depict the Battle of the Spurs (1302). Tree-ring dating in the Oxford Research Laboratory for Archaeology and the History of Art confirmed that the trees from which the carved planks were cut were growing in the late twelfth century.

the occasional exceptional item: Magdalen has the Prince Arthur tapestries, a collection of Turkish pottery, and an Assyrian bas-relief. Even the new graduate colleges are building collections of which Oxford may be proud.

The question may be asked, 'Why should a university collect anything?' The need for books is fairly straightforward: they have been for centuries and probably still are the primary vehicle for the transmission of information and thought from one generation or from one geographical area to another. But why the need to collect objects? Here again, the reasons are mainly those of scholarship, though also sometimes of connoisseurship: objects are the visible evidence of history and the raw material for the compilation of the various branches of the history of man and of natural history (and hence science) that are now a major part of the proper study of an academic institution. As such, the varied collections of the University have been in actual use, for teaching as for research, since the late sixteenth century and continue to do service today.

8

The University's Contribution to the Life Sciences and Medicine

PAUL WEINDLING

IN all ancient universities each age has tended to pursue the types of science and medicine most appropriate to its culture and social characteristics. Yet distinctive and developing continuities can be discerned which link Oxford's medieval origins with our modern scientific age. The endeavours of late-medieval classical scholars, known as humanists, to establish the original texts of philosophers like Aristotle, Galen, and Hippocrates stimulated studies of the natural world and the human body. Such scholarship has sustained values linking medieval and modern medicine, medicine being one of the four essential branches of medieval learning. From the fourteenth century, when two Doctors of Medicine were included among the fellows of New College, to the early twentieth, when William Osler (1849–1919) consciously promoted the ideal of the humanist physician, Oxford medicine is best understood in the context of the tradition of classical scholarship and the Christian sense of duty to relieve suffering. The medical sciences and kindred disciplines like biology, anthropology, and psychology have been shaped partly by philosophical ideals deriving from classical studies and partly by new philosophies based on experiments, field studies, and physical and mathematical models.

Osler believed that his Oxford precursors, Thomas Linacre (c.1460–1524), William Harvey (1578–1657), and Thomas Sydenham (1624–89), represented the fusion of arts, letters, and practice to which all physicians were to aspire. Other philosophically inclined medical researchers, such as the physiologists John Scott Haldane (1860–1936) and Charles Sherrington (1857–1952), were agreed on the need to provide an intellectually stimulating scientific education. For Osler and other later idealists Linacre, Harvey, and Sydenham embodied the humanist ethos of Oxford; but all three men also spent much of their lives in London, and Linacre and Sydenham at least aimed to

HOW THE EYE FUNCTIONED was crucial to Roger Bacon's search for experimental knowledge. His account was influenced by the Arabian mathematician Alhazen and the Persian physician Avicenna, both of whom were writing in the early eleventh century. In his *Opus Maius* (revised 1267) Bacon here illustrates the curvature of the eye. He foresaw the magnifying properties of convex lenses.

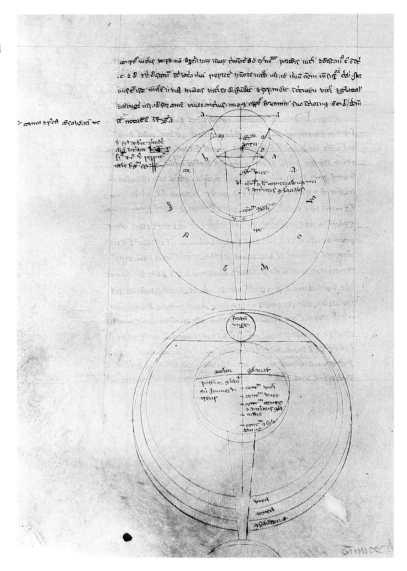

engage the University with wider intellectual and social movements. Accordingly, this chapter adopts a broad view, including men (and a very few women) educated in Oxford, or who moved to Oxford at the height of their powers as teachers and researchers, or who were simply resident in Oxford owing to the attractions of the University and its colleges.

Impressive breadth and diversity have transcended conventional disciplinary boundaries in the University, which has tended to look quizzically at the dawning of the modern faith in experiments and numbers. Thus, in the seventeenth century medical humanism led to a concern with the religious and philosophical bases of science and medicine. In the early nineteenth century harmonizing such sciences as biology and geology with the Scriptures was felt to be more important than accumulation of experimental data. In the late nineteenth century laboratory expansion took place slowly because of agonized debates over animal experimentation, which did the academic community much credit. During the twentieth century Oxford scientists have tackled such sensitive issues as race, intelligence-testing, contraception research, and the social determinants of scientific achievement. The lectures named after G. J. Romanes (1848–94) and Herbert Spencer (1820–1903), two inspirational evolutionary philosophers, offer annually the opportunity for reflection on human and ethical dimensions of the sciences. The ethos of the University has never been that of a teaching factory producing a standard academic product. Rather, individuals have been initiated into learning and research by being encouraged to think critically about the fundamental assumptions of their discipline. Reflection, scepticism, and faith feature as much in the history of Oxford biology and medicine as anatomical dissection, physiological experimentation, and therapeutic innovations.

Medieval medicine as a university study was based on commentaries on ancient texts which were of philosophical and theological significance. Indeed, in the thirteenth century there were a number of Oxford-educated physician bishops. Nicholas of Farnham (d. 1257) combined the practice of physic at the royal Court with philosophy, diplomacy, and a career in the Church, becoming Bishop of Durham. There were distinguished figures at Oxford who were knowledgeable about physic but were not members of a medical faculty, and indeed played a part in the wider world of religious politics. Both Robert Grosseteste (1175–1253) and Roger Bacon (1220?–c.1292) also studied at Paris and joined the Franciscan order. Grosseteste was Chancellor of the University, and from 1235 as Bishop of Lincoln continued to keep a watchful eye on Oxford affairs. He was a seminal influence on Roger Bacon, whose wide-ranging interests included optics, alchemy, and astrology while in Oxford during the 1250s; Bacon then returned to Paris and was imprisoned for apparently heretical beliefs.

It was only in the fourteenth century that the first medical degrees were conferred at Oxford, mainly on holders of first degrees in the Arts or theology. Most Oxford medical men relied on fellowships in the Arts or ecclesiastical positions for their income. Merton College was strong in medicine during the fourteenth century, and New College had eight medical fellows during the fifteenth. At Merton John of Gaddesden (c.1280–1361) wrote a widely respected synthesis of the traditional corpus of Galenic medical texts: his *Rosa Anglica* earned the praise of Edward, the Black Prince, and of Geoffrey Chaucer, but was criticized as out of touch with the newer Continental learning.

Although the University traditionally licensed a small number of physicians and surgeons to practice, there was a novel attempt at control over all the many varieties of medical practice: in 1421 physicians petitioned Henry V to restrict the practice of physic to those licensed by an English university. Linacre considered that humanist medical education should be a prerequisite for the medical practitioner. He became a fellow of

CLASSICAL SCHOLARSHIP JOINED WITH CHRISTIAN PIETY in this frontispiece (*above*) to Linacre's translation of Galen's *On the Method of Medicine* (1530). Above the public anatomy stand notable ancient physicians, Christ healing a leper, and the patron saints of physicians (St Cosmas and St Damian).

THE FORTRESS OF HEALTH (*right*) as conceived in 1631 by the mystic physician Robert Fludd. From north, south, east, and west evil angels unleash demons and plagues. They are combatted by the physician using divine powers to restore the sick to health.

All Souls in 1484, and spent over a decade in Italy studying medicine and the classics. As was characteristic of the time, he followed a multiple career as a physician, scholar, and clergyman. He was a founder of the College of Physicians in London in 1518, encouraged Henry VIII to establish the Regius Chair of Medicine, and bequeathed money to found medical lecturerships. He promoted the use of improved humanist editions of classical texts on medical theory and practice. Yet, in view of his friendship with Thomas More (1478–1535), the Oxford-educated humanist, scholar, lawyer, and ill-fated statesman, it is appropriate to characterize Linacre's vision of medical education as Utopian in paying more attention to the ideal of the academically trained physician than to the actual medical practice of the time.

During the sixteenth and seventeenth centuries Oxford medical graduates produced writings of great diversity, ranging from humanism to astrology. Robert Burton (1577–1640), author of the literary and medical classic *The Anatomy of Melancholy*, was a

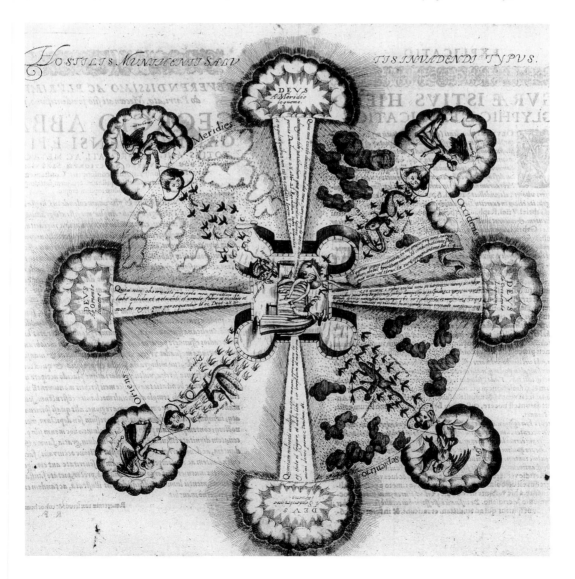

Student of Christ Church, a beneficiary of its ecclesiastical patronage, and a benefactor of the Bodleian Library. In 1624 the Tomlins Readership in Anatomy was established, and after 1636 the statutes of Archbishop William Laud (1573–1645) ensured that anatomical demonstrations regularly took place. The Physic (now Botanic) Garden was opened in 1632. Oxford libraries continued to build up substantial holdings of medical books, and Laud's bequest of Arabic books stimulated study of the Islamic enrichment of the ancient Greek medical classics. But it was not until the 1640s that Oxford could claim to equal the scientific reputation of other European universities. New experimental methods probed such fundamental physiological processes as respiration, the nature of the blood, and the structure of organs. When the royalists sought refuge in Oxford in the early 1640s, notable groupings of scientists and doctors coalesced. William Harvey, the discoverer of the circulation of the blood, was transplanted to the Wardenship of Merton College. His treatise *De Generatione Animalium* of 1651 provided an account of life from conception to the fully formed animal, and reaffirmed the Aristotelian view of embryological growth as an epigenetic process of continuing unfolding. Harvey inspired a circle of physiologists, including Nathaniel Highmore (1613–85), Walter Charleton (1619–1707), and Ralph Bathurst (1620–1704), who contributed to a renaissance of English anatomy and physiology. A sign of the new vigour of medical science at Oxford was a substantial increase in medical graduates.

Although the royalist defeat meant the departure of Harvey, medical activity was intensified by an influx of Puritan reformers supporting experimental philosophy, as well as ideals for universal learning and the prolongation of life. The zeal for learning and practical experiments of the Puritan academics John Wilkins (1614–72) at Wadham and Jonathan Goddard (1617?–75), Harvey's successor at Merton, bore fruit in the Oxford Experimental Philosophy Club during the 1650s. The Club was a nursery for the Royal Society, established in London in 1660. While the interests of the Oxford virtuosi ranged from husbandry to mathematics, a priority was to establish a theological basis for 'experimental divinity' (a contemporary term for natural science). William Petty (1621–87), who was Reader in Anatomy and a talented statistician, outlined an ambitious scheme for a teaching hospital. The treatise on the anatomy of the brain by Thomas Willis (1621–75) was beautifully illustrated by Christopher Wren (1632–1723). Willis discovered the arterial circle at the base of the brain in 1664. Robert Boyle (1627–91), the chemist and Christian philosopher, while resident in Oxford from 1654 to 1668, was interested in the properties of air, and this gave rise to remarkable cooperative experiments carried out by Robert Hooke (1635–1703) and John Mayow (1640–79) on the chemical basis of respiration. Richard Lower (1631–91) described how venous blood became red after passing through the lungs, and experimented on blood transfusion. This brilliant circle encompassed both royalists and Anglicans like Willis, and Puritans and Parliamentarians like Sydenham, fellow of All Souls between 1648 and 1655 and a relentless critic of excessively academic university studies without clinical experience. Such intellectual polarities typify Oxford's creative pluralism. During the

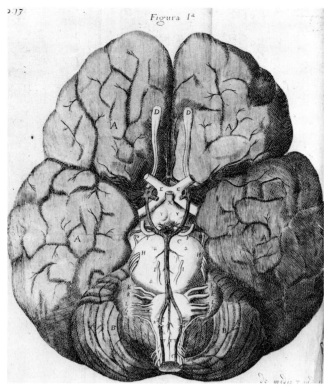

'EVERYTHING FROM AN EGG' (*left*) was the motto inscribed on the frontispiece to Harvey's book *On the Generation of Animals* (1651). The egg is being opened by Jove, and among the escaping animals is a tiny human being. Harvey followed Aristotle in suggesting that the various parts of an organism are not preformed, but are developed in succession in the growing embryo.

BRAIN ANATOMY (*right*) was pioneered in Restoration Oxford by Thomas Willis. His treatise of 1664 was illustrated by Christopher Wren, who was present at the dissections of numerous animals and human cadavers. The drawing is of a human brain.

1660s the momentum was sustained. From 1677 to 1690 Robert Plot (1640–96) ran an Oxford Philosophical Society which met, after 1683, in the newly constructed Ashmolean Museum. John Locke (1632–1704), while a student and lecturer in Oxford from 1652 until 1667, was deeply influenced by the great array of scientific activity. Locke's commitments to medical science and practice can be seen as contributing to his empirical philosophy, which has been a cornerstone of Western thought.

Although the momentum of the new experimental philosophy was not sustained in the eighteenth century, Oxford acquired a hospital and an anatomy school, and (except for a spell in the mid-century) botanical studies flourished. As the result of a legacy from a wealthy apothecary and amateur botanist, William Sherard (1659–1728), John James Dillenius (1687–1747) was appointed to the revived Chair of Botany in 1734, and his collecting activities were ably demonstrated when his herbarium was catalogued by a later professor, Sydney Vines (1849–1934). The wealthy medical graduate John Radcliffe

ROBERT PLOT (*above*) pioneered investigations into the exploitable natural resources of the English counties. His *Natural History of Oxfordshire*, published in 1677, led to his appointment as the first Keeper of the Ashmolean Museum. In its new chemical laboratory he undertook analyses of Oxfordshire's medicinal springs.

DR JOHN RADCLIFFE PORTRAYED IN THE IMAGE OF AESCULAPIUS (the Greek god of medicine) by Francis Bird (*right*). In this statue in Radcliffe Quad at University College, the snake sloughing its skin is a symbol for the renewal of youth. Radcliffe challenged the tenets of Galenism and upset colleagues in Oxford. He moved his practice to London, yet his legacies have contributed greatly to science and medicine in Oxford.

(1650–1714) enriched the University: he endowed travelling fellowships for aspiring doctors, and library facilities in the Radcliffe Camera, which became known as 'the Physic library' by the middle of the century. In 1770 the trustees of his estate decided to build (in addition to an observatory) the Radcliffe Infirmary. Although not formally connected to the medical Faculty, this offered University teachers and Faculty members the chance to acquire clinical experience as honorary physicians. George Henry Lee, the third Earl of Lichfield (1718–72), established a University professorship for the delivery of clinical lectures. The Lichfield Professor developed a system of ward teaching. Medicine became a seed-bed for other natural sciences, such as chemistry and botany. John Freind (1675–1728), who briefly lectured on chemistry in Oxford, wrote the first English-language history of medicine while imprisoned in the Tower of London for Jacobite activities. He promoted the idea of establishing an anatomy school at Christ Church, a scheme which was finally realized in the 1760s. The fiery Thomas Beddoes (1760–1808), after medical studies at Oxford, returned to a Readership in Chemistry in 1788. A year later, after the French Revolution, he was to be found in association with Samuel Taylor Coleridge (1772–1834) and Humphry Davy (1778–1829). Studies of Mediterranean and Middle Eastern flora were made by John Sibthorp (1758–96), who was a founder member of the Linnaean Society formed in 1788 (see above, p. 245). Sibthorp favoured applied botany and rural economy, and bequeathed money to found a chair in these disciplines. Utility and the practical application of science for humane purposes characterized eighteenth-century medicine and natural history.

There is a remarkable parallel between the Christian humanists of the mid-seventeenth century and the scientific defenders of scriptural literalism in the early nineteenth. William Buckland (1784–1856), Professor of Geology until 1845, and his successor John Phillips (1800–74) advocated the use of fossils in stratigraphy. Buckland imaginatively reconstructed the forms, habits, and environment of prehistoric iguanodons and pterodactyls. His studies were part of a broader movement among scientists who accepted that the world was older than the Bible said it was, but still sought to defend faith in Christian providence. Buckland and John Kidd (1775–1851), the Regius Professor of Medicine from 1822, wrote studies of natural theology in the popular series of treatises founded by Francis Henry Egerton, eighth Earl of Bridgwater (1756–1829), 'on the power, wisdom and goodness of God as manifested in the creation'. The entomologist Frederick William Hope (1797–1862), who for a time served as a curate, gave his collection of insects to the University and endowed a Chair of Zoology. Charles Daubeny (1795–1867), an Oxford MD who at times held Chairs of Chemistry, Botany, and Rural Economy, believed that science was of practical utility and that it contributed to an education in theology. The mathematician and philosopher Baden Powell (1796–1860) argued in 1855 for a more liberal approach to studies of evolution—that freedom to discuss the evolutionary implications of research in physiology and geology would not detract from God's glory as the first cause of Creation. The way was clear for a naturalistic approach to studies of evolution, mind, and matter.

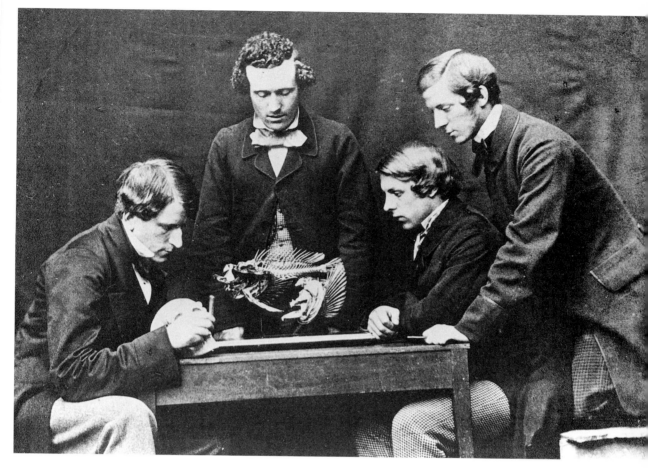

DR ROLLESTON EXAMINING A HUMAN SKULL in the Christ Church Anatomy School in 1858. Two years later Rolleston presided at the Oxford meeting of the British Association when Samuel Wilberforce (the Bishop of Oxford) and T. H. Huxley debated the Darwinian theory with reference to the structural differences between the brains of men and monkeys. The photograph was taken by Charles Dodgson (Lewis Carroll).

In the late seventeenth century John Locke had been caught up in the contrasting currents of traditional philosophy and the new experimentalism. There was a similarly turbulent ebb and flow of opinions on evolution and experimentalism during the nineteenth century. The confrontation with revealed religion forced scientists to muse not only over the details of specific researches but also on the nature, practices, and scope of legitimate scientific enquiry. Under Henry Acland (1815–1900), appointed Regius Professor in 1861, Oxford medicine again linked hands with the ideal of a liberal education. Acland believed that Oxford medical students should receive a broad and basic scientific qualification if they were to prove superior when they proceeded to clinical training in London, and thus become the élite of the medical profession. He took an interest in the sanitary conditions of Oxford, and in 1877 established a Diploma in Preventive Medicine and Public Health. He passed for an academic reformer, but he was

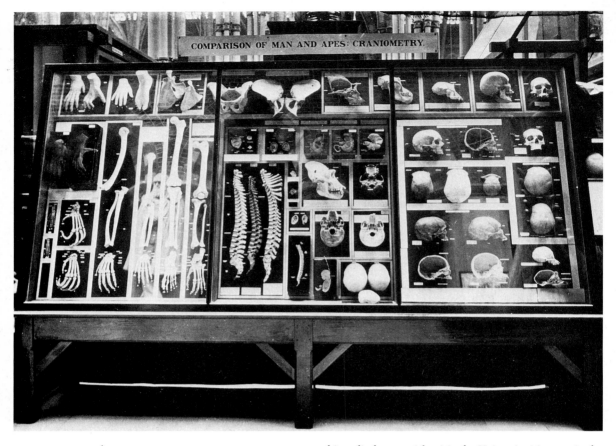

COMPARISON OF MAN AND APES: CRANIOMETRY.

MAN'S RELATIONSHIP TO THE APES was presented in a display-case (*above*) in the University Museum in the 1890s. The measuring of skulls (craniometry) led to studies correlating brain-shape and -height with intelligence. The Oxbridge undergraduate, it was sometimes claimed in the early years of the twentieth century, was an 'A1' type of superior physique and mental capacity.

THE DECORATIVE IRON AND GLASS of the University Museum (*right*), opened in 1860, proved that modernity could be blended with traditional forms and that Gothic art could find expression in 'railway materials'. Sited round this 'cathedral' of the natural-history collections were lecture-theatres and laboratories.

not a supporter of specialization. His views on the unity of the sciences were embodied in the University Museum. This cathedral of the sciences was opened in 1860, when it echoed to the clash between Thomas H. Huxley (1825–95) and Bishop Samuel Wilberforce (1805–71) over Charles Darwin's theory of natural selection. The museum reveals the academic and aesthetic spirit of John Ruskin (1819–1900), of whom Acland was a close friend. Ruskin was one of the many Oxford academics—also including Charles Dodgson (Lewis Carroll, 1832–98) and C. S. Lewis (1898–1963)—who opposed animal experimentation.

Throughout the late nineteenth and early twentieth centuries Oxford was strong in comparative anatomy, under the leadership of George Rolleston (1829–81), a disciple of

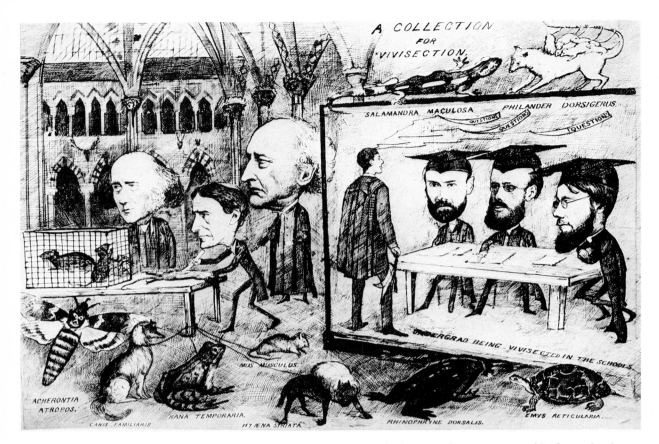

ANTI-VIVISECTION CAMPAIGNS found much support in Oxford. Among the University notables featured in this cartoon of 1883 are the Professor of Medicine, Henry Acland, the physiologist Burdon-Sanderson (shown dissecting a rat), and the Dean of Christ Church, H. G. Liddell (an enthusiastic amateur scientist). The collection of animals is being equated with the trials of an undergraduate at a termly examination or 'collection'.

Huxley. Embryology and studies of heredity flourished. At the time zoological studies of evolution involved dissection, microscopical observations of the resulting series of slides, and theoretical deduction. E. Ray Lankester (1847–1929) and Edward B. Poulton (1856–1943) did much to provide an empirical basis for Darwinian evolutionary theory, and from 1899 Walter F. R. Weldon (1860–1906) was a pioneer of statistical studies of evolution. Judicious compromise over vivisection facilitated the inauguration of a Faculty of Medicine in 1885. John Burdon-Sanderson (1828–1905) was Waynflete Professor of Physiology from 1882 and Regius Professor of Medicine from 1895. He initiated a distinguished and continuing tradition of research on muscular activity, and attempted to modernize the teaching of physiology and pathology. He also served on Royal Commissions on hospitals for infectious diseases, and on the consumption of tuberculous meat and milk.

The growth of the British Empire during the later nineteenth century fostered the rise of the new disciplines of anthropology, geography, and forestry, and helped to make

Oxford aware of its role in the wider world. On presenting to the University his extensive collections, Augustus Henry Lane Fox Pitt-Rivers (1827–1900) stipulated that regular instruction be given in anthropology. This discipline reinforced Victorian convictions in the law of progress from the primitive to the civilized. Edward Burnet Tylor (1832–1917) was the first Reader in 1884. Tylor's study of *Primitive Culture* examined the evolutionary basis of law, morality, and religion with studies of animism, magic, and a range of superstitions. His library was the nucleus for a Department of Social Anthropology, established in 1914.

Evolutionary concerns with the distribution of plants and animals prompted the Linacre Professor of Human and Comparative Anatomy, Henry Nottidge Moseley (1844–91), to support moves for establishing geography in Oxford. Halford John Mackinder (1861–1947) was appointed Reader in Geography in 1887, with financial assistance from the Royal Geographical Society. He claimed that the Oxford-educated humanist scholar Richard Hakluyt (1552?–1616), who wrote on the history of voyages of discovery, was his predecessor. As a student Mackinder had been much influenced by Darwinism and anthropology, and he had a missionary zeal for establishing geography as a bridge between the natural sciences and the humanities. His activities led to the

THE DEPARTMENT OF HUMAN ANATOMY was established as a result of the division between human and comparative anatomy in 1881. Arthur Thomson (*standing, centre*) taught for several years in a temporary iron-roofed extension. Thomson also taught anatomy to artists and was a keen anthropologist.

THE OXFORD FORESTRY INSTITUTE
evaluates tree species for their economic
and ecological value. The *acacia tortilis*, or
umbrella thorn, provides seed-pods for
livestock feed and wood for charcoal. It is
a fast-growing tree with potential for
widespread use in Africa and the Middle
East.

founding of the Oxford School of Geography in 1899, but his interests were so broad—
spanning political activism as a Liberal Unionist MP and as Director of the London
School of Economics—that the infant subject required several acts of emergency resus-
citation by the Royal Geographical Society. He was succeeded in 1905 by Andrew John
Herbertson (1865–1915), whose zoological studies had led him to biogeography and
climatology. These complemented the work of the Oxford Forestry Institute, founded
in the same year. Its first director, William Schlich (1840–1925), and his successor
Robert Scott Troup (1874–1939) had considerable experience in the Indian Forest service, and the new institute maintained close ties with the India Office. The institute

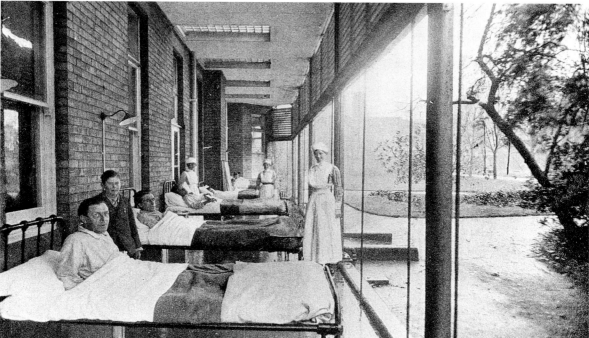

WILLIAM OSLER founded the Oxfordshire Association for the Prevention of Tuberculosis in 1909. After organizing an exhibition in the Examination Schools, the Association established a network of outpatient dispensaries, and provided open-air treatment balconies at the Radcliffe Infirmary. It also educated people on the need for a wholesome diet and for good personal hygiene.

encouraged experimental studies of growth-rates and of the regeneration of tree species. The diplomas in anthropology, geography, and forestry were useful in training colonial cadets and officers.

The early twentieth century found Oxford biology and medicine in an expansive and purposeful mood. The sense of moral purpose was evident in Osler's medical humanism, as he prescribed the reading of classical and Renaissance authors as a character-building exercise for future doctors. His practical achievements included a system of rural tuberculosis dispensaries in Oxfordshire, which became a model for the nation.

CHARLES SHERRINGTON (*back row, left*) with the physiology finalists of 1920. During the First World War the student population was reduced but the number of women students increased. Women had to undertake anatomical dissections in a room apart from men, and were instructed in surface anatomy down to the level of the umbilicus. Sherrington also had two women laboratory technicians.

Charles Singer (1876–1960) was attracted to Oxford by Osler with a post nominally in pathology, but actually in the history of biology and medicine. In 1914 he organized a room for the study of the history of science in the Bodleian. Such new branches of learning illustrate how the University's strong literary, theological, and political traditions enriched medicine and allied sciences so that they retained distinctive links to their past besides encouraging fruitful applications in the present. The Reader in Physiology, Haldane, combined experimental physiological research and utilitarian work in industrial health with a holistic Christian philosophy. Just as scientists made philosophical contributions, so the philosopher F. C. S. Schiller (1864–1937), a pioneer of pragmatism, was a keen eugenicist, advocating biological solutions to social problems, and was a leading figure in psychical research.

Experimental psychology came to Oxford with the appointment of William Mac-Dougall (1871–1938) as Wilde Reader in Mental Philosophy in 1903. Henry Wilde (1833–1919) had endowed the readership in 1898, and although nominally in the Faculty of Arts, MacDougall—much to his benefactor's irritation—migrated to the Department of Physiology. He combined interests in evolutionary biology, anthropology, and physiology, and studied the relations of body and mind and social behaviour. Although there was no formal degree course in psychology, MacDougall attracted a handful of enthusiastic students who also served as experimental subjects; among the latter was Cyril Burt (1883–1971), the psychologist who masterminded the eleven-plus examination, which became such a notorious feature of the operation of the Education Act of 1944.

Oxford medical scientists were active in seeking practical applications for their research skills during the Great War. The standards laboratory, instituted in 1915 by the pathologist Georges Dreyer (1873–1934), became a leading centre in the Empire for serological diagnosis of diseases like syphilis. Dreyer promoted the inoculation of all troops with typhoid-paratyphoid vaccine and, joining the Royal Air Force, conducted research in aviation medicine. The physiologist Sherrington studied industrial fatigue and for a time worked incognito as an unskilled workman at the Vickers-Maxim shell factory. He also advised the Government on the problems of alcoholism and tetanus. The zoologist Edwin Stephen Goodrich (1868–1946) studied grain-pests and weevils in wheat. The psychologist MacDougall advised on psycho-neurotic soldiers.

During the 1920s new sources of public and private funds for medical research were available: the recently established Medical Research Council saw Oxford and Cambridge as a reservoir of élite talents, and efforts were made to co-ordinate projects with the Rockefeller Foundation and other private trusts. In 1920 Edward Whitley (1879–1945), a wealthy amateur biochemist, was helping Sherrington to teach the rising numbers of students, and he donated money for a Chair in Biochemistry. The first holder of the post was Benjamin Moore (1867?–1922), an authority on TNT poisoning. His successor was Rudolph Peters (1889–1982), whose work on the vitamin B complex was relevant to interwar problems of nutrition. The department's work greatly benefited from donations by the Guinness family, Lord Nuffield (1877–1963), and the Rockefeller Foundation. The year 1926 saw the opening of a large modern Department of Pathology, made possible by the bequest of Sir William Dunn (1833–1912). Pharmacology thrived, and Oxford was the cradle of the British Pharmacological Society. Archibald Garrod (1857–1936), the Regius Professor of Medicine and a pioneer of studies of the genetic basis of metabolic anomalies, advocated the application of biochemistry to medicine. From 1934 Wilfrid Le Gros Clark (1895–1971) provided evolutionary perspectives on human anatomy. He drew on his studies of primates in writing extensively on the evolution of man. One of the brightest stars in Oxford's intellectual firmament between the wars was the Professor of Physiology, Sherrington, who resumed studies on the reflex activity of the nervous system. With John Eccles (b. 1903) he developed the concept of the motor unit, for which Sherrington was awarded the Nobel Prize in 1932. This work was part of a much broader synthetic study of the integrative action of the nervous system, around which Sherrington built an outstandingly successful research school. Sherrington's influential belief in the coexistence of the physical and psychic fits into the continuing vitalist tradition in Oxford biology.

Biology was a central resource, not only for medicine but also for a range of disciplines such as anthropology, psychology, and the social sciences. The central evolutionary tenets of biology were undergoing substantial modifications. Zoology flourished under Goodrich with innovative work on heredity and experimental embryology. Gavin de Beer (1899–1972) scrutinized the relations between embryology and evolution, and investigated the development of the vertebrate skull while in Oxford until 1938. Julian Huxley (1887–1975), who worked in Oxford until 1925, was an enthusiast for studies of evolution, experimental embryology, ecology, and animal behaviour. De Beer and Huxley modernized Darwinian embryology, with its antiquated notions of the embryo recapitulating the stages of evolution, by studying the role of genes and hormones and with embryological experiments. In 1927 the appointment of Arthur Tansley (1871–1955) marked Oxford's recognition of ecology as a scientific discipline in the plant sciences. Charles Elton (1900–91) established the Bureau of Animal Population and developed animal ecology on the basis of concepts like food-chains, habitat niches, and the natural regulation of numbers. Oxford became a permanent centre for ornithology. In 1921 enthusiastic undergraduates formed an Oxford Ornithological Society, which shifted the foundations of ornithology from collecting to study of the balance of birds in relation to their habitat. This led to the founding of the Oxford Bird Census, which established the first British co-operative trapping-station on Christ Church Meadow in 1927. From 1932 this was supported by the British Trust for Ornithology; in 1938 the University provided support as a memorial to the late Chancellor, Lord Grey of Fallodon (1862–1933), and the Edward Grey Institute of Field Ornithology was established.

There were enterprising efforts in applied biology. John Baker (1900–84) researched into sexual physiology, and developed the chemical contraceptive Volpar (derived from the phrase 'voluntary parenthood'). The Imperial Forestry Research Institute, established in 1924 with support from the Rajah of Sarawak and the Colonial Office, acted as a training centre for colonial forest officers, and so had enormous impact on global ecology. Geography and anthropology moved in the direction of the Arts and Humanities. Lieutenant-Colonel Kenneth Mason (1887–1976) was the first Professor of Geography, appointed in 1932. He had been superintendent of the Survey of India, and had mounted expeditions to the Himalayas. Geographers stressed the relevance of their subject to international relations and to social and economic problems, as with the compilation of *A Survey of the Social Services in the Oxford District* in 1938. With the appointment of Alfred Reginald Radcliffe-Brown (1881–1955) in 1937 the Department of Social Anthropology became a fully fledged institute for the comparative study of human cultures and social systems. Radcliffe-Brown had considerable expertise in field work and hoped to establish social anthropology as 'a theoretical natural science of society'. Sherrington's neurological concepts shaped the views on human perception of E. E. Evans-Pritchard (1902–73), who was in Oxford from 1935 to 1940 and again as Professor of Social Anthropology from 1946. Evans-Pritchard studied magic and witchcraft among African peoples, and did much to break down the assumed differences between primitive and modern thought. An Institute of Psychology was established in 1936 with support from the Rockefeller Foundation and from a private benefactor. This enabled psychology to be taught first to graduate students, and from 1947 as part of a combined honours school with physiology and philosophy.

The momentum for establishing a centre of postgraduate medical education and clinical research in Oxford came from outside the University towards the end of the 1920s from the Rockefeller Foundation and leading London practitioners. The interest of William Morris (Lord Nuffield) was aroused in 1930. In 1936 a benefaction of £2 million from Morris (on which see pp. 33–34) gave a boost to clinical medical research, and advanced plans for a postgraduate medical school in Oxford. Departments were established for anaesthetics, clinical biochemistry, orthopaedics, medicine, ophthalmology, pathology, surgery, and obstetrics and gynaecology. The Nuffield Institute for Medical Research was centred on a radiological research unit, which pioneered X-ray cinematography and made the first radiological demonstration of foetal circulation in 1939. Clinical Chairs were endowed in Medicine, Surgery, Obstetrics, and (for the first time in Britain) Anaesthetics, and subsequently in Orthopaedics. Hospital facilities were expanded with the Nuffield Orthopaedic Centre. These initiatives laid the foundations for outstanding developments in Oxford medicine during the Second World War.

Between 1939 and 1945 the sense of commitment to the war effort inspired a brilliant burst of creative endeavour in Oxford medicine. Yet it was initially scientific interest in substances which could break down the cell walls of bacteria that led Ernst Chain (1906–79), a refugee chemist from Berlin, and Howard Florey (1898–1968) to begin research on penicillin. Only when penicillin was shown to be of therapeutic use in the clinic did its application to the war effort become an urgent priority. Ethel Florey

THE CHEMICAL STRUCTURE OF PENICILLIN needed to be discovered in order to facilitate its production. Here, in 1942, Edward Abraham (*left*) and Ernst Chain (*second from right*) confer with Wilson Baker and Robert Robinson of the Dyson Perrins Laboratory.

(1901–66) helped to organize clinical trials in the Radcliffe Infirmary. In order to facilitate large-scale production it was necessary to determine the molecular structure of penicillin. The chemists at the Dunn School collaborated with Robert Robinson (1886–1975) and other chemists in the Dyson Perrins Laboratory, but Robinson did not accept the structure suggested by Edward Abraham (b. 1914) of the Dunn School. The controversy was resolved by a crystallographic study by Dorothy Hodgkin (b. 1910) on material provided by Abraham.

Among numerous other war-related achievements in chemotherapy, the success of the Army Malaria Research Unit at Oxford in pioneering mepacrine as a substitute for quinine must be singled out. Pharmacology flourished under Harold Burn (1892–1981), who was expert in methods of biological assay. Peters conducted biochemical research on the effects of chemical burns and gas warfare, and on deficiencies of vitamin B. Robert Macintosh (1897–1989) and Hans Epstein (b. 1909) developed a simple but accurate apparatus for the administration of volatile anaesthetics. Many biologists and medical scientists focused on wounds and injuries. St Hugh's College housed a Military Head Injuries Unit, and the results of head wounds were carefully indexed and analysed. Hugh Cairns (1896–1952), the Nuffield Professor of Surgery, was horrified at the brain injuries of army motor-cycle dispatch riders, and he led a campaign for compulsory crash-helmets. Peter Medawar (1915–87) experimented in the use of fibrinogen in natural plasma as a 'glue' for joining the ends of cut nerves, and with J. Z. Young (b. 1907) provided biological rationales for improved techniques in skin-grafts. Joseph Trueta (1897–1977), an orthopaedic surgeon and refugee from Spain, contributed to research on traumatic shock. Le Gros Clark at the Department for Human Anatomy improved understanding of the regeneration of damaged muscles. A Burns Research Unit was located at the Radcliffe Infirmary. Biochemists studied the effects of injury, and a German refugee, Ludwig Guttmann (1899–1980), was among those involved in research on nerve injuries. His work led him to establish

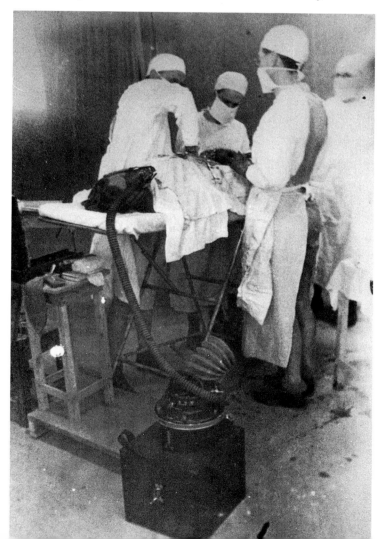

THE OXFORD VAPORIZER was developed during the Second World War in order to give reliable anaesthetics in field hospitals without the use of cumbersome cylinders of compressed gases. It was produced by Morris Motors and presented to the armed services by Lord Nuffield. Here it is seen in Burma in 1944.

THE FIRST FOUR-MINUTE MILE was
the achievement of Roger Bannister, then
a medical student and today Master of
Pembroke College. On 6 May 1954 he ran
the distance in 3 minutes 59.4 seconds at
the University Athletic Club ground in
Iffley Road. Since the nineteenth century
sports have figured prominently in
University life, and have been the
primary means of maintaining student
health and fitness.

Stoke Mandeville as a national centre for spinal injuries. Janet Vaughan (b. 1899) contributed to the organization of blood transfusions and to nutritional research on
hunger oedema.

The emerging welfare state confronted Oxford science and medicine with new
opportunities and problems. The creation of the National Health Service meant that
many more well-trained medical specialists were needed. The University expanded
with increased State funding for undergraduates and graduates, and for scientific and
medical research. What was at first a wartime improvisation in 1939 led to the establishment of a clinical school in 1946. Wartime planning of a National Health Service
accelerated the founding of an Oxford Institute of Social Medicine in 1942, which was
supported by the Nuffield Provincial Hospitals Trust. John Ryle (1889–1950), the first
professor, developed studies of social, occupational, and psychosomatic factors in dis-

ease. This was part of an adventurous new concept of the role of medicine in society. In the institute's brilliant but short-lived first phase of existence Ryle studied the health, growth, and development of the pre-school child in Oxford. Alice Stewart (b. 1906) detected the carcinogenic effects of low-dose radiation on the foetus. Hugh Sinclair (1910–90) inaugurated the Oxford Nutrition Survey, monitoring the effectiveness of wartime food policy; he identified certain fats as essential for a healthy diet, and considered that heart and other diseases could be prevented by dietary improvements. Richard Doll (b. 1912) has been an outstanding exponent of epidemiology, with researches on lung cancer and asbestosis. The statistical methods of clinical trials have also been much improved in more recent years. Oxford has maintained the National Registry of Childhood Tumours since 1962, and has been the leading centre for studies of perinatal epidemiology, combining the talents of clinicians, midwives, and social scientists.

In the Faculty of Physiological Sciences the momentum of research in neurophysiology was sustained, and has provided a focus not only for physiologists but also for psychologists and for those specializing in other branches of medical and biological research. The Departments of Human Anatomy under Le Gros Clark, Pathology under Florey, and Biochemistry under Peters thrived with enlarged resources for research. The pharmacologist Burn took an interest in the autonomic nervous system. Studies by H. F. K. Blaschko (b. 1900) of adrenalin and of the biosynthesis of catecholamines had immense benefits for the pharmacology of the central nervous system. Edith Bülbring (1903–90), who like Blaschko brought to Oxford the advantages of a rigorous German scientific education, studied how muscle contractions were activated. Cephalosphorin, an antibiotic alternative to penicillin, was discovered and developed by Abraham and Guy Newton (1919–69). It has been widely used, and profits from its sale have been ploughed back into a trust fund supporting further medical research. Le Gros Clark revived the study of physical anthropology, and in 1953, together with Joseph Sidney Weiner (b. 1915), exposed the Piltdown fraud, concerning the supposed discovery in 1912 of the skull of a remote ancestral form of man. Le Gros Clark also established the African origin of *Homo sapiens*.

In biological sciences there was a profound contrast between the whole-animal biology and the atomistic reductionism of genetics and biochemistry. Alister Hardy (1896–1985) came to Oxford with the resolve to encourage field studies in ecology and behaviour. He was an expert on the movement of plankton under the sea, and maintained the emphasis on whole-animal biology. He encouraged the Dutch biologist Nikolaas Tinbergen (1907–88) to join the Department of Zoology in 1949. Tinbergen felt he had a mission to introduce the central European science of animal behaviour (which he called 'ethology') into the English-speaking world, and Oxford gave him the freedom to develop studies of instinct and social behaviour. Ecological ethology influenced the work of the ornithologist David Lack (1910–73), who built on foundations laid by Charles Darwin's study of variation among the finches of the Galapagos

Islands. An observer of nature in the wild rather than an experimentalist, he studied ecological isolation in island bird populations as well as the local nesting-patterns of swifts (in the tower of the University Museum) and robins (in nearby Wytham Woods). His general studies of population ecology emphasized population density as a factor in animal evolution. Edmund Brisco ('Henry') Ford (1901–88) developed the science of ecological genetics with research on wild populations of butterflies and moths. Geoffrey Blackman (1903–80) reinvigorated the School of Agriculture with interdisciplinary teamwork on herbicides, combining the talents of chemists, physiologists, biochemists, and statisticians. It was said that he changed the colour of the British landscape by eliminating the red of the poppy and introducing the yellow of oil-seed rape.

Geography developed in historical directions under its professors Edmund William Gilbert (1900–73) and then Jean Gottmann (b. 1915), who had considerable experience of international administration and politics. His study *Megalopolis*, depicting the urbanized north-eastern seaboard of the United States, had a profound effect on urban studies. Social geography began to burgeon in Oxford, and at the same time environmental

NIKO TINBERGEN (photographed here in 1964) was a meticulous observer of animals in the wild. His studies of instinct were based on worldwide analyses of the behaviour of birds (especially gulls), and he related behaviour to physique and evolution.

HALFORD MACKINDER undertook the first ascent of Mount Kenya from this base camp in 1899. As director of the first School of Geography in a British university, he propounded a geopolitical interpretation of the relations between the heartland and the coastland—regions accessible to horsemen and shipmen, or, as it appeared during the Second World War, when he was still active, Russians and Americans.

concerns led to a strengthening of physical geography with an especial focus on the problems of erosion in arid regions. Geography has recovered something of Mackinder's synthetic spirit through the notion of environmental change.

A new phase in zoology came with the appointment as Linacre Professor of Zoology of John Pringle (1912–82), who was noted for his work on the myogenic rhythm of insect muscles. Pringle nurtured the Oxford Enzyme Group, which advanced understanding of basic protein chemistry using X-ray crystallographic research methods. Pringle aptly referred to 'the two biologies', drawing a contrast between holistic studies of evolution and animal behaviour, and the atomism of molecular biology. Here there were echoes of the seventeenth-century dispute between Aristotelian theology and the new mechanistic philosophy. A historical defence of the cell as a higher unity against biochemistry and genetics was mounted by Baker, who emphasized the indebtedness of present-day science to the seventeenth-century microscopists.

The application of the physical sciences to biological problems meant that research became more abstract and technical, but required greater resources in terms of equipment, personnel, and accommodation. Close ties with the Medical Research Council and medical research charities provided the necessary support, and a new breed of professors were adept fund-raisers and managers. Hans Krebs (1900–81) brought his MRC unit for the study of cellular metabolism to Oxford in 1955, and with Hans Kornberg (b. 1928) discovered the glyoxylate cycle. Donald Woods (1912–64) established the central role of nucleic acid in the metabolism of the cell. Research into nucleic acid was initiated with measurements of amounts of DNA. James Gowans (b. 1924) studied the physiology of the lymphocyte. Neuro-endocrinology was developed by Geoffrey Wingfield Harris (1913–71). Work was initiated on the physiology of vision, and Oxford was a leading centre for neuro-biological research. That the Chair of Genetics moved from zoology to biochemistry in 1970 was indicative of the increasing dominance of the physical sciences. New disciplines included molecular biophysics (1966), cellular physiology, and immunochemistry under the biochemist Rodney Porter (1917–85), who was awarded a Nobel Prize for his studies of immunoglobulins.

The 1960s saw Oxford's emergence as a major international centre for clinical medicine. Among the achievements of clinical medicine have been the management of inflammatory bowel disease, the treatment of diabetic coma, and the discovery of the genes for adult polycystic kidney disease (the commonest inherited disorder of the kidney), and for haemoglobin and Christmas diseases. Anaesthetists have examined the physiology of mechanical ventilation, and the interaction between anaesthetic agents and drugs used for treating high blood pressure. Pharmacological achievements include the discovery of the mode of action of aspirin, the first receptor-labelling experiments, and research into the effects of taking cannabis. While fundamental scientific problems have shaped research strategies, some work has had clinical spin-offs, such as the L-Dopa therapy for Parkinson's Disease. Clinical neurologists achieved the first recording of sensory-evoked potentials from the spinal cord, and undertook the first national epidemiological study of Creutzfeldt–Jakob brain disease. Clinical psychiatrists developed effective psychological treatments for anxiety disorders and identified the syndrome of bulimia nervosa. The research base of clinical medicine has been strengthened by the recently opened Institute for Molecular Medicine, which, thanks to the proximity of the modern John Radcliffe Hospital, will reinforce the humane alliance between fundamental scientific research and clinical practice.

The distinction of twentieth-century Oxford as a research university is attested by its contribution to the careers of several Nobel Laureates in Medicine and Physiology, and to four in Chemistry, which were awarded to researchers interested in biochemistry or (as Frederick Soddy, 1877–1956) in socio-economic problems. Cyril Hinshelwood (1897–1967), Hodgkin, Eccles, Florey, Medawar, and Soddy were undergraduates at Oxford; Eccles, Medawar, the pharmacologist John Vane (b. 1927), and the Hepatitis B researcher Baruch Blumberg (b. 1925) gained Oxford doctorates, although only Eccles remained in the Department of Physiology, his Nobel Prize-winning work arising

ARISTOTLE'S *NATURAL HISTORY* has been a potent force in biological studies. Knowing little about ovulation and fertilization, doctors of medicine supposed that the entry of the semen into the woman actually started off the formation of an embryo. The illumination is taken from a thirteenth-century copy of a Latin translation which was acquired by Merton College before 1375.

FLORA GRÆCA

Sibthorpiana.

CENTURIA SEXTA.

1826.

ATHENÆ.

directly out of this Oxford experience. Florey returned to Oxford armed with a Cambridge Ph.D. to undertake his collaboration on penicillin research with the Berlin-trained Chain. Oxford has attracted other Prizewinners when the originality of their work was already apparent, as in the cases of Krebs, Porter, Sherrington, Tinbergen, and Soddy, whose discovery of the radioactive decay of isotopes was used to determine the geological age of rocks and fossils before his interests shifted to economics. Oxford has also provided hospitality to overseas researchers at crucial stages in their careers, as to Ragnar Granit (b. 1900), who as a post-doctoral researcher learnt the techniques of electrophysiology, or to refugees like physiologist Severo Ochoa (b. 1905) and the pharmacologist Otto Loewi (1873–1961).

The integration of research, based in departments and laboratories, and of clinical medicine, based on the hospital wards, into the teaching life of the college-based University has at times been problematic. The balance between teaching and research can be precarious, but the increasing activity in research has benefited Oxford's role as a teaching university, as readers and professors in new disciplines have progressed from lecture courses to establishing diplomas and undergraduate schools. The Diploma in Anthropology dates from 1905, and that in Forestry from 1906, although the Diploma in Ophthalmology, instituted in 1910, lasted only a short time. The year 1886 saw the inception of Natural Sciences Schools, when a course in animal morphology attracted students of good quality. Some subjects have struck roots at the undergraduate level. New Honour Schools were established in Geography in 1934 and Psychology in 1947. But proposals for a Final Honour School in Anthropology were rejected in 1895 and again in 1949–50. From 1970 an undergraduate School of Human Sciences has provided a bridge between the humanities and sciences. While medical students have taken honours degrees in a range of subjects, most have been in Physiological Sciences, which has given them a scientific edge over colleagues trained entirely in teaching hospitals. Oxford can be seen to have been in advance of the trend towards an increasingly scientific type of clinical medicine. The Nuffield Reader in Pathology Emeritus, A. H. T. Robb-Smith (b. 1908), has analysed the careers of Oxford graduates in medicine: between 1901 and 1960, of 1,973 graduates 40 per cent went into general practice, 26 per cent became hospital physicians, 14 per cent became surgeons, 9.5 per cent became pathologists or engaged in medical research, and 10.5 per cent had administrative positions or were in the armed forces. Oxford, therefore, has contributed much to health care.

Oxford biologists and medical scientists have been leading statesman of science in learned societies, and have acted as Government advisers, popularizers, and campaigners for the funding of British science. In these roles they are very much like the humanist medical reformers of the sixteenth and seventeenth centuries. Some, like the

JOHN SIBTHORP travelled to Greece and the eastern Mediterranean in 1786–7 and 1794–5 in order to identify the six hundred plants described by Dioscorides in the first century AD. In his will he made the publication of the *Flora Graeca* the first charge upon his estate (it appeared in ten volumes between 1806 and 1840).

FAMILY TREE OF SCIENCE DEPARTMENTS TO THE 1980s
giving a date at which a Department may be said to have been established

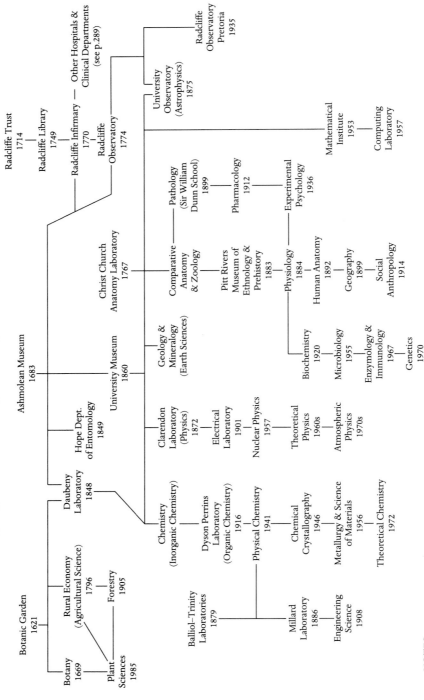

NOTES

There is no easy correlation in Oxford between Chairs, Final Honour Schools, and administrative Departments.

Words placed in brackets are new names for old Departments.

JULIAN HUXLEY WITH A FIRE SALAMANDER featured in *Animal Patterns*, a television series of 1953. Huxley left Oxford and achieved fame as a popularizer of biology and eugenics. His radio broadcasts included his role as the scientific authority among the 'Brains Trust' panel of academic experts.

biologists David Lack and Alister Hardy, have continued earlier concerns with science and theology, collecting evidence of religious experiences. Tansley not only took a broad interest in sciences concerning the conservation of wild life, but also had a vision of science as promoting spiritual values of a high order. The role of the State and the social responsibility of scientists have been controversial. Here there has been a spectrum of opinion. Arguments for science as part of a planned economy were advocated by J. B. S. Haldane (1892–1964), who studied 'Greats' and Natural Sciences at Oxford. His radical views were countered from 1940 by an Oxford-based group, the Society for Freedom in Science. Initiated by the biologist J. R. Baker, among its activists were the botanists Cyril Darlington (1903–81) and Tansley, and the philosophically inclined physical chemist Michael Polanyi (1871–1976), who condemned the subordination of science to central State planning.

The geneticist Darlington (who came to Oxford in 1953 as Sherardian Professor of

Botany) prescribed compulsory sterilization as a solution to the world's population and ecological problems, and the biochemist Krebs advocated socio-biological explanations of juvenile delinquency. Julian Huxley, whose education and first appointments were at Oxford, was a brilliant popularizer of biology, ethology, and eugenics: he became first Secretary-General of Unesco and contributed to its statement on race differences in 1951. Oxford men have taken a lead in international enterprises—not only in research, but also in the sphere of welfare and social security. This is exemplified by Harold Butler (1883–1951), a Prize Fellow of All Souls, who was one of the prime movers in the International Labour Office before returning to Oxford in 1939 as first Warden of Nuffield College. Concern with domestic social reform is exemplified by William Beveridge (1879–1963), who as a Balliol undergraduate developed an interest in this area, and while Master of University College wrote the *Report on Social Insurance and Allied Services* (1942), which gave a considerable boost to planning of the postwar welfare state. Just as Oxford scientists have contributed to the humanities, so historians and educationalists have made contributions to such fields as the training of nurses and to more equitable health-service provision.

Today's plethora of scientific institutes and clinical facilities defies any facile characterization. Indeed, a sprinkling of social scientists, historians, philosophers, and geographers further enhance the pluralism and vitality of Oxford life sciences and medicine. Just as the Renaissance humanists transcended disciplinary boundaries, so these latter-day advocates of interdisciplinary approaches would concur in the view that science and medicine reflect cultural values. This outlook gives renewed significance to the past visions and achievements of Oxford scientists in earlier centuries. At its best, medical and scientific education at Oxford has served not only to initiate students into the corpus of medical knowledge of each respective period, but also to question and evaluate. This has led to ever increasing extensions of knowledge and to an understanding of broader human issues concerning nature, health, and healing.

9

The University's Contribution to the Modern Physical Sciences

PAUL HOCH

DESPITE the occasional presence of many interesting and creative characters, Oxford was scarcely to be reckoned a major centre in the physical sciences until well into the present century. In the 1800s it could hardly be mentioned in the same breath as the main German and Scottish universities, Paris, or even Dublin; and in the last third of the nineteenth century it could not bear comparison with Cambridge, Manchester, Vienna, or the Zurich polytechnic. The medieval and early modern beginnings of the subject in the collegiate University were well and truly noted by the first Curator of the Oxford Museum of the History of Science, R. T. Gunther (1869–1940), in his fourteen-volume *Early Science in Oxford*. Important figures in the early traditions include the thirteenth-century monk Roger Bacon (1220?–92), the sixteenth-century alchemist/magus and student of St John's, Robert Fludd (1574–1637), and the seventeenth-century sceptical chemist Robert Boyle (1627–91) and his assistant Robert Hooke (1635–1703). The latter was a Christ Church graduate and afterwards Professor of Geometry at Gresham College in London and Secretary of the Royal Society. While he was at Oxford he built a 'pneumatical engine' and helped Boyle to develop the new 'mechanical philosophy'. Boyle himself was not a member of the University, though his group—which later formed the nucleus for the Royal Society—met regularly in the 1650s, originally at Wadham College, and included the Savilian Professors of Geometry and Astronomy, whose chairs had been founded as early as 1619 by Sir Henry Savile (1549–1622), Warden of Merton College. In the second half of that century Edmund Halley (1656–1742) published his first papers as an Oxford student, and made his first serious astronomical observations in St Helena, before becoming Savilian Professor of Geometry in 1704. His prediction of the return of his Great Comet in 1758 was to be an important confirmation of Newton's gravitational theory.

By the end of the seventeenth century scientific research in Oxford—such as there

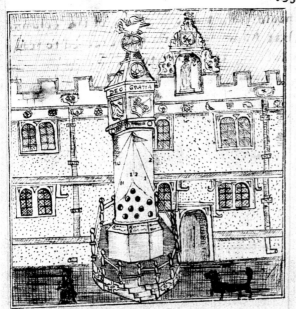

But more artificial is the description of a Cylindrical dial at right angles to the horizon; such as is to be seen in ẙ Colossus of Art in Areâ quadratâ C.XC. whose varietie of invention is such, that if the Authors name had been conceald, I should

A POLYHEDRAL AND CYLINDER SUNDIAL (*left*) erected at Corpus Christi College in 1579 illustrates the geometrical virtuosity of its designer, Charles Turnbull. It bears twenty-seven different forms of sundial, together with tables of astronomical and calendrical information. This manuscript drawing by Robert Hegge shows the pillar as it was about 1625. A restored version still stands in the college quadrangle.

THE SCIENTIFIC KNOWLEDGE gained from the voyages of discovery features prominently in the frontispiece (*right*) to Sir Francis Bacon's English-language *Proficience of Learning* published at Oxford in 1640. The ideas contained in the book were the basis for the experimental enthusiasm which characterized science in Oxford and London during the following decades.

was—was closely connected with the collecting, preservation, and teaching activities of the Ashmolean Museum on Broad Street, which was opened on 21 May 1683 (see pp. 100–1). This was to be the centre of science teaching in the University until 1860, when a new University Museum was opened near to the University Parks, and out of which the present 'Science Area' emerged. The latter term indicates the circumscribed, and apparently specialist, position of science within what was until well into the present century a predominantly ecclesiastical and Arts-dominated collegiate university. This

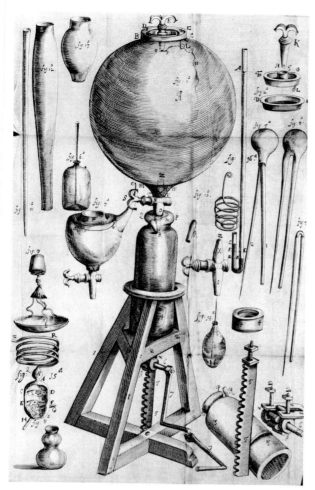

ROBERT BOYLE'S AIR PUMP (*left*), made by his assistant Robert Hooke in about 1658, was used for a series of experiments which laid the foundation of pneumatic chemistry in England and led to the formation of Boyle's Law. The instrument does not survive, but Boyle's illustration, published in 1660, is sufficiently detailed for working replicas to have been made.

ROBERT HOOKE'S INGENUITY is well illustrated by his sketch (*below*) of an experiment he devised in 1663 for measuring the force of falling bodies. A steel ball drops on to a balance, lifting larger weights: the greater the height it falls from the greater the weight lifted. Understanding the physics of falling bodies helped pave the way for Isaac Newton's discoveries.

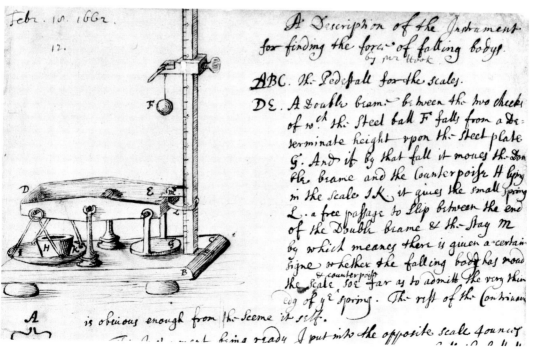

changed only grudgingly and gradually over a very long period. As late as 1964 a former physics student (later professor at Bristol), John Ziman (b. 1925), noted that 'In Oxford it sometimes seems that even pure science still has to struggle for recognition . . . The schools of physics and chemistry [have become] amongst the largest and most important in the country, yet at some High Tables, their Professors are often spoken of as dangerous power-hungry "administrators" by the Fellows of the ancient colleges.'

The founder of the original Museum, Elias Ashmole (1617–92; see above, pp. 245–6), was a former lawyer, Collector and later Controller of the Excise, Civil War ordnance officer (on the royalist side), Windsor Herald, genealogist, folklorist, cataloguer of natural and antiquarian 'rarities', alchemist, astrologer, speculative Freemason, and an early member of the Royal Society. This was a period in which natural philosophy was

Nunc mea, mox hujus; sed postea nescio cujus.

E. Ashmole

Astra regunt homines

Mercurio-philus Anglicus

London
Printed for Richard Mynne

These Hieroglyphicks vaile the Vigorous Beames
Of an vnbounded Soule: The Scrowle & Scheme's
The full Interpreter: But how's conceald.
"Who through Ænigmaes lookes, is so Reveal'd.
I: Crofs: sculp: T: W: M: D:

Fraxinus in silvis pulcherrima, ———
Alpa in terris operosissima, ———   Virg: Eg: 7
Centum puer Artium.

ELIAS ASHMOLE's interest in astrology, alchemy, and arcane symbolism is revealed in the frontispiece to his *Fasciculus Chemicus* of 1650 (*left*). His horoscope, in lieu of a portrait, bears the motto 'astra regunt homines' (the stars rule men). Although Ashmole ruled his own life with the casting of horoscopes, he also promoted the sceptical and empirical approach to learning which was to discredit such preoccupations.

THE OLD ASHMOLEAN BUILDING (*far left*), which now houses the Museum of the History of Science, was the first purpose-built public museum in Britain. The museum itself occupied the top floor, while the middle floor was a venue for scientific lectures, and the basement was the University chemical laboratory. Completed in 1683, the building is depicted here in an engraving of 1685.

less divided into separate disciplines than it has since become and not so clearly distinct from other approaches to knowledge. The foundation statutes of Ashmole's Museum declare that 'knowledge of Nature' should be attained by 'inspection of Particulars', such as those contained therein. Collecting and exhibiting were integral with research and teaching—demonstrations were crucial for everything. The first Keeper of the Museum, Robert Plot (1640–96), also obtained a University Chair of Chemistry, at first connected to the Museum. He served briefly as Secretary to the Royal Society, but was best known for his natural-history studies of Oxfordshire (see above, p. 276) and later of Staffordshire, at a time when such subjects embraced the beginnings of what we would now call geology and palaeontology. He was also a part-time alchemist, pursuing the 'menstruum'—an elixir of life—which he planned to market. His assistant and eventual successor as Keeper, the Celtic scholar Edward Lhuyd (1660–1709), produced the illustrated fossil catalogue *Lithophylacii Britannici Ichnographia* (1699), a significant work of early palaeontology. Among other subsequent assistants, James Sadler (1753–1828) became prominent as England's first hot-air balloonist, possibly an indirect result of the Museum's interest in pyrotechnics and gases. Nevertheless, by this point the Museum's main teaching was devoted to experimental philosophy and astronomy within the context of the School of Natural History, with anatomy and chemistry dispensed to medical students in the basement laboratory. The latter embraced a range of concerns which developed into separate biomedical subjects, as well as zoology and mineralogy.

At the beginning of the eighteenth century the fifth holder of the Sedleian Chair of Natural Philosophy, Sir Thomas Millington (1628–1704), still favoured traditional and outmoded Aristotelian approaches. The subject was revolutionized by the experimental and 'Newtonian' emphases of his Deputy, John Keill (1671–1721), who lectured in the Old Schools (now the Bodleian) Quadrangle. The emphasis was on Boyle's procedure of teaching physical laws through practical demonstrations—an approach emulated during the second decade of the century by the Museum Keeper, John Whiteside (1679–1729). The latter could also be regarded as the founder of physics-teaching in the University, for his courses began a programme continued to the present day. The Savilian Professor of Astronomy, James Bradley (1693–1762), also gave very well-attended

EDWARD LHUYD (*right*), the second Keeper of the Ashmolean Museum, strove to achieve systematic collection and classification, and helped to initiate the disciplines of palaeontology and philology. The only portrait of Lhuyd is this miniature painted about 1723 in the initial letter of his eulogy in the Ashmolean Museum's Book of Benefactors.

THE RADCLIFFE OBSERVATORY (*far right*) was founded in 1771 after Thomas Hornsby persuaded the Radcliffe Trustees to devote some of their considerable wealth to the subject of astronomy. This print of 1814 from R. Ackermann's *History of the University of Oxford* shows the interior, with some of the smaller instruments. The building is now part of Green College.

courses in both astronomy and experimental philosophy within the Natural History School, but most of his observational research was conducted outside Oxford, some of it as Astronomer Royal at Greenwich. He made one of the first calculations of the velocity of light, and also of the effect of the moon's gravity on the declination of the earth's axis.

The chemistry teachers in the Museum basement after Plot were all medical men. The Radcliffe Infirmary opened in 1770, sending an increased number of students for chemistry instruction at the Museum. This led to the establishment of a Readership in Chemistry 'to revive the study of medicine in this Place', according to Martin Wall (1747–1824), its first incumbent. The Radcliffe Observatory, initiated under the same foundation by Bradley's pupil and successor Thomas Hornsby (1733–1810), contained some of the best equipment of its era. It was attached to the Chair of Astronomy, but did not formally become a part of the University until 1839. Hornsby was also Reader in Experimental Philosophy from 1763, and as such responsible for tuition in what we would now call physics. From 1782 he held the Sedleian Chair of Natural Philosophy.

The Chemistry Readership was eventually upgraded to the Aldrichian Chair in 1803. Its first incumbent was John Kidd (1775–1851), later Regius Professor of Medicine, whose appointment led eventually to the development of separate courses in Zoology and Mineralogy. His more substantial publications include *Outlines of Mineralogy* (1809) and *A Geological Essay on the Imperfect Evidence in Support of a Theory of the Earth* (1815). He was also a determined advocate of the phlogiston theory of combustion, long after it had been discredited by Lavoisier (1743–94) and others. Kidd's successor, Charles Daubeny (1795–1867), pioneered the development of an interdisciplinary organic chemistry, applying it to agriculture. He simultaneously held the Chairs in Botany and Rural Economy, and eventually (in 1848) moved his chemical teaching to a new, private laboratory at the Botanic Garden. His influence was undoubtedly stronger on science education in Oxford than in active research—a judgement that must also hold for many of his professorial contemporaries. One of his admirers, the former Director of the Science Museum in London, Sherwood Taylor (1897–1956), claims that 'Unlike so many Oxford men of science, he never fell behind the times and never relaxed his efforts to rouse the complacent college tutors to the importance of scientific knowledge.' One of his more controversial works, at least within the University, was his *Brief Remarks on the Correlation of the Natural Sciences Drawn up with Reference to the Scheme for the Extension and Better Management of the Studies of the University, now in Agitation* (1848). He also produced some substantial, if to a degree misguided, scientific works. For example, his *Description of Active and Extinct Volcanoes* (1826) supported a later superseded chemical theory of volcanic action put forward by Humphry Davy (1778–1829); and his *Diluvial Theory* (1831) accounted for the supposed geological effects of the imagined biblical deluge from the days of Noah. He published in all some 176 scientific papers and a useful, if scarcely original, *Introduction to the Atomic Theory* (1831). The Daubeny Laboratory—over whose portals was subsequently engraved Roger Bacon's SINE

A BURNING LENS, by focusing the sun, provided precise heat for chemical experiments in the age before the Bunsen burner. This 16-inch-diameter lens and stand was supplied in 1791 to Thomas Beddoes, the Reader in Chemistry, by the London glass-manufacturer William Parker and Son. It was part of the improved equipment ordered by Beddoes's laboratory assistant James Sadler.

EXPERIENTIA NIHIL SUFFICIENTER SCIRI POTEST ('nothing may be sufficiently known without [practical] experience')—was used by scores of Magdalen students, and also provided University instruction in quantitative analysis until the 1920s.

When Daubeny vacated the Museum its basement was assigned to the new specialist in Mineralogy, Nevil Story-Maskelyne (1823–1911), who presided over his subject for the next two generations. The new incumbent in Chemistry was Benjamin Brodie (1817–80), a former pupil of the pioneering German organic chemist Justus von Liebig (1803–73). Arriving in 1855, he found at first neither space nor equipment, and was for several years forced to take refuge in a specially built basement laboratory at Balliol while awaiting the construction of a more substantial facility. His research was noteworthy for its determined opposition to the early atomic theory long accepted by Daubeny. He was nevertheless respected for his studies of the alkaline peroxides, and was also among the first to express his chemical transformations in stochiometric form (including the relative numbers of all the constituent molecules which combine to produce the reaction).

SIR BENJAMIN COLLINS BRODIE, the son of a distinguished surgeon of the same name, became in 1855 the first non-medical man since the seventeenth century to occupy Oxford's Chair of Chemistry. This portrait of Brodie with his balance, made about 1847 by Nevil Story-Maskelyne, later Professor of Mineralogy, is itself an early product of the most outstanding chemical discovery of the age—photography.

After the Napoleonic Wars Mineralogy and Geology were both split off from the chemical part of the medical syllabus, with the establishment of separate readerships. These were both held by William Buckland (1784–1856), who is generally considered to be among the founders of both historical geology and fossil palaeontology. His two appointments brought him only £100 each per annum and, like many another scholar in the natural sciences, he derived the bulk of his income from ecclesiastical preferments—in his case the living of Stoke Charity in Hampshire and a canonry at Christ Church. In addition, as was common practice at the time, he received fees for his lectures, which, up till the 1830s, enjoyed considerable popularity. In his inaugural lecture, *Vindiciae Geologicae*, he claimed that his subject 'is founded upon other and nobler views than those of mere pecuniary profit and tangible advantage', and should therefore be 'admitted to serve at least a subordinate ministry in the temple of our Academical Institutions'. Unfortunately, in the ecclesiastically orientated Oxford of the first half of the nineteenth century even this apparently modest inclination did not pass unchallenged. He felt he had to walk a thin line between the new Natural Science, the 'natural theo-

WILLIAM BUCKLAND was a pioneer in the study of dinosaur fossils, and, as this lithograph of 1823 'from Nature' by George Rowe suggests, a magnetic lecturer who attracted large audiences and introduced the University to the study of historical geology. Curiosity led him to cook and taste, systematically, the flesh of the entire living animal kingdom.

logy' of William Paley (1743–1805), in which science was tolerated so long as it expounded the glories of God's creation, and the later religious fervour of the rising Oxford Movement of Edward Bouverie Pusey (1800–82) and John Henry Newman (1801–90). Hence his seeming obsession with the Flood, which is manifest in his two principal books, *Reliquiae Diluvianae* (1823) and *Geology and Mineralogy Considered with Reference to Natural Theology* (1836). Happily, he eventually abandoned the deluge—despite increasing pressure from Oxford fundamentalists—when he became converted to the alternative Ice Age glaciation hypothesis of Louis Agassiz (1807–73). Nevertheless, he not only managed to keep his standing in the Church, but in 1845 even became Dean of Westminster. Among his contributions to palaeontology was an early description of the so-called megalosaurus, and also a sophisticated deduction, from 'coprolitic' (excrement) strata, of the diet of ichthyosaurs.

From 1832 to 1860 the experimental philosophy and geology of the School of Natural History were given more spacious quarters next door to the Museum, in the Clarendon Building. In 1839 Robert Walker (1801–65) was appointed to the Readership in Experimental Philosophy. This was a period which William Tuckwell, in his *Reminiscences of Oxford* (1900), described as one of 'prescientific science'. He recalled Walker as a very active demonstrator who 'constructed and exploded gases, laid bare the viscera of pumps and steam engines . . . manipulated galvanic batteries, magic-lanterns, air-guns'. Nevertheless, from 1849 Walker was actually barred from treating his subject mathematically, as that province belonged to the mathematics professors. The latter included the Savilian Professor of Geometry from 1828 to 1860, the Revd Baden Powell (1796–1860), who was well known for his book *The Undulatory Theory of Light* (1841), as well as for his many papers on radiant heat and the dispersion of light in the *Philosophical Transactions of the Royal Society*. He also expounded on the relationship between religion and science, and especially on *The Present State and Future Prospects of Mathematical and Physical Studies in the University of Oxford* (1832), which was then becoming quite a controversial topic. With the help of Daubeny and the University Commissioners, he eventually succeeded in his campaign to have the place of science upgraded.

A key step was the establishment in 1850 of the Honour School of Natural Science, which—the 1850 Commissioners noted—should be built around 'a great Museum for all departments of Physical Science'. The latter, the previously mentioned University Museum, was erected alongside the Parks and opened in 1860. It had facilities for the physical sciences of chemistry, experimental philosophy, mineralogy, and geology, as well as a small observatory for the Professor of Astronomy. Sherwood Taylor noted that 'The notion that a scientific professor should, if he wished, carry out research was of course accepted even in the earliest times, but the University had not as a rule provided any place where such research might be done.'

In the case of chemistry a small laboratory was built adjoining the new Museum. Thanks to the influence of John Ruskin (1819–1900), this was modelled on the Abbot's kitchen at Glastonbury Abbey, and almost from the outset proved cramped and inadequate. Prompted by the Commissioners, the University encouraged the colleges to make provision for instruction in Natural Science. Balliol therefore, as previously noted, established a chemistry laboratory in its cellars. One of its most successful graduates was Augustus Vernon Harcourt (1834–1919), who moved to a readership at Christ Church in 1859 and whose pupils in turn stocked the other college laboratories. Although at first working at the new Museum, he was given the use of expanded facilities for a laboratory at Christ Church in 1863, which he applied to inorganic chemistry and elementary physics. His research focused on rates of chemical change, and helped to establish the law of mass action on a quantitative basis. A new wing was added to the University Museum's chemistry laboratory in 1878, which with subsequent extensions eventually became the present Inorganic Chemistry Laboratory. In 1879 Trinity and Balliol jointly established a new college laboratory on the site of a disused stable, which became a centre for the study of chemical kinetics and spectroscopy, as well as for the teaching of physical chemistry to students, such as the later proponent of the theory of atomic isotopes, Frederick Soddy (1877–1956). Harcourt's most outstanding student

THE UNIVERSITY MUSEUM was intended to house the entire corpus of scientific knowledge. Behind a Gothic and godly façade, everything was presented within the context of the divine creation. This engraving from the *Illustrated London News* of 5 November 1859 shows the semi-detached chemical laboratory or 'Abbot's Kitchen' to the right of the main building, with the Museum House beyond.

was the future advocate of bridging chemistry to physics, Nevil V. Sidgwick (1873–1952). Other college laboratories were established before the First World War at Queen's and Jesus.

In 1872 Experimental Philosophy was expanded into a newly built Clarendon Laboratory, adjacent to the new Museum; this was two years before an equivalent facility was completed at Cambridge. Funds for the new building came from the Clarendon Press, based originally on the substantial profits of the multi-volume *History of the Rebellion and Civil Wars in England* (whose publication began in 1702). In 1875 the small astronomy annexe to the Museum was replaced by a University Observatory, built further into the Parks to facilitate untroubled observation. Two thirteen-inch reflecting telescopes were presented to the University by Warren de la Rue (1815–89), an astronomer and chemist. Important work on comparative stellar brightness was done by Charles Pritchard (1808–93), who was Savilian Professor of Astronomy from 1870. He first applied astronomical photography to the measurement of stellar parallax. The new Observatory was also the origin of an astrophysics department separate from the Clarendon Laboratory's experimental philosophy (later physics). The older Radcliffe Observatory was moved to Pretoria in 1935 (and its former site now forms part of the present Green College). The University Observatory in the present century became a centre for solar observation and solar physics, under the leadership of Henry Plaskett (1893–1980).

Brodie's successor in what was now the Waynflete Chair of Chemistry arrived in the Abbot's Kitchen in 1872. He was William Odling (1829–1921), an effective controversialist, though the department's chemist historian Dr Bowen (1898–1980) tells us that 'he did not consider that active research was part of his professional duties'. He was especially sceptical of molecular theories. In 1912 he was succeeded by the energetic W. H. Perkin, jun. (1860–1929), later President of the Chemical Society. Together with his students Perkin pursued an exhaustive programme of research, especially on the aromatic compounds, and was responsible for building the Dyson Perrins Laboratory of Organic Chemistry (with the help of funding from the well-known Perrins Worcester Sauce family). During the First World War the department was organized into teams to help industry produce dye-stuffs, solvents, pharmaceuticals, and explosives. One of the Balliol chemistry tutors, Harold Hartley (1878–1972), Head of the Balliol–Trinity laboratory, was particularly active in chemical warfare, and emerged as a brigadier general, later going into industry. His most outstanding student at Balliol was C. N. Hinshelwood (1897–1967).

After the war the department expanded rapidly. In 1919 a new Chair in Inorganic and Physical Chemistry was set up for Soddy. Two years later he was awarded a Nobel Prize for the theory of isotopes he had developed before the war at Glasgow. Unfortunately, like all too many professorial appointees, he came to office well past his prime as a researcher, and thereafter was best known for his feuding with other professors. Sidgwick became leader of an impressive subdepartment of physical organic chemistry, producing wide-ranging research in all aspects of the subject. The tragedy for Oxford was

THE DYSON PERRINS LABORATORY, opened in 1916, was modelled upon the chemistry laboratory at Manchester University—not surprisingly, perhaps, when one considers that W. H. Perkin was persuaded to leave his well-found laboratory in Manchester in order to come to Oxford and revive the fortunes of his subject.

CYRIL HINSHELWOOD'S WORK carried him from his investigation into the *Kinetics of Chemical Change in Gaseous Systems* (1926) to the adaptation of bacteria to their chemical environment— from the world as a molecular chaos to the growth and structure of the living cell.

that he was passed over for the chair to which Soddy was elected. Nevertheless, he produced his then influential *Electronic Theory of Valency* (1927), based on the Bohr–Rutherford atomic theory—though, ironically, the latter had just been made obsolete by the development of the new quantum mechanics. His subsequent *magnum opus* was the two-volume *Chemical Elements and their Compounds* (1950). One of his early students was H. T. (later Sir Henry) Tizard (1885–1959), who worked with him in the Daubeny Laboratory. Tizard was from 1942 President of Magdalen College, and from 1945 Chief Scientific Adviser to Prime Minister Clement Attlee.

On Perkin's death in 1929 he was succeeded as Professor of Chemistry by his former pupil and collaborator Robert Robinson (1886–1975), later President of the Royal Society and Nobel Laureate. In the Second World War the Dyson Perrins Laboratory did significant work on fuels, war gases, and drugs, including penicillin and the antimalarials. The current Waynflete Professor of Chemistry and Head of the Laboratory is Jack E. Baldwin (b. 1938), who since 1987 has also been Director of the Interdisciplinary Research Centre for Molecular Sciences, sponsored by the Science and Engi-

ASSORTED OXFORD CHEMISTS photographed in the teaching laboratory of the Old Chemistry Department (now the Inorganic Chemistry Laboratory) in 1926. The elderly organic chemist W. H. Perkin sits by an unidentified graduate student, with the physical chemist E. G. J. Hartley standing behind and the inorganic chemist Bertram Lambert peeping over the bench.

neering Research Council. The centre also included the formerly independent Laboratory of Molecular Biophysics, for long headed by Sir David Phillips (b. 1924), who is also head of the Advisory Board for the Research Councils. His laboratory pioneered the use of synchrotron radiation for a variety of crystallographic studies—for example, in relation to the foot-and-mouth disease virus, antibody modelling, and the domain structures of proteins (leading to a better understanding of their role in blood-clotting).

In 1937 the Chair of Physical Chemistry passed to Hinshelwood, known for his book *The Kinetics of Chemical Change in Gaseous Systems* (1926), which grew out of work he began as a research student in the Balliol–Trinity laboratory. In 1941 he and his group moved into a new, large Physical Chemistry Laboratory provided by Lord Nuffield (1877–1963), with other physical chemists joining him from the college laboratories. His work on reaction kinetics was eventually rewarded with a Nobel Prize. He also doubled as President of the Classical Association! He was succeeded in 1964 by Rex E. Richards (b. 1922), best known for his pioneering work on nuclear magnetic resonance analysis of proteins. He obtained funding and facilities to double the capacity of the department.

Another of the most outstanding Oxford scientists of the interwar period and after was the future Royal Society Research Professor and Nobel Laureate Dorothy Crowfoot Hodgkin (b. 1910). She began reading chemistry in 1928 at Somerville, which is named after the great early-nineteenth-century scientist Mary Somerville (1780–1872). (The latter was not a student of the University, as women were not then admitted.) Hodgkin was inspired by the Christmas lectures delivered by W. H. Bragg (1862–1942), entitled 'Concerning the Nature of Things', to devote her upper-level Chemistry practical work to the subject of X-ray crystallography. After graduation she went for two years to Cambridge to work with the young crystallographer J. D. Bernal (1901–71), and together with him obtained the first X-ray photographs of a protein crystal, for which they later received the Nobel Prize. They also helped form the Cambridge Stu-

N. V. SIDGWICK poses at a blackboard in the Balliol–Trinity Laboratories. The photograph was taken in 1910, the year in which he published *The Organic Chemistry of Nitrogen*, a textbook which was revised and still in use fifty years later. Throughout his career he was a great synthesizer of chemical knowledge.

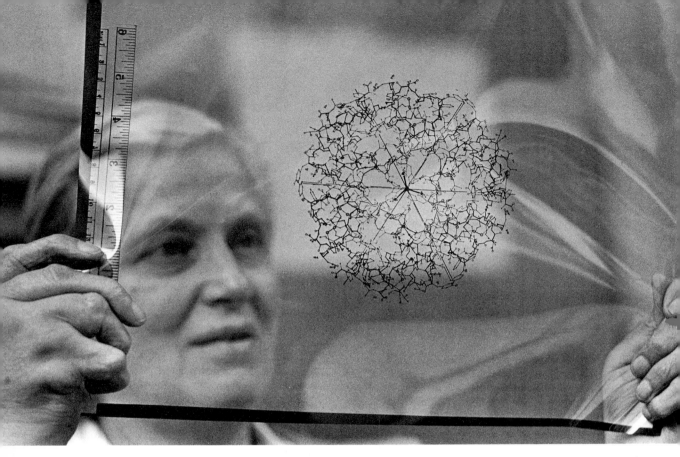

DOROTHY HODGKIN's predecessors had already constructed models representing the ways in which atoms and molecules are joined together. She showed that it was possible, using X-ray diffraction of crystals, to formulate three-dimensional models of the chemical structure of the molecules themselves (including those of penicillin, vitamin B12, and insulin).

dents Anti-War Committee, which later metamorphosed into the 'Social Function of Science' movement. She then obtained a research fellowship with teaching responsibilities at Somerville, and later helped build up the Chemical Crystallography Laboratory in co-operation with H. M. 'Tiny' Powell (1924–91). As a woman she was long officially barred from meetings of the prestigious Oxford-based Alembic chemistry club, a discriminatory policy which unfortunately continued until 1950.

In 1966 Professor Powell estimated that the combined School of Chemistry had about seven hundred honours students (not counting those in Biochemistry and Metallurgy), and no fewer than six professors—no one of whom was in theoretical or quantum chemistry. The overwhelmingly experimentalist emphasis gave the department an outdated appearance (especially if we recall that the California Institute of Technology had already included theoretical chemists like Richard Tolman, 1881–1948, and Linus Pauling, b. 1901, in the 1920s). However, in addition to Sidgwick's early work on the theory of valency, mention should be made of the even more theoretical work on the same subject in the 1930s in Cambridge by Charles A. Coulson (1910–74), later Rouse

Ball Professor of Mathematics, and after the war the investigations of J. W. Linnett (1913–75) into molecular wave functions. In 1972 Coulson transferred from Mathematics to a newly created Chair of Theoretical Chemistry, but died a couple of years later.

The Clarendon Physical Laboratory was for long a teaching rather than a research institution. Things might have been different if the Chair of Experimental Philosophy to which Robert Walker was appointed in 1860 had been offered, upon his death a few years later, to the outstanding German mathematical physicist Hermann von Helmholtz (1821–94), who was then visiting Oxford. In the event, from 1865 the new professor was Robert Bellamy Clifton (1836–1921), who had graduated as a first-class mathematics student ('Wrangler') at Cambridge, and served as the first Professor of Natural Philosophy at Owen's College, Manchester. He maintained, according to a recent historical article by Professor Brebis Bleaney (b. 1915), that 'the wish to do research betrays a certain restlessness of mind'. He did not suffer from this condition himself, and at Oxford his main efforts went towards the important task of educating future science schoolmasters. The only significant research completed in his fifty-year tenure was carried out in 1895 by C. V. Boys (1855–1944) of the Royal College of Science in South Kensington, who had temporarily abandoned London for Oxford because there was too much vibration around his London laboratory to measure the gravitational constant 'G'. Addressing the Universities Commission of 1877, Clifton spoke mildly in favour of research. He argued strongly for two additional professorships in his subject, and the Commissioners recommended the establishment of one in electricity—though this was not implemented until twenty-four years later. J. S. Townsend (1868–1957), who actually performed many of the experiments on electronic discharges in gases at Cambridge with which J. J. Thomson (1856–1940) is credited, was finally elected to this second chair in 1900. A second laboratory, to be devoted to the study of electricity, was built for him with funds provided by the Drapers' Company. Completion was unfortunately delayed till 1910, by which time Townsend too was past his peak of productivity in research. Nevertheless, in those days before compulsory ages of retirement he was to linger on for another thirty-two years. His best-known hobby-horse was his repeated claim that the electron collision experiments for which James Franck (1882–1964) and Gustav Hertz (1887–1975) received the Nobel Prize— and which provided confirmation of the old quantum theory—were completely erroneous. Of the new quantum mechanics of the mid-1920s he resolutely and for ever after refused to take any notice. The University managed to persuade him to retire only when, during the Second World War, he was prosecuted for disrupting a radio course for servicemen. The sort of attitudes that got him into trouble were perhaps visible almost two generations earlier, when between 1903 and 1905 students noticed that six successive courses of lectures by Clifton and Townsend were given—concurrently!—at 12 noon on Tuesdays and Saturdays. The Electrical Laboratory's outstanding success was the X-ray spectroscopy experiments in 1913–14 of the young H. G. J. Moseley

(1887–1915), which enabled him to place the elements of the periodic table in their correct order. He was never a member of staff of the University, and a year later was killed at Gallipoli.

Clifton's successor from 1919, F. A. Lindemann (1886–1957), later Lord Cherwell, became Churchill's scientific adviser in the Second World War and was accused by Tizard of squandering lives and resources on a futile strategic bombing campaign. Before the First World War he had done experimental work on specific heats under Walther Nernst (1864–1941) in Berlin, which provided an early confirmation of the quantum theory of Max Planck (1858–1947). In his first year at Oxford he reputedly designed a very sensitive new photocell to detect starlight. After this he did no further experimental work in his very long tenure, but through his organizing and fund-raising efforts he helped lay the basis for a substantial research expansion. His great coup, after

H. G. J. MOSELEY was the outstanding scientist of his generation, and his death in the Great War was a tragedy for Oxford and the scientific world. He is seen here in 1910 shortly after graduating from Trinity College. In the few remaining years of his life he was to establish the atomic number of the elements, the foundation upon which nuclear physics and atomic chemistry rest.

FRANZ EUGEN SIMON, the thermo-dynamician, left Germany in 1933 and moved to Oxford, where he pioneered the study of low-temperature physics. He became a naturalized British subject in 1938, but a year later, when war broke out, he, like other refugees, was not entrusted with official secrets and was barred from Oxford's radar facility. His mind turned instead to the development of an atomic bomb, which was not at that time an official project.

the rise of a Nazi Government in Berlin, was the recruitment of one of Nernst's out-standing students Franz Simon (1893–1956) and his collaborators Kurt Mendelssohn (1906–80) and Nicholas Kurti (b. 1908), who together founded the Oxford low-temper-ature school based on the helium expansion and adiabatic demagnetization techniques they brought over from Germany. Even before their arrival, Derek Jackson (1906–72), a wealthy horse-racing enthusiast and part-owner of the *News of the World* newspaper, in 1928 made what is reputed to be the first experimental spectroscopic determination of a nuclear spin. Later, in collaboration with H. G. Kuhn (b. 1904), a refugee and former student of James Franck at Göttingen, he examined Doppler broadening with atomic beams. Their close collaboration was particularly remarkable, as Jackson was then the brother-in-law of Sir Oswald Mosley (1896–1980), supporter of Hitler and leader of the British Blackshirts. Kuhn retained a strong respect and affection for Jackson, and later wrote his Royal Society memoir. A new Clarendon Laboratory was built in 1939 and important war work was done in the next few years on radar development, infrared detectors, and uranium separation by gaseous diffusion. A significant postwar success was the discovery in 1945 of ferromagnetic resonance by James H. Griffith (1908–81), later President of Magdalen College. Work was also done on paramagnetic relaxation and nuclear magnetic resonance, and in 1951 the first successful nuclear alignment was achieved. A High Magnetic Field Laboratory was built in the 1950s, and further effort was put into experimental examination of nuclear moments and various areas of solid-state physics. Anatole Abragam (b. 1914), who worked in the Clarendon in this period, subsequently became head of the French national laboratory in nuclear magnetism. From 1946 to the mid-1950s work in nuclear physics and orientation was led by another former refugee, Hans von Halban (1908–64), who also played a significant role in the wartime atom-bomb project.

There was no chair of theoretical physics associated with the Clarendon Laboratory till the end of the Second World War, when the two physics laboratories were merged, and Townsend's Wykeham Chair was converted to this purpose. In his book on *The Physical Significance of the Quantum Theory* (1932) Lindemann expressed strong misgivings about the probability interpretation of the new wave mechanics. Nevertheless, the following year he helped recruit the theory's main articulator, Erwin Schroedinger (1887–1961), to a supernumerary fellowship at Magdalen College. In the event Schroedinger had little contact with the Clarendon, and departed for his native Austria only three years later. The Hungarian and Berlin theorist Leo Szilard (1898–1964) was brought into the Clarendon in the mid-1930s as a nuclear experimenter, but left in 1938 for America. Between 1933 and 1936 two other Berlin theorists, Fritz London (1900–54) and his brother Heinz (1907–70), did significant theoretical work on superconductivity, a subject which was further explored by Mendelssohn. However, upon the expiry of his three-year fellowship Fritz left for the Continent and eventually for America, while Heinz moved his studies to the more theoretically orientated Wills Laboratory at Bristol. With the assignment of the Wykeham Chair to theory in 1945, Simon pressed strongly for the appointment of Rudolf Peierls (b. 1907), a former student of Werner Heisenberg (1901–76). Peierls had made important contributions to the theory of electrons in solids, magnetism, and the atomic nucleus, and was at that time Professor of Mathematical Physics at Birmingham. When Lindemann declined to make such an appointment, Simon attributed this to motives bordering on xenophobia, and Peierls did not actually obtain the post until 1963. Under him, and his Royal Society-sponsored colleague R. H. Dalitz (b. 1925), Oxford theoretical physics came into its own, but maintained an autonomy separate from the experimenters in the Clarendon. Many believe that Simon too, as a former professor in Breslau and subsequently the leader of low-temperature research in the Clarendon, would have made an outstanding Director of the laboratory. Upon Cherwell's retirement in the mid-1950s Simon was in fact elected to this post, but died before he could assume it. The Chair of Experimental Philosophy then went to the microwave spectroscopist Brebis Bleaney, under whom both student numbers and research expanded very rapidly.

From 1957 Simon's personal chair was assigned to nuclear physics, and Denys

Wilkinson (b. 1922) was appointed. At first use was made of accelerator facilities at the relatively nearby Harwell and Aldermaston atomic laboratories. In 1962, after considerable controversy both in the Oxford community and with the Ministry of Science, Oxford obtained its own substantial accelerator facility—though research in particle physics still had to be conducted at the European Centre for Nuclear Research (CERN) and the Rutherford Laboratory. Under Wilkinson nuclear physics was also a separate department, but enjoyed an especially close liaison with theoretical physics under Peierls. The other main stream of physical research was in atmospheric physics, under G. M. B. Dobson (1889–1976), who originally came to Oxford in 1920 as a lecturer in Meteorology. On the basis of his original experiments on meteor trails, with the help of Lindemann he postulated a temperature rise in the upper atmosphere due to ultraviolet absorption by ozone layers, whose density and seasonal variations he subsequently examined. After the war he used a variety of new instruments to obtain artificial satellite data for use in meteorology. One of Dobson's collaborators and eventual successors, John T. Houghton (b. 1931), became Director of the Meteorological Office. This led indirectly to the formation of the Robert Hooke Institute as a joint venture of the Met Office, with a revamped Oxford Department of Atmospheric, Oceanic, and Planetary Physics. At the Clarendon, from 1978 Bleaney was succeeded as Director by the neutron diffraction specialist E. W. J. Mitchell (b. 1925), later chairman of the Science and Engineering Research Council and a leading proponent of the new university-based interdisciplinary research centres.

Despite eventual experimental successes, progress in physics was for long somewhat inhibited by its distance from mathematics and—as with chemistry—by a general shortage of theory. One can contrast this with Cambridge physics, which as early as the mid-nineteenth century was strongly dominated by graduates of the Mathematical examination ('Tripos'), especially under the leadership of the outstanding mathematical physicists Maxwell (1831–79) and Rayleigh (1842–1919). As late as 1930 Oxford's Savilian Professor of Geometry, G. H. Hardy (1877–1947), wrote that if Oxford was to have a first-rate mathematics school it must 'persuade the University (or rather the Colleges) that such a school is an asset'. He then returned to Cambridge. Dr Margaret Rayner (b. 1929) has noted that for long 'research experience was not required (or possibly even expected) of mathematics tutors, whose responsibility lay almost entirely within their own colleges'. Of the then professors, three out of four were from Cambridge, including Hardy. Another of them, A. E. H. Love (1863–1940), was Sedleian Professor of Natural Philosophy from 1898 for two generations. He had published his famous *Treatise on the Mathematical Theory of Elasticity* in 1893, and is still known for the application of his 'Love waves' to seismology. The third Cambridge-educated professor was E. A. Milne (1896–1950), who was elected in 1928 after doing important work on stellar atmospheres. But by 1932 he had become obsessed with his own 'kinematical relativity' as an alternative to Einstein's General Theory, though his efforts met with little approval. His successor as Rouse Ball Professor, Charles Coulson, did more than

SIR MICHAEL ATIYAH, author of K-Theory and joint author of the Atiyah–Singer index theorem of 1962, has crossed mathematical boundaries and linked the separate disciplines of geometry, topology, algebra, and calculus. He is pictured here in the Mathematical Institute in 1989. He is Director of the Isaac Newton Institute in Cambridge.

anyone to effect a bridge between mathematics and the physical sciences. Even so, as late as 1950 the mathematicians were still housed rather uneasily in the Radcliffe Science Library.

In 1953 a new Mathematical Institute was established across Parks Road in a building recently vacated by the Institute of Social Medicine. It helped to bring together the various college mathematicians but soon became overcrowded. It nevertheless boasted in J. H. C. Whitehead (1905–60), Waynflete Professor of Pure Mathematics since 1947, one of the outstanding topologists of the day, who attracted students from all over the world. A new building was repeatedly promised, but not made available (in St Giles') until 1966. Dr Rayner notes: 'It took thirty-six years for the mathematicians to establish the kind of Institute that had been envisioned [by Hardy] in 1930.' By way of comparison, in the same period Richard Courant (1888–1972) alone established *two* world-leading mathematics institutes—at Göttingen and at New York University; clearly he worked in what were then much more sympathetic environments. Nevertheless, following the University expansion of the 1960s and 1970s, by 1989 Oxford Mathematics embodied ten professors, two readers, and no fewer than forty-five lecturers—and was doing world-class work in most areas of the discipline. The Rouse Ball Professor since 1973 has been the mathematical physicist Roger Penrose (b. 1931), who is best known for his two-spinor formulation in general relativity, the subject disavowed by Milne. A related development was the establishment in 1957 of a first-class Computing Laboratory. Mathematical tools and modelling also found important application in Mathematical Economics, Biomathematics, and in a joint School of Mathematical Logic.

The father of Oxford metallurgy—and of scientific metallurgy in Britain—was William Hume-Rothery (1899–1968). Asked to explain his predilection for developing the physical and chemical basis of his subject, he recalled that he had started as 'an Oxford chemist trained in the Chemistry School where the question "Why is this like this?" was continually asked . . . The metallurgist [then] asked *how* to make an alloy strong—the chemist asked *why* is the alloy strong?' He was encouraged by Soddy to work on intermetallic compounds, and studied this topic for a time at the Royal School of Mines. Attempting to understand the conditions under which such compounds were formed led him, upon his return to Oxford in 1925, to consider the role played by their electronic structure. He was advised by Sidgwick that the best theory of electronic conduction available was the electron lattice theory for metals expounded by Lindemann in the *Philosophical Magazine* in 1915. This was a very strange claim, as that particular theory had never had many successes or adherents. Nevertheless, Hume-Rothery's efforts to reinvigorate the discredited theory—despite the advent of the new quantum mechanics—led him to formulate his famous 'phase rules' for the formation of alloys. As late as 1929, while writing a book on various alternative theories of what he called *The Metallic State* (published in 1931), he confessed his difficulties in keeping up with the latest quantum mechanical theory: certainly it must have placed quite a strain on his limited mathematics. Nevertheless, when his book appeared it included (in an appendix contributed by a visiting post-doctoral student at Cambridge) a précis-

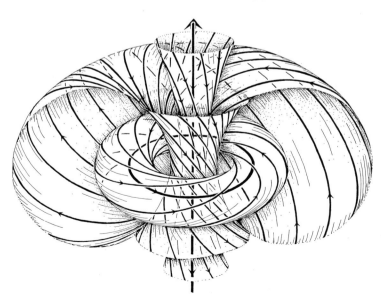

A TWISTOR is a pattern of linked circles, moving along its axis at the speed of light, developed by Professor Roger Penrose, which describes the structure of the angular momentum of a spinning massless particle, such as a photon. The object is to place relativity theory and quantum theory upon the same mathematical basis and to reformulate the geometry of space–time and the physics taking place within it.

translation of the dissertation which Felix Bloch (b. 1905) wrote for Heisenberg upon electronic conductivity in a periodic potential similar to that of a metal. Even if he was still not entirely convinced by the new approaches, Hume-Rothery was at least fully committed to a *theoretical* explanation of the observable properties of metals and alloys, and was deeply critical of the unscientific approaches of previous generations of trial-and-error metallurgists. His work proved to be an important bridge between the new theoretical physics and the new scientific metallurgy he and his students created. The transition to the new physical metallurgy is clearly visible in his *Electrons, Atoms, Metals*

ISAAC WOLFSON, who endowed the first Chair of Metallurgy in 1956, is shown the intricacies of a lathe during the opening ceremonies for the department's first home, the Hume-Rothery building, in 1960.

and Alloys (1948), written in the form of a colourful dialogue between an 'old metallurgist' and a young one of the new scientific generation.

The School of Metallurgy at Oxford arose largely out of Hume-Rothery's efforts. From 1925 to 1929 he held only a demonstrator's position at Magdalen, and was allowed only one bench in Professor Perkin's Dyson Perrins chemistry laboratory. In 1929 he was appointed to a research fellowship sponsored by the Armourers and Braziers Company, and moved to what was then the Old Chemistry Department. In 1932 he was appointed to the short-term Warren Research Fellowship of the Royal Society—and held it for twenty-three years! Although this was probably one of the most important research posts in Oxford, the University's contribution to it was virtually nil. An endowed readership was created for him by the Pressed Steel Company in 1954, followed three years later by his appointment as the first Wolfson Professor of his subject. After the establishment of the readership, Simon pressed strongly for the creation of a metallurgical research centre along the lines of the famous theoretically orientated Institute for the Study of Metals at Chicago, but this was thought insufficiently practical by British industrialists, who pressed instead for a teaching department to provide them with future manpower. As in the case of the Engineering School (below), there was opposition to such industrially relevant activities within the Oxford community. A new specialization was created in 1956, and at first given the slightly pretentious title of Science of Metals—though this was eventually changed back to Metallurgy some years later. In the meantime the Hume-Rothery building was opened for the new subject in 1960. Peter Hirsch (b. 1925), who had obtained the first electron diffraction photographs of dislocations in metals at Cambridge in the late 1940s, came as professor in 1966. In 1973 the title of the degree was broadened to 'Metallurgy and Science of Materials'.

In 1925 R. T. Gunther wrote, 'British geology owes so much to Oxford men that it would not be far off the mark to call Oxford the cradle of the science in this country.' In addition to Plot, Lhuyd, and Buckland, he no doubt had in mind the formulator of the uniformitarian thesis, Charles Lyell (1797–1875), who had graduated in classics from Exeter College in 1819. Lyell subsequently returned briefly to Oxford to study Law, but in an article on 'The State of the Universities' in the *Quarterly Review* (June 1827) he expressed considerable scepticism about both teaching and scholarship at his old university. Gunther noted too that whatever the accomplishments of Oxford geology, no other science 'has received so little recognition, financial and otherwise, from the University'. As late as 1950 the University's contribution to the department was only a few hundred pounds a year.

The Victorian department was dominated by John Phillips (1800–74) and Sir Joseph Prestwich (1812–96). Between 1896 and 1936 the chair in the subject was occupied by W. J. Sollas (1849–1936), a man well known for the breadth of his scientific interests, but not one able—in the face of college indifference—to build up his subject. Upon his death the chair passed to one of his demonstrators, in what has been described as a typical internal appointment. The new man, J. A. Douglas (1884–1978), undoubtedly did good work for the Anglo-Persian Oil Company in the Middle East and in India, but was less well known in academic journals. His chief concern was to obtain better quarters for his subject than the minimal ones provided in the University Museum. He was offered the Old Clarendon Laboratory, but the conversion was delayed by the Second World War and not completed until 1948–9. Upon his retirement in 1950 he was succeeded by the well-known mountaineer and explorer L. R. Wager (1904–65), who had also, like his predecessor, made substantial contributions to igneous petrology. He proceeded to further refocus the department's research towards his own interests—a development not universally welcomed by his colleagues. Nevertheless, E. A. Vincent (b. 1919) was appointed to a lecturership to develop the chemical side of the discipline. At that time the department was classified not in the Faculty of Physical Sciences but in Biological Sciences—presumably mainly because of its past association with palaeontology, though this also reflected its lack of contact with mathematics and physics. Vincent recalls pointing out the anomaly to the professor, who, however, preferred to remain with the biologists, 'who think in the same woolly-minded way that we do'. It was not till 1970 that the department was reassigned to Physical Sciences. In 1953 the department tried to strengthen itself in geochemistry with the appointment of a Reader in Mineralogy, L. H. Ahrens, but he moved on to a chair in another university only three years later. This was said to be the result of his firm conviction that the existing system for assigning college fellowships strongly discriminated against the less popular scientific subjects. Vincent then succeeded to this readership, but got no fellowship either. In addition to petrology, important research focuses were established in sedimentology, geochemistry, and in isotopic geochronological dating. Some lunar and meteoritic samples were analysed, in addition to terrestrial material. In 1959 E. Ronald Oxburgh (b. 1934) was appointed as departmental demonstrator. He had changed to Geology after passing Classical Mods. He was an early and enthusiastic proponent of plate tectonics, but when he wanted to start research in the Alps the professor discouraged him on the grounds that there was still 'good work to be done in the Scottish Highlands'. In 1964 Oxburgh obtained the first college tutorial fellowship in the subject, at St Edmund Hall. Two years later he helped develop a geothermal map of Britain. He eventually moved on to head the Earth Sciences department at Cambridge, and is now Chief Scientific Adviser to the Ministry of Defence. Vincent succeeded to the Oxford chair in 1967, by which time the department had evolved from a Victorian department of natural history, characterized by collecting and description, to a sophisticated geochemical and geophysical laboratory, and its members had been promoted to chairs at Manchester, Hull, Durham, Birmingham, Columbia, Alberta, and Cambridge. It has since become an internationally respected Department of Earth Sciences.

Engineering as a university subject was spurred into being by the burgeoning nineteenth-century railway industry. Courses were begun in London and Durham in the 1830s, with the first chairs established at Cambridge (1837), Glasgow (1840), University

THE ASTROLABE, imported from the Islamic world in the eleventh century, became the pre-eminent instrument for mathematical and astronomical computation. This example of *c*.1350 belonged to the Merton College school of astronomers, who made Oxford one of the scientific centres of Europe in the fourteenth century. It is similar to that described by Geoffrey Chaucer, whose *Treatise on the Astrolabe* was written at Oxford in 1387.

College, London (1841), Trinity College, Dublin (1842), Queen's College, Belfast (1843), the Royal School of Mines (1853), and Edinburgh (1868). At Oxford the subject grew out of a grant of £8,000 that one Thomas Millard (d. 1871), not a member of the University, left to Trinity College. In 1886 part of this was applied to building a one-storey 'mechanical workshop' (later known as the Millard Engineering Laboratory) in Dolphin Yard between Trinity and Balliol. F. J. Jervis-Smith (1848–1911), a vicar from Taunton in Somerset, was brought in to lecture in Experimental Mechanics, and from 1888 also in Engineering. He did significant research in specialized instrumentations, wireless telegraphy, photography, and also in experimental physics. Upon his retirement in 1908 the University finally founded a chair and a department. The first professor, Charles Frewen Jenkin (1865–1940), was the son of the first holder of the engineering chair at Edinburgh—which is perhaps indicative of the generation lag between the Scottish universities and Oxford in the physical sciences. Jenkin had a respectable scientific background, having passed the Mathematical Tripos at Cambridge, which no doubt made him seem an ideal choice to electors concerned that only the *science* of engineering be taught. In his inaugural lecture, *Engineering Science* (1908), the theoretical (and respectably non-utilitarian) aspects of his subject were emphasized: 'What we propose to teach, then, in Oxford is the Science or Theory of Engineering, and to leave the experience . . . to a subsequent apprenticeship.' A serious problem was noted: 'The only building provided for the Engineering Department is the Millard Laboratory. It is small and somewhat shabby. Of equipment there is almost none.' An early demonstrator was D. R. Pye (1886–1960), a fellow of New College, later Provost of University College, London, and President of the Institute of Mechanical Engineers. Unfortunately, when he resigned his college fellowship in 1919 it was to be forty years before any other engineering lecturer or demonstrator received one.

There was considerable opposition to the expansion of the department on to a permanent site. Indeed, there were some who believed that Engineering, like the railway, would be 'more at home' beside the canal, and that it should on no account be placed anywhere near the Parks. This undoubtedly reflected opposition to Engineering as an Oxford subject, an antipathy which lasted at least until the 1950s. In a rejoinder which he issued in November 1912 the Wykeham Professor of Physics, Townsend, concluded that people who thought in this way might as well say that 'an Engineering Laboratory would be more at home in any other part of England than in Oxford . . . The idea that any modern science can be taught without laboratory instruction could not possibly be entertained, except by an expert on education trained in the Oxford school of philosophy.' On the other hand, supporters of the new Engineering expansion 'consider that it is a reproach to the University that for such a long time Oxford has contributed so little to the advance of scientific knowledge, and that the majority of the clever men

A PRECISION DRIFT CHAMBER under construction in the Nuclear Physics Laboratory in 1990. A total of 25,000 accurately placed and tensioned wires make it possible to measure the direction and momentum of charged particles. When finished, the chamber was sent to Hamburg for use in a European project.

A RESEARCH STUDENT in the Department of Earth Sciences (*above*) displays the results of calculations in which variations of gravity over the oceans are derived from measurements of the position of the ocean surface by satellite altimeters. The information is used in studying the history of the ocean basins and in investigating the pattern of convection occurring within the solid earth.

THE ENGINEERING DEPARTMENT has made a long-standing contribution to the development of the gas turbine by Rolls-Royce (*right*). Short-duration experimental techniques have been used to study the heat transfer and fluid mechanics in the high-pressure turbine—the hottest part of the engine—with the aim of improving engine efficiencies and life.

educated in Oxford are kept for the first twenty-two years of their lives in absolute ignorance of the world they live in'. After some further battling, what is now the Jenkin Building was erected opposite the Parks (though almost immediately activity was suspended on account of the First World War).

The 1920s brought a substantial expansion in teaching, and also in research, which was centred around refrigeration, electrical circuits, vibrations, and mechanics. Jenkin moved on to the Building Research Station at Watford in 1929, and was succeeded by R. V. (later Sir Richard) Southwell (1888–1970), another Cambridge mathematician (who had also read Mechanical Sciences). He had also been in charge of the aeronautics department at the National Physical Laboratory, and before that had been at the national aeronautics research establishment at Farnborough. He persuaded the Rhodes Trustees, and subsequently the chairman of Metal Industries, to finance an

Oxford readership in his department. He specialized in the mathematical theory of structures, the impact testing of materials, and the theory of fracture. His *Introduction to the Theory of Elasticity for Engineers and Physicists* (1936) built on Love's earlier *Treatise* (fourth edition, 1927). Much of the original work of his research group is collected in *Relaxation Methods in Theoretical Physics* (1946). By then he had left Oxford (in 1942) to become Rector of Imperial College, London. A number of his students went on to professorships in their own right, one became Vice-Chancellor, and two became prominent engineering leaders at Rolls-Royce—with whom the department's relations have remained extremely close until the present day. One of the department's outstanding undergraduate students was Ann Pellew (b. 1915) of St Hugh's College, who obtained a First in 1939 as Oxford's first female engineering graduate, before going on to a very successful career at Farnborough.

An expert in the mathematical theory of electricity and electron diffraction who came to Oxford in 1941 was the Austrian refugee Hans Motz (1909–87). During the war

ANN PELLEW photographed in flying-kit at the Royal Aircraft Establishment in Farnborough in 1954. She was awarded the Queen's Commendation for her work on the Comet disasters, in the course of which she risked her life forty times. In a quieter moment she became British gliding champion in 1966.

he served as a consultant to the Admiralty on the generation of microwaves for radar sets. At the end of the war, in May 1945, he wrote to his sponsors in the Society for the Protection of Science and Learning regarding his prospects at Oxford: 'my impression [is] that the chances of permanent establishment of a foreigner . . . are small. The University seems very anxious to preserve the pattern of its old tradition and suspects, rightly or wrongly, that people from outside might become promoters of undesirable changes.' A few months later he left for a lecturership at Sheffield. However, the Scottish-trained Alexander Thom (1894–1985) was elected as Southwell's successor. This represented a considerable departure from the previous professorial tradition of Cambridge mathematicians. In the early 1950s, while a visiting research associate at Stanford, Motz extended his Oxford work on microwaves to produce the first relativistic microwave source or 'undulator' (as he called it), and many years later, in 1976, also at Stanford, the free electron laser. In the improved atmosphere generated by Thom, Motz agreed in 1954 to return to Oxford, as a reader, and produced his outstanding *Electromagnetic Problems of Microwave Theory* (1957). In 1973 he was elected the University's first Professor of Electrical Engineering. Perhaps more than anyone else, he spanned the gap between science and engineering.

In 1955 a Committee on the Future of Engineering Science was appointed by the Hebdomadal Council, recommending—amidst considerable opposition—a doubling of the department's size and substantial further building. Among the leading opponents were the Professors of Physics and Chemistry, Lord Cherwell and Sir Cyril Hinshelwood. The former believed that the practice of engineering should be taught in technical colleges, with the theoretical aspects at Oxford presumably falling to his own department. Hinshelwood worried that the additional burdens of a huge engineering staff would undermine the Oxford college system, since finding additional college fellowships seemed at that time impossible. Despite these concerns, the expansion soon got under way, with the nine-storey Thom building erected in the late 1950s. The year 1959 also brought the first of a substantial series of college fellowships. Upon Thom's retirement in 1961 he was succeeded by Douglas Holder (1923–77), formerly of the National Physical Laboratory's aerodynamics division. A new Chair—in Structural Engineering—and a new Honour Moderations were soon established. A joint Honour School of Engineering and Economics was set up, and a one-year diploma in plasmas. In 1971 the redundant power station at Osney was purchased, and became the Southwell Laboratory for large-scale research, especially in wind-tunnel aerodynamics. A new Holder Building was erected in 1976, shared between Engineering and Metallurgy. From 1979 to 1990 the head of Engineering was Professor Peter Wroth (1929–91), who established further Honour Schools in Engineering and Computer Science, and in Electronic and Structural Materials Engineering. An Honour School in Engineering, Economics, and Management was created in the late 1970s. The management teaching is the responsibility of Templeton College, which also provides advanced programmes for industrial, financial, and public-service managers. Like many of the physical sci-

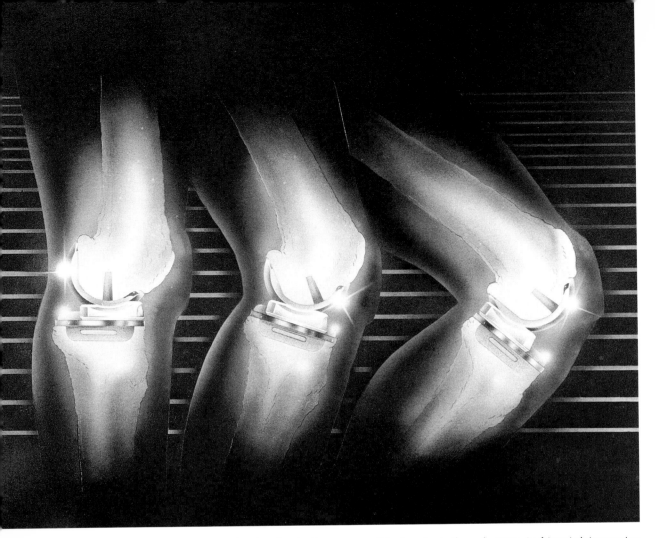

THE OXFORD KNEE was developed in the Department of Engineering in the early 1970s. As this artist's impression shows, it embodies a floating meniscal bearing made of polyethylene, which moves backwards and forwards as the knee is flexed. To this has now been added a femoral component with spherical internal geometry which minimizes bone resection.

ences and Engineering, the new Management courses have had to overcome a certain amount of scepticism—especially about their more utilitarian aspects. They are now set for substantial expansion.

The history of Engineering is almost a summation of University attitudes towards the modern physical sciences. Even after making allowance for the fact that the agricultural depression of the 1880s and 1890s reduced the revenues at the disposal of the colleges, it is difficult to avoid the conclusion that, with few exceptions, Oxford was late, slow, and niggardly in taking up these subjects, which also suffered in the nineteenth century from the indifference of a collegiate and a teaching university towards research. Not only was there strong opposition from college Arts dons (and clerics) to

University laboratories, but there was considerable animosity from pre-existing mathematical or scientific disciplines towards younger rivals. In the mid-nineteenth century experimental philosophy (physics) was handicapped by a long-running jurisdictional battle with mathematics. This was followed by another with the different varieties of chemistry (which were better established in the colleges), and even up to the end of the Second World War by yet another dispute with mathematics about the control of 'mathematical' (or, as some said, 'theoretical') physics. The old Clarendon Laboratory under Lindemann—replaced only on the eve of the Second World War—never did have an electricity supply, because that was the province of Townsend and his Electrical Laboratory.

In retrospect the truly surprising thing is how the opposition was eventually worn down, not just by the repeated threats of Royal Commissions, but even more decisively by what Professor J. K. Galbraith (b. 1908) has called *The New Industrial State* (1967) of the postwar period. During the last war Oxford played a leading part in the British aeronautics, radar, and atomic programmes, and continued afterwards to have close relations with the national research establishments at Farnborough, Malvern, Harwell, and later Aldermaston. Its relations were hardly less cordial with—among others—Imperial Chemical Industries, Rolls-Royce, and the Morris Motors of Lord Nuffield. Given this situation, it was probably inevitable that the modern industrial state—including its University Grants Committee, Research Council, and other components—would use its money and overwhelming influences gradually to reshape the University to meet its new needs. This included a gigantic externally funded postwar expansion of the Sciences, in particular, eventually, of Engineering. Management is now set to follow the same pattern. Opposition from the Arts has been somewhat muffled by their own considerable expansion, and by the establishment of new graduate colleges to provide many of the required college fellowships in the newer subjects. The fact that a number of college heads have now come from the Sciences, or from Engineering, shows that at Oxford this particular long-running battle has been decisively and conclusively won.

The Growth of an International University

JOHN DARWIN

IN the middle of the nineteenth century Oxford was a very different university in almost all respects from what it had become by the middle of the twentieth: in its size, in the scope of its studies, and in the kind of students it attracted. First and foremost, Oxford then existed as an academy for the English ruling élite and for those who aspired to join it. It offered formal instruction, primarily in the classics, of a kind designed to complete the classical education provided in the major public schools. Its students, if assiduous, were steeped in the major texts of ancient history and philosophy and equipped for life with an inexhaustible fund of classical tags. This, in an age when classical literature retained immense prestige, was a highly functional preparation for a career in politics, law, the civil service, or even the justices' bench in the rural counties, where the landed class maintained supremacy in local affairs. An advanced classical education was still regarded as the key to intellectual sophistication and a necessary entrée for membership of the leisured class from which was drawn the social and political leadership of mid-Victorian Britain, as well as the expanding bureaucracies of the Empire. Oxford was also the great academic stronghold of the Established Church. But what the University offered was not just the academic equipment for a future career in Church or State, but the opportunity to mix socially with those who, whether by talent or hereditary right, were bound for high places. In the societies and clubs, sporting, political, or intellectual, with which Oxford abounded, friendships were made and alliances formed as if in preparation for later careers. Oxford undergraduate life served quite self-consciously as a threshold for entry into the 'adult' political and intellectual world of the metropolis.

Preoccupied with this highly specialized and prestigious social role, mid-Victorian Oxford was not, in the modern sense, a centre of research. Still less was it concerned to compete with the great universities of Europe or to develop systematically its expertise

VISCOUNT MILNER, a graduate of Balliol and a fellow of New College, personified the links between Oxford and the Empire at the turn of the century. As High Commissioner of South Africa between 1897 and 1905, he recruited a 'kindergarten' of aides, largely from Oxford. He was a Rhodes Trustee, and at the time of his death had just succeeded Lord Curzon as Chancellor. This portrait of him is by J. Guthrie.

in the study of other languages and cultures (except the classical). Its major academic innovation after 1850 was to gear itself for the competitive academic examinations used increasingly from mid-century onwards to recruit the higher echelons of the civil service at home and in the Empire. To some extent this may have encouraged a more serious, meritocratic, and middle-class tone in Oxford life, especially in those colleges, like Balliol, where academic achievement was regarded as the essential prelude to worldly success in Government and politics.

Rationally organized in its own terms, Oxford nevertheless struck foreigners as a quintessential example of the baffling eccentricity of English institutions. It was a university town, but even the most persistent visitor was unlikely to discover a university campus. In the University there were professors who enjoyed international fame but who played no part in the teaching of its students and were despised by those who did.

There were prize fellowships whose holders lived and worked elsewhere. There was a syllabus which, in the most industrialized and capitalist country in the world, was dominated by ancient history and philosophy, reflecting profound contempt for merely vocational subjects. And undergraduate life often seemed devoted to organized sport and less organized frivolity, since social status rather than academic merit was the key to admission.

Not surprisingly, perhaps, Oxford as a university invited ambivalent and contradictory responses from foreign visitors and academics. As the finishing-school of a ruling class whose imperial power expanded dramatically in the nineteenth century, it commanded respect and aroused curiosity. As a centre of learning, even if of a somewhat eccentric English kind, it was of some interest to foreign scholars. Its peculiar teaching practices, so different from those of most contemporary universities, were intriguing. Hippolyte Taine (1828–93), who was the most authoritative French interpreter of English society and culture of his day, came to Oxford in 1871 to deliver a series of lectures. He was ravished by Oxford's architectural beauty and the sensations of 'poetic solitude' he experienced in rambling about the city. But, he complained, Oxford was 'trop beau' and too much taken up with a worldly social life: it was impossible to work there as you could in Germany. Despite meeting a number of leading secular academics, with whom he enjoyed a rapport, Taine was struck by 'the profoundly ecclesiastical character of this university' and also commented unfavourably on the inegalitarian distinction by type of gown between different classes of undergraduates (the scholars and commoners).

A later visitor, Woodrow Wilson (1856–1924), was also captivated by the charm of college quadrangles and gardens. 'A mere glance at Oxford', he wrote home in July 1896, 'is enough to take one's heart by storm.' If he could secure a post in Oxford, he declared, he would return home only to pack his possessions. But though Wilson became a great admirer of the tutorial system practised in Oxford, with its emphasis on close personal supervision by the tutor, and sought to introduce it at Princeton when he became President of the College, it was not an uncritical enthusiasm. 'The English make an old-fashioned mistake about it,' he told an (American) audience in 1902: 'They appoint their tutors for life and their tutors go to seed.' Wilson expressed the contradictory emotions felt by many foreign and especially transatlantic visitors: delight at the visual beauty; amusement at quaint customs; admiration for the intensity and thoroughness of the teaching system; but equally a certain astonishment at the apparent disdain for modernity and at the absence of amenities and facilities taken for granted at universities elsewhere. This attitude was delightfully satirized by the Canadian Stephen Leacock (1869–1944). The students, he told readers in *My Discovery of England* (1922), worked under distressing conditions: 'The lack of an adequate building fund compels them to go on working in the same old buildings which they have had for centuries.' As for Oxford's syllabus, 'the programme of studies is frankly laughable . . . there is less applied science than would be found with us in a theological college'.

RUDYARD KIPLING AND MARK TWAIN were among those to receive honorary degrees at the Encaenia—a combination of formal academic ceremony and garden party all in full academic dress—in 1907. Here the Chancellor of the University, Lord Curzon, a former Viceroy of India, makes his way up the High Street.

Leacock's irony masked an uncritical admiration for Oxford which came perhaps most easily to those little acquainted with its peculiarities as an educational institution but profoundly impressed by its aura of confidence, its sempiternal antiquity, and its rejection of crass materialism. Oxford's medievalism, ecclesiasticism, and lack of practicality touched a romantic chord. In 1907 Mark Twain (1835–1910), a bitter if inconsistent critic of the social values of the 'gilded age' in the United States, received the offer of an honorary doctorate from the Chancellor, Lord Curzon (1859–1925), with a delight fortified by his resentment at the honouring of dozens of lesser literary fry by American universities. In his *Autobiography* one of the most popular authors in the English-speaking world handsomely repaid the debt, with an unsolicited testimonial all the more remarkable from so irreverent a source. 'I am quite well aware,' he wrote, 'and so is America, and so is the rest of Christendom—that an Oxford decoration is a loftier distinction than is conferrable by any other university on either side of the ocean, and is worth twenty-five of any other, foreign or domestic.' Perhaps Twain's death three years later denied us a new masterpiece, *Huck Finn at Balliol*.

Mark Twain's praise may have been exaggerated. But there was no doubt of Oxford's distinctive character among the major universities of the world (there was of course a family likeness with Cambridge). Unlike many universities in other countries, Oxford had not been founded (though it had been favoured) by the State. Nor was it governed by a board of wealthy non-academic trustees, as was common among the private foundations of the United States. It was instead a self-governing corporation of academics who enjoyed an enviable autonomy from State and benefactors alike. In the 1870s Government had intervened to abolish the requirement that the fellows of colleges remain unmarried and take holy orders, and also imposed administrative changes to strengthen University, as opposed to college, finances. But the academics were left in undisturbed control of the syllabus, admissions, appointments, and the criteria of academic merit and advancement. The day-to-day government of the University was theirs. For practical purposes that largely meant that it was left in the hands of the colleges, for Oxford notoriously was really a loose confederation of colleges with only a skeletal centre to administer the few common services: chiefly, the Bodleian Library, the museums, the Press, examinations, and the conferment of degrees, as well as the proverbially under-attended lectures of its proverbially undervalued professors.

After autonomy, Oxford's second distinctive characteristic was the prime importance of the colleges in providing instruction through their band of tutorial fellows and by means not so much of lectures as of the tutorial, in which teacher and taught wrestled together with the standard controversies of their subject. It was of course the colleges, and not the University, which enjoyed income from endowments and had first call on the loyalty of old members and potential benefactors. Oxford graduates at home and abroad looked back nostalgically—if they looked back at all—to their college community, not to the amorphous entity that was the University. In the late nineteenth century the social character of many colleges was still heavily influenced by the clerical atmosphere Taine had noticed. The old requirement that tutors be clergymen had been abolished, but the social consequence of the old system, the prevalence of unmarried fellows living in college on close terms with their undergraduate charges, survived the legal change and was still as much the hallmark of the Oxford 'system' as the tutorial or the relative insignificance of the University at large.

Academic autonomy and the sense of apartness that it encouraged, and the strength of the colleges as academic and social units, conspired to create a peculiar ethos and structure in Oxford which had a powerful and limiting effect on its appeal to students from overseas, on its influence as a model of higher education outside the United Kingdom, and on its claim to be a great international centre of scholarship. If the colleges were the dominant force in the University, their overriding preoccupation was the teaching and preparation of undergraduates for the 'Schools', the final degree examinations. They had little incentive to diversify the undergraduate syllabus, in which classical history and philosophy still remained supreme at the end of the nineteenth century, with Anglo-centric history and English literature gradually becoming more popular. Their function was not the education of scholars but the equipping of young men with a form of mandarin literacy so that they could compete for posts in the Indian and home civil services, where entry was by competitive examination chiefly in those subjects taught at Oxford and Cambridge. The introduction of new subjects or any drastic widening of the old undergraduate syllabus was likely to be a source of trouble

CORNELIA SORABJI was the first Indian woman student at Oxford, where she studied at Somerville College. By special permission she attended lectures at All Souls and at Balliol, and took the Bachelor of Civil Law examination in 1893. She became an eminent lawyer in India and an influential writer on the emancipation of women from purdah.

and expense, if it meant the recruitment of additional tutors and the honing of a new range of teaching skills.

By the same token colleges were disinclined to regard the pursuit of research as an important function of their tutors. The reforms that had rolled through the Oxford colleges in the nineteenth century had had the effect of strengthening the tutorial fellows, who actually gave instruction, against other classes of fellows, who might be absent or merely ruminative. Many abuses of college funds were corrected; but the result was to reinforce the tendency of colleges to concern themselves single-mindedly with teaching a very narrow range of disciplines through tutors whose teaching and pastoral burdens were too heavy to encourage original work. Among many college tutors there was even perhaps a certain mistrust of research as mere selfishness. This was best left, one remarked, to professors. Up to 1914 the tutor who lived in college and gave himself unstintingly to teaching remained the ideal. In turn, this immensely powerful tutorial ethic helps to explain why colleges so often preferred to appoint as fellows their own graduates, whose loyalty could be relied on and whose character was known, and why they were unlikely to choose from those who, however talented academically, lacked direct experience of the Oxford teaching method. Teaching thus became an inbred system in which the inflow of new ideas from outside Oxford was reduced to a trickle.

Thus, even at the time of Mark Twain's encomium there were powerful reasons why Oxford as a university seemed curiously limited as a centre of learning and almost indifferent to many branches of study regarded elsewhere as essential at a place of higher education. The idea that the University existed to promote research, or to attract and instruct graduate students, was scarcely recognized at all. The preoccupation with undergraduate teaching, the supreme importance of college instruction, the marginality of professors, the individualism bred by a highly decentralized academic structure, meant inevitably that the research seminar never became the academic focus that it had become in German or American universities. Indeed, to acquire basic research skills it was often necessary to travel abroad: thus the historian H. A. L. Fisher (1865–1940) went to the École des Chartes in Paris and others went to Germany. Even in the 1920s the Royal Commission on Oxford and Cambridge set up at the end of the First World War chided the University for its excessive preoccupation with undergraduates and urged it to think more of becoming a major international centre for research and graduate work. In an authoritative book, *Universities: American, English, German* (1930), Abraham Flexner (1866–1959) mixed a highly sympathetic appreciation of Oxford's academic values with sharp criticism of its failure to attend to graduate studies, and the parochialism of college attitudes. In these circumstances, for all its prestige and romantic charm, Oxford's academic influence and its ability to attract students and academic staff from other countries—crucial tests in the twentieth century of international status in higher education—were bound to be somewhat circumscribed. The iron grip of its late-Victorian ethos had to be broken if Oxford was to play a wider and richer role in international life.

But it would be wrong to suppose that late-Victorian Oxford was entirely parochial and self-sufficient, or that its students were insularly English. The University contained many scholars of international standing, among them the lawyers Frederick Pollock (1845–1937) and W. S. Holdsworth (1871–1944), the historians James Bryce (1838–1922) and R. H. Tawney (1880–1962), the philosophers T. H. Green (1836–82) and F. H. Bradley (1846–1924), and the Orientalist D. S. Margoliouth (1858–1940). The absence of research seminars and the relatively small output of original work did not reflect a lack of scholarship or learning. Scholarly discussion was often informal, and scholars moved easily between disciplines. Tutors who earned their bread and butter teaching classics to undergraduates might, like Margoliouth, be major figures in different fields 'on the side'. Others who may have published little that was original were engaged in textual scholarship. This was a major intellectual preoccupation of the later nineteenth century, when the authenticity of many important literary, philosophical, and historical texts was being challenged with new techniques largely pioneered in Germany. Yet others contributed to the collective scholarship behind the *Dictionary of National Biography* or the *Oxford English Dictionary*.

Secondly, Oxford may have been self-absorbed, but even in late-Victorian times it was not insensitive to the world beyond British shores. Classical scholars were influenced by European ideas and methods. The University bestirred itself to offer honorary degrees to distinguished foreign artists and men of letters, Turgenev and Rodin as well as Mark Twain among them. Despite its idiosyncratic features as a teaching institution, Oxford seems to have attracted a considerable number of students from overseas, even before the arrival of the Rhodes Scholars in the early years of the new century. In 1897 some 11 per cent of those entering the University had been born abroad (although half of them may have been the sons of British expatriates who had since returned home).

Finally, it should not be forgotten that an important part of Oxford's impact outside the United Kingdom was through the work of the University Press. By 1914 the Press had established branches in India, the United States, Canada, and Australia, and had diversified its output considerably with textbooks, children's books, standard authors, and popular editions like the 'World's Classics'. But perhaps the most vital contribution that the Press made to Oxford's academic reputation internationally was through its ability to publish scholarly monographs that remained in print for many years. In the age before Government support for research, and before a wider market for academic publications had come into existence, the Press played a key role in financing the publication of Oxford scholarship and disseminating its influence abroad.

From these late-nineteenth-century beginnings Oxford was gradually transformed into an international university of a recognizably modern type. Students from overseas, especially from the United States, arrived in larger numbers and with greater impact. Among them the proportion of graduate students grew steadily, reflecting Oxford's enhanced attractiveness as a centre for postgraduate research. The range of disciplines

AMERICAN INTEREST IN OXFORD grew rapidly after the First World War with the regular selection of Rhodes Scholars and the growth of academic exchange. The film *A Yank at Oxford*, made in the late 1930s and starring Robert Taylor, Vivien Leigh, and Maureen O'Sullivan, showed that its eccentricities were now thought suitable for mass entertainment.

of graduate and undergraduate students expanded, and to teach them staff were recruited from outside the old confines of the Oxford colleges. The systematic study of the rest of the world was broadened and deepened, while the strengthening of both natural and social sciences in Oxford stimulated participation in global networks of information and the comparative study of social institutions. Oxford remained an eccentrically organized university by international standards, but by the second half of the twentieth century its staff, students, range of academic interests, and concern for organized postgraduate study all reflected deliberate adjustment to an international role, and an acceptance that the University must compete with other major centres of higher education abroad in the promotion of research and in the diversity and sophistication of its portfolio of disciplines. It was no longer enough to teach the ruling élite of Britain and the British Empire. Increasingly it was an international élite of scholars and students which had to be drawn to Oxford as much by the scope of its interests and the reputation of its original work as by its romantic charm or the fame of its undergraduate teaching.

But Oxford's route to academic modernity was characteristically indirect. There was no great plan to remodel its academic structure and syllabus since then, as now, the University's internal government, the great virtue of which is to disfavour hierarchy or the growth of a self-important academic bureaucracy, was ill adapted to carry through great programmes of change and reform. If nothing else, the decentralization implicit in its collegiate organization imposed a gradualism scarcely distinguishable from immobility. Oxford's movement towards a wider syllabus, the organization of graduate work, and the introduction of a more positively international element into its staff and student body arose not from local initiative but from external impulses and benefactions. Perhaps ironically, it was Oxford's links with the British Empire which contributed most in the first half of the twentieth century to widening the University's academic and social outlook.

In 1922 the University Press, in a volume commemorating its history since 1478, could proclaim that 'Oxford is proud to consider itself as *par excellence* the Imperial University . . . Imperial subjects are an important and growing branch of study at Oxford.' Of course, as we have seen, Oxford had been for centuries the academy of a ruling élite, some of whom had served in the far-flung colonial administration of the British Empire. But the idea that Oxford should actually train young men specifically for a career in India or Africa, or that the University should become a reservoir of practical expertise in all the varied social, economic, and political problems of colonial government, was much more recent. Such ideas were a radical departure from the prevailing ethos of Victorian Oxford, and strikingly modern in their assumptions about the social purpose of a university.

The original impetus behind this novel conception arose from the British connection with India. In 1875 the Professor of Sanskrit, Monier Williams (1819–99), persuaded the University to allow new entrants into the Indian Civil Service (then virtually an all-British service) to spend their probationary year of instruction in Oxford. Staff were to be recruited to teach them, and the BA syllabus modified to make provision for Indian studies as a division of Oriental studies. Then in 1875 the University approved a plan for establishing an Indian Institute, to be funded partly by Government and partly by princely benefactors in India, where Indian studies and the training of the probationers were to be concentrated.

In many ways this ambitious attempt to introduce a new and outward-looking element into the University, that might have bypassed the natural conservatism of the colleges, turned out to be a false start. Indian studies folded up as a degree course within a few years when Government changed the regulations on the age of entry into the Indian Civil Service. Indian history at Oxford suffered from the appointment of retired British officials to teach it and from its tendency to become official history. Indian students who came to Oxford in increasing numbers after 1900 shunned the Institute as the eyes and ears of the India Office in London. Later attempts to establish a more sympathetic base for Indian studies in Oxford came to nothing, and in the 1940s India's drive towards independence seemed to remove the urgency of funding the study of its history, culture, and politics. Nevertheless, Oxford's involvement with India did leave some important legacies. The resources of the Indian Institute Library, later transferred to the Bodleian, have helped make Oxford one of the most important centres for the study of Indian history outside the subcontinent. Indian history entered the undergraduate syllabus in modern history long before the history of other parts of the Third World. The practice of bringing probationer British officials bound for India to Oxford for a year popularized the idea, now commonplace, that the University offered useful international expertise of a practical kind, and stimulated interest in contemporary problems overseas. Last, but certainly not least, the Indian connection brought to

TOURING HIS DISTRICT AND DISPENSING JUSTICE to the Indian population were regarded as the most important function of the British official in India. Julian Cotton, a graduate of Corpus Christi, entered the Indian Civil Service in 1893 at a time when it was an increasingly popular destination for the ablest products of Oxford and Cambridge. This photograph was taken in 1900.

THE INDIAN INSTITUTE was founded by Monier Williams, who intended that, as well as being a centre of Oriental studies, it should house 'a complete collection of specimens of products of India'. The provincial authorities in India were asked to send local artefacts, and a torrent of miscellaneous material, hard to arrange and even harder to display, poured into the Institute.

Oxford the academic study of forestry, with its beginnings in the training of young men for the Indian forest service. Here too the original design for a practical service course to meet an imperial need led eventually to the creation of an academic discipline of whose global importance we are only just becoming aware.

It was an imperial initiative of a quite different kind which was to help transform Oxford much more dramatically after 1900 and open it up to a wider range of overseas influence and concerns. In 1873 Cecil Rhodes (1853–1902), already at twenty a wealthy diamond magnate from the Cape, came back to Oxford to gain a degree. Rhodes developed a deep sentimental attachment to Oxford, and also a conviction that the classical history and philosophy that were then its staple fare enlarged the mind and sharpened

CECIL RHODES on trek. 'The great Amalgamator' was to exercise almost as great an influence on Oxford as on South Africa. His will created the Rhodes Trust, which founded the Rhodes Scholarships and Rhodes House—home, now, to a major library and archive for Commonwealth and American studies.

the wits. But when he made his will (and Rhodes made several) he thought not simply of a generous benefaction to his old college—though the Rhodes building in the High Street marks his generosity to Oriel. By the time of his final will he had come to envisage a phalanx of young men (women were added later) who would come to Oxford from the United States and the white colonies—Canada, Australia, New Zealand, and South Africa—and return home two or three years later imbued with the fraternal loyalty of the Anglo-Saxon nations (there were also to be scholars from Germany). Rhodes hoped that those from the Empire countries would dedicate themselves to the unity of the Empire. To carry out this programme, he nominated a loyal and determined group of trustees. Within a few years of his premature death in 1902, and without apparently any consultation with the University (as opposed to the individual colleges they were to enter), the first Rhodes Scholars began to arrive.

Rhodes's dream of his scholarships as a seed-bed of eager imperialist missionaries may have turned out to be far-fetched. But if returning Rhodes Scholars were often sceptical about Empire they proved a valuable advertisement for Oxford. Straight away, the new scholars were a powerful reinforcement to the number of overseas students in the University. Between the wars the 196 Rhodes Scholars usually made up a third of the total of overseas students, which fluctuated between 525 and 600 in an overall student population that rose from four to five thousand. The proverbial athletic prowess of Rhodes Scholars and the wise arrangements for their integration into the various college communities ensured their social acceptability and enhanced their prestige in undergraduate society. The result was to diffuse acquaintance with overseas countries, especially the United States, widely through Oxford and in return to make Oxford familiar to many communities throughout the world for whom it had previously been remote, mysterious, and even sinister. In one sense Rhodes Scholars were pioneers who were able to show others that the road to Oxford was less baffling than they

A RHODES SCHOLAR, as shown in the *New Yorker* in 1936. The reputation established by Rhodes Scholars for an enviable combination of academic and athletic talent played an important part in making undergraduate society in Oxford more cosmopolitan. Far from being tolerated outsiders, Rhodes Scholars came to be seen as an élite within the University.

thought and the Oxford syllabus less bizarre than they feared. The presence of Rhodes Scholars from the United States spurred the University into recognizing that it must offer the equivalent of the doctoral degree that could be gained elsewhere for advanced study, since many American Scholars preferred postgraduate work to a second BA and expected a qualification comparable with that offered by the major graduate schools at home. So in 1917 the D.Phil. came into existence: belated but significant acceptance by the University that promoting postgraduate research and awarding degrees commensurate with those of other major institutions abroad were now indispensable to its status.

The creation of the Rhodes Scholarships was the first fruit of Rhodes's will. In the first forty years of their existence some two thousand students were brought to Oxford from the United States, Germany, and countries in the British Commonwealth. But the Rhodes Trustees contributed in other important ways to widening the University's interests and equipping it as a great research centre for the study of the modern world. After a period of uncertainty, the Trustees decided in the mid-1920s to embark on the construction of Rhodes House to serve as the centre for the study of the Empire in Oxford, and to accommodate the growing library on colonial topics which they had helped to build up. Of course, Britain's changed international circumstances have rendered obsolete part of the original intention that Rhodes House should make Oxford 'a home for the study of Imperial problems in Government and Administration'. But the real legacy of its founders is a library that is the major focus in Oxford for the study of Commonwealth countries and, to a growing extent, of the United States, as well as housing a rich collection of archival materials, especially in African history. Just as the Indian Institute Library remains as a superb academic legacy of the defunct imperial purpose of the Indian Institute, so Rhodes House Library reflects the reincarnation of an old imperialist project as an academic resource which now attracts scholars and students from all over the world.

Although the grandiose ideas of the early Rhodes Trustees were not realized, the encouragement they gave to the study of the contemporary world, especially the study of Africa and Asia, was of major significance in the slow transformation of Oxford from a university almost entirely devoted to teaching undergraduates through the college system and within a narrow and conservative syllabus. The existence of Rhodes House encouraged the idea of Oxford's becoming the centre for colonial studies, where colonial officials could be trained in a range of disciplines with a practical application, including economics, anthropology, and public administration. Rhodes's great friend Alfred Beit (1853–1906) endowed a professorship for the study of colonial (later Commonwealth) history. The Rhodes Trustees financed the early fieldwork of Margery Perham (1895–1982), who became the major academic authority on the problems of colonial government in Africa. During the Second World War African and colonial studies in Oxford received a powerful stimulus partly because of the political sensitivity of colonial issues in Anglo-American relations. It became important to show that colonial problems were being systematically studied and that the responsibilities of colonial rule were being taken seriously. Money was found for new posts in colonial economics, law and anthropology. A Committee for Colonial Studies was set up in the University. In 1946 an Institute for Colonial Studies was established, subsequently incorporated into the new foundation of Queen Elizabeth House (1953). In the same year money from the Northern Rhodesian copper industry funded a new Rhodes Professorship in Race Relations. Just in time for the decline and fall of the British Empire, colonial and Commonwealth studies had established themselves firmly as a major academic presence in Oxford.

The concern with colonial affairs was thus the foundation of much of Oxford's more recent involvement in the academic study of the Third World. Colonial economics became development economics, and Oxford is now a major centre of development studies, with its academic headquarters at Queen Elizabeth House. The influence of the new academic fields in colonial history and economics, African politics and sociology, Indian history and colonial public administration was diffused into the syllabuses of graduate and undergraduate studies. It was therefore very largely by this colonial back door that the University first came to widen its study of the world, and to see itself as offering to scholars and students from overseas something more than its prestigious undergraduate syllabus.

The Rhodes connection brought one other benefit of inestimable importance to the University. Before 1904 there were numerous American visitors to Oxford, but Oxford

JOHN D. ROCKEFELLER, a pioneer of the American oil industry, made over much of his personal fortune to the Rockefeller Foundation, established in 1913. In the 1930s Rockefeller contributions towards the New Bodleian, the Institute of Experimental Psychology, Social Studies, and better chemistry laboratories played a key role in strengthening Oxford's academic resources. This cartoon appeared in the *Chicago Tribune*.

HENRY FORD aboard his first Ford car in 1896. He took a keen interest in education—usually with an emphasis on 'learning by doing'. The Ford Foundation was set up in 1936 to manage his philanthropic activity. In the postwar years Oxford became a significant beneficiary of its generosity especially to the Historic Buildings Appeal (1958) and towards the foundation of Wolfson College (1966).

remained something of an enigma. But once the scholarship scheme was properly under way Oxford became for a widening circle of influential Americans a deserving object of the philanthropic tradition which benefited American universities so greatly. Oxford was a major beneficiary of the generosity of the Rockefeller Foundation, which gave large sums to help build the New Bodleian, promote social studies, encourage experimental psychology, support the expansion of clinical medicine, and help pay for the new Law Library. In 1958 the Ford Foundation gave a million dollars to the Oxford Historic Buildings Appeal, and subsequently further sums to promote the study of European politics. By the permanent transatlantic bond which he had encouraged the University to make, Rhodes, on its behalf, had cast his bread upon the waters. Great universities need great tycoons.

There were of course other ways in which academic life in Oxford responded directly to the great cultures of the world and contributed to their exploration. The Taylor Institution, opened in 1835, was founded to forward the study of modern languages, but for long remained an independent body only loosely connected with the University. In the mid-1920s its position was regularized and its building expanded. Nevertheless, in many ways Modern Languages were still something of a Cinderella subject: even in the 1930s there were few college tutors to teach them and they hardly competed in academic prestige with Greats, Modern History, or even English. Perhaps for Modern Languages, as for the study of modern Europe generally, the real turning-point came with the Second World War and its tense aftermath. The struggle for Europe enormously enhanced the value of scholarly knowledge of its recent history and politics, while the rapid expansion of Soviet influence into eastern Europe created a vast new area of study for which academic provision seemed urgently necessary.

In the early 1920s the first Professor of International Relations at Oxford, Alfred Zimmern (1879–1957), had urged in his inaugural lecture that the University pay more attention to international affairs. Oxford, he said, had a mission to civilize barbarians 'in the shape of the international economic forces which mould our material existence . . . as a nursery of statesmen, close to the busy world and yet beyond it, she can develop a graduate school of government without stiffening theory into dogma'. In the interwar years nothing came of Zimmern's idea, but in 1947 Llewellyn Woodward (1890–1971), his successor as Professor of International Relations, repeated the call in even more urgent language: 'Our maps do not show us the extent to which the civilized area of the world has receded,' he declared; the world faced 'the decline of civilization as we know it'. A little academic experimentation in Oxford might be thought an inadequate remedy for such a drastic condition, but Woodward pressed the case for change. Citing the 'excellent provision' for colonial studies in Oxford, to show its practicality, he urged the creation of an institute for postgraduate work in international studies to be modelled on the Russian Institute at Columbia University in the United States.

Woodward did not get his institute, but in other respects his warnings fell on receptive ears. In the early postwar years financial assistance to the University by central Government increased sharply. The Scarbrough Commission, a Government inter-departmental committee, urged the University to expand its interest in Slavonic and Oriental studies, a direct reflection of the rising importance of these regions in Government eyes. A number of new posts were created, including a new Professorship in Modern History, which Woodward himself occupied. In 1946 the Maison Française was established as a French cultural institute in Oxford, as part of the University, not as an agency of the French Government. But, characteristically, Oxford's major postwar expansion in international studies came about not through Government initiative or the creation of a research institute but almost incidentally, through a private benefaction and in the form of a new college. Antonin Besse (1877–1951) of Aden offered the University £1½ million in 1948 to build a new postgraduate college, one third of whose members were to be French, and to finance expansion at other colleges with a view to increasing the number of French students there. After some negotiation the restriction on the choice of students was lifted and agreement was reached on the foundation of a new college, to be called St Antony's, formally chartered in 1950. By this bizarre colonial route the chance had come to widen the University's interests, not by the obstructed path of internal reform but by a new creation.

From the first, St Antony's was cosmopolitan in tone and far-flung in its interests. It was self-consciously different from the traditional undergraduate colleges, and one early president of its Junior Common Room fiercely resisted proposals for a college blazer and (worse still) college cuff-links. Academic specialists were recruited from within and outside Oxford to develop Soviet, Far Eastern, and Middle Eastern studies. In 1953 the Rhodes Professorship of Race Relations was associated with the college—a modish subject seen by some as the key to the evolution of the Commonwealth as the vehicle of post-colonial British influence. But just as important as these new academic enterprises was the fact that the student population of the college was predominantly from overseas. For its minority of British graduate students it was a place to encounter unfamiliar cultures, histories, and ideologies made the more accessible by personal contact. To the University at large it brought a welcome infusion of new academic interests and the stimulating influence of different academic traditions. Together with the creation of the Rhodes Scholarships, it might well be thought that the establish-

ANTONIN BESSE was a businessman of French extraction living in Aden while it was still a British colony. Evelyn Waugh met him there, and wrote a delightful account of an outing they made together in his travel book *Remote People* (1932). Besse gave over a million pounds to found St Antony's College, and is seen here with his wife on the occasion of his honorary doctorate in 1951.

ment of St Antony's has done more than anything else to make Oxford an international university in the recruitment of its students and the range and variety of its academic activities. But St Antony's also exhibits the unpredictable fortune of so many academic foundations in Oxford. Endowed by Besse with the idea of promoting closer Anglo-French academic relations, the college has never developed interests in France on the same scale as those in Soviet, German, or Middle Eastern Studies. As Rhodes, had he lived, would have discovered, founders propose, the academic Fates dispose.

Before the general check to the expansion of higher education in Britain which set in in the early 1970s, there was one more small wave of expansion which further extended the international range of the University. In the 1960s additional Government funding made possible the setting up of a Latin American Centre (also based at St Antony's) and the strengthening of Chinese and Middle Eastern Studies, together with a sprinkling of other posts to reinforce the teaching of international subjects in history and social studies particularly. Meanwhile, at Nuffield College another important centre of graduate studies had developed after 1945 with special interests in European politics, Commonwealth history and politics, and development economics, as well as in the broad range of social studies. And in recent years, in belated recognition of Zimmern's hopes, Oxford has also developed a successful school of international relations attracting graduate students from all over the world. With some 1,400 graduate students from overseas making up 40 per cent of the University's postgraduate population and with a portfolio of specialisms bringing it into touch with most of the world's regions and major cultures, Oxford has become academically more outward-looking and diverse than ever before. This has powerfully reinforced the much older tradition of undergraduate interest in international affairs that was particularly evident during the 1930s in the Oxford Union debates and in the remarkable attendance at Zimmern's lectures on contemporary international politics (which regularly drew audiences of over 100 between 1930 and 1934); and which revived sharply in the 1960s, with the stimulus of the Vietnam war.

Thus far we have discussed Oxford as if it were a university given over entirely to the Arts and Social Studies. Certainly this was the impression outsiders often had of the University, especially before the Second World War; nor was it entirely misleading, since the number of students reading for science degrees was comparatively small and the prestige of their subjects unfairly depressed. Perhaps apocryphally, the wife of one Warden of All Souls was credited with the remark that a clever classicist could 'get up' science in a fortnight. (Frederick Lindemann, 1886–1957, later Lord Cherwell, the source of this story, claimed, less plausibly, to have replied: 'What a pity your husband has never had two weeks to spare.') Even after the Second World War, the six largest undergraduate degree courses were still in non-scientific subjects, and it was not until the 1980s that the total of postgraduate and undergraduate students in the Sciences and Medicine approached parity with those in Arts and Social Sciences.

Behind these crude statistics lay a dramatic expansion of the sciences in Oxford since

JEAN MONNET (*centre*), who played a key role in the establishment of the Common Market, seen here with Edward Heath and the Warden of Nuffield College in 1965. Harold Wilson, the Prime Minister, and James Callaghan were also present. They asked how an application to join the Common Market would be received, and were told 'It all depends how you asked'.

the early part of this century: in numbers, in their intellectual impact on the University, and in the prestige and academic distinction they have contributed to it. Large and important Schools of Mathematics, Physics, Chemistry, Physiology, Clinical Medicine, Biochemistry, and Engineering Science were built up, together with smaller departments of international distinction. Long before their student numbers had grown to modern proportions, the sciences in Oxford had acquired an international reputation. In the Arts the growth of wider and more international academic interests was, as we have seen, a slow and sometimes painful process, often dependent upon external stimulus and required to accommodate to local intellectual and pedagogic tradition. In the sciences too a distinctive local approach to teaching and research could often be seen. But by their very nature the sciences were far more open to intellectual influences from abroad, and their practitioners necessarily more conscious of an academic world extending far beyond the limits of the United Kingdom, let alone of Oxford. Well before most non-scientists discovered the attractions of the international conference, their scientific counterparts were used to international gatherings where ideas were exchanged and reputations built or broken.

But the course of scientific expansion in Oxford was characteristically idiosyncratic and accident-prone. In the mid-nineteenth century Oxford had appeared briefly to draw ahead of Cambridge in its provision for the natural sciences with the opening of the University Museum in 1860. But in the later part of the century Cambridge's scientific pre-eminence grew inexorably. There the university authorities used the system of college taxation recommended by the University Commission of 1872 to found new posts in the sciences. In Oxford the colleges had been expected to support the expansion of science, but the financial stringency which accompanied the agricultural depression of the 1880s and 1890s made them reluctant to do so. As a result, it proved very difficult to build up departments large enough to press a strong claim on such University funds as were available. There was also the accident of personality. Oxford had established a modern physics laboratory, the Clarendon, before the great Cavendish Laboratory at Cambridge. But its professorial director in the years before 1914, R. B. Clifton (1836–1921), was little interested in its research potential and even took to closing it for part of the week; the University authorities too seemed indifferent to the Clarendon's potential. It was in the college laboratories (there were to be six in all) that teaching and research were often liveliest, while in a college like Magdalen (which had its own laboratory) there was a substantial intake of undergraduates for Science degrees before 1914 and a tradition of vigorous tutoring in the sciences.

Even before 1914, as the previous chapters have shown, Oxford was not without some international distinction in science and medicine. In Ray Lankester (1847–1929) it had for a time one of the best-known zoologists of the day as Linacre Professor from 1891 to 1898. Sir William Osler (1849–1919) was attracted to Oxford from across the Atlantic, and held the Regius Professorship of Medicine from 1904 to 1919. His *Principles and Practice of Medicine* was a standard work in the English-speaking world for thirty years. Most important of all, perhaps, the small size and the intimacy of the early science departments created opportunities for undergraduates to participate in the research work of the laboratories and even to initiate scientific enquiries of their own. Frederick Soddy (1877–1956) (a Nobel Prizewinner in Chemistry), N. V. Sidgwick (1873–1952), Henry Tizard (1885–1959), and Julian Huxley (1887–1975) all began their careers in scientific research while still being taught as undergraduates. This tradition, established in Oxford's scientific 'dark age' before 1914, has remained a feature of the distinctive culture in which British scientists are brought up, and helps to account for the fact that their discoveries, in the pure sciences at least, have by international standards been out of all proportion to their numbers.

The First World War was a turning-point in public attitudes to scientific research. The outbreak of war in 1914 found Britain with insufficient capacity to manufacture explosives and propellants, and exposed the Empire's damaging dependence upon Germany for pharmaceutical, optical, and photographic products. The shell shortage of 1915 led to the formation, by the State, of a new chemical giant, ICI. British chemists exchanged their laboratories for the munitions factories and saved the British Army. For the next fifty years Britain's safety, and even survival, was thought to depend upon investment in the natural sciences. This led to the beginnings of regular Government support for the universities, and some limited public funding of scientific research. It was in this new climate in the interwar years that the sciences in Oxford broadened their base, physically and intellectually, established an international reputation across a range of disciplines, and widened their contacts with the scientific community in Europe and the United States.

Inevitably, however, progress was slow and uncertain. Throughout the interwar years the number of college tutors in science subjects was still very small and, because of the difficulty of obtaining college fellowships, many scientists remained outside the real centre of institutional power in the University. Some leading scientists with independent means, like Thomas Merton (1888–1969), became impatient with Oxford's cumbersome decision-making processes and preferred to withdraw to their own private laboratories, often at a considerable distance. Those who stuck it out were sometimes forced to depend on hand-to-mouth financial gifts and a desperate search for sponsorship or funding which consumed vast amounts of time and energy.

Nevertheless, there can be no mistaking the gains made by Oxford science between the wars. Chemistry became, as might have been expected in a generation brought up on tales of the shell shortage, the most popular Science degree course. What the Great War began, Soddy and Cyril Hinshelwood (1897–1967), successively Professors of Chemistry, continued. Both won Nobel Prizes (Soddy in 1921, Hinshelwood in 1956). Over the same period N. V. Sidgwick's work on the electronic theory of valency, published in 1927, brought him—and Oxford chemistry—international recognition. By the time of his death in 1952, remarked Sir Henry Tizard, then the elder statesman of British science, Oxford had become the leading school of chemistry in the world with major laboratories provided by Dyson Perrins (1864–1958) and Lord Nuffield (1877–1963). Other centres of research activity of international significance were to be found in zoology, ecology, and genetics. Before his departure to London in 1925, Julian Huxley taught a powerful group of young zoologists. Oxford zoology became identified with an emphasis on field research and the study of animal communities. The work of Charles Elton (1900–91) on animal populations, and of E. B. Ford (1901–88), who founded ecological genetics, made Oxford a major centre of ecological studies, including, with the advent of A. G. Tansley (1871–1955) to the Chair of Botany in 1927, plant ecology. Oxford zoologists played an important part in the adaptation of the Darwinian theory of natural selection to the new discoveries of genetics. Thus, without the local prestige and scale of operations which characterized the natural sciences in Cambridge, what emerged in Oxford between the wars was a cluster of research fields in which Oxford scientists established international distinction and, in some cases, preeminence. The number of postgraduate students increased, and in 1934 the Radcliffe Science Library was expanded.

An even more striking contributor to the new status of science in interwar Oxford than either Soddy or Hinshelwood was Frederick Lindemann, elected Professor of Natural Philosophy (i.e. Physics) in 1919 at the age of thirty-three. Lindemann was a passionate, combative champion of scientific and technological education who combined private wealth, a cosmopolitan background, and considerable personal eccentricity. He had been brought up in England but educated in Germany, where he had studied at what was then the great centre of theoretical physics at Berlin. There he met Nernst (1864–1941), Max Planck (1858–1947), and Einstein (1879–1955), and became interested in low-temperature physics. But Lindemann owed his fame, and perhaps his Oxford chair, to his startling wartime career at the Royal Aircraft Establishment at Farnborough. Having calculated mathematically how an aircraft could be brought out of a spinning nosedive, until then regarded as fatal to aircraft and pilot, Lindemann tested his theories personally, repeatedly piloting an aircraft into and out of a spin to demonstrate the infallibility of his technique. When he came to Oxford, he brought with him his interest in aircraft, a network of industrial connections made at Farnborough, and his pre-war interests in the quantum theory and low-temperature physics, as well as a certain arrogance and mystique.

In Oxford Lindemann revived the moribund Clarendon Laboratory and the study of physics. By his social and industrial connections he was able to attract private funding and eventually to pay for a new Clarendon Laboratory which opened in 1939. Although he lost interest in his own research, he encouraged and promoted low-temperature physics and made the Clarendon one of the world centres in this field by the end of the interwar years, as well as the leading laboratory for high-resolution spectroscopy. But Lindemann's main contribution to raising the international profile of Oxford physics was his energetic campaign to bring to Oxford academic refugees from Hitler's Germany, gleaning money from private sponsors to pay their salaries. With physicists like

Simon (1893–1956), Kurti (b. 1908), Mendelssohn (1906–80), and Kuhn (b. 1904), Lindemann achieved a vital intellectual transfusion at a key moment in Oxford's development into a major centre of scientific research. Here the personal factor was crucial. It was Lindemann's original interest in low-temperature experiments (a product of his years in Berlin), his wide European connections and contacts, and his entrepreneurial skill in reviving the Clarendon which enabled Oxford to take such fruitful advantage of the German intellectual diaspora in the 1930s. Then, during the Second World War, Lindemann became Winston Churchill's personal scientific adviser. Oxford's élite, the Heads of Houses and the Hebdomadal Council, now forgave Lindemann his years of morbid sensitivity to the slights inflicted by the colleges upon his scientists. Oxford had always prided itself upon its intimate connections with the world of public affairs. This world now included a scientific dimension. In that case, as even Arts men acknowledged, it had better be an Oxford one. Oxford science had already arrived upon the international scene: now it had arrived in Oxford as well.

In the late 1930s and early 1940s, in a different field from Lindemann's, one of the greatest achievements of modern science was accomplished in Oxford, the benefits of which were to be felt by millions of people in every part of the world. Significantly, it was the work of a scientist who had been drawn to Oxford from the other side of the globe. Howard Florey (1898–1968) had come to Oxford as a Rhodes Scholar from South Australia in the early 1920s. After academic appointments in Cambridge and Sheffield, he returned to Oxford as Professor of Pathology in 1935. Building on the vast mass of his own experimental data in animal physiology, Florey began to explore the therapeutic potential of the penicillin mould that Alexander Fleming (1881–1955) had discovered some ten years before, but whose medical possibilities as an anti-infection agent had never been developed. It is easy to forget today that only sixty years ago any serious infection was a major threat to human life almost as much in the developed as in the undeveloped world: the drugs available to doctors by the 1930s, though not ineffective, lacked the enormous efficacy of antibiotics. Florey's genius lay in recognizing penicillin as the most promising of possible sources of counter-infection therapy, if only the intractable problems of turning it into a usable medicine could be overcome. After arduous experimentation and clinical testing, Florey and his team at last learnt how to use penicillin without poisoning the patient—the major risk in all life-saving drugs—and, just as vital, how to prepare it in a stable form and in adequate quantities to be widely available for hospital use. By 1942 Florey knew enough to be able to advise Fleming himself on how to use penicillin to overcome an apparently hopeless case of meningitis in a friend. Thereafter it was used to save countless lives in the Allied armies during wartime and became the basis for the antibiotic revolution that has since transformed medicine at every level. For this work Florey and his Oxford collaborator, Ernst Chain (1906–79), like Fleming, received a Nobel Prize in 1945.

Florey's achievement dramatized the way in which the sciences in Oxford, so long the Cinderella subjects in the University, could win enormous fame for it, as well as

THE PROCESSION OF BOATS. At the end of each day's bumping-races in Eights Week the flags of the competing colleges were run up on the Barges and the crews processed past them, and before the spectators, in salute. In 1858, when this picture was painted by G. Howse, Exeter College went Head of the River and the average weight of the eight oarsmen was ten stone five and a half pounds.

confirming the immense social usefulness of its research activity not just in Britain but in the world as a whole. In the years after the Second World War enthusiastic recognition of the social importance and strategic value of scientific research led successive British Governments to increase greatly their spending on higher education, especially in the sciences. Oxford's annual grant from the Government rose from just under £600,000 in 1947–8 to over £3 million by 1961–2. In the 1950s and early 1960s State funding paid for new laboratories for Organic and Inorganic Chemistry, as well as new buildings for Metallurgy, Engineering, Biochemistry, Zoology, and Geology. Oxford was one of the select group of five universities chosen for the installation of the very costly apparatus required for research in nuclear physics. With this physical expansion came at last a rapid increase in student numbers. Between 1951 and 1971 the number of undergraduates entering the University each year to read for a degree in the sciences rose from 364 to 1,003, or from some 21 per cent of all undergraduate entrants to 38 per cent. Among postgraduates the proportion rose less dramatically, but from a higher starting-point: from some 33 per cent just after the Second World War (compared with only 13 per cent in the 1920s) to 40 per cent in 1964–5 and 42 per cent in 1989–90. Even so, the increase in absolute numbers was considerable: by 1989 there were five times as many science postgraduates in Oxford as there had been in the later 1940s. Among these, postgraduate students from overseas have been a steadily growing band, and by 1989 made up a third of the total. The postwar years have also seen the spectacular growth of several sciences scarcely represented in Oxford before 1939—like Biochemistry and Engineering Science—and the rise of Mathematics and Physics to be the largest of the undergraduate Schools in the sciences, supplanting Chemistry. Oxford thus acquired after 1945, in contrast with its earlier history, an academic sector in pure science comparable in its share of students with that of most British universities of a similar size. But the University has remained reluctant to develop as strongly in applied science and technology, where other British universities have been able to recruit large numbers of overseas students. In a striking parallel with the Arts and social studies, the postwar years saw cautious experimentation with new disciplines on a small scale broaden out into the diversified and internationally sensitive syllabus and research interests characteristic of the University by the 1970s and 1980s.

The expansion of subjects and disciplines is, however, only part of the story. Foreign students may have come to Oxford to sample its academic offerings. But in an academic community where purely formal instruction was only part of the educational process,

CRICKET (*above left*) is a sport in which university amateurs, mainly batsmen, can perform at international level—witness, among others, Colin Cowdrey and Imran Khan. University cricket has been played in the Parks since 1881, and T. G. Jackson's pavilion is sited at the same distance from the wicket as the pavilion at Lord's.

THE PLEASURE PUNT (*below left*) is derived from a traditional Thames craft. The boat is handled with a pole, and for more than a century punting on the River Cherwell has been a favourite pastime in the humid Thames Valley summer.

FREDERICK LINDEMANN (later Lord Cherwell), the Professor of Natural Philosophy (Physics), championed the expansion of the sciences in Oxford. He was passionately concerned about air defence. Winston Churchill selected him to become his personal scientific adviser, and the two men are seen here together in Norfolk in 1941, watching a demonstration of a new anti-aircraft device.

and where the instinct among students for forming societies, clubs, and cliques has always been highly developed, their wider experience of life in Oxford was just as important as tutorial and lecture. We know relatively little about the life of students from abroad towards the end of the last century. Balliol, however, established an early reputation for cosmopolitanism. Even after 1900 there was uncertainty about how best to provide for students from Africa and Asia. In 1920 the Master of University College proposed the funding of a special hostel or college for Indian students, where they 'could form a society with sufficiently homogeneous antecedents to secure an esprit de corps and a good fellowship comparable to the traditions of a normal college'. Perhaps fortunately, this idea was still-born.

Of all foreign students who came to Oxford before the Second World War, those arriving as Rhodes Scholars had perhaps the best chance of settling in quickly and happily. Since the vast majority were white, there were few barriers of racial prejudice to overcome. Sporting prowess yielded its usual dividend of esteem. The emphasis placed by the selection boards on qualities of character and leadership was also likely to produce confident young people well adapted to the social challenge of a competitive and cocksure undergraduate society. Foreign students from Afro-Asian backgrounds often had more ambivalent feelings. G. K. Chettur (1898–1936), who came to Oxford from India in the early 1920s, looked back nostalgically to his golden days as secretary of the Majlis (the Indian society in Oxford) and to his elegant rooms in New College. But even he remembered how many of his Indian friends seemed reluctant to move out of their own circle, and recalled his own outrage at a play he saw in Oxford which crudely caricatured the Indian student 'in Baboo Jabberjee style'. A year or two later Solomon Bandaranaike (1899–1959), a premier in the making, arrived from Sri Lanka (to find himself a *de facto* Indian in English eyes). Bandaranaike was a forceful and ambitious young man who was delighted at the opportunity to cross swords with British politicians at the Union. 'Oxford,' he recalled, 'and particularly the Union, profoundly influenced my entire career and outlook.' But like Chettur he discovered that many of his Indian friends seemed unable to mix in a wider society. Unlike Chettur, he was more inclined to blame this on local prejudice than on the social shortcomings of the visitors. 'The average Englishman' (Bandaranaike was presumably referring to his student

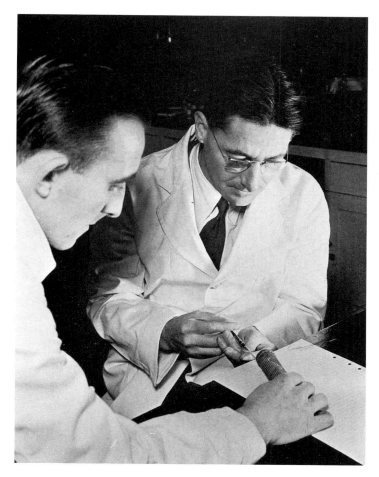

HOWARD FLOREY, a Rhodes Scholar from South Australia who became Professor of Pathology, injecting a solution into a mouse's tail. In collaboration with Ernst Chain, Florey was able, by extremely skilful laboratory testing and clinical trials, to transform Alexander Fleming's penicillin mould into a usable drug that was to save thousands of lives in the Second World War and since.

THREE MAJOR FIGURES IN
INTERNATIONAL POLITICS, Bob Hawke
(University College, 1953–6), later Prime
Minister of Australia (*above left*), S. W. R. D.
Bandaranaike (Christ Church, 1919–24),
subsequently Prime Minister of Sri Lanka
(*above right*), and Tom Mboya (Ruskin
College 1955–6), one of the leading figures
in Kenyan politics in the 1950s and 1960s
(*right*).

contemporaries) 'hedges himself in with numerous sub-conscious barriers—his traditions, his codes of behaviour and action . . . his natural reserve and intense race-consciousness.' Another premier-to-be, the historian Eric Williams (1911–81) from Trinidad, who was both an undergraduate and graduate student in Oxford, insisted in his memoirs some thirty years later that racial prejudice had denied him success in the prize fellowship examination at All Souls (as if anything so predictable could at the time have explained an All Souls election) and had driven him to seek an academic career in the United States.

It is difficult to assess testimony of racial prejudice, though we would be wise to assume that for Africans and West Indians particularly it was perhaps even harder than for Indians to feel that vital combination of acceptance and respect by their peers which made the inevitable strains of life in a demanding foreign institution bearable. There was a subtle but important connection between the constitutional status of the student's home and his social status in Oxford—if only in his own mind. Interestingly,

SENSATIONAL CHARGE AGAINST A CLUB

Well Treated by All Undergraduates in University

But Coldness Shown to Coloured Men at the Carlton

Mr. D. F. Karaka.

MEN'S LIFE MADE A 'LIVING HELL'

THE condemnation of the colour bar by Mr. D. F. Karaka, the first Indian to hold the office of President of the Oxford Union, at the closing debate of the term last night, proved the biggest sensation in the University since the famous King and Country debate.

Although his condemnation has been received with unanimous approval, his reference to the Oxford Carlton Club is being keenly criticised in many quarters.

A member of the Carlton Club said to-day that it had become a tradition that coloured undergraduates should not be admitted as members.

D. F. KARAKA was the first Indian to be elected President of the Oxford Union (in 1934). One newspaper said haughtily and distastefully that the office would 'no longer be held in such high esteem'. Karaka's cool dismissal of this 'ungracious remark' won him widespread support, and his subsequent claim that the Oxford Carlton Club practised a colour bar was a local sensation.

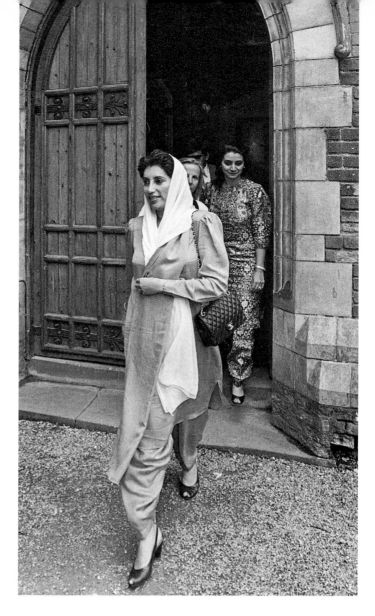

BENAZIR BHUTTO, then Prime Minister of Pakistan, visiting her old college, Lady Margaret Hall, in July 1989. Miss Bhutto's father, Zulfikar, had been at Christ Church. She herself read Philosophy, Politics, and Economics between 1974 and 1977, and achieved the distinction often coveted by those intent on a political career: she was elected President of the Union.

British policy towards India was debated at the Union on a number of occasions between the wars, ending almost invariably in victory for those who championed the cause of Indian nationalism. In 1934 the President of the Union, Dooso Karaka (1911–74), was himself an Indian. In an atmosphere of this sort, Indian students were unlikely to feel that Oxford undergraduate society was entirely cold and unfeeling, and for some Oxford's left-leaning political clubs offered an attractive social outlet. In the postwar years the number of overseas students increased, and with the onset of de-colonization the political and ideological climate was generally much more sensitive to the aspirations of foreign students from Third World countries. On the other hand, the rapid change in the status of many Afro-Asian countries and the prevalence of highly charged racial issues in the international politics of the 1960s meant that Afro-Asian students were still less likely to feel so easily at home as those from Europe, the United States, or the 'old' Commonwealth.

Thirty years ago an elaborate survey by the student magazine *Isis* threw up a number of familiar complaints about life in Oxford for the overseas student. A Spanish student grumbled that instead of the sunlit days by the river that he had been led to expect, Oxford had turned out to be a collection of 'grim, wet, Gothic museums'. Others complained of the squalor of some college rooms (not without justice in the 1960s) and the unpalatable food. The social chasm of the vacation, when the colleges closed their doors and undergraduates were expected to leave Oxford, was another grievance. So was the lack of a students' union for the whole University, which made it difficult to meet other foreign students and make friends of the opposite sex. (It might be added that even British students who came as postgraduates to Oxford from other universities also complained of social isolation.) English 'reserve' remained a barrier to easy social contact. No doubt such a survey repeated today would yield some similar reactions, but in certain respects life for the overseas student has changed for the better. College accommodation is generally of far better quality, and more plentiful, than thirty years ago, and often more flexible. Self-catering facilities have made the defects of college cuisine more bearable. Perhaps most important of all, the much larger proportion of postgraduates among foreign students and their tendency to congregate in certain subjects has permitted a far more effective 'colonization' of Oxford than was possible for overseas undergraduates with eight-week terms and a more strictly college-bound life. The growth of new all-graduate colleges like Wolfson, Linacre, and St Cross has filled a social void and replaced the lonely digs in an Oxford surburb. The observer today is more likely to be struck by the vigour, self-confidence, and optimism of the overseas student community than by its unease or lack of acceptance. Indeed, at the time of writing the very sharp decline in the numbers of home-grown graduate students in the Arts and social sciences has meant that in many fields of advanced study the majority are from overseas. In a curious reversal of roles, it is the British graduate student, depressed by poverty and lack of opportunity, who looks on enviously at the comparative wealth and superior prospects of his overseas counterparts.

What have been the results of this long experience of attracting students and more senior scholars? What influence, if any, has Oxford exerted on the world outside Britain? As we saw at the beginning of this chapter, Oxford enjoyed an international reputation long before it had made much concession to the importance of becoming more international in its interests and more accessible to scholars and students from abroad. To a large extent, perhaps, it owed its fame to its association with a ruling class which was admired and disliked abroad probably in equal measure. Its peculiar teaching system acquired vicarious prestige. In 1930 Harvard adopted the 'Harvard House Plan' apparently in partial imitation of the Oxford college system, just as earlier Woodrow Wilson had adapted the tutorial method to Princeton. But although

LESTER PEARSON served in the Canadian army in the First World War, before reading history at St John's College. He became successively an academic, a diplomat, and a politician. As Canadian foreign minister he was a major international figure in the 1950s, serving as President of the United Nations General Assembly (as shown here) in 1952–3. He was Prime Minister of Canada from 1963 to 1968.

graduates of Oxford were to be found in almost every country of the British Empire before 1939, as well as in many others, and although they were especially likely to be found in education, the Oxford model of a university has never been implanted overseas. The reasons are not difficult to understand. For the secret of Oxford's peculiar structure and ethos lay in its origins and growth over centuries into a very loose confederation of self-governing academic corporations, scarcely supervised by the State and certainly not funded by it. Moreover, the colleges had been able to cut themselves free from their benefactors and escape the influence of external trustees. It was hardly likely that these conditions would replicate themselves in colonial societies, where in other circumstances the influence of Oxford as a model might have been powerful. Funds were limited. The pressure on Government to interfere was strong. The demand by local communities for a voice in their local university was irresistible. A collegiate structure appeared an expensive folly, full academic self-government on the Oxford model an absurd concession to pedagogic self-importance. Instead, for the most part new universities in the countries of the Empire and Commonwealth followed the model of Britain's civic universities, with departments rather than colleges as the key components, and a centralizing bureaucracy to match.

Nor was Oxford well suited to the task of acting as godfather to the new universities that sprang up in many British dependent territories after the Second World War. There was a brief wartime association with Makerere University College in Uganda, when a committee was established in Oxford to advise on curriculum and examinations, to arrange inspection, to despatch visiting lecturers, and to assist with continuing academic study in Britain. But these functions were soon handed over to the Inter-University Council and Oxford's special relationship lapsed. Usually it was London University, with its long experience of validating degree courses in university colleges in Britain, as an examining rather than a teaching body, and with its long tradition of offering external London degrees, which came far more naturally than Oxford to the task of aiding the development of higher education overseas—or certainly of offering a practical model of university organization.

Influence perhaps should not be judged crudely by imitation. It remains an article of faith in the University that, apart from the quality of the writing and research it encourages, it also exerts a strong if unquantifiable influence in the diaspora of the undergraduate and postgraduate students who pass through its colleges and faculties—an ever increasing proportion of them from overseas countries. The University and its colleges have long depended, and are likely to depend even more in the future, on the respect, sympathy, and loyalty of former students. Influence of this sort is based in part on Oxford's reputation for expertise in the sciences and the vast range of academic studies bearing on the life and culture of many societies around the world. Part of it also derives from the successful modern adaptation of the old tradition of close contact between student and tutor or supervisor, which remains the hallmark of the University at postgraduate and undergraduate level, and one of its main attractions to students from other countries. And part of it comes, perhaps, from something older still: the

WILLI BRANDT was Chancellor of the Federal Republic of Germany between 1969 and 1974. His *Ostpolitik* played a notable role in encouraging *détente* in Europe in the early 1970s. He received an honorary doctorate in January 1970, and is seen here afterwards at a reception in Christ Church.

THE CROWN PRINCE OF JAPAN. After receiving an honorary doctorate in September 1991, the Crown Prince visited the Nissan Institute in North Oxford. Throughout the 1980s the academic study of Japan, and especially of its history and politics, has been of growing importance in the University.

surviving charm of Oxford's physical environment and the effervescent life of its student body, memorable, competitive, and invigorating. Indeed, we may suspect that much of what makes Oxford attractive and influential abroad really derives from its continuing success in drawing to itself some of the ablest products of *British* schools. For Oxford, with its collegiate structure and its tutorial system still geared primarily to the needs of undergraduates, and dependent on their quality, there has always been a close connection between its academic reputation at home and its success as an international university. If one conclusion can be drawn from Oxford's often unpredictable development since mid-Victorian times it is that the status of an international centre of higher education can be assured only by continual adaptation and by finding the intellectual and physical resources to match the most successful centres elsewhere. Equally, much of what Oxford has to offer British students pursuing British careers derives from its openness to foreign intellectual influences, and its involvement in disciplines for which national boundaries do not signify. Oxford's future, therefore, can only lie in continuing the role it has come to assume more and more consciously since the end of the First World War, of being both a great national and international university: both a great exporter and a great importer of ideas at the highest academic level. Easier said, of course, than done.

Further Reading

Aston, T. H. (general ed.), *The History of the University of Oxford* (Oxford): i. *The Early Oxford Schools*, ed. J. Catto (1984); iii. *The Collegiate University*, ed. J. McConica (1986); v. *The Eighteenth Century*, ed. L. S. Sutherland and L. G. Mitchell (1986).

Bender, T. (ed.), *The University and the City, from Medieval Origins to the Present* (New York and Oxford, 1988), not about Oxford but useful for comparison with other university towns in Europe and America.

Fasnacht, R., *A History of the City of Oxford* (Oxford, 1954).

Mallet, Sir Charles, *A History of the University of Oxford*, 3 vols. (London, 1924–7).

Thompson, F. M. L. (ed.), *The University of London and the World of Learning, 1836–1986* (London, 1990), for comparison.

University of Oxford, *Report of [Franks] Commission of Inquiry*, 2 vols. (Oxford, 1966).

Victoria County History of Oxfordshire, iii. *The University of Oxford* (Oxford, 1954).

1. CITY AND UNIVERSITY

Andrews, P. W. S., and Brunner, E., *The Life of Lord Nuffield: A Study in Enterprise and Benevolence* (Oxford, 1955).

Barnett House, Oxford, *Survey of the Social Services in the Oxford District*, 2 vols. (1939).

Betjeman, J., *An Oxford University Chest* (London, 1938).

Butler, C. V., *Social Conditions in Oxford* (London, 1912).

Graham, M., 'The Suburbs of Victorian Oxford: Growth in a Pre-industrial City' (D.Phil. thesis presented to the University of Leicester, 1985).

—— and Tomlinson, S., *Town and Gown: Eight Hundred Years of Oxford Life. Catalogue of an Exhibition in the Bodleian Library, Oxford* (Oxford, 1982).

Hassall, T. G., 'Archaeology of Oxford City', in G. Briggs, J. Cook, and T. Rowley (eds.), *The Archaeology of the Oxford Region* (Oxford, 1986).

Hibbert, C. (ed.), *The Encyclopaedia of Oxford* (London, 1988).

Martin, A. F., and Steel, R. W. (eds.), *The Oxford Region: A Scientific and Historical Survey* (Oxford, 1954).

Morris, J., *Oxford* (London, 1965).

Newman, R. J., *The Road and Christ Church Meadow: The Oxford Inner Relief Road Controversy 1923–74. A study of the Relationship between Central and Local Government* (Minster Lovell, 1988).

Overy, R. J., *William Morris, Viscount Nuffield* (London, 1976).

Platt, C., *The Most Obliging Man in Europe: Life and Times of the Oxford Scout* (London, 1986).

Scargill, D. I., 'Conservation and the Oxford Green Belt', in R. T. Rowley (ed.), *The Oxford Region: Papers Presented to a Conference to Mark One Hundred Years of Adult Education in Oxford* (Oxford, 1980).

Whiting, R. C., 'Oxford between the Wars: Labour and the Motor Industry', in R. T. Rowley (ed.), *The Oxford Region: Papers Presented to a Conference to Mark One Hundred Years of Adult Education in Oxford* (Oxford, 1980).

2. THE UNIVERSITY AND THE NATION

Brockliss, L., Harriss, G., and MacIntyre, A. D., *Magdalen College and the Crown* (Oxford, 1988).

Brooke, C., Highfield, R., and Swaan, W., *Oxford and Cambridge* (Cambridge, 1988).

Cobban, A. B., *The Medieval English Universities: Oxford and Cambridge to c. 1500* (Aldershot, 1988).

Curtis, M. H., *Oxford and Cambridge in Transition 1558–1642* (Oxford, 1959).

Green, V. H. H., *A History of Oxford University* (London, 1974).

Kearney, H. F., *Scholars and Gentlemen: Universities and Society in Pre-industrial Britain, 1500–1700* (London, 1970).

Rowse, A. L., *Oxford in the History of the Nation* (London, 1975).

Stone, L. (ed.), *The University in Society: Oxford and Cambridge from the Fourteenth to the Early Nineteenth Century* (Princeton, 1975).

Ward, W. R., *Georgian Oxford: University Politics in the Eighteenth Century* (Oxford, 1958).

—— *Victorian Oxford* (London, 1965).

3. THE ARCHITECTURE OF THE UNIVERSITY AND THE COLLEGES

Arkell, W. J., *Oxford Stone* (London, 1947).

Colvin, H. M., *Unbuilt Oxford* (New Haven, 1983).

—— 'Architecture', in L. S. Sutherland and L. G. Mitchell (eds.), *The Eighteenth Century* (The History of the University of Oxford, 5; Oxford, 1986).

Davis, R. H. C., 'The Chronology of Perpendicular Architecture in Oxford', *Oxoniensia*, 11–12 (1946–7).

Gee, E. A., 'Oxford Masons 1370–1530', *Archaeological Journal*, 109 (1952).

Goodhart-Rendel, H. S., 'Oxford Buildings Criticised', *Oxoniensia*, 17–18 (1952–3).

Kersting, A. F., and Ashdown, J., *The Buildings of Oxford* (London, 1980).

Newman, J., 'The Physical Setting: New Building and Adaptation', in J. McConica (ed.), *The Collegiate University* (The History of the University of Oxford, 3; Oxford, 1986).

Pantin, W. A., 'The Halls and Schools of Medieval Oxford: An Attempt at Reconstruction', *Oxford Historical Society*, NS 16 (1964).

Reed, D., and Opher, P., *New Architecture in Oxford* (Oxford, 1977).

Royal Commission on Historic Monuments, *Oxford* (London, 1974).

Sherwood, J., and Pevsner, N., *The Buildings of England: Oxfordshire* (Harmondsworth, 1974).

4. THE UNIVERSITY'S CONTRIBUTION TO RELIGION

Chadwick, O., *The Spirit of the Oxford Movement* (Cambridge, 1990).

Courtenay, W. J., *Schools and Scholars in Fourteenth Century England* (Princeton, 1987).

Dent, C. M., *Protestant Reformers in Elizabethan Oxford* (Oxford, 1983).

Ellis, I. P., *Seven against Christ: A Study of 'Essays and Reviews'* (Leiden, 1980).

Engel, A. J., *From Clergyman to Don: The Rise of the Academic Profession in Nineteenth Century Oxford* (Oxford, 1983).

Gilley, S., *Newman and his Age* (London, 1990).

Green, V. H. H., *Religion in Oxford and Cambridge* (London, 1966).

Morgan, R. (ed.), *The Religion of the Incarnation: Anglican Essays in Commemoration of Lux Mundi* (Bristol, 1989).

Rashdall, H., *The Universities of Europe in the Middle Ages*, new edn., ed. F. M. Powicke and A. B. Emden (Oxford, 1936).

Robson, J. A., *Wyclif and the Oxford Schools: The Relation of the 'Summa de ente' to Scholastic Debates at Oxford in the Later Fourteenth Century* (Cambridge, 1961).

Roper, H. R. T., *Archbishop Laud 1573–1645*, 2nd edn. (London, 1962), ch. 8, 'Oxford'.

5. THE UNIVERSITY'S CONTRIBUTION TO CLASSICAL STUDIES

Boardman, J., '100 years of Classical Archaeology in Oxford', in D. Kurtz (ed.), *Beazley and Oxford* (Oxford, 1985).

Bowra, C. M., *Memories 1898–1939* (London, 1966).

Brink, C. O., *English Classical Scholarship: Historical Reflections on Bentley, Porson and Housman* (Cambridge and New York, 1986).

Bywater, I., *Four Centuries of Greek Learning in England* (Oxford, 1919).

Clarke, M. L., *Classical Education in Britain 1500–1900* (Cambridge, 1959).

Dodds, E. R., *Missing Persons: An Autobiography* (Oxford, 1977).

Farnell, L. R., *An Oxonian Looks Back* (London, 1934).

Jones, H. S., 'The Foundation and History of the Camden Chair', *Oxoniensia*, 8–9 (1943–4).

Lloyd-Jones, H., *Blood for the Ghosts: Classical Influences in the Nineteenth and Twentieth Centuries* (London, 1982).

Pattison, M., *Memoirs* (London, 1885).

Sandys, J. E., *A History of Classical Scholarship*, ii–iii (Cambridge, 1908).

Weiss, R., *Humanism in England during the Fifteenth Century*, 3rd edn. (Oxford, 1967).

Wilamowitz-Moellendorf, U. von, *Geschichte der Philologie*, in A. Gercke and E. Norden (eds.), *Einleitung in die Altertumswissenschaft*, 2nd edn. (Berlin and Leipzig, 1921), translated as *History of Classical Scholarship* by A. Harris, ed. H. Lloyd-Jones (London, 1982).

6. OXFORD'S CONTRIBUTION TO MODERN STUDIES IN THE ARTS

Barker, N. J., *The Oxford University Press and the Spread of Learning, 1478–1978* (Oxford, 1978).

Burrow, J. W., *A Liberal Descent: Victorian Historians and the English Past* (Cambridge, 1981).

Chester, Sir Norman, *Economics, Politics and Social Studies in Oxford, 1900–85* (London, 1986).

Engel, A. J., *From Clergyman to Don: The Rise of the Academic Profession in Nineteenth Century Oxford* (Oxford, 1983).

Firth, Sir Charles, *Modern History in Oxford, 1841–1918* (Oxford, 1920).

——*Modern Languages at Oxford, 1724–1929* (Oxford, 1929).

Lawson, F. H., *The Oxford Law School, 1850–1965* (Oxford, 1968).

Palmer, D. J., *The Rise of English Studies: An Account of the Study of English Language and Literature from its Origins to the Making of the Oxford English School* (University of Hull Publication; London, 1965).

Proceedings of the British Academy, 1903– (valuable for obituaries of individual scholars of the Academy's fellowship).

Slee, P. H., *Learning and a Liberal Education: The Study of Modern History in the Universities of Oxford, Cambridge and Manchester, 1800–1914* (Manchester, 1986).

Sparrow, J., *Mark Pattison and the Idea of a University* (Cambridge, 1967).

Sutcliffe, P. H., *The Oxford University Press: An Informal History* (Oxford, 1978).

7. THE COLLECTIONS OF THE UNIVERSITY

Anon., *Pietas Oxoniensis: In Memory of Sir Thomas Bodley, Knt. and the Foundation of the Bodleian Library* (Oxford, 1902).

Anon., *Catalogue of a Loan Exhibition of Silver Plate Belonging to the Colleges of the University of Oxford* (Oxford, 1928).

Blackwood, Beatrice, *The Origin and Development of the Pitt Rivers Museum* (Occasional Papers of the Pitt Rivers Museum; Oxford, 1974).

Craster, Sir Edmund, *History of the Bodleian Library, 1845–1945* (Oxford, 1952).

Daniel, G., *A Short History of Archaeology* (London, 1981).

Davies, K. C., and Hull, J., *The Zoological Collections of the Oxford University Museum* (Oxford, 1976).

Gunther, R. T., *Early Science in Oxford*, iii (Oxford, 1925).

Impey, O., and MacGregor A. (eds.), *The Origins of Museums* (Oxford, 1985).

MacGregor, A. (ed.), *Tradescant's Rarities* (Oxford, 1983).

Morgan, Paul, *Oxford Libraries Outside the Bodleian: A Guide* (Oxford, 1973).

Ovenell, R. F., *The Ashmolean Museum, 1683–1894* (Oxford, 1986).

Philip, I. G., *The Bodleian Library in the Seventeenth and Eighteenth Centuries* (Oxford, 1983).

Piper, Sir David, *The Treasures of Oxford* (New York, 1977).

Poole, Mrs Reginald Lane, *Catalogue of Portraits in the Possession of the University, Colleges, City, and County of Oxford*, 3 vols. (Oxford, 1912–26).

Simcock, A. V., *The Ashmolean Museum and Oxford Science, 1683–1983* (Oxford, 1984).

—— *Robert T. Gunther and the Old Ashmolean* (Oxford, 1985).

Vernon, H. M., and Vernon, K. D., *A History of the Oxford Museum* (Oxford, 1909).

Walker, T. (ed.), *University of Oxford Botanic Garden*, guide (Oxford, 1989).

8. THE UNIVERSITY'S CONTRIBUTION TO THE LIFE SCIENCES AND MEDICINE

A County Hospital 1920–1988: A Collection of Essays about the History, Changes and Development of the Hospitals in Oxford (Oxford, 1988).

Dewhurst, K. (ed.), *Oxford Medicine: Essays on the Evolution of the Oxford Clinical School to Commemorate the Bicent[en]ary of the Radcliffe Infirmary, 1770–1970* (Oxford, 1970).

Maddison, F., Pelling, M., and Webster, C. (eds.), *Linacre Studies: Essays on the Life and Work of Thomas Linacre, c. 1460–1524* (Oxford, 1977).

Simcock, A. V., *The Ashmolean Museum and Oxford Science, 1683–1983* (Oxford, 1984).

Sinclair, H. M., and Robb-Smith, A. H. T., *A Short History of Anatomical Teaching in Oxford* (Oxford, 1950).

Webster, C., *The Great Instauration: Science, Medicine and Reform 1626–1660* (London, 1975).

9. THE UNIVERSITY'S CONTRIBUTION TO THE MODERN PHYSICAL SCIENCES

Bleaney, B., 'Physics at the University of Oxford', *European Journal of Physics*, 9 (1988).

Bowen, E. J., 'The Development of the University Laboratories', in E. J. Bowen, Sir H. Hartley, and H. M. Powell, *Chemistry in Oxford* (Cambridge, 1966).

Crombie, A. C., *Oxford's Contributions to the Origins of Modern Science: A Paper* (Oxford, 1954).

Heilbron, J. L., *H. G. J. Moseley: The Life and Letters of an English Physicist 1887–1915* (Berkeley, 1974).

Hoch, P. K., and Yoxen, E. J., 'Schroedinger at Oxford: A Hypothetical National Cultural Synthesis which Failed', *Annals of Science*, 44 (1987).

Howatson, A. M., 'A Century of Oxford Engineering', unpublished lecture.

Hunter, M. C. W., *et al.*, *Elias Ashmole 1617–1692: The Founder of the Ashmolean Museum and his World* (Oxford, 1983).

Powell, H. M., 'Oxford Chemistry 1966', in E. J. Bowen, Sir H. Hartley, and H. M. Powell, *Chemistry in Oxford* (Cambridge, 1966).

Rayner, M., 'Mathematics in Oxford since 1914', unpublished lecture.

Rose, J., and Ziman, J. M., *Camford Observed* (London, 1964).

Rupke, N. A., *The Great Chain of History: William Buckland and the English School of Geology, 1814–1849* (Oxford, 1983).

Sherwood Taylor, F., 'The Teaching of Science at Oxford in the Nineteenth Century', *Annals of Science*, 8 (1952).

Simcock, A. V., *The Ashmolean Museum and Oxford Science, 1683–1983* (Oxford, 1984).

Vincent, E. A., 'Geology and Mineralogy at Oxford, 1936–1986', unpublished lecture.

10. THE GROWTH OF AN INTERNATIONAL UNIVERSITY

Ashby, E., *Universities: British, Indian, African. A Study in the Ecology of Higher Education* (London, 1966).

Aydelotte, F., *The American Rhodes Scholarships* (Princeton, 1946).

Bandaranaike, S. W. R. D., *Speeches and Writings* (Colombo, 1963).

Birkenhead, Lord, *The Prof in Two Worlds: The Official Life of Professor F. A. Lindemann, Viscount Cherwell* (London, 1961).

Chettur, G. K., *The Last Enchantment: Recollections of Oxford* (Mangalore, 1934).

Crosby, L. A., Aydelotte, F., Valentine, A. C. (eds.), *Oxford of Today* (Oxford, 1927).

Engel, A. J., *From Clergyman to Don: The Rise of the Academic Profession in Nineteenth Century Oxford* (Oxford, 1983).

Flexner, A., *Universities: American, English, German* (New York, 1930).

Gunther, A. E., *Robert T. Gunther: A Pioneer in the History of Science, 1869–1940* (Oxford, 1967).

Howarth, J., 'Science Education in Late-Victorian Oxford: A Curious Case of Failure?', *English Historical Review*, 102 (1987).

Macfarlane, R. G., *Howard Florey: The Making of a Great Scientist* (Oxford, 1979).

Madden, A. F., and Fieldhouse, D. K. (eds.), *Oxford and the Idea of Commonwealth* (London, 1982).

Mansbridge, A., *The Older Universities of England: Oxford and Cambridge* (London, 1923).

Report of the Royal Commission on Oxford and Cambridge Universities, Cmd. 1588 (1922).

Symonds, R., *Oxford and Empire: The Last Lost Cause?* (Basingstoke, 1986).

Williams, Eric, *Inward Hunger: The Education of a Prime Minister* (London, 1969).

Chronology

727	Foundation of St Frideswide's Priory
912	First written reference to Oxford
919	Oxford known to be fortified, by this time, with walls
1002	St Brice's Day massacre of the Danes in Oxford
1005	St Ebbe's Church dedicated
1035	St Martin's Church at Carfax granted to Abingdon Abbey
1050	The Saxon tower of St Michael in the Northgate built
1071	The west end of Oxford remodelled to accommodate a motte and bailey castle
1086	Domesday Book records that the burgesses enjoy the right of pasture over Port Meadow. First record of St Peter in the East
1100	St Aldate's Church existed by this time. St Cross Church, Holywell, built
1122	First recorded Mayor of Oxford. All Saints Church founded (closed 1971)
1123	St Giles' Church building begun
1129	Oseney Abbey founded
1130	Henry I builds Beaumont 'Palace' outside the north wall
1142	Aubrey de Vere III created an earl and chooses the title of Oxford
1143	Queen Matilda escapes from Oxford Castle across the ice
1155	Henry II confirms the privileges of the Guild Merchant of Oxford
1187	The University is in being with its several faculties
1193	Golden Cross Inn opened
1199	Town's earliest surviving charter
1209	First recorded clash between town and gown: many scholars flee and some are thought to have found their way to Cambridge and to have started a new university there
1214	The Legatine Ordinance, the earliest of the University's charters, makes the town pay a penance of 52 shillings a year for the riots in 1209
1221	The Black Friars arrive
1224	First recorded Chancellor of the University. The Grey Friars arrive
1231	Every student is required to put his name on the roll of a Master
1244	The Chancellor secures the right to handle all cases of debt involving students
1248	After further disturbances between town and gown the Mayors of Oxford are compelled every year on assuming office to take an oath to uphold the privileges of the University. Earliest record of the Proctors
1249	University College founded
1255	The University secures a role in the supervision of the sale of food and drink
1258	Parliament meets at Oxford
1263	Balliol College founded

1264	Scholars dispersed to make way for the King's headquarters in his war with the barons: the Provisions of Oxford promulgated. Merton College founded
1277	The Benedictine houses of the southern province resolve to open a house of studies in Oxford: in 1283 a small priory is founded as a cell of Gloucester Abbey
1280	Rewley Abbey founded
1290	The concept of privileged persons established in law
1291	Durham College founded for the Benedictine monks of the northern province
1295	The town elects burgesses to Parliament for the first time
1300	Mitre Inn opened
1314	Exeter College founded
1320	Tackley's Inn built
1326	Oriel College founded
1334	Masters and Scholars resolve to abandon Oxford for Stamford, but the King instructs them to return (see also 1827)
1341	Queen's College founded
1355	St Scholastica's Day riot leads to the effective subjugation of the town to the University: the University thereafter appoints the Clerks of the Market and has sole control over weights and measures
1362	Canterbury College founded for the monks of Christ Church, Canterbury
1379	New College founded
1396–7	First reference to the stone quarries at Headington
1427	First record of the University Chest with the five keys. Lincoln College founded
1435	St Mary's College founded for the Augustinian canons
1437	St Bernard's College founded for the student monks of the Cistercian Order
1438	All Souls College founded
1448	The Registers of Congregation begin
1458	Duke Humfrey's Library opened. Magdalen College founded
1478	First record of printing in Oxford
1483	Richard III visits Oxford
1487	First mention of real tennis at Oxford
1488	Henry VII visits Oxford
1496	John Colet returns to Oxford from Italy
1499	Erasmus comes to Oxford for the first time
1502	The Lady Margaret Professorship of Divinity, the oldest existing chair, founded
1509	Brasenose College founded
1517	Corpus Christi College founded
1530	Henry VIII asks the University to pronounce upon the validity of his marriage to Catherine of Aragon
1534	The University's seal affixed to the decision of thirty theologians that the Bishop of Rome has no greater jurisdiction in England than any other foreign bishop
1535	Thomas Cromwell, now Vicar General, appoints a Cambridge-trained lawyer, Layton, to visit Oxford, where he condemns the whole monkish community: within a few years the religious houses have been dissolved and Canterbury, Durham, Gloucester, St Bernard's, and St Mary's Colleges have disappeared
1538	The friars are dispersed
1542	Diocese of Oxford created

1546   Regius Professorships of Divinity, Civil Law, Medicine, Greek, and Hebrew founded. Christ Church founded

1549   Visitors appointed by Edward VI bring new statutes laying down the length of terms, the hours of lectures, etc.

1554   Upon the accession of Mary a new Commission is issued to remodel the University. Trinity College founded

1555   Latimer and Ridley burnt outside the town ditch in what is now Broad Street. St John's College founded

1556   Cranmer martyred. Cardinal Pole's Injunctions—a last attempt to drive Protestant heresies out of the University and colleges

1559   Visitors appointed by Queen Elizabeth scrap Pole's Injunctions: Catholics ejected and Protestants restored to their positions

1565   First matriculation registers

1566   Queen Elizabeth visits Oxford

1571   Jesus College founded

1577   Black Assize: jail fever kills the Lord Chief Baron of England, the High Sheriff of Oxfordshire, and 300 others

1580   Convocation decrees that all students must reside in hall or college

1581   New matriculation statute requiring subscription to the Thirty-nine Articles and to the Queen's supremacy

1592   Second visit of Queen Elizabeth. The city expands by purchasing Northgate Hundred

1600   The West Gate removed

1602   Bodleian Library opened

1604   The University secures the right to elect burgesses of its own to Parliament

1605   James I visits Oxford and grants the borough a charter of incorporation; the King's Arms public house is then built in honour of James I

1610   Water is piped over 2,000 metres from Hinksey Hill to Carfax Conduit

1613   Wadham College founded

1619–26   Savilian Professorships of Geometry and Astronomy, Sedleian Professorship of Natural Philosophy, White's Professorship of Moral Philosophy, Camden Professorship of Ancient History, Tomlins Lecture (later Professorship) in Anatomy, and Heather Professorship in Music founded

1624   Town and gown co-operate with others in improving navigability of the Thames. First record of St Giles' parish wake, which evolved into St Giles' Fair. Pembroke College founded

1630   Archbishop Laud elected Chancellor

1631   Hebdomadal Board appointed

1632   Botanic Garden opened

1633   First meeting of the Board of Delegates of the Press

1636   Laudian Code accepted by Convocation. Charles I visits Oxford

1642   Charles I enters Oxford after the battle of Edgehill and makes his headquarters there

1646   Oxford besieged: in April Charles escapes, in June Oxford surrenders to the Parliamentary army

1647–9   Parliamentary Visitation: all but three Heads of Houses replaced

1649   Oliver Cromwell pays a state visit to the University, and (1650) is elected Chancellor

1652   A second Board of Visitors appointed

1654   A third Board of Visitors appointed

1660   At the Restoration of the Stuart monarchy a new Commission is appointed and all the surviving ejected Heads are reinstated

1661	The Earl of Clarendon, now Chancellor, visits Oxford
1663	Visit of Charles II
1665	Court and Parliament moved to Oxford to escape the plague in London
1667	The 'flying' coach to London established
1674	Anthony Wood published *Historia et Antiquitates Universitatis Oxoniensis*. The first Oxford Almanack published
1675	David Loggan, appointed Engraver to the University in 1669, produces his *Oxonia Illustrata*
1681	Charles II's fourth parliament meets at Oxford
1683	On the day the Whig martyr Lord Russell is beheaded Convocation condemns Whig opinions 'destructive to the sacred persons of Princes', and books by Hobbes, Milton, and others are burnt in the Schools Quadrangle. Ashmolean Museum opened
1688	James II dissolves the Corporation and rules the town through nominated Commissioners. He attempts to subvert the liberties of Magdalen College
1691–2	Anthony Wood publishes *Athenae Oxonienses*
1695	The Lamb and Flag public house opened
1699	Oxford ragwort found growing in Botanic Garden
1711	Robert Harley becomes the first Earl of Oxford of the second creation
1714	Worcester College founded
1724	In an attempt to win University minds over to the Hanoverian succession, George I founds the Regius Professorship of Modern History
1731	James Fletcher leases a bookshop which became Parkers
1738	Boswells established
1740	Hertford College founded (dissolved 1805, refounded 1874)
1748	Holywell Music Room opened
1753	*Jackson's Oxford Journal* begins publication (till 1909). Blackstone delivers his lectures on the Laws of England
1768	The parliamentary representation of the town sold to the Duke of Marlborough and the Earl of Abingdon
1770	The Radcliffe Infirmary opened
1771	The Mileways Act brings town and gown together for the improvement of the streets. The Old Bank in High Street founded
1772	North and East Gates removed
1774	New Covered Market constructed
1778	New Magdalen bridge completed. The canal opened as far as Banbury
1782	Morrell's brewery in St Thomas Street begins trading
1784	James Sadler ascends in a hot-air balloon—the first Englishman to do so
1788	Mallams, estate agents and auctioneers, founded. Haydn composes the Oxford Symphony, No. 92; this was performed when he received the degree of D.Mus. in 1791
1789	Carfax Conduit removed (it stands now at Nuneham)
1790	Oxford Canal joined to the Midland canal network
1795	William Hall buys the Swan's Nest brewery
1797	Rowell & Son, gold- and silversmiths, established
1800	William Baker, furnishers, founded
1802	The first examination Honours list published
1805	The County Gaol built in the Castle grounds

1807   The examination Honours list divided into separate class lists for Literae Humaniores and Mathematics

1812   The water colourist William Turner, known as William Turner of Oxford, returns to Oxford from London

1814   Rudolf Ackermann's *History of the University of Oxford: Its Colleges, Halls and Public Buildings* published

1815   Brasenose the first recorded Head of the River crew

1818   Oxford Gas Company founded to supply gas to lamps in the streets

1822   Beaumont Street laid out

1825   The town released from its annual St Scholastica's Day penance. Oxford Union Society founded

1825–35 St John Street laid out

1826   The University Press begins to move from the Clarendon Building to Walton Street. Oxford Lunatic Asylum opened, later the Warneforde Hospital

1827   Candidates for a degree cease to have to swear an oath not to attend or give lectures at the pretend University of Stamford. First Varsity cricket match

1829   First Oxford and Cambridge Boat Race, at Henley

1832   Cholera epidemic (followed by others in 1849 and 1854)

1833   John Keble's Assize Sermon starts the Oxford Movement

1835   Municipal Corporations Reform Act enfranchises the ratepayers; St Clements added to the town. Joseph Thornton's bookshop opened

1836   The New Theatre, now the Apollo, founded in George Street

1837   *Oxford City and County Chronicle* (later the *Oxford Chronicle*) founded in the Liberal interest

1841   County Hall erected in New Road

1843   Martyrs' Memorial finished

1844   The Great Western Railway reaches Oxford at Grandpont

1850   First Royal Commission of Inquiry into the University set up. Honour school of Natural Science founded

1851   The London and North Western Railway reaches Oxford from Bletchley

1851–4   The University Galleries, now part of the new Ashmolean Museum, opened

1853   Park Town laid out. The first class lists in Natural Science and in Law and Modern History published

1853–7   Rev. Edward Bradley of University College, Durham, publishes *The Adventures of Mr. Verdant Green*

1854   The University reformed by Act of Parliament: the Hebdomadal Board becomes the elected Hebdomadal Council, and Dissenters are permitted to matriculate and take degrees; executive Commissioners are appointed to see to the necessary changes in University and college statutes. The ratepayers adopt the Public Libraries Act: the first librarian is B. H. Blackwell

1855–60 University Museum built

1855   Act of Parliament allows St John's College to develop its estate in North Oxford

1857   Delegacy of Local Examinations founded

1858   Salter Bros. steamers founded

1859   The mayor's oath, instituted in 1248, is abolished by Act of Parliament

1861   Thomas Hughes publishes *Tom Brown at Oxford*

1862   St Philip and St James consecrated. The *Oxford Times* founded

1864   First Varsity athletics match

1865   A Local Board of Health established. Oxford School of Art founded. Matthew Arnold refers to Oxford as the 'home of lost causes'. C. L. Dodgson publishes *Alice's Adventures in Wonderland*, featuring Alice Liddell, daughter of the Dean of Christ Church

1866 The Randolph Hotel opened

1868 The Oxford Police Act provides for a joint town and University force. Henry Taunt publishes his shilling series of photographic views of Oxford. Delegacy of Non-Collegiate Students, later (1930) St Catherine's Society and (1963) St Catherine's College, founded

1869 St Barnabas' Church opened

1870 The University *Gazette* founded. The first class list in Theology published. Keble College founded, the first to be built of brick

1871 Parliament abolishes all remaining religious tests, and Dissenters are allowed to become fellows of colleges. Second Royal Commission of Inquiry appointed to inquire into the revenues of the University and the colleges. C. L. Dodgson publishes *Through the Looking-glass and What Alice Found There*. Kingerlee, builders, founded

1872 Separate class lists published for Law and for Modern History. Oxford Co-operative and Industrial Society founded. Wingfield Home opened to convalescents. First Varsity Rugby Football match

1873 First class list for the degree of Bachelor of Civil Law published. A sewerage system is laid to discharge wastes into the Thames below Oxford. Oxford and Cambridge Schools Examination Board founded

1874 Matthew Arnold writes of 'that sweet city with her dreaming spires'. John Ruskin inspires teams of undergraduates to labour on the road to Hinksey. Sales of Frank (i.e. Sarah Jane) Cooper's marmalade begin. First Varsity Association Football match. Hertford College re-established by Act of Parliament, 37 and 38 Vict., c. 55

1875 Oxford High School for Girls founded

1876 Clipsham stone introduced to Oxford by Sir Thomas Jackson

1877 Executive Commissioners appointed to carry out the recommendations of the Second Royal Commission of Inquiry: the colleges are taxed to provide a Common University Fund. Arthur Shepherd buys a men's and boys' outfitters shop. Cowley Barracks opened

1878 Wesley Memorial Church opened. Lady Margaret Hall founded. City of Oxford High School for boys opened

1879 Blackwell's founded. Somerville College founded. The Society of Home Students, now St Anne's College, founded

1881 Horse-drawn trams appear on the streets

1883 The University establishes a new system of faculty organization. The *Oxford Magazine* founded

1884 Oxford Historical Society founded. Oxford University Dramatic Society formed

1885 Minty Furniture founded in High Street. Infectious Diseases (now the Rivermead) Hospital opened

1886 Oxford Eye Hospital opened. St Hugh's College founded

1887 The first class list in Oriental Languages (from 1896 Oriental Studies) published. Walters of The Turl founded

1888 Payne & Son, goldsmiths, open their premises in the High Street. Mrs Humphry Ward publishes *Robert Elsmere*, portraying the world of T. H. Green, Mark Pattison, and Walter Pater

1889 Oxford becomes a county borough

1890 Oxford Electric Company founded

1891 School of Art becomes Oxford City Technical School. Construction of Pitt Rivers Museum completed

1892 The University starts a Day Training College for Teachers. *Isis* founded

1893 The names of women candidates printed in the class lists for the first time. St Hilda's College founded

1894 The new Ashmolean Museum opened. C. B. Fry captains Oxford in athletics, cricket, and association football

1895–6	St Martin's Church demolished and Carfax widened
1896	Oxford Bach Choir formed. Thomas Hardy publishes *Jude the Obscure*
1897	The first class list in English Language and Literature published. The new Town Hall opened
1898	Morris Garages opened
1899	Ruskin College established to provide residential education for working men and women
1905	The first class list in Modern Languages published
1909	The Chancellor, Lord Curzon, publishes his *Principles and Methods of University Reform*, the clearest account of the government and organization of the University
1910	Oxford Electric [Cinematograph] Theatre opened
1911	Max Beerbohm publishes *Zuleika Dobson*
1912	H. E. Salter publishes *Records of Medieval Oxford*, the first of a score of works elucidating the early history of town and University. The General Board of the Faculties is instituted. Morris makes his first car
1919	The third Royal Commission set up with H. H. Asquith in the chair
1920	*Cherwell* begins publication
1923	Statutory Commissioners appointed to carry out the recommendations of the Asquith Commission. The first class list in Philosophy, Politics, and Economics published. Oxford Playhouse opened
1924	Museum of the History of Science opened in the old Ashmolean Museum building
1925	Herbert Henry Asquith becomes the first Earl of Oxford of the third creation
1926	Pressed Steel Company comes to Oxford. Osler Hospital opened
1927	The class List in Natural Science is divided into separate class lists for Animal Physiology, Botany, Chemistry, Engineering Science, Geology, Physics, and Zoology. Oxford Preservation Trust founded
1928	Major boundary extension. *Oxford Mail* begins publication
1929	St Peter's Hall founded. The Black Friars return to Oxford (see 1221 and 1538)
1930	Oxford Ice Rink opened in Botley Road. Oxford Society formed
1931	Wingfield-Morris Orthopaedic Hospital established
1933	The first class list in Geography published
1934	Royal Oxford Hotel built. Oxford City Technical School becomes the Schools of Technology, Art, and Commerce
1935	Dorothy Sayers publishes *Gaudy Night*
1936	*Oxoniensia* begins publication
1937	Nuffield College founded
1938	John Betjeman publishes *An Oxford University Chest*
1939	The first class list in Agriculture published. Crematorium opened. Slade Hospital opened
1940	Churchill Hospital opened. New Bodleian Library completed with the aid of the Rockefeller Foundation
1942	Oxford Committee for Famine Relief (Oxfam) formed
1945	The first class list in Forestry published. The Maison Française established. Evelyn Waugh publishes *Brideshead Revisited*
1948	Pergamon Press founded as Butterworth-Springer. St Antony's College founded
1949	The first class list in Psychology, Philosophy, and Physiology published
1951	The first class list in Biochemistry published
1952	The first class list in Music published
1954	Foundation stone of new College of Technology, Art, and Commerce laid by Lord Nuffield

1955 St Giles' School of English founded, followed by many other English-language schools for foreigners

1957 After seven centuries the last surviving medieval hall, St Edmund Hall, becomes a full college

1959 Cutteslowe Walls dividing Council estates from middle-class houses of Urban Housing Company demolished. Oxford Instruments Group founded

1960 The first class list in The Science of Metals, subsequently Metallurgy, and subsequently Metallurgy and the Science of Materials, published. College of Further Education opened

1960–5 Cowley Centre built

1962 Linacre College founded

1964 The Franks Commission appointed by the University

1965 St Cross College founded

1966 The first class list in Engineering Science and Economics published. Museum of Modern Art opened. Conference of Colleges established. Wolfson College founded

1967 Simon House opened as a night shelter

1970 The first class lists in Mathematics and Philosophy and in Modern History and Modern Languages published. The College of Technology becomes the Polytechnic. Radio Oxford begins broadcasting

1970–2 Westgate Centre built

1971 The first class lists in Modern History and Economics and in Physics and Philosophy published. John Radcliffe Maternity Hospital opened

1972 The first class lists in Agricultural and Forest Sciences, in Human Sciences, in Philosophy and Theology, and in Physiological Sciences published

1973 The first class list in Experimental Psychology published

1974 Local government reorganization puts an end to separate University representation on the City Council

1975 The first class lists in Classics and Modern Languages and in Philosophy and Modern Languages published. Museum of Oxford opened

1979 John Radcliffe Hospital opened. Green College founded

1980 The first class list in Engineering, Economics, and Management published

1981 The first class lists in Ancient and Modern History and in Metallurgy, Economics, and Management published

1983 The first list of Bachelors of Fine Art published

1984 City Council Ice Rink opened. Stanford University opens premises in Oxford

1986 The first class list in Pure and Applied Biology published. Oxford United promoted to the First Division

1987 The first class list in English and Modern Languages published. Dillons open a bookstore in Oxford

1988 The first class list in Mathematics and Computation published

1989 The first class lists in Electronic and Structural Materials Engineering and in Engineering and Computing Science published

1990 Rewley House for extramural students becomes a full college with the help of the W. K. Kellogg Foundation

Glossary of Terms Used in the Book

admissions system	In some countries success in the examinations for the baccalaureate entitles a student to attend a university: in Britain the universities themselves decide whom they will admit. In Oxford decisions to admit undergraduates or to refuse admission are taken by the colleges.
Aldermen	senior municipal officers next below the mayor. They disappeared when local-government was reorganized in 1974.
Ashmolean Museum	The Ashmolean Museum in Broad Street was opened in 1683. In 1894 a new Ashmolean Museum was opened behind the University Galleries in Beaumont Street. The building in Broad Street, which houses the Museum of the History of Science, is often referred to as the old Ashmolean. The new Ashmolean has been combined with the University Galleries to form what we now understand by the Ashmolean Museum.
Bachelor	a person who has taken a first degree at the University.
bailiffs	the executive agents who carry out the decisions of the municipal government.
burgesses	citizens of a borough in possession of political rights, two of whom might be selected to serve as burgesses, i.e. Members of Parliament. The Members elected to Parliament to represent the University were also referred to as burgesses.
canon	a clergyman living within the precinct of a cathedral or, nowadays, if not living within it, attached to it.
Canon Professors	holders of chairs attached to the Cathedral and to Christ Church.
chair	A professor is said to hold a chair: the chair in Inorganic Chemistry etc.
Chancellor	once the effective and now the honorific head of the University, elected by members of Convocation.
Chichele Professor	Henry Chichele (1362?–1443) founded All Souls College: a Chichele Professor, however, is one whose chair, attached to the college, was created comparatively recently at the prompting of the Commissioners appointed by Parliament.
class	(1) a small group of students receiving instruction in slightly more formal circumstances than those of a seminar; (2) a first, second, or third class in an examination.
clerk	a person in minor orders, hence, at a time when the University was part of the Church, a student.
college	Like the University, each college is a self-governing corporation, and the degree of independence enjoyed by the colleges distinguishes Oxford and Cambridge from all other Universities.
commoner	an undergraduate member of a college who did not hold a scholarship and did not, therefore, receive his 'commons' (or subsistence) at the expense of the foundation, but had to pay for them.

Common University Fund   instituted by the University Reform Act of 1877, 40 and 41 Vict., c. 48, to receive taxes levied upon the income of the wealthy colleges for the benefit of the University. It has since become, in addition, a means of transferring money from the University to the colleges.

Congregation   a meeting of the resident Masters of Arts engaged in the work of the University. Congregation meets in the Sheldonian Theatre.

Convocation   a meeting which all Masters of Arts of the University are entitled to attend whether resident or not. Formerly a means of bringing up yesteryear's graduates to oppose change, since the reforms carried out by the Commissioners named in the Act of 1923, 13 and 14 Geo. 5, c. 33, it has been a harmless body which elects the honorific Chancellor and the Professors of Poetry.

corporation   a body of persons, created by royal charter or parliamentary statute, constituting an artificial person authorized to make contracts, sue and be sued, etc.

Delegates   members of the University appointed to manage the University Press, the system of local examinations available to secondary schools, etc.

discommon   exercise the ancient right, now obsolete, of the University authorities to prevent a tradesman from dealing with undergraduates.

doctors   those holding the highest degrees of the University, the Doctorates of Letters, of Civil Law, of Science, etc. Not to be confused with the thousands of successful graduate students who, in the twentieth century, have received the degree of Doctor of Philosophy.

dons   It is not clear how this Spanish title has come to be used to describe the Heads, fellows, and tutors of colleges and indeed the whole teaching staff of the University.

down   When undergraduates leave Oxford they are said to go down.

endowed college   a college which has been given lands or other forms of property to provide it with a permanent income.

faculty   a department of study at the University, and the body of teachers belonging to it. In medieval times there were Faculties of Arts and Medicine, Civil Law, and Theology. Today we speak generically of the Arts Faculties, English Language and Literature, Law, Social Studies, etc., and the Science Faculties, Biological Sciences, Clinical Medicine, Physical Sciences, etc. The structure of the modern faculty with its faculty board dates from 1883.

fellows   The fellows of a college are, together with the Head, the constituent members of the corporate body with a right to vote upon all issues and a duty to administer in accordance with trust-deeds the property by which the educational work of the college is supported. Colleges also elect other categories of fellow, like Honorary Fellows and Emeritus Fellows, who do not participate in the deliberations of the corporate body. See also supernumerary fellowships.

finals   examinations for the Bachelor of Arts degree taken by undergraduates after three or four years' study.

freshers   men and women newly arrived at the University.

gentleman-commoner   a commoner of superior social rank to whom in the seventeenth and eighteenth centuries colleges offered privileges.

graduates   (1) used generally for those with first degrees, who may be scattered over the whole world; and (2) more specifically for graduate students, those with first degrees who are in residence continuing to study at the University for higher degrees.

hall	either (1) a residential hall, of which there were hundreds in the earlier centuries of the University's existence; or (2) the dining-hall of a college.
Heads of Houses	A House is a college, and one college, Christ Church, has a Dean, who is also the Dean of the Cathedral; six—Balliol, Pembroke, St Catherine's, St Cross, St Peter's, University—have a Master; seven—Corpus Christi, Magdalen, Rewley House, St John's, Templeton, Trinity, Wolfson—have a President; ten—Brasenose, Hertford, Jesus, Lady Margaret Hall, Linacre, St Anne's, St Edmund Hall, St Hilda's, St Hugh's, Somerville—have a Principal; three—Oriel, Queen's, Worcester—have a Provost; two—Exeter, Lincoln—have a Rector; and eight—All Souls, Green, Keble, Merton, New, Nuffield, St Antony's, Wadham—have a Warden.
Hebdomadal Board	meeting weekly in term time, the University cabinet which was instituted by the Chancellor, Archbishop Laud, in 1631, and consisted entirely of heads of colleges.
Hebdomadal Council	the new University cabinet, now an elected body, representative of heads, professors, and masters, established by Act of Parliament in 1854, 17 and 18 Vict., c. 81.
higher degrees	There are higher degrees appropriate to every faculty, but the vast majority of graduate students are working either for a one-year degree, the Master of Studies or the Master of Science, or a two-year degree, the Master of Letters or the Master of Philosophy, or a three-year degree, the Doctor of Philosophy.
honours	Honours degrees were introduced in 1801 to enable the University to recognize merit greater than that required to pass an examination.
Humfrey	The name of the library given to the University by Humphrey, Duke of Gloucester (1391–1447), is spelt Humfrey.
keeping terms	In order to keep terms undergraduates must reside in Oxford for at least six weeks in each of three eight-week periods at Michaelmas (which is roughly autumn), Hilary (winter), and Trinity (spring).
liberal arts	liberal as opposed to mechanical; in the medieval university the term referred to the *trivium*, grammar, logic, and rhetoric, and the *quadrivium*, arithmetic, geometry, music, and astronomy.
literae humaniores	the study of the Greek and Latin classics, literature, philosophy, and history.
Masters	Masters of Arts: in Oxford those with Bachelor's degrees are not required to sit a further examination before receiving their Master's degrees—the passage of time (seven years from matriculation) and the payment of a small fee is sufficient. In former centuries Masters of Arts, who had completed the required courses of study at the University, were held to have acquired a licence to teach.
matriculation	the act of placing one's name upon the register of the University.
mayor	the chief public officer of the borough, appointed for one year.
Members	Members of Parliament.
Moderations	or Mods, in many faculties the first public examination, taken at the end of two, three, or in the case of Greek and Latin Literature five terms.
muniment	a document, often a title-deed, preserved with care in order to prove ownership.
personal chairs	a chair conferred upon an individual scholar which terminates with his departure: the contrast is with an endowed chair, to which a new appointment is made when it falls vacant.
Prelims	in some faculties the first public (or preliminary) examination, usually taken at the end of one or two terms.

privileged persons	in previous centuries tradesmen and craftsmen who were declared by the University to come under University jurisdiction rather than that of the town.
Proctors	the officers of the University police, who have been in existence since the thirteenth century: in the last twenty years they have found a new role, asking challenging questions about the administration of the University on behalf of the teaching staff.
Regent Masters	Masters of Arts who presided over disputations, or debating exercises in which the parties formally expounded, attacked, and defended a proposition or thesis, a duty discharged for a few years only after graduation.
Regents	Masters of Arts under whom, in the days before there were colleges, undergraduates enrolled.
Regius Professor	the holder of a chair founded by the Crown, and to which the Crown usually still makes the appointment.
scholasticism	the mixture of Christian theology and Aristotelian philosophy taught in the medieval university.
school	(1) a place from which applicants seek admission to the University, as in comprehensive school, grammar school, public school, secondary school, etc.; (2) a room or building in which a specific discipline is taught, as in the School of Moral Philosophy in the Schools Quadrangle; (3) the course of study prescribed by a faculty: the school of modern history, the engineering school, etc.; and (4), in the plural, final examinations and the building, the Examination Schools, in which these take place.
scout	a male servant employed by a college to look after the young gentlemen on a staircase.
seminars	a small group of persons meeting, often with a visiting speaker, to study together in a more open and speculative manner than in a class.
senior members	a term whose use gathered pace in the confrontational atmosphere of the late 1960s, distinguishing all those who teach and sit upon the governing bodies of the University and colleges from all those under instruction who do not.
servitorships	undergraduate places given to those who, in return for waiting upon the fellows of a college, received their board and tuition free.
State scholarships	instituted after the First World War, when the State undertook, for the first time, to help (some) children whose parents could not afford the cost to come to university—not, of course, to Oxford only.
statutes	the rules laid down, nowadays under parliamentary authority, for the government of the University and, separately, for each college. The University is continually modifying its statutes, and colleges may alter theirs subject to the consent of the Privy Council.
student	There are still people alive who think the world has never been the same since undergraduates became known as students.
Student	in effect, a fellow of Christ Church.
studium generale	a medieval expression for a university. It used to be thought that this meant an institution in which every branch of learning was studied. It is now accepted that it means a place of learning to which students resort from all parts of the country and beyond. And yet, somehow, the point is never quite settled, for, as Gladstone said in 1892, 'it always seems as if the word University, soaring above the plane of antiquarian learning ... was fitted, and as it were predestined, to convey the idea of its ultimate function as the treasure-house of all knowledge'.

subscription	the act of declaring one's acceptance of and belief in the Thirty-nine Articles of Religion which were drawn up in 1571 as the basis of the Anglican creed.
supernumerary fellowships	a way of associating distinguished scholars with colleges and giving them dining rights etc. without making them full members of the corporate body.
'The …'	The principal streets in Oxford are often spoken of as The High, The Turl, The Broad, etc., rather than as High Street etc.
tutor	a fellow (and occasionally a non-fellow) appointed by a college to look after the studies and (diminishingly) the morals of undergraduates.
tutorial	sometimes referred to as a tute, an hour set aside for an undergraduate or two undergraduates to take work to a tutor and submit it for comment and discussion; undergraduates in Oxford have one or two tutorials a week.
undergraduate	between matriculation and graduation a student is an undergraduate.
Union, the	Not to be confused with a Poor Law union or with a trade union, the Oxford Union Society was established in 1825 to enable undergraduates to debate political motions; in organization and conduct it is modelled upon Parliament itself.
university	a corporate body which establishes chairs and faculties, matriculates students, conducts examinations, and confers degrees. Although Oxford University is also frequently spoken of as a federation of colleges, the interests of the University do not always coincide with those of the colleges. From the seventeenth to the nineteenth centuries the preponderance of power lay with the colleges; in the twentieth century it has been returning, slowly, to the University.
up	From whatever part of the world and from whatever altitude they set out, undergraduates come up to Oxford at the beginning of each term.
varsity	university.
Vice-Chancellor	the prime minister or president of the University, appointed for four years.
Visitor	In the first five hundred years of its existence the University underwent Visitations intended to secure compliance with the wishes of the Crown. Nowadays each college has a Visitor, who is part outside inspector, reminding the members of the governing body of their duty to obey the college statutes, and part court of last resort to decide disputes among members of the college. Some other institutions also have Boards of Visitors.
Wayneflete Professor	or, nowadays, more often Waynflete Professor: a professor attached to Magdalen College whose chair is associated with the name of the founder, William of Wayneflete, rather than the name of the college which he founded.
Wykeham Professor	a professor attached to New College whose chair is associated with the name of the founder, William of Wykeham, rather than with the name of the college which he founded.

Acknowledgements of Sources

The editor and publishers are very grateful for the help and advice of many college and city librarians and archivists in Oxford, and of staff in the University museums and departments. They wish to thank the following who have kindly given permission to reproduce the illustrations on the pages indicated:

Aerofilms 92, 102; The Warden and Fellows of All Souls College, Oxford 89, 208, 221; Ashmolean Museum, Oxford 9, 39, 44, 47, 50, 91, 105, 142, 166, 167, 170, 177, 181 both, 185, 186, 187, 195, 243 left, 244, 246, 249, left, 254, 258, 260 right, 262, 263, 264, 306; Associated Press / Topham Picture Source 79, 354; Balliol College, Oxford 66 top, 198; Dr R. D. Barnes of the Oxford Forestry Institute 284; B. T. Batsford 4, 29; Derek Bayes 294; The Bettmann Archive 352; Biomet Ltd. 334; Bodleian Library, Oxford 3 (GA Oxon. 4° 369 pl. 12), 6 right (MS Douce 104), 10 top (Wood 276(b) f. xxx) 13 (GA Oxon. a 80 fo. 27r), 14–15 (AII.13 pl. 2), 17 (GA Oxon. 4° 99 p. 98), 20 (GA Oxon. 4° 369 pl. 19), 22 right (GA Oxon. a 38 fo. 34), 23 (GA Oxon. a 72 p. 70), 24 (GA Oxon. c 81 no. 382), 26 (GA Oxon. 4° 99 p. 9), 28 (GA Oxon. a 81), 30 (Minn Collection neg 1/1), 32 bottom (N.Oxf. A5 4 Nov. 1921), 46 (GA Oxon. B 109 (b) fo. 80), 58–9 (MS Top. Oxon. C 16 no. 65), 61 (GA Oxon. 8° 926 (10) facing t/p), 64 bottom (GA Oxon. a 72 fo. 78), 68 (GA Oxon. 4°417) 70 bottom (GA Oxon. 4° 405), 70 bottom, 84 (M Gough Oxon. 50 fo. 18r), 85 Arch. Antiq., A II, 97 (GA Oxon. 4°795/2) 101 (GA Fol. B 33), 103 (GA Oxon. B 109 (b) opp. p. 237), 107 left (GA Oxon. B 109a fo. 258), 112 (MS Top. Oxon. d 501 fo. 89r), 129 (MS. Mus. Sch. C 377 fo. 4r), 133 (G.5 2 (1+2) Th.), 139 (B21, 10(3) Th.), 146 (GA Oxon. 4° 412 p. 2), 149 (GA Oxon. 4° 414 p. 529), 150 (GA Oxon. 4 417 p. 1070), 152 (GA Oxon. 4° 414 p. 424), 161 (MS. Canon. gr. 97 fo.86v), 162, 164 (MS. Auct.F.2.13 fo.47r), 172 (MS. Canon. Class. Lat. 30 fo 1r), 174 (GA Oxon. 4° 412 fo. 67r), 175 (GA Oxon. a 44 p. 120), 179 (JJ Coll. Ox. 8, Ox. Sch. 2), 182 (MS.Gr. Class. a 1(p) (8)), 202, 223 (Rhodes House, Perham MSS.), 235 (MS. 264 fo. 170v), 237 (Don e 232 TP), 238 (Arch. Ac 11.TP), 240 (MS. Pococke 375 fos. 3v–4r), 247 (Mus. Ashmole 1758 fos. 13v–14r), 272 (Vet.E.I.c.5 (3) TP), 273 (P2, 2(1) Med pp. vi–vii), 275 left (4 H 34 Art. Seld. Fp), 275 right (Lister B66 Pl 12–13), 282 (GA Oxon. 4° 417 p. 1084), 302 right (Brox B 48.3 TP), 305 (Ashm. 1664 fo. 3r), 307 (GA Oxon. b 109 (b) pl. opp. p. 240), 311 (GA Oxon. a 38 fo. 35), 347, 365 (NGA Oxon. A108 9.3.1934).

© The British Council 1989, photo by Anita Corbin and John O'Grady; British Library 2 right (MS Add 49999 fo. 29), 64 top, 270, 346; British Museum 62 (no. 12283), 63 (no. 244481); Camera Press 199, 220, 222; Campaign for Oxford (photo: Rob Judge) 210; Centre for Oxfordshire Studies 21, 35, 70 top, 71, 108, 285 both, 339; Governing Body of Christ Church, Oxford 52 (photo: Bodleian Library, Oxford MS 375/1r) 255; The Master and Fellows of Corpus Christi College, Cambridge 132; The President and Fellows of Corpus Christi College, Oxford 163 (Thomas Photos) 183 both (photos: Bodleian Library MS.C.C.C. d 515 fo.75r and v), 188 (photo: Bodleian Library C.C.C. Archives K1000 (B)/6), 302 left (M.S.C.C.C. 40 p. 135); Country Life 100; DIA (photo: Bodleian Library, Oxford GA Oxon. 8° 1055 (21)) 19; Sir William Dunn School of Pathology, Oxford 240, 363; Department of Earth Sciences, University of Oxford 330; Fitzwilliam Museum, Cambridge 48; Hulton Picture Company 67, 153, 213, 292, 299, 364 bottom right; Department of Human Anatomy, University of Oxford 283; Illustrated London News 313; Trustees of the Imperial War Museum, London 362; Jan and Krystyna Kaplan 156; Sir Anthony Kenny of the Rhodes House Trust 364 top left; A. F. Kersting 6 left, 90, 94 top, 97 top, 98, 111, 115, 116, 135, 281; The Provost and Scholars of King's College, Cambridge 211; The Rector and Fellows of Lincoln College, Oxford 197; The President and Fellows of Magdalen College, Oxford 7 bottom, 54, 107 right, 145; Raymond Mander and Joe Mitchenson Theatre Collection 184; Mansell Collection 75, 141, 148; The Warden and Fellows of Merton College, Oxford (photos: Bodleian Library) 42 bottom (Merton Charter 370), 124 (MS Merton Coll.269 fo. 248r); Methodist Church Archives and History Committee at the Museum of Methodism (photo: Thames and Hudson) 143; Dr K. M. E. Murray (Thomas-Photos) 228; Museum of the History of Science 260 left, 276, 279, 304, 309, 310, 316, 317, 320.

National Library of Scotland 204; National Library, Prague 127; National Portrait Gallery, London 60, 131; Natural History Museum, London 259; The Warden and Fellows, New College, Oxford (photos: Martin Mitchell) 22 left, 42 top, 80, 268, (photo: Bodleian Library, Oxford MS New Coll. C.288 4r) 43; The New Yorker Magazine, Inc., drawing by Robert Day © 1936, 1964 349; The Warden and Fellows of Nuffield College, Oxford 32 top; Nuffield Department of Anaesthesia 291; Philip Opher 117, 119, 314; The Provost and Fellows of Oriel College 10 bottom, 267; Oxfam 154, 155; Oxford City Council 12, 18, 36–7 (photo: Bodleian Library, Oxford G54 C17 49.6. f/p. 152); Oxford and County Newspapers 78, 80, 158, 192, 224, 326, 356, 369; Oxford University Museum 243 right, 251, 280; Professor Roger Penrose 325; Pitkin Pictorials 1; Pitt Rivers Museum, Oxford 249 right, 256; Popperfoto 364 top right; Billett Potter 82, 157, 219, 318, 366, 370; Private collection (photo: Courtauld Institute of Art) 165; The Trustees of the Regimental Museum Oxfordshire and Buckinghamshire Light Infantry 27; Research Laboratory for Archaeology, Oxford 194; The Reverend J. S. Reynolds 151; Professor A. S. Robertson (photo: John McMaster) 191; Rolls-Royce 331; Royal Commission on the Historical Monuments of England 2 left, 88, 114 (Crown Copyright); The President and Council of The Royal Society 303 both; St Catherine's College Archives 118; The Master and Fellows of St Cross College, Oxford and the Trustees of the late Sir William Coldstream (photo: Chris Andrews) 266; The President and Fellows of St John's College, Oxford 7 top; Virginia G. Schendler 214; School of Geography, University of Oxford 295; Scottish National Portrait Gallery 337; Lady Simon (photo: Physics Photographic Unit) 321; The Principal and Fellows of Somerville College 341; Mrs Elizabeth Speakman (photo: Bodleian Library S. Hist.930.1, opp. T.P)205; Arthur Strong 212; Wim Swaan 5, 40, 87, 94 bottom, 113, 120; Syndication International 77, 332; The Curators of the Taylor Institution 215; Turner Entertainment Company © 1938, Ren. 1965 Metro-Goldwyn-Mayer Inc. All rights reserved 344; University Laboratory of Physiology, Oxford 286; University Library, Cape Town 348; UPI/Bettmann Newsphotos 368; Weidenfeld and Nicolson Ltd. (photo: Penny Tweedie) 99, 277; Gunnar Westrup 227; Workers' Educational Association 66 bottom; The Provost and Fellows of Worcester College, Oxford (photo: Bodleian Library GA Oxon. 4° 1064) 106.

We have been unable to trace the copyright-holder of the drawing on p. 226 but if notified we shall be pleased to amend the acknowledgements in any future edition.

Index